A MEXICAN FAMILY EMPIRE
The *Latifundio* of the Sánchez Navarros, 1765–1867

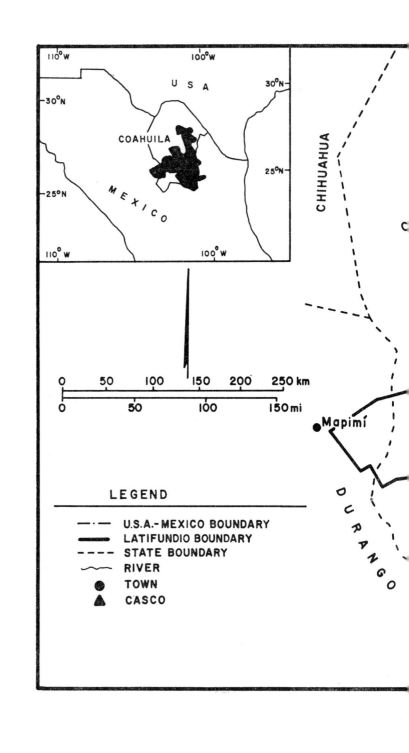

110°W   100°W

U S A

30°N   30°N

-30°N

COAHUILA

25°N

M E X I C O

-25°N

110° W   100° W

0   50   100   150   200   250 km

0   50   100   150 mi

Mapimí

DURANGO

LEGEND

—·—   U.S.A.-MEXICO BOUNDARY
▬▬▬   LATIFUNDIO BOUNDARY
- - - -   STATE BOUNDARY
〜〜   RIVER
●   TOWN
▲   CASCO

The *Latifundio* of the Sánchez Navarro Family

(map by Carlos Parra)

A Mexican Family Empire

The *Latifundio* of the Sánchez Navarros, 1765–1867

CHARLES H. HARRIS III

UNIVERSITY OF TEXAS PRESS • AUSTIN AND LONDON

THE PUBLICATION OF THIS BOOK WAS ASSISTED BY A GRANT FROM
THE ANDREW W. MELLON FOUNDATION

Portions of chapters 1, 6, and 12 of this book first appeared as a paper presented
to the IV International Congress of Mexican History and are used with the permission of the University of California Press.

Library of Congress Cataloging in Publication Data
Harris, Charles Houston.
    A Mexican family empire, the latifundio of the Sán-
chez Navarros, 1765–1867.

    Bibliography: p.
    Includes index.
    1. Latifundio—Mexico—Coahuila—Case studies.
2. Sánchez Navarro family. I. Title.
HD329.C6H37   301.35′1′09721   74-28274
ISBN 0-292-75020-X

For T. F. M.

CONTENTS

TABLES

ACKNOWLEDGMENTS

One of the most pleasant aspects of finishing a book is having the opportunity to thank those who helped make it possible. This study was undertaken at the suggestion of Thomas F. McGann, to whom I owe a profound debt of gratitude. My deep appreciation also goes to Nettie Lee Benson, Donald D. Brand, Karl M. Schmitt, Stanley E. Hilton, Louis R. Sadler, and Jack McGrew, who read portions of the manuscript and provided valuable criticism. Research in Mexico was made possible by an NDEA–Fulbright-Hays grant. Lic. Juan Sánchez Navarro, Lic. Carlos Sánchez Navarro, Doña Blanca Villar Villamil de Sánchez Navarro, and Doña Luz Sánchez Navarro de Mac Gregor graciously facilitated my research on their distinguished family. The directors and staffs of the Latin American Collection at the University of Texas, the Archivo General de la Nación, the National Archives, the Huntington Library, the Archivo General del Estado de Coahuila, and the Archivo General del Estado de Nuevo León were extremely helpful. To my wife goes my gratitude for reasons that she knows best.

INTRODUCTION

The importance of the hacienda has been admirably expressed by Jacques Lambert, who states, "Nothing has had a more widespread and lasting effect on Latin America's social and political history than the large estate."[1] This is certainly the case for Mexico, a country that was dominated for four hundred years by the landed estate, whose most significant form was the *latifundio*, a holding usually composed of two or more haciendas. Yet our knowledge of the hacienda is woefully inadequate. As Charles Gibson points out, we lack not only information but also a secure conceptual frame. He adds, "My own feeling is that the hacienda is a crucial institution, that for various reasons its study has been slighted, and that we would be well advised to make a concerted effort toward solving the historical problems that it raises."[2]

Fortunately, an encouraging beginning toward solving these problems has been made by Gibson himself and especially by François Chevalier, whose classic work on colonial Mexico will long remain the standard against which other hacienda studies are measured.[3] And a growing number of scholars are making significant contributions toward illuminating various aspects of the hacienda.[4] But perhaps, as has recently been suggested, the time has come to abandon the term *hacienda studies* altogether, on the ground that it is too restrictive.[5]

In addition to approaching the topic from such standpoints as labor systems or regional variations, we must examine the interaction between the activities of the landowners—the *hacendados*—and the evolution of the hacienda itself.

In this connection, J. H. Hexter's comments about the English landed aristocracy would appear equally valid for Mexico: "It seems to me that if we were to examine the story of the overmighty subject we might learn a great deal about the way the English magnate transformed his landed wealth into power by successive adaptations to emergent circumstances. . . . When we seek what underlay the excessive power wielded by these overmighty subjects we discover that it was in all cases similar: all of them used their lands as a base from which to move to a position of command or control over men."[6] In Mexico, because many estates were really owned by families rather than by individuals, the approach suggested by Hexter might better be applied to the "overmighty family," that is, to the "wealthy and powerful family blocks whose members aid and abet each other in both business and politics."[7]

Such a study is made possible by the Sánchez Navarro papers, located at the University of Texas at Austin. This magnificent archive —the largest collection of hacienda materials in the United States— comprises some 75,000 pages of manuscripts spanning the period from 1658 to 1895. Not only is there a detailed calendar, but the papers also include personal letters, business correspondence, hacienda reports and inventories, wills, land titles, and court records.[8]

As in my two previous studies of this family, the present work employs a topical approach.[9] While this approach necessarily involves a certain amount of repetition, the scope and complexity of the Sánchez Navarros' affairs preclude a strictly chronological treatment. A topical framework permits a detailed analysis of how the family built up and operated their estates and of how they exercised their resultant economic, social, and political power. The geographical and chronological boundaries of this study permit analysis of both continuity and change in Mexico's evolving socioeconomic structure during one of the most decisive periods in her history—the era of transition from colony to nation.

The case study of the Sánchez Navarros calls into question many of the earlier generalizations made about the Mexican hacienda, such as the assertion that haciendas were "only in a limited way subject to the rules of economic enterprise, management for profit, and sale for gain. They were held because of family tradition, as means of social prestige, and managed with as little risk as possible."[10] The Sánchez Navarros simply do not conform to this stereotype. They were motivated by more practical considerations than prestige and tradition. The point is an important one, for the Sánchez Navarros were not merely another elite landowning family: in less than a century this remarkable clan amassed a domain approaching the size of Portugal. Their *latifundio* was the largest ever to have existed not only in Mexico but also in all of Latin America.

PART ONE

THE COLONIAL PERIOD (1765–1821)

1. The Family and the Land

Santiago de la Monclova was an unlikely place in which to make a fortune. Set among low hills beside a tree-lined river, it was a drab village of crude adobe buildings clustered around a dusty plaza. The population in 1767 consisted of some hundred families plus thirty-five soldiers of the presidio, or garrison, and their dependents; the chief characteristic of the inhabitants was their poverty. Reflecting this, the most imposing of the one-story structures in the town was the governor's residence, a crumbling ruin only partially habitable.[1]

Such was the capital of one of the backwaters of New Spain, the frontier province of Coahuila, or, as it was formerly known, Nueva Extremadura. To become parish priest of Monclova was hardly a choice assignment, but for Father José Miguel Sánchez Navarro it proved to be the opportunity to build an economic empire. Assisted by his relatives, he established a *latifundio* that was to make him one of the wealthiest landowners in northern New Spain.

When José Miguel Sánchez Navarro began forming the *latifundio* in 1765, the province of Coahuila extended northward to the Presidio de San Sabá and the Medina River, in what is now Texas. Nueva Vizcaya bounded Coahuila on the west and south, the line running from the confluence of the Conchos and Río Grande south to the settlement of Mapimí and from there east to the Hacienda de Anhelo. The Nuevo Reino de León and the Colonia de Nuevo Santander bordered Coahuila on the east.[2] In 1787 an administrative reorganization added to Coahuila the districts of Parras and Saltillo, previously part of Nueva Vizcaya.

The watershed of the Sierra Madre Oriental bisected Coahuila from the Río Grande southeast to Saltillo, forming two distinct geographical regions. The area to the southwest was much higher, reaching an elevation of more than three thousand feet above sea level. Only a few oases, such as Parras and Patos, relieved the bleakness of this arid region with its landscape of desert vegetation and sterile mountains. Occasional streams trickling down the western slope of the Sierra Madre flowed into brackish lagoons in the Bolsón de Mapimí, the trackless wilderness forming the entire western portion of Coahuila. In contrast, the region to the northeast of the watershed consisted largely of semiarid plains sloping gradually down to the Río Grande.[3] Breaking the monotony of these vast steppes were a few low sierras and several rivers meandering down from the Sierra Madre Oriental. The Nadadores, with its tributary the Monclova, flowed to the northeast, joining the Sabinas running to the southeast through the Valley of Santa Rosa. The combined rivers became the Salado, which continued on a southeasterly course until it reached the Río Grande.

When the Spaniards settled Coahuila in the late seventeenth century they had congregated along the fertile river valleys, founding the capital of the province in 1689 near the sites of several earlier but unsuccessful settlements beside the Monclova River. From the beginning the handful of Spaniards had to defend their homes against the constant attacks of hostile Indians, mainly Apaches, who nearly destroyed Monclova itself in 1721. The Bolsón de Mapimí represented the greatest danger from the Indians, for it was their exclusive preserve.[4] The Apaches also swept across the Río Grande to invade Coahuila from the northwest. When Nicolás de Lafora, a military engineer, traveled through the province in 1767 on an inspection tour, the Indians were temporarily at peace. Lafora, nevertheless, was of the opinion that the only hope for Coahuila's prosperity lay in subduing the savages. If this were not done, he wrote, the ruin of the settlers was inevitable.[5]

At the time of Lafora's visit there were few colonists available to fight off the Indians. The inhabitants of Coahuila numbered fewer than eight thousand settlers scattered on various haciendas and ranchos or clustered around a handful of villages, missions, and presidios.[6] Connecting the centers of population was a rudimentary network of roads whose hub was Saltillo. A wagon track linked Monclova with Saltillo to the south and the presidios to the north, while east-west communications were along a road passing through Parras, Patos, and Saltillo to Monterrey.

The principal natural resource of Coahuila was its land. The Spaniards had been disappointed to find only small deposits of precious metals. Although a few silver mines operated in the vicinity of Monclova and Santa Rosa, mining constituted an insignificant economic activity. Most of the inhabitants had necessarily turned to agriculture for their livelihood. The river valleys were well suited to farming, but the settlers faced serious problems in their attempt to wrest a living from the soil. Besides frequent Indian raids they had to contend with a scarcity of water, for Coahuila underwent periodic droughts. With its semiarid plains supporting only sparse vegetation, Coahuila was best suited to ranching on an extensive scale.[7] Ranchers acquired the vast tracts they needed either by means of *mercedes*, royal deeds granted as a reward for services to the crown, or by purchasing unused crown lands, called *tierras realengas*, at public auction.

The land itself was relatively valueless without water, and a struggle developed early for control of the meager water resources. This scramble centered along the riverbanks. Because the crown owned all running water, land grants did not carry with them riparian rights unless specifically mentioned. Individuals, therefore, usually had to secure additional *mercedes* in order to utilize the rivers for irrigation. The degree to which water was prized is indicated by the fact that irrigation rights were granted for a specified number of days, hours, and even minutes during the month, a practice dating back to Rome and one that continued through the nineteenth century.[8]

The raising of livestock was not only a means to wealth but also the mark of social prestige in a society that was extremely status conscious.[9] In Coahuila, as in other areas of New Spain, farmers and small-scale ranchers were fighting a losing battle against the encroachment of powerful *hacendados*. Though settlement of Coahuila dated only from the late seventeenth century, the trend toward *latifundios* had reached the point that in 1766 the governor complained that a handful of *hacendados* had virtually taken possession of the province.[10]

The most important *latifundio* in Coahuila was the Marquisate of Aguayo. Francisco de Urdiñola—a Basque who began as an obscure common soldier, became a wealthy miner and rancher, and served as governor of Nueva Vizcaya—formed the nucleus of this enormous landholding.[11] His properties included mines and haciendas at Bonanza, Mazapil, and Río Grande in Zacatecas, but most of his holdings lay in the section of Nueva Vizcaya that became part of Coahuila in 1787. Urdiñola began to acquire land in 1583 from the original settlers of Saltillo and Parras, eventually amassing a *latifundio* that extended north from Saltillo into the province of Coahuila, west to Parras, and south into Zacatecas, embracing some 11,626,850 acres.[12] The center of Urdiñola's *latifundio* was the splendid Hacienda de San Francisco de los Patos, forty miles west of Saltillo.

After Urdiñola's death in 1618, his estates descended undivided for several generations through the female line for lack of male heirs. His great-granddaughter married and moved to Spain, where in 1682 her husband obtained the title of Marquis of San Miguel de Aguayo y Santa Olalla. After his death she created the *mayorazgo* of Aguayo, entailing the *latifundio*, which descended to their daughter. In 1712, the daughter went to New Spain with her third husband, José Ramón de Azlor y Virto de Vera, second Marquis of Aguayo, who devoted himself to administering his wife's princely inheritance.[13] Except for the years 1719 through 1722, when he served as governor of Coahuila and Texas, he managed his wife's properties until his death at Patos in 1734.

Under the direction of Azlor y Virto de Vera the *latifundio* entered a period of consolidation and expansion. One of his first actions was to tighten the stranglehold that the Aguayos already had over the town of Parras. The Marquisate extended to the outskirts of the village and included the springs providing most of the town's water. Besides restricting the grazing land available to the townspeople, the Marquis raised the price at which he sold them water for irrigating their vineyards.[14] He then safeguarded the House of Aguayo's monopoly over the water supply at Parras by obtaining in 1717 a *composición*, or grant of clear title, from the crown covering all the lands and water rights then composing the Marquisate.[15]

Not only did the Marquis clear the titles to the *latifundio* but he was also instrumental in extending its western boundary from Parras to the Sierra de Mapimí, slightly west of the modern city of Torreón.[16] This immense area consisted of unused crown lands that the House of Aguayo acquired between 1717 and 1760 through a series of royal deeds. The land was largely desert, and the crown sold it for a nominal price, as when Aguayo bought 222,000 acres for a mere 250 pesos in 1731.[17] The total amount of land acquired by this process was enormous. On paper the area equalled 982,100 acres, but because of primitive surveying methods the actual extent proved to be 2.2 million.[18]

Azlor y Virto de Vera simultaneously expanded the *latifundio* northward into Coahuila. He secured a grant in 1716 for 104,000 acres on the northern boundary of the Aguayo estates. While the Marquis was fulfilling the complicated legal requirements for obtaining formal possession of his grant, the governor of Coahuila and the citizens of Monclova in 1733 raised bitter objections that brought matters to a standstill. The impasse ended when the Marquis renounced his claim to the disputed area near Monclova. At the same time, however, he applied for additional crown land to the northeast because his flocks numbered 180,000 head and urgently needed additional watering places.[19] Aguayo was primarily interested in acquiring title to the three widely separated water holes in the area, but he laid claim to all the intervening territory. The matter was still pending when the Marquis died in 1734.

The following year his elder daughter, now the Marchioness of Aguayo, married José Francisco Valdivielso, created first Count of San Pedro del Alamo in 1734 and owner of vast estates in Nueva Vizcaya. Valdivielso established a sheep-raising *latifundio* that extended over some 1,096,680 acres and whose headquarters were the Hacienda de Santa Catalina del Alamo in Durango.[20] The matrimonial alliance thus united two of the largest landholdings in northern New Spain. Not content with this enviable situation, the newlyweds determined to expand their properties. The Marchioness and her husband pressed her late father's pending claim, and in 1744 the land in Coahuila was finally surveyed, a procedure that frequently consisted of only a visual estimate. The surveyors calculated the territory to be 861,780 acres, most of it waterless; in 1746, the Marchioness received title and formal possession.[21] This huge addition to their *latifundio* by no means satisfied the House of Aguayo's hunger for land. They attempted in 1765 to incorporate the unused crown lands between the Presidio de Santa Rosa and the Río Grande.[22] Failing in this, the Aguayos subsequently secured permission from other *hacendados* to graze their flocks between Monclova and Santa Rosa, and also along the Sabinas River.

In the 1760's the Marquisate of Aguayo, which sprawled across more than 14,688,630 acres—the equivalent of some 22,950 square miles—was nearly two-thirds the size of Portugal. To protect this domain from recurrent Indian raids, the Aguayos maintained a force of *escolteros*, or private cavalry. Great herds of cattle and horses roamed the Marquisate, but sheep raising was the principal activity, and travelers estimated the flocks at 200,000 to 300,000 head.[23] The Aguayos' wealth enabled the family to develop even the recently acquired sections of their *latifundio*, such as the Hacienda de Cuatrociénegas.[24] They also fostered a certain amount of industry on their properties. The Hacienda de Santa María de las Parras had 200,000 grapevines and produced both wine and brandy for sale in central New Spain.[25] The Hacienda de Patos boasted the first *obraje*, or woolen textile mill, in Nueva Vizcaya, supplying felt hats, coarse cloth, and other woolen stuffs for the peons.[26]

The headquarters of the Marquisate were still at Patos, whose inhabitants numbered over one thousand two hundred in 1765.[27] Responsibility for operating the Marquisate rested with an *administrador*, or general manager, since the Aguayos, in common with many other members of the colonial nobility, had become absentee landlords whose existence revolved around the viceregal court in Mexico City. The Aguayos' primary interest in the *latifundio* was in the revenue it produced, and their visits to the landholding consisted of annual vacations spent at Patos.

Compared with the gigantic Marquisate of Aguayo, other rural property in Coahuila seemed insignificant, although several estates were impressive in their own right. On the southern boundary of the Marquisate was the *latifundio* belonging to the Jesuit College of Parras. Following their usual pattern, the Jesuits built the landholding in order to support their educational activities. They began acquiring land in 1729 at auction for insignificant sums: 34,678 acres in 1731 for 50 pesos, 300,000 acres in 1741 for 480 pesos. In this manner their properties, whose seat was the Hacienda de Los Hornos, eventually grew to 682,000 acres. But the Jesuits lost the fruits of their labor: in 1767 they were expelled from New Spain, and the crown leased out the *latifundio* to a succession of individuals for a pittance.[28]

North of Monclova the Garza Falcón family had monopolized land along the Sabinas River, in the fertile Valley of Santa Rosa near the presidio of the same name. The Garza Falcóns had been prominent in Coahuila for decades, several members of the family having served as governors in the 1720's and 1730's. With the permanent establishment in 1739 of the Presidio de Santa Rosa, its commander was authorized to grant land to the settlers. As it happened, the commander was Captain Miguel de la Garza Falcón, who promptly began issuing *mercedes* to his brothers: 109,120 acres to one brother in 1739 and 230,450 acres to another in 1740. By granting land to each other the Garza Falcóns soon built a sizeable holding, which they further expanded by buying out other settlers. Their *latifundio* eventually comprised some 457,160 acres. Moreover, they controlled much of the precious water in the Sabinas River; their Hacienda de San Juan de Sabinas dominated the left bank, and their other estate, Nuestra Señora de los Dolores, the right.[29]

Still another *latifundio* had taken form in 1741 when Captain José Vázquez Borrego, a restless frontiersman, arrived in Coahuila with his servants and livestock.[30] Intent on becoming a substantial landowner, he purchased the Hacienda del Alamo northeast of Monclova on the Nadadores River, enlarged his properties by means of a *merced*, and founded the Hacienda de Encinas as the headquarters of his land-holding.[31] At the same time he was busily obtaining vast tracts of *tierras realengas* to use for grazing. In 1745 he secured clear title to 849,850 acres, bought from the crown for 980 pesos, and the following year a similar transaction raised his holdings to their maximal extent—1,300,800 acres.[32] Around 1750, however, his *latifundio* was reduced by nearly one-half, to 707,000 acres.

This drastic reduction occurred because Vázquez Borrego decided to transfer part of his operations to a region less frequented by hostile Indians, the province of Nuevo Santander, where he obtained title to some 377,000 acres.[33] He simultaneously ceded 693,000 acres in Coahuila to a royal official in Saltillo, who founded on this tract the Hacienda de Sardinas on the northern boundary of the Marquisate of Aguayo.[34]

It was not uncommon for priests as well as laymen to be landowners in Coahuila. The practice was as old as the founding of Saltillo in 1575, for the chaplain who accompanied the founders became an important *hacendado* in the neighborhood.[35] The practice still prevailed in the eighteenth century. A curate owned over 17,000 acres near Candela in 1750. A much larger tract belonged to the chaplain of the Presidio de Santa Rosa, who raised livestock as a sideline. This enterprising priest obtained in 1741 some 96,000 acres of crown lands on the Sabinas River, establishing the Rancho de San Francisco Javier de la Escondida.[36]

Another rancher-priest was Father José Flores de Abrego, curate of Monclova for nearly sixty years.[37] In marked contrast to those who acquired their rural properties in extensive tracts, Flores de Abrego built a *latifundio* in piecemeal fashion through purchases spanning decades, a procedure imposed by the pattern of land tenure in the vicinity. Much of the land around Monclova had been granted to the original settlers in relatively small parcels of 6,675 to 30,000 acres. With the passage of time some of these properties had become successively fragmented through inheritance. Beginning in 1714 Flores de Abrego patiently bought out the various heirs to several of these properties, which he consolidated into the Hacienda de Cieneguilla.[38]

He employed the same technique north of Monclova at the confluence of the Nadadores and Monclova Rivers, fashioning his purchases into the Hacienda de Adjuntas.[39] As a result of his numerous real estate transactions, when Flores de Abrego died in 1755 he left a *latifundio* comprising a respectable 139,160 acres.[40]

Appointed to succeed Flores de Abrego as curate of Monclova was Father José Miguel Sánchez Navarro. Making brilliant use of his predecessor's technique for acquiring property, José Miguel and his relatives were to effect a drastic reduction in the number of Coahuilan *hacendados*.

The young curate's lineage was ancient, dating back to thirteenth-century Spain where the Sánchez Navarros had distinguished themselves fighting against the Moslems. The family name was carried to the New World by Captain Juan Sánchez Navarro, who emigrated to New Spain around 1550, drifted to the northern frontier, and was among the founders of Saltillo in 1575.[41] The captain took an active part in the life of the new community. He engaged in ranching, constructed on the outskirts of Saltillo the first gristmill in the region, and found time to participate in local government as a town councilor.[42] By the time of his death around 1600, Sánchez Navarro had established a family whose descendants, intermarrying with the Arizpe and Rodríguez families in Saltillo, played a dynamic role in the development of Coahuila.[43]

During the seventeenth century Saltillo remained the home of the Sánchez Navarros, who devoted themselves to the profession of arms or to operating the family mill.[44] As the frontier moved north, however, a few Sánchez Navarros moved with it. Sergeant Diego Luis Sánchez Navarro was a member of the expedition that in 1674 founded the settlement of Nuestra Señora de Nueva Extremadura near the future site of Monclova. When Monclova itself was founded in 1689, he received a grant of land in the vicinity and settled there, ending his career with the rank of captain.[45] Juan Bautista Sánchez Navarro was one of those commissioned in 1698 by the governor of Coahuila to build the Misión de Dulce Nombre de Jesús de Peyotes north of Monclova.[46]

As the eighteenth century opened, the Sánchez Navarros enjoyed considerable social status as one of the first families of Coahuila who were, for good measure, *hidalgos*, or nobles. As was natural in a widespread clan, the position of the members varied. Some were common soldiers, such as Joaquín and Cristóbal, who participated in founding the Presidio de Santa Rosa where they settled after retiring from the army.[47] Others were priests, among them Leonardo and José Martín, the latter serving as curate of Saltillo.[48] The family fortunes declined for a time, as evidenced by the sale of the flour mill in 1705,[49] but by mid-century the Sánchez Navarros' wealth was solidly established due to the enterprise of the head of the clan, Captain Cristóbal José. He was proprietor of an orchard, a vineyard, and a small ranch near Saltillo; but his principal interest was in mining. As of 1749 he had brought into production in the Nuevo Reino de León a profitable silver mine, where he was establishing a rudimentary smelter, or *hacienda de beneficio*, which he named San Nicolás de la Laguna. Cristóbal José was a person of consequence, as shown by the governor's allowing him to administer civil and criminal justice to his large labor force without interference from the local authorities.[50] Cristóbal José was a man of many parts, not the least of his accomplishments being the fathering of eleven children—six daughters and five sons.

The eldest son, José Miguel, was born in Saltillo in 1730 and studied for the priesthood at the Colegio de Nuestra Señora de Guadalupe, in Zacatecas. At the age of twenty-five he became the curate of Monclova.[51] The immense moral authority inherent in his new position as parish priest made him one of the most influential members of that community. Though plagued by ill-health during much of his life, José Miguel displayed unusual energy. Besides ministering to his parishioners, in 1758 he initiated the construction of a new church; he would spend decades supervising this project, which proceeded slowly due to the poverty of the Monclovans.[52]

Although he was a competent priest, José Miguel's real interest was business; fortunately for him, there was no prohibition against a cleric engaging in commerce. Monclova might be a dreary little village, but it was strategically located on the trade route between Saltillo and the northern presidios, besides being the capital of Coahuila and the commercial center of the province. José Miguel was quick to realize that this situation, combined with his position in the community, presented him with potentially lucrative business opportunities. Shortly after his arrival he began supplementing his income through retail trade.[53] To put his commercial enterprises on an organized footing he purchased a corner lot on the plaza next to the church and built a small store, which within a few years featured dry goods packed in by mule the dusty 125 miles from Saltillo.[54] He expanded his holdings in 1760 by acquiring two additional lots and a house near the church.[55]

Needing help in these diverse activities, José Miguel sent to Saltillo for his business-minded brother José Gregorio, who assumed management of the store while the curate remained the silent half of an informal partnership.[56] The needs of the townspeople and surrounding haciendas provided a gratifying volume of business, and the store prospered under José Gregorio's direction.[57] His appointment in 1762 as executive officer of the local militia cavalry unit reflects the considerable status and influence José Gregorio had attained in the community.[58]

Commerce, however, was not the sole basis of the Sánchez Navarros' fortune. Rather, their economic empire was to rest upon the twin pillars of commerce and ranching. The profits from the store enabled José Miguel to broaden the base of the Sánchez Navarros' activities by launching a new enterprise in the form of sheep raising.

The curate's involvement in ranching was a direct outgrowth of his tenure as the provincial tithe administrator between 1762 and 1773.[59] His post was a strategic one since the tithe, which constituted the principal source of Church revenue, was one of the most important taxes collected in New Spain. The general population had to pay the tax, in kind, on virtually all products of agriculture and grazing.[60] The chief agricultural product in Coahuila was maize, while lambs and kids represented the bulk of the tithe from grazing.[61]

José Miguel's job was a difficult one, entailing not only the supervision of agents actually gathering the tax but also arranging the sale of the commodities collected. To expedite the handling of the tithe José Miguel began operating trains of pack mules and oxcarts, using them to haul freight for his store as well.[62] As a general rule he was able to dispose of part of the tithe within Coahuila itself simply by selling the commodities back to the *hacendados* who had produced them. On occasion his zeal in marketing the remainder of the tithe resulted in disputes with the civil authorities. For example, in 1769–1770 the governor banned the export of wheat and corn because of a grain shortage, but José Miguel nevertheless tried to sell these commodities in Nuevo León where they commanded a higher price.[63]

He had good reason to be zealous regarding the tithe: it was an extremely lucrative business. When Father Juan Agustín de Morfi, the most perceptive traveler in Coahuila during the colonial period, passed through Monclova in 1777, he commented on this matter. Morfi noted that, although the curacy at Monclova was worth two thousand pesos a year, that sum would not even pay the household expenses of the curate, who had made a fortune of eighty thousand pesos from administering the tithe, despite having suffered continual losses from Indian raids.[64]

It is impossible to determine the accuracy of Morfi's figure, but José Miguel did manage to make a double profit from the tithe. He received a commission of 8 percent and then compounded his gains by speculating with the sale of the tithe commodities, particularly the livestock. With capital from the store José Miguel himself bought some of the tithe sheep, paying their local market price of around 4 reals each and duly turning the money in to the Bishopric of Guadalajara. Using this technique the curate rapidly built a flock of his own: by 1763 his sheep already numbered 5,523 head.[65] At the same time he realized a substantial profit by selling part of his growing flocks to buyers outside Coahuila, and he also used the animals he bought from the tithe to pay for some of his purchases; for instance, he once acquired a Negro slave for 200 pesos, paying 25 pesos in cash and the balance in 350 tithe sheep and goats at 4 reals a head.[66]

The tithe might be enriching José Miguel, but it was producing little revenue for the Church. It should be noted, however, that the ecclesiastical authorities in Guadalajara had been aware of the curate's activities and had even given their permission for him to sell livestock.[67] When José Miguel began administering the tax, the commodities yielded some 4,736 pesos. After expenses, including José Miguel's commission, the Bishopric of Guadalajara received only 3,919 pesos.[68] In 1773, the last year of the curate's administration, the tithe produced only some 3,560 pesos net. Though José Miguel had been speculating with the tithe, there was certainly no dramatic increase in the Church's revenues after his administration ended. The Church then farmed out the tax, receiving some 4,000 pesos in 1774 and 1775 and only 3,000 pesos in each of the two succeeding years.[69]

While he was building his flocks José Miguel began investing in rural property. As an outgrowth of his commercial activities, in 1764 he bought a small farm near Monclova, using the land to pasture his herd of mules and to raise wheat by means of irrigation.[70] Since he did not own a ranch, his close friend the *mayordomo* of the Aguayo Hacienda de Carmen allowed the curate to graze his sheep at that hacienda, where the *mayordomo* himself had a personal flock.[71]

The next step of course was for the Sánchez Navarro brothers to acquire ranch land, and in 1765 they began buying small tracts in the vicinity of Monclova.[72] The brothers organized their ranching operations on the basis of another informal partnership. Each of the Sánchez Navarros retained title to his own property, but for their mutual benefit they managed their holdings as a unit. Since ranching was a full-time job, José Miguel once again turned to his family, bringing in another brother, Manuel Francisco, and putting him in charge of the nascent *latifundio*.

In his capacity as curate, José Miguel also helped Manuel Francisco become a landowner. One of the curate's duties was that of directing a lay brotherhood, whose only asset was a tract of land. In 1770 José Miguel secured the bishop's permission to sell the tract in order to benefit the brotherhood. The curate duly publicized the sale and solicited bids. When the appointed day arrived, it was Manuel Francisco who entered the high bid—150 pesos—and obtained title to 12,526 acres and ten days' water rights at the confluence of the Nadadores and Monclova rivers, in the Valley of Adjuntas.[73]

Here the brothers established their headquarters—the Hacienda de San Ignacio del Paso Tapado, located on the right bank of the Monclova River near the Nadadores. Having centered their activities in the Valley of Adjuntas, the brothers determined to gain control of the entire valley. They were in the enviable position of being able to finance their purchases with money derived from the store and from José Miguel's speculation with the tithe. The Sánchez Navarros were therefore able to buy land whenever it became available.

A major opportunity presented itself in 1772. Much of the Valley of Adjuntas was part of the landholding formed by José Miguel's predecessor as curate of Monclova, who had bequeathed the land to his nephew. When the latter died in 1772, the executor of the estate —none other than José Miguel—sold most of the property at auction to satisfy creditors, among whom were José Gregorio as well as José Miguel himself. The town crier publicized the sale in vain for twenty days before a prospective buyer, backed by a merchant-rival of the Sánchez Navarros, submitted a bid of 3,750 pesos. It seemed as though the land would slip from the avid grasp of the three brothers, but they had no intention of losing the chance to add a considerable block of real estate to their holdings. On the final day, with the possibility of being outbid eliminated, José Gregorio appeared and offered 100 pesos more than the rival merchant. José Miguel ceremoniously delivered the deeds to José Gregorio in February, 1773.[74]

The new property was diverse: one block consisted of a flour mill, a house, and an orchard in Monclova. These urban holdings were located, conveniently enough, next to the Sánchez Navarro store.[75] Second, there was a majority interest in the Hacienda de Cieneguilla across the river from Monclova. Most important, the transaction included four tracts totaling 85,270 acres in the Valley of Adjuntas.[76]

In this manner the brothers consolidated some of their holdings in the valley, where with the addition of José Gregorio's real estate they now owned some 104,470 acres. And by 1774, through a purchase of crown lands, José Gregorio increased their holdings by an additional 39,024 acres. Located in eastern Coahuila near Candela, this tract provided the Sánchez Navarros with a winter range for their flocks.[77] The Hacienda de Tapado had become the headquarters of a sizeable landholding.

José Gregorio, though basically a merchant, had been instrumental in forming the *latifundio*, but he was not to see its continued development, for he died at the end of 1774. His death marked the close of an era in the rise of the Sánchez Navarro empire. By the terms of the merchant's will, the bulk of his property went to his two brothers, with the curate receiving all real estate, thus preserving the integrity of the landholding.

Until 1774 the Sánchez Navarros had been able to attend personally to their business enterprises. The merchant's death not only raised the critical problem of replacing him but also brought out the growing need for additional personnel to assist in handling the brothers' affairs. In recruiting subordinates, José Miguel habitually turned first to his family. There was no lack of relatives, for the term *family* was used in its most extended sense. Besides the immediate relatives of José Miguel and Manuel Francisco, the family included collateral relatives, in-laws, and people who were merely relatives of relatives.

The undisputed leader of the Sánchez Navarros by 1774 was José Miguel. As the eldest son he had become the head of the family several years earlier upon the death of his father, whose ranch near Saltillo he had inherited. Since José Miguel was the shrewdest and wealthiest of the Sánchez Navarros, as well as a priest, he received the respect of the more distant relatives. The curate was not only the head of the extended family but also the *patrón* to whom his kinsmen-clients looked for protection and assistance.[78]

A strong feeling of family loyalty existed among the Sánchez Navarros. While José Miguel and his brothers had been prospering in Monclova, they had not forgotten those of their relatives whose economic situation remained somewhat precarious. Perhaps it would be more accurate to say that they had not been allowed to forget their relatives, for the brothers received a steady stream of requests for aid, to which they responded with gifts of money and merchandise. They were also afforded ample opportunity to make loans to needy relatives, and José Gregorio had meticulously recorded these transactions in the account books at the store.[79]

The less affluent members of the clan reciprocated in several ways the financial assistance they received. The sisters in Saltillo frequently sent small gifts of sweetmeats to their brothers in Monclova, and the austere bachelor existence of José Miguel and his brothers was brightened when their youngest sister arrived from Saltillo early in 1774 to be their housekeeper. In this connection, although the Sánchez Navarros had become men of substance in Monclova, they had not permitted a crowd of hangers-on to join them; the sister was the only relative to live with them until 1774. Their attitude contrasted markedly with that of many other *hacendados* who prided themselves on maintaining a numerous entourage in lavish style.[80]

Instead of using his relatives to demonstrate his status, José Miguel employed them in a much more practical way—from them he received a constant flow of information, a mixture of family gossip and news of value in his clerical and business affairs. Relying primarily on his family connections, José Miguel was building a network of business agents and informants. He had, in fact, already embarked on a policy that combined family loyalty and long-range business planning, that of sending talented nephews to college. Beginning in 1771 he had been paying more than seven hundred pesos a year to educate José Vicente Arizpe at the seminary in Guadalajara.[81] Other nephews would follow Arizpe, becoming priests and lawyers. As they attained responsible positions, José Miguel's investment in their education was to return handsome dividends.

Following José Gregorio's death, however, it was Manuel Francisco who did the most to advance the Sánchez Navarros' fortunes. In 1775 he married the daughter of one of the leading local *hacendados*, Juan Manuel Palau. The latter had settled in the Valley of Santa Rosa, where he had married into the prominent Garza Falcón family.[82] Through his wife Palau had inherited the Hacienda de Nuestra Señora de los Dolores, which the Garza Falcóns had founded in 1745. Although his wealth had dwindled as a result of Indian depredations, Palau was still a man of standing in the community.[83]

His principal asset was the huge Hacienda de Dolores, or Hacienda de Palau as it was commonly called, located in the most fertile region of Coahuila. The *casco*, or headquarters complex, of Dolores was hardly impressive. The main house was small and primitive, and the only protection against raids was a breastwork in front of the door. Dolores, which had once boasted large herds of horses, was on the verge of ruin, for the Indians were systematically stripping the estate of livestock. Nevertheless, the hacienda was potentially a source of great wealth, for its rich and well-watered soil produced crops of excellent quality, such as sugar cane twelve feet high.[84] As Palau's son-in-law, Manuel Francisco stood to inherit this estate.

Instead of helping Palau to rebuild the hacienda, Manuel Francisco continued to devote himself to the Sánchez Navarros' enterprises. His new prospects did little to alter his relationship with José Miguel, for Manuel Francisco's role remained that of a younger brother and junior partner; José Miguel was the one who made the important decisions concerning the Sánchez Navarros' affairs. And one of his decisions was that Manuel Francisco would take over management of the store in addition to operating the *latifundio*.

That landholding increased dramatically around 1782, when Manuel Francisco inherited the 217,418-acre Hacienda de Dolores upon Palau's death. But with the hacienda he also inherited a long-standing dispute with the Vázquez Borrego family over its eastern boundary, a dispute characteristic of the hacienda system. Because authorities at both the provincial and viceregal levels issued *mercedes*, the grants sometimes overlapped. The boundaries of haciendas, moreover, were defined in the vaguest of terms, which provided a fertile field for litigation. Whenever possible, boundaries were fixed in relation to prominent landmarks, but with the passage of time the names of some landmarks changed, further confusing the situation.

In this instance the dividing line between the Hacienda de Dolores and the Vázquez Borregos' Hacienda del Alamo ran along the crest of a hill called Cacanapos. Unfortunately, two hills only a short distance apart had both become known as Cacanapos. Palau had claimed the easternmost Cacanapos as the boundary, the Vázquez Borregos the westernmost.[85] Palau had taken the matter to court in 1762 but had lost the case. The issue lay dormant until 1788, when the Vázquez Borregos moved livestock into the disputed area. Manuel Francisco immediately sued, alleging that his neighbors had invaded his Hacienda de Dolores by taking advantage of the confusion over which Cacanapos actually constituted the boundary.[86]

Manuel Francisco having initiated a legal battle against the Vázquez Borregos, the Sánchez Navarro brothers widened the scope of the conflict by filing a second suit against their neighbors in 1788. This dispute concerned water rights and a tract of land on the boundary between the Vázquez Borrego *latifundio* and the Sánchez Navarros' Hacienda de Tapado. The brothers charged their neighbors with trespassing and with obstructing their use of the Nadadores River. Both parties then produced *mercedes* to justify their actions.

The Sánchez Navarros' lawyer disclosed the crux of the dispute when he argued that the Vázquez Borregos were entitled only to the water that the Sánchez Navarros did not use. When the latter had purchased their land in the Valley of Adjuntas, most of the tracts had carried with them water rights. Manuel Francisco had interpreted this to mean that he could consolidate the water rights and draw from a single point on the river. Accordingly, he was building a dam on the Nadadores below its confluence with the Monclova. The Vázquez Borregos were understandably disturbed at the prospect since most of their *latifundio* lay downriver.[87]

The two lawsuits that the Sánchez Navarros initiated in 1788 became enmeshed in the ponderous machinery of the legal system. There was considerable difficulty merely in finding the proper tribunal to hear the cases. The governor of Coahuila declared himself unable to rule on the disputes, so they were transferred to the High Council of Finance in Mexico City. Since the cases did not involve the royal treasury, the Council transferred them to the Real Audiencia, the supreme court of New Spain. This body declared that Coahuila was no longer under its jurisdiction and ordered the cases sent to the Audiencia of Guadalajara. That tribunal in 1795 ruled in favor of the Sánchez Navarros and ordered the governor of Coahuila to execute the judgment. As was to be expected, the Vázquez Borregos appealed the decision, and the matter bogged down in such complicated legal maneuvering that not until 1802 did the cases finally reach the governor.[88]

But by then yet another conflict had arisen between the two *hacendado* families, who were on the verge of a range war. A strip of Vázquez Borrego land separated the northern and southern sections of the Sánchez Navarro *latifundio*. Within this corridor at a place called Oballos were extensive salt licks, which the Vázquez Borregos had long permitted the Sánchez Navarros to use. Embittered by losing the costly lawsuits, the Vázquez Borregos prohibited passage of their adversaries' flocks in 1802. The Sánchez Navarros' response was ruthless—on Manuel Francisco's orders his shepherds reached Oballos by running forty thousand sheep across the Vázquez Borregos' best range.

The Vázquez Borregos' initial reaction was to file a suit demanding compensation for their devastated rangeland.[89] But upon further reflection they decided that although they might win this battle they were losing the war, because the governor was moving to enforce the Audiencia's ruling despite the delaying tactics of the Vázquez Borregos' lawyer. Consequently, the Vázquez Borregos began to sound out their opponents regarding the possibility of reaching a compromise.[90] Their first attempts failed because of José Miguel's intransigence, but a compromise was finally reached in 1804 to the relief of all concerned.

This case illustrates the exasperatingly slow legal process in New Spain, which encouraged private settlements of this kind. Evidencing the parties' dread of future litigation were the harsh penalties specified if the agreement were ever violated. The party committing the infraction would have no legal recourse and would have to pay a fine of three thousand pesos plus the expenses of the injured party, who could enforce the agreement through the courts.

The settlement ending sixteen years of expensive litigation was a victory for the Sánchez Navarros. The Vázquez Borregos conceded every legal point at issue in both lawsuits and in addition granted their opponents unconditional use of the water, pastures, and salt licks on their *latifundio* for a fifteen-year period. In return the Sánchez Navarros granted the Vázquez Borregos an interest-free loan of fifteen thousand pesos for a term of fifteen years. The crucial point, though, was that as security for the loan they obtained a mortgage on the Vázquez Borrego *latifundio*.[91]

By this pact the Sánchez Navarros joined the northern and southern sections of their landholding. And, as a nephew had pointed out in urging José Miguel to accept the settlement, in all probability the

Vázquez Borregos would be unable to repay the loan, and the junction could then be made permanent.[92] The financial resources accruing from their commercial activities were thus instrumental in enabling the Sánchez Navarros to win their struggle against the Vázquez Borregos who, like most *hacendados*, had considerable land but little capital.

These resources had also been decisive in the expansion of the Sánchez Navarro *latifundio* by more peaceful means, for the brothers often took land in settlement of debts. This practice delineates the boundaries of family loyalty, because when the debtors were relatives the Sánchez Navarros took the land perhaps reluctantly but they nevertheless foreclosed. One such instance involved a cousin, Francisco Javier de Arizpe. Owner of a ranch in the Valley of Adjuntas, he had incurred a sizeable bill at the brothers' store; by 1775 his debts exceeded one thousand four hundred pesos. After carrying him on the books for nine years José Miguel demanded payment. Unable to comply, Arizpe in 1784 signed over his ranch to satisfy seven hundred pesos of the debt, and the Sánchez Navarros added another 55,850 acres to their Hacienda de Tapado.[93]

Another case of land acquisition at the expense of relatives concerned José Castilla y Terán, a Spanish cavalry officer who married a niece of the Sánchez Navarros. The Spaniard owned most of the Hacienda de Señor San José east of Monclova, and on one occasion he borrowed 645 pesos from José Miguel. But when Castilla y Terán died in 1791 the debt was still outstanding, and the curate sued. In settlement of his claim José Miguel secured title to the late Spaniard's 140,920 acres.[94] This addition represented a major step toward joining the winter range near Candela to the rest of the Sánchez Navarro *latifundio*.

The center of that landholding remained the Valley of Adjuntas. The brothers finally secured virtual control of the valley through two purchases by which they rounded out the boundaries of Tapado. Both transactions involved small, independently owned properties. José Miguel paid 125 pesos in 1798 for a wedge-shaped tract containing 6,881 acres. Manuel Francisco did even better, for in 1801 he contributed another 6,675 acres, taken in settlement of a debt, for which he paid exactly 25 pesos plus the cost of drawing up the deed of sale.[95]

José Miguel likewise had an eye for a bargain, and that same year he snapped up the Rancho de San Francisco Javier de la Escondida. The ranch had been established by the chaplain of the Presidio de Santa Rosa, who had mortgaged it to a merchant as security for a loan. The principal plus the accrued interest had raised the total debt to 4,581 pesos by 1801.[96] Since the creditors lived in the city of San Miguel el Grande, they arranged to have José Miguel collect for them. Instead, the curate offered them 450 pesos in cash if they would cede him their rights as creditors. They agreed, signing over the mortgage. When José Miguel foreclosed on the ranch he added an impressive 100,200 acres to the Sánchez Navarro holdings near Santa Rosa.[97]

By 1805 the *latifundio* had grown to some 671,438 acres, but in that year Manuel Francisco died, and the resultant crisis threatened the integrity of the landholding. Manuel Francisco left his estate to his children, the rural properties going to his eldest son, twenty-three-year-old José Melchor. To prevent the fragmentation of the landholding, the curate presented his nephew José Melchor with a most attractive proposition: if the younger man agreed to manage the *latifundio* as well as José Miguel's other interests he would be the curate's sole heir. Not surprisingly, José Melchor readily accepted.[98] The team of José Miguel and his nephew was to prove even more formidable than that originally composed of the curate and his brothers.

Having again preserved the integrity of the landholding José Miguel could continue the process of consolidating it. Around the turn of the century he had begun to buy up water rights and small tracts still in the hands of independent landowners. The only factors needed to implement this policy were patience and money, both of which the curate had in abundance. The more these small properties became fragmented through inheritance the easier it became for José Miguel to absorb them piecemeal. By 1819 he controlled most of the water rights on the Nadadores and Monclova rivers.[99] He had also been acquiring property on the southern and eastern fringes of the *latifundio*, particularly at the Hacienda de San José de las Higueras east of Monclova. That estate had once been named the Hacienda de Señor

San José, and the curate had added most of it to the *latifundio* in 1792 after José Castilla y Terán's death. He had since been chipping away at the remainder.[100]

An extremely important tract at San José de las Higueras passed into José Miguel's hands in 1820 as a result of the misfortunes of his nephew Juan Ignacio de Arizpe, the tax collector and administrator of the tobacco monopoly for Coahuila and Texas. A careless administrator, Arizpe had on occasion borrowed from the curate to cover shortages in his accounts.[101] But the real crisis occurred in 1801, when Arizpe made the disconcerting discovery that he was short 12,300 pesos. In desperation he again turned to José Miguel, offering all his assets as collateral for a loan. The curate agreed, and Arizpe signed over two flour mills, a store, and four houses in Monclova, several hundred head of livestock, and two tracts of rangeland, one of them at San José de las Higueras.[102]

Having temporarily staved off financial disaster, Arizpe's problem became that of repaying the loan. José Miguel charged him 5 percent annual interest, carefully recording Arizpe's installments in a special account. To reduce his indebtedness the tax collector even supplied building materials for José Miguel's favorite project, the construction of the new church in Monclova. But he made little headway because at the same time he continued to borrow money from José Miguel to purchase rural property as well as to cover recurrent shortages in his accounts. By the time he died in 1818, Arizpe owed the curate a total of some 21,800 pesos.

José Miguel therefore retained both the property his nephew had mortgaged in 1801 and that which Arizpe had subsequently accumulated.[103] And the tract that counted was the rest of San José de las Higueras. This acquisition represented a real triumph for the curate—after decades of maneuvering he had at last joined the winter range near Candela to the main body of the *latifundio*.

While enlarging the landholding to the east of Monclova, the Sánchez Navarros had also been expanding its northern boundary. In 1820 they were embroiled in a particularly bitter and complicated lawsuit with the Elizondo family over the Hacienda de San Juan de Sabinas. The dispute had its origins in a transaction that José Miguel concluded in 1808, when he loaned Ignacio Elizondo ten thousand pesos at 5 percent annual interest.[104] With the money Elizondo bought the western half of San Juan de Sabinas in 1809 from the Garza Falcóns, its founders. The huge hacienda covered 234,144 acres, and Elizondo's half included the *casco*, together with water rights on the Sabinas River.[105] The new *hacendado* began operations on an impressive scale, constructing a chapel, restoring the rest of the rundown *casco*, and rebuilding the irrigation system.[106] Elizondo did not live to implement all his plans, but after his death in 1813 his heirs continued to operate the western half of San Juan de Sabinas.

The eastern half of that hacienda—some 117,072 acres—passed into the Sánchez Navarros' hands in 1814 when the curate's nephew José Melchor purchased it from the Garza Falcóns.[107] From the beginning there was trouble between José Melchor and the Elizondos over the water rights. Despite an agreement in 1815 to share the water, each party claimed three-fourths of the flow in the Sabinas River.[108] Matters came to a head in 1819. The Elizondos had built a log dam across part of the river to divert water to their property, and José Melchor smashed the installation. He defended the action on the ground that lack of water was causing crop failures not only on his part of San Juan de Sabinas but also across the river at Soledad, a hacienda that Manuel Francisco had founded in the late 1780's. Furthermore, José Melchor alleged that in smashing the dam he had acted legally since the *alcalde*, or mayor, of Santa Rosa had authorized the move. The Elizondos readily admitted that the official had ordered the destruction of their dam. They contended, however, that in so doing the *alcalde* was hardly acting on the merits of the dispute—he was José Melchor's brother![109]

The Elizondo family appealed the *alcalde*'s order, but while the case was in the courts the Sánchez Navarros launched a legal counterattack in 1819 that made the entire question of water rights academic. They employed their favorite tactic, that of foreclosure. Acting for his uncle the curate, José Melchor demanded repayment of the principal and interest on the loan made to Ignacio Elizondo in 1808. Since Elizondo's heirs had been able to meet only a fraction of this obligation, the Sánchez Navarros quickly secured a judgment granting them the western half of San Juan de Sabinas. The Elizondos desperately began a series of legal maneuvers to delay execution of the ruling.[110]

Supremely confident of ultimate victory, José Melchor was determined to break his adversaries. Not being content to leave matters in the hands of his lawyer in Monterrey, he eagerly took a personal hand in the proceedings. When in 1820 the governor dispatched a special commissioner on fact-finding trips to San Juan de Sabinas the *hacendado* not only accompanied him but also made the journeys as pleasant as possible. He furnished an armed escort, at times numbering sixteen *vaqueros*, as a precaution against Indian attacks along the road. He supplied all necessary provisions, as well as two women servants to prepare the meals. He even furnished a pack mule to carry the official's bed.[111] José Melchor could well afford to be lavish in his efforts to influence the commissioner, and he was prepared to spend whatever it took to ruin his opponents.

Yet the hapless Elizondos were by no means the only ones against whom José Melchor was raging. Ever since 1817 he had been engaged in another acrimonious dispute over water rights farther up the Sabinas River. A priest named José Antonio Quirós and his partner, one José María Echais, had occupied a tract at the headwaters of the river. The earthen dam they built near the source of the Sabinas allowed only a trickle of water to flow downstream, and the crops at José Melchor's Hacienda de Soledad were failing.

He sued the partners in 1818 and for good measure filed claim to their land, asserting that they had no legal title to it. Quirós and Echais refused to appear in court at Santa Rosa, so José Melchor's brother the *alcalde* obligingly went to their property and forced them to increase the flow of water downriver. Shortly afterward, in June, 1818, the two partners appealed to the Audiencia of Guadalajara, complaining that the *alcalde* had trespassed and had arbitrarily restricted their water rights. On learning of this move José Melchor promptly retained an attorney in Guadalajara. Fearing that the partners were seeking a quick judgment, the *hacendado* instructed his lawyer to delay the proceedings at all costs until the Audiencia could hear his side of the dispute.[112]

Even as he prepared his case against Quirós and Echais, the *ha-*

cendado was busily pressing yet another lawsuit. As had been predicted, when the fifteen thousand pesos that the Sánchez Navarros had loaned the Vázquez Borregos in 1804 came due in 1819, the latter could not pay. José Melchor, again representing his uncle, sued to have the debt satisfied with the Vázquez Borregos' property. The first step was to seize the debtors' livestock and other chattels; accompanied by a special commissioner and an armed escort, José Melchor made several sweeps through the Vázquez Borrego estates in 1820–1821 collecting livestock.[113] Foreclosing on the *latifundio* itself would be the next order of business.

The impending foreclosures against the Vázquez Borregos and the Elizondos meant that the Sánchez Navarros were well on the way to doubling the size of their domain, which by 1821 already covered more than 800,000 acres. Furthermore, once the suits against Quirós and the Elizondos were successfully concluded, the Sánchez Navarros would dominate the Sabinas River the way they already controlled the Nadadores and the Monclova.

On the eve of independence the Sánchez Navarros' only rival for hegemony in Coahuila was the Marquis of Aguayo. Vast as the Sánchez Navarro holdings had become, they were still greatly overshadowed by the Aguayo landholding of nearly fifteen million acres containing nearly 213,000 head of livestock.[114] Despite these impressive statistics the Marquis's wealth was more apparent than real. The Aguayo properties at one time had produced princely revenues, which the Aguayos spent on a princely scale. They owned, for example, not one but four palatial residences in Mexico City.[115] But progressive mismanagement of their *latifundio* resulted in bankruptcy by 1818, with a group of creditors taking over the administration of the estates.[116]

The Sánchez Navarro properties by contrast were not only free from debt but also returned a profit, a situation due in large measure to the personal attention that the family had lavished on their landholding.

2. Ranching

Ranching in Coahuila, as in the other northern provinces of New Spain, was essentially a struggle against drought and Indians. Of the two, Indians constituted the more serious problem, with only short and infrequent interludes of peace interrupting their devastating incursions. Despite this hostile environment, by 1774 the Sánchez Navarros were engaged in ranching on a large scale, an accomplishment attributable in large measure to careful planning.

José Miguel exercised close supervision over ranching as he did over the family's other enterprises. Directing operations from his home in Monclova, the curate made decisions on the basis of information contained in a steady flow of letters from Manuel Francisco, who managed the landholding.

Manuel Francisco was a *hacendado*, but he had little time to enjoy the luxurious indolence commonly associated with this social class. Since he was responsible for the day-to-day operation of the *latifundio*, his life centered around building the flocks, making improvements at the *casco* of Tapado, and above all trying to please the curate, who was an exacting taskmaster. Following the merchant José Gregorio's death in 1774, Manuel Francisco was forced to redouble his efforts since the curate then had him manage the store as well as the *lati-*

fundio. Under José Miguel's direction he did a creditable job of running both enterprises simultaneously; nevertheless, he continued to spend most of his time at Tapado, for he was a rancher at heart.

Rising above a vast prairie, the *casco* of Tapado resembled a fortress. Enclosing the one-story buildings was a high and solidly built adobe wall. From a fortified watchtower at the northeast corner musketry could enfilade the wall to protect the *casco*'s single gate.[1] In the event of Indians forcing the massive gate, the defenders could still resist from the ranch house itself since the building had been designed primarily for defense. The substantial structure was built in the form of a square around a spacious patio, with the area between the rear of the house and the outer wall forming a large corral. Whenever a raid was imminent, large numbers of livestock were herded into the patio and corral for safekeeping.

Manuel Francisco's efforts at Tapado received favorable comment from Father Morfi, who visited the hacienda in 1777. The priest's overall impression was that the rude but functional *casco* demonstrated the Sánchez Navarros' lack of imagination as well as their indifference to comfort. But at the same time the hacienda evidenced the brothers' wealth and their determination to protect their property, an attitude worthy of imitation throughout the province. Morfi's major criticism was that the absence of an orchard, or of even a single tree to provide shade for the livestock, constituted a notable oversight on the part of *hacendados* who otherwise understood their own interests so well.[2]

In the years following Morfi's visit the Sánchez Navarros continued to make physical improvements at Tapado. For instance, they added a store and a large shed in 1780. Four years later José Miguel built a chapel and cemetery because Indians made the roads too hazardous for his peons to travel to Monclova to receive the sacraments. The curate became quite enthusiastic about the project, even traveling in his coach to Tapado to oversee the final stages of construction and to officiate at the dedication of the chapel.[3]

From this time on, José Miguel's visits to Tapado became much more frequent, as a result of reorganization in the managerial structure of the Sánchez Navarros' enterprises. After Manuel Francisco inherited the Hacienda de Dolores it became manifestly impossible for him to rebuild that estate, manage the rest of the *latifundio*, and operate the Monclova store as well. Consequently, the curate decided to put a nephew in charge of the store, leaving Manuel Francisco free to concentrate on the expanded *latifundio*. And during those times when Manuel Francisco had to be at Dolores the curate himself assumed part of the managerial burden by personally supervising operations at Tapado. José Miguel's heightened interest in the landholding even extended to learning the practical aspects of ranching.

Ecclesiastical preferment ended José Miguel's active participation in ranching. The curate received a royal commission in 1790 as canon in the recently created Bishopric of Linares and moved to Monterrey, the see of the diocese.[4] He still remained abreast of matters in Coahuila through correspondence with his brother, for the Sánchez Navarros reverted to their original pattern of management with Manuel Francisco operating the *latifundio* under José Miguel's direction.

The curate's absence gave Manuel Francisco the opportunity to concentrate on developing the northern section of the landholding, which was his personal property. Having installed his family in Santa Rosa, he spent much of his time at the Hacienda de Dolores. Endeavoring to make more productive use of this enormous acreage, he established a second *casco*—Soledad—a few miles northeast of Dolores on the Sabinas River.

In addition, Manuel Francisco expanded the managerial structure by placing a *mayordomo* in charge of his two estates.[5] This *mayordomo* and the foreman of Tapado were responsible for routine operations, Manuel Francisco alternately supervised the two sections of the landholding, and José Miguel made the policy decisions. This arrangement continued even after the latter retired from his post in Monterrey and returned to Monclova in 1795.

The mechanics of ranching were relatively simple; the requisite elements were, of course, land, water, and livestock. The Sánchez Navarros had certainly missed no opportunity to acquire land. Moreover, during normal years the brothers had an adequate water supply from the two rivers flowing through the center of their landholding. The Sánchez Navarros had also been building their flocks, for sheep were the mainstay of the *latifundio*. José Miguel had owned a total of 5,523 sheep in July, 1763; in August, 1774, despite heavy losses among the flocks during the spring, the lambs alone numbered 14,135 head.[6] The animals thrived in the semiarid climate of Coahuila and were much more profitable than cattle. Not only did they produce two crops a year—lambs and wool—but also there was a ready market for both wool and mutton.

The Sánchez Navarros had amassed their livestock in several ways, the most important being José Miguel's purchases of tithe sheep and goats. The brothers augmented the natural increase of these flocks by acquiring sheep from other *hacendados*; some of these sheep were purchased and others were received as payment in kind for goods sold at the Monclova store.[7] The fact that José Miguel was the provincial tithe collector until 1774 strengthened the brothers' bargaining position when buying livestock from other ranchers. Because of droughts in Coahuila, *hacendados* faced recurrent shortages of corn for their peons' rations, and it was José Miguel who decided to whom the tithe corn would be sold. On several occasions he helped the Vázquez Borregos to cope with such shortages by selling them tithe commodities.[8] In return, the Vázquez Borregos sold him sheep at less than their market value.[9]

For years the Sánchez Navarros had also realized a tidy profit by renting out part of their growing flocks. Sometimes the lessee paid cash; at other times, payment was in the form of additional animals.[10] The brothers thus increased their livestock without effort, while protecting their investment by having others assume responsibility for safeguarding a part of their flocks.

One of the attractions of sheep raising was that it required only a minimal outlay for equipment. The most essential item was sheepshears, which the Sánchez Navarros were buying from the Aguayo Hacienda de Patos as early as 1770.[11] The few other implements used in ranching—such as axes, copper cauldrons for rendering tallow, and knives for slaughtering sheep—were available through the Sánchez Navarro store in Monclova. *Yerba de Puebla*, the poison commonly used against predators, had to be imported from the center of the viceroyalty and supplies of it were sometimes slow in arriving.[12]

This minor problem was an exception: procurement of equipment and supplies usually posed little difficulty.

The cycle of operations revolved around the flocks of *churro* sheep —an ugly, but hardy, breed that produced excellent mutton but mediocre wool.[13] The pattern of herding the flocks conformed to the ancient Spanish practice of transhumance, the periodic and alternating movement of sheep between two areas with different climates.[14] During the winter, the sheep went to the mountains around Candela; later, when the *latifundio* expanded northward, the sierras near Santa Rosa were also used for this purpose. During the summer the flocks were herded down to the river valleys after seasonal rains had revived the pasture along the Nadadores and the Sabinas.[15] The flocks were kept in the same general area as they grazed and were referred to collectively as the *hacienda de ovejas*. The tens of thousands of animals making up the *hacienda de ovejas* were divided on the basis of both number and type. Each shepherd had a flock that rarely exceeded two thousand head and was usually composed of a certain type: yearlings, two-year-olds, or three-year-olds. There were also separate flocks of breeding rams, aged slaughter ewes, and nursing ewes with their lambs.

A high point in the year was the lambing season, usually in January and July. To assist the shepherds during this critical period a crew of peons was dispatched from Tapado. The three or four weeks of the lambing season represented a time of intense activity for these *ahijadores*, or lambers. They first erected corrals of brush in which to confine the ewes while they dropped their lambs. The *ahijadores* then kept moving through the flocks, driving in ewes ready to give birth and assisting with the difficult births. If the weather turned unusually cold during January, the *ahijadores'* work became especially difficult, as they had to spend much of their time caring for the new-born lambs, which easily became chilled. Sheepmen dreaded such a drop in temperature, for lambs perished by the hundreds in the space of a few hours. Some of these losses were compensated for by the number of twins born—10 to 20 percent of the lamb crop.[16] Lambing concluded with the branding of the new crop and the castration of the yearlings destined for slaughter.[17]

The flocks dispersed until the next major phase of the operations cycle, the shearing, which normally took place at Tapado in March and again in August. The shearers worked rapidly. Each man selected a bleating animal from the sheepfolds, dragged it backward by a hind leg to a covered shed adjoining the corrals, and began shearing. Holding the struggling animal down by placing a knee on its hindquarters and an arm around its neck, the shearer clipped the greasy coat, which fell away in a solid sheath. Hovering nearby were young boys who applied either a tarry mixture or the fruit of a liliaceous plant called *cebadilla* to the many nicks on the animal; if this were not done, blowflies would lay their eggs in the open wounds, which in a few days would be covered by a mass of worms feeding on the sheep's flesh. After the worm medicine had been applied to the foreman's satisfaction, the terrified animal was released to join its fellows.[18]

Upon completion of the August shearing, the pace of activity slowed until the annual roundup and branding of the horses, mules, and cattle in January. During the same month, a flock of several hundred sheep and goats was slaughtered at Tapado.[19] The climax of January's activities was the lambing season, marking the beginning of the annual operations cycle.

Despite José Miguel's insistence on record keeping, the method of accounting for the sheep was actually a rather loose one. There was, for example, no standardized format for reports: data on the flocks were merely part of the information on hacienda affairs contained in the stream of letters the curate received. Each lamb crop was always counted, and, periodically, so was the entire *hacienda de ovejas*, normally at shearing time. But during the rest of the year the supervisory personnel only reported losses, both for sheep and other livestock. The Sánchez Navarros, therefore, had only a general idea of the number of animals they owned at any given time. The lamb crop is the best available indicator for the size of the flocks, as shown in table 1.

The flocks required constant attention not only because of the natural stupidity of sheep but also because of the hazards inherent in ranching. A case in point was the lambing season in January, 1792, when the crop exceeded 14,000 head. Manuel Francisco's initial pleasure quickly turned to dismay; throughout January and Febru-

TABLE 1
Sánchez Navarro Flocks in the Colonial Period

Date	Lamb Crop	Total Sheep
July, 1763		5,523
August, 1774	14,135	
July, 1776	4,800	
January, 1780	6,500	
October, 1787	8,000+	
January, 1788	14,000+	
July, 1790	4,000	
October, 1791	9,000+	
January, 1792	14,000+	85,000
December, 1795	heavy losses	
June, 1811	11,000+	
October, 1812	16,000	
May, 1813	10,000	
November, 1813	16,000+	
June, 1814	12,500	
October, 1814	14,500	
November, 1815	11,200	
January, 1816	15,000	
May, 1816	8,000	
January, 1817	7,365	
October, 1817	4,520	

SOURCE: SNP (2505), (713), (3508), (3454), (3444), (3433), (1731), (824), (2469), (1863), (1898), (1893), (1908), (1854), (1905), (1911), (1059), (1855), (1937), (2431), (1800), (1839), (100), (586), (10), (3038), (2872), (3561), (2877), (2198), (1316).

ary, hard freezes and blinding snowstorms hit the *latifundio*, and, despite the *hacendado*'s best efforts, the flocks suffered grievously with more than 8,000 lambs dying. Nor were losses confined to the lambs: slaughter ewes perished by the hundreds. Moreover, wolves were also making inroads on the flocks, and poison was in critically short supply. Manuel Francisco reported this melancholy state of affairs to José Miguel, but the Sánchez Navarros were hardly on the verge of ruin—their flocks still numbered some 85,000 head.[20]

In comparison with the *hacienda de ovejas*, the rest of the livestock was relatively unimportant. As early as 1768, José Gregorio began grazing horses on the first tract of land the brothers acquired. The merchant continued to breed horses and mules, both pack animals and fine coach mules. By his death in 1774, he had amassed a herd of some 200 head.[21] In succeeding years this herd increased several-fold but still represented only a sideline.[22] The same was true for cattle; as late as 1787, the Sánchez Navarros' range cattle numbered only 782 head. Yet a certain amount of diversification was taking place, for at Tapado there were also several score of oxen, plus a herd of 200 milch cows. Their milk went to make cheese for sale at the Monclova store, providing a small but steady source of income.

The very fact that the Sánchez Navarros concentrated on raising sheep made their livestock less attractive to the Apaches than that of some other *hacendados*. Although the Indians stole various kinds of animals, they had a decided preference for horses and mules, prizing them not only as mounts but also for meat.[23] The brothers' herds were therefore a much less tempting target than was, say, the Marquis of Aguayo's livestock, which included thousands of horses and mules. Nor was the Sánchez Navarros' Hacienda de Tapado as exposed to depredations as were estates on the periphery of Spanish settlement. These factors help to explain the brothers' success, for Indian attacks constituted the gravest problem facing Coahuilans.[24]

When the Sánchez Navarros began ranching in the mid-1760's, the fragile peace with the Apaches was shattered and the nomads again devastated the province. The long-suffering citizens naturally looked to the royal garrisons for protection, but the available troops were pitifully inadequate. Only three presidios existed in Coahuila—at Río Grande, Santa Rosa, and Monclova—and each was garrisoned by a mere handful of soldiers.[25] The best the troops could do was to protect these settlements and send small detachments in belated pursuit of raiders. Reducing the effectiveness of even these limited measures was the deplorable state of the army's equipment. Besides having wretched horses the troops were short of gunpowder. The governor reported in 1770 that the Monclova garrison had been without powder for over three years; the men there made do with what they could borrow from the Presidio de Santa Rosa.[26] If the military could do little to contain the Indians, the citizenry could do even less, for most Coahuilans lacked weapons. The governor appealed for help to the viceroy, who promised to provide two hundred muskets.[27]

In the meantime, the Apaches continued their depredations, and the outlying haciendas bore the brunt of these forays. Because of their proximity to the Indians' strongholds, the ranches in the Valley of Santa Rosa and the Marquis of Aguayo's Haciendas de Cuatrociénegas and Carmen were especially vulnerable, suffering repeated and costly raids. But most of the damage consisted of loss of livestock rather than lives. This was not the case at another of the Marquis's ranches, which was completely destroyed by Apaches who killed thirteen people and captured ten; nor was it true when a war party massacred fourteen shepherds at Mesillas. Civilians composed most of the casualties in this savage frontier warfare, but the army also suffered bloody defeats, such as the ambush of a forty-man column, from which seventeen troopers escaped alive.[28]

The army attempted to stem the tide by sending in reinforcements, and by 1774 the defenses of Coahuila were somewhat stronger, at least on paper; a new post at the settlement of San Fernando de Austria raised troop strength in the province to 171 officers and men.[29] Yet by then the Marquis of Aguayo, for one, had had enough. Losses at the hands of the Apaches forced him to abandon several ranches, among them the Hacienda de Joya, which had the only well for some sixty miles on the road between Saltillo and Monclova. Capitalizing on this situation, the Apaches began laying ambushes at Joya; many a parched traveler expecting to find water found death instead.

In view of Aguayo's withdrawal, the governor strongly recommended to the viceroy that the abandoned estates be divided among settlers who would defend them. Aguayo protested, arguing that the withdrawal was only temporary and that he intended to reoccupy the properties with a force of *escolteros* strong enough to protect his interests until a proposed line of presidios could defend the province adequately. Accepting these arguments, the viceroy rejected the governor's proposal for land reform.[30]

In the midst of this depressing situation, the Sánchez Navarros had been resolutely defending their own interests. José Miguel in 1769 had demanded military escorts for his pack trains engaged in collecting the tithe. The ecclesiastical authorities in Guadalajara exerted pressure on his behalf, and the viceroy ordered a reluctant governor to detail some of his few troops for this purpose.[31]

Protecting the *latifundio* was a much more difficult proposition. Though the Sánchez Navarros took the precaution of keeping some of their stock near the *casco* of Tapado the Apaches made a surprise attack on the night of March 11, 1770, and ran off a herd of horses and mules. The Indians also captured and tortured the three *vaqueros* on guard duty; two of the horribly mutilated men died during the night, while the third lingered in agony until he died the following morning.[32]

Repeated incursions cost the brothers additional servants and livestock during 1771.[33] In December, 1775, a war party stole nineteen horses and forty-eight mules from Tapado. In May, 1776, Apaches struck the *hacienda de ovejas*, killing four shepherds and capturing two youths, who subsequently managed to escape. Indians returning from a successful foray again swept down on the flocks in June, killing another shepherd and taking a captive. In December, marauders escaped with four droves of Sánchez Navarro mules.[34]

The Apaches became so bold that in March, 1777, they raided the settlement of Santa Rosa, where they butchered five of the townspeople. Manuel Francisco responded to the deteriorating situation by feverishly strengthening the defenses of Tapado. Spurring him on was a report from the *mayordomo* of the Hacienda de Sardinas, who wrote in July: "We're surrounded by Apaches; they're being seen every day. I expect them to steal all our livestock because in view of what happened at Santa Rosa the province is defenseless and there is nowhere to look for help."[35]

Throughout 1778 the Indians continued to ravage Coahuila. Relief came at last in 1779, when the governor concluded an alliance with the Mescalero Apaches, who agreed to fight as mercenaries against the Lipan Apaches. Confronted by this alliance the latter found it prudent to make peace in 1780. Yet the peace treaties proved short-lived, for in 1781 the Apaches resumed hostilities.

Initially, their most destructive raids were against haciendas around

Parras and Saltillo, but by 1784 the Sánchez Navarros' properties were also under attack. In May, Apaches slaughtered 112 sheep from one of the flocks.[36] Depredations became increasingly serious during the next few years. In December, 1785, the foreman of Tapado urgently requested a shipment of gunpowder; and in February, 1786, Manuel Francisco had to assign several armed men to guard the flocks at the lambing pastures, where the Indians had raided during the last two full moons.[37] That month they even attacked Tapado, driving off a herd of horses.

José Miguel immediately notified the governor of this latest outrage, and that official expressed his sympathy but observed philosophically that the Indians "always emerge triumphant and with profit" from their forays.[38] To make matters worse, the Apaches were taking a heavy toll of the Sánchez Navarros' shepherds, leading Manuel Francisco to comment that "these wretches are bearing the brunt of the raids. May God grant that the savages cease inflicting such casualties."[39] José Miguel did not confine himself to lamenting the situation; instead, the curate prepared to smite the ungodly by sending additional muskets, ammunition, and gunpowder to Tapado.[40]

As Father Morfi had observed, the Sánchez Navarros defended their properties with greater determination than did most other ranchers; but the brothers nevertheless continued to take heavy losses, especially in 1790 when the current wave of incursions reached its climax. During the month of March alone, Apaches killed fourteen of the workers at Tapado, besides plundering a train of Manuel Francisco's oxcarts on the road between Tapado and Santa Rosa. In April the Indians wantonly slaughtered five hundred sheep at Tapado, and in May they killed two herders and carried off a youth.[41]

The casualty figures for Coahuila as a whole were alarming: in March, 1790, the Apaches killed forty persons, wounded two, and stole 812 horses.[42] In attempting to combat these incursions, the authorities were hampered by the apathy of the citizens, many of whom fatalistically accepted the Indian menace as a calamity visited on them by God. The governor finally had to resort to such drastic measures as fining *hacendados* who failed to arm their servants, especially those tending livestock. On the other hand, the governor also found it necessary to impose punishments on the servants themselves—they habitually neglected to carry weapons even when these were available.[43] Nor were urban dwellers capable of an aggressive defense, judging from a 1791 census of the able-bodied men in Monclova and its environs. Of 444 individuals, 149 were weaponless. Moreover, in a situation where only cavalry were effective against the highly mobile Indians, the townspeople could muster only 287 horses.[44]

Fortunately the Monclovans did not have to take the field to any extent, for depredations began to diminish sharply toward the end of 1791. The authorities had finally found a solution to the problem of frontier defense: as the regular troops defeated the Indians in battle, they collected, resettled, and provisioned the nomads in reservations located near the presidios.[45]

With the typical frontiersman's distrust of Indians, Manuel Francisco viewed their current inactivity as the probable prelude to a new, and even more devastating, wave of depredations. A flurry of minor raids did occur in January, 1792, involving the theft of livestock from the vicinity of Santa Rosa and other presidios.[46] But despite these incidents, and occasionally others of a similar nature, the frontier at last entered an era of relative peace.[47]

The Indian menace might have declined, but there remained the specter of recurring drought, the other scourge of northern ranchers. The lack of vegetation that Father Morfi observed around Tapado was not due entirely to the Sánchez Navarros' oversight—a drought was scorching Coahuila. Traveling from Monclova to Tapado, Morfi himself had commented on the blighted countryside, noting that little rain had fallen during the last four years.[48] The drought had begun in 1774, just as the Sánchez Navarros had built their ranch into a large-scale operation.

Sheep were able to withstand drought much better than cattle. They devoured weeds that cattle would reject and could forage in terrain too rough for the larger animals. More importantly, sheep had recourse to several substitutes for water. The flocks could survive for weeks at a time on the moisture obtained by licking dew from vegetation, by eating succulent desert flowers, or by feeding on the roots of the spiky *sotol* plant, which the shepherds dug up and split open for them.[49]

Nevertheless, these measures could not be employed indefinitely, and the onset of the drought marked the beginning of a period when the brothers lost much of their livestock. The surviving records are fragmentary, but if the losses they report are projected for the duration of the drought it must be concluded that the *hacienda de ovejas* suffered severely. By 1775 the accustomed lambing pastures could not be used, because the flocks were being driven from place to place in search of water. During the July, 1776, lambing season alone, 866 sheep died, and the lamb crop barely reached 4,800 head.[50] As Morfi observed, the drought continued to sear Coahuila during 1777. Thus, while the number of sheep that perished cannot be precisely determined, the Sánchez Navarros suffered crippling losses. The drought finally broke in 1778, and Manuel Francisco stoically set about rebuilding the flocks.

He succeeded despite the recurrence of drought in 1784–1785, in 1790, and again in 1798–1802. The latter was especially serious, approaching in intensity the ruinous drought of 1774–1777. By February, 1802, the seventy yoke of oxen at Tapado had been reduced to twenty, and many of these were too weak for plowing. By April, thirty-five dairy cows had died, and the rest were too thin to be milked. Several thousand sheep had also died, not only from the drought but also from an epidemic that had broken out in some flocks at the beginning of 1802.[51] In an atmosphere of deepening gloom José Miguel traveled to Tapado to inspect the situation. While he and Manuel Francisco were conferring, rain came at last.

The remedy, however, was worse than the disease; it seemed as though every drop of rain lacking for the last few years fell at once. A torrential thunderstorm burst over Monclova on the afternoon of May 25, 1802, and the rains continued unabated until June 3; violent storms again drenched the area from June 23 to July 3. The terrified townspeople attributed the ending of the disastrous rains to the intercession of their patroness the Virgin of Zapopan, whose image they had in desperation carried in a solemn procession to the crest of a nearby hill. The deluge had been a catastrophe. Besides the total loss of crops, more than 150 of the adobe buildings in the town had disintegrated under the relentless downpour; of those still standing, most were without roofs.[52] As reports began to trickle in, it was learned that a major disaster had occurred throughout a wide area; every settlement between Monclova and Monterrey had likewise been devastated.[53]

The Sánchez Navarros had suffered a serious setback. Besides their losses at Monclova, operations on the *latifundio* had been disrupted, the flocks were in worse shape than ever, and the *casco* of Tapado, which was built of adobe, had been heavily damaged.[54] Moreover, the brothers were unable to confront this crisis with their customary energy. For one thing, they were advancing in years: José Miguel was now seventy-two and Manuel Francisco fifty-nine. Yet their progressively poor health, rather than their age, was the real problem. José Miguel suffered from an assortment of ills, among them gallstones, the loss of most of his teeth, and arthritis in his hands; Manuel Francisco had a painful condition in his legs that often made it impossible for him to mount a horse.

The solution was to have Manuel Francisco's two eldest sons assume part of the managerial burden. The younger, José Miguel's namesake, helped administer the haciendas near Santa Rosa. He appears to have been a compassionate *hacendado*, for in September, 1802, he had to borrow money from his uncle the curate because he had allowed persons leasing small parcels of land to postpone paying their rent until the next maize harvest.[55] His twenty-year-old elder brother, José Melchor, was made of sterner stuff. José Melchor assumed primary responsibility for managing Tapado in the summer of 1802, and his guiding principle was to tighten administration in order to maximize profits.[56] He was a harsh disciplinarian and on several occasions found himself in difficulties with the governor for mistreating peons.[57] Nonetheless, José Melchor did begin to rejuvenate the management of the landholding, completely overshadowing his younger brother.

Having divested himself of the crushing responsibilities under which he had worked for decades, the weary Manuel Francisco retired to his home in Santa Rosa. His participation in *latifundio* affairs was now limited to advising his sons as they served their apprenticeship. But Manuel Francisco was not destined to enjoy his well-earned leisure for long. His health was rapidly failing; in February, 1805, at the Hacienda de Dolores, the grizzled rancher died at the age of sixty-two, leaving José Melchor to carry on.[58]

José Melchor's accession as the curate's junior partner restored a firm hand to the management of the Sánchez Navarros' properties. As we have seen, the curate agreed to make José Melchor his sole heir if the younger man would operate the family's commercial enterprises. José Melchor's youthful energy was tempered by José Miguel's business acumen and experience, the two men constituting a formidable team.

Symbolizing José Melchor's policy of making the landholding more productive was the construction of a new *casco* on the left bank of the Nadadores, some four miles downriver from Tapado.[59] The site was chosen with an eye to better utilization of the Ojo Caliente, a hot spring located a mile and a half to the southwest. This permanent spring was to be the principal source of water for the new hacienda, thereby lessening the Sánchez Navarros' dependence on the Nadadores with its seasonal fluctuations.

The new *casco*, named Nuestra Señora de las Tres Hermanas, was built on a much grander scale than Tapado. The ranch house was conventional in design: a one-story structure in the form of a quadrangle around an extensive patio. The patio was connected to the front gate with a passage large enough to accommodate vehicles. Under José Melchor's direction work continued intermittently for decades, and Hermanas eventually reached impressive proportions. Two wings, each built around a large plaza, were subsequently added to the main house. The northern wing contained offices, quarters for the administrative personnel, and installations for processing sugar cane, while the southern wing had tenements for peons, as well as several granaries. A carriage house was also built at the rear of the main house.

Hermanas thus evolved into an enormous structure enclosing three quadrangles and having a façade measuring 250 yards. Among the outbuildings were a small chapel for the peons and clusters of huts where some of the workers lived. Surrounding the entire *casco* was a thick stone wall, ten feet high. Unlike Tapado, Hermanas was built entirely of stone, which precluded a repetition of the storm damage the adobe buildings at Tapado had suffered in 1802.[60]

In designing such an imposing structure, José Melchor was looking ahead to the day when he would inherit the landholding, and he was building a residence befitting the scion of the Sánchez Navarro family. This motive undoubtedly became stronger after his marriage in 1807 to María Francisca Apolonia de Beráin, a young lady from a moderately well-to-do family in Santa Rosa.[61]

Until the day of his inheritance, however, José Melchor's job was to manage the *latifundio* as efficiently as possible. He spent a good deal of time in the saddle making a circuit between the Tapado-Hermanas complex and his own Soledad and Dolores haciendas. His usual procedure was to spend some time at each *casco* supervising activities and issuing instructions for the operation of that hacienda until his next visit. He varied the pattern by riding out to inspect the flocks as they moved across the range. José Melchor made a point of keeping his uncle informed, almost on a daily basis, of developments on the landholding. The administrative personnel at the haciendas also sent a stream of reports to the curate, who still handled the Sánchez Navarros' financial affairs but, because of age and poor health, now rarely left Monclova.

In marked contrast to his father's situation, José Melchor had a much freer hand in operating the *latifundio*. One way in which he exercised this authority was by trying to eliminate incompetent subordinates. Besides dismissing or reassigning several of the overseers at Tapado, he fired two foremen in succession before he found one to his liking.[62] Although this reshuffling of personnel caused some initial confusion, in the long run it did make for greater efficiency. José Melchor was determined to get as much work as possible from each employee, not only because there existed a chronic labor shortage on the *latifundio*, but also because he had very ambitious plans for the landholding. The construction of Hermanas remained his favorite project, but in addition he was vitally interested in expanding the acreage under cultivation.

One of the most widely accepted generalizations about the hacienda
is that the goal of every *hacendado* was to make his properties self-
sufficient. But there is increasing evidence that this assertion needs
further investigation. A recent study of the important sugar-producing
Hacienda de Atlacomulco in Morelos demonstrates that "self-
sufficiency was neither achieved nor expected" on that estate.[63] Although the Sánchez Navarros did not operate plantations like Atlacomulco, they really did not strive to achieve self-sufficiency either.
As we shall see, they were content to purchase most of the manufactured articles, clothing, and textiles required. The only area where
self-sufficiency counted was in raising enough maize for the peons'
rations.

For the first few years of Tapado's existence, the grain required at
that hacienda came from the curate's farm near Monclova.[64] The Sánchez Navarros subsequently raised crops at Tapado itself, though, at
the time of Morfi's visit in 1777, only a small area was under cultivation. Most of the fields were devoted to maize, the practice in Coahuila being to raise two crops a year. By the beginning of 1780, the
Sánchez Navarros had dug an irrigation ditch and had planted thirty-
five acres in wheat.[65] Though used in emergencies for the peons' rations, wheat was primarily a cash crop. With most of the production
earmarked for the brothers' flour mill in Monclova, wheat represented
yet another step in the integration of their business enterprises.

The expanding agricultural activities at Tapado received a sharp
setback during the drought of 1784–1785, which produced a general
crop failure.[66] But within two years the situation had improved appreciably, for two hundred acres were planted in wheat, of which Tapado produced two crops a year.[67] The increased yields at Tapado reflected the generally improved condition of agriculture in Coahuila,
whose governor reported an abundant grain harvest in 1787 and excellent prospects for the coming year.[68]

Yet, because of recurring drought, agriculture remained a precarious undertaking. Following the abundant harvests of the late 1780's,
there occurred a crisis in 1790. Drought drastically curtailed the grain
supply, and the governor prohibited the shipment of flour outside the
province. Adding to the threat of famine was the abnormally small

amount of maize available for planting. Timely rains averted disaster, and in January, 1791, the governor rescinded his ban on grain exports.[69]

By this time the Sánchez Navarros had made considerable progress, because both Tapado and Dolores produced bumper crops of wheat and corn.[70] Tapado in fact produced a variety of crops. In 1792, a favorable year, the tract at the Ojo Caliente alone yielded 2,228 bushels of maize. As for wheat, the only specific reference is to a planting of thirty acres, though there were presumably other fields devoted to this grain. Besides the staple crops, the hacienda had small fields of beans, chile, squash, and sugar cane, and a vineyard was established with cuttings brought from Monclova.[71]

After several years of favorable conditions drought again ruined agriculture in Coahuila. By 1798 the wheat harvests at Tapado were negligible, and the Sánchez Navarros found themselves forced to purchase wheat despite the exorbitant price it commanded.[72] Yet the brothers persisted in planting on schedule in a gamble that the rigorous drought would break. The scant rainfall during the next three years did little to alleviate the situation: by February, 1801, Manuel Francisco was merely trying to salvage a few of the irrigated fields at Tapado.[73]

José Miguel redoubled his efforts to purchase grain but met only with frustration. The agricultural crisis was taking on biblical overtones; as if the devastating drought were not enough, a plague of locusts descended on the croplands in the central part of the province.[74] And even those areas free of locusts had some other calamity to report. At the Hacienda de Patos, for instance, a combination of drought and a plant fungus called *chahuistle* destroyed most of the standing wheat.[75] The drought extended as far away as Monterrey where the price of corn soared in the fall of 1801 and winter of 1802.[76]

When relief came in the summer of 1802, in the form of the torrential downpours already mentioned, the deluge also extended as far as Monterrey. The combination of drought and floods resulted in a general shortage of grain in Monclova, Monterrey, and Saltillo, where the fortunate few who had reaped a decent harvest were reportedly becoming wealthy.[77] The Sánchez Navarros were in no position to profit from the situation, for the wheat crop at Tapado had been very scanty, and José Miguel was still attempting to arrange purchases of grain. He had his business agent in Saltillo investigate the possibilities there, but the reply was far from encouraging; wheat was so scarce that the municipal authorities prohibited its leaving the city.[78] José Miguel himself made inquiries at the Hacienda de Patos, only to learn that no wheat was available from that source. In addition to drought and fungus, the crop at Patos had suffered from a fierce hailstorm in May just before harvest time, and the yield was only a third of the previous year's disappointing harvest. To meet the shortage the *administrador* of Patos planned to buy maize from central New Spain at the Saltillo fair in September.[79] The curate presumably had to do likewise.

Thus, when the youthful José Melchor took over the operation of the *latifundio* in the aftermath of the 1802 crisis, one of his chief concerns was to expand the acreage under cultivation in order to stockpile grain reserves for the next siege of drought. He plunged into his duties with enthusiasm, though he complained constantly about the magnitude of the task confronting him. With the return of favorable weather in 1803, he repeatedly complained to his uncle that there were simply not enough peons at Tapado to harvest the bumper crops, let alone attend to the other chores.[80] And there was no end of other chores because José Melchor frequently initiated projects that spread the available manpower even more thinly.

Realizing that irrigation was the key to success in agriculture, he decided on a major expansion of the irrigation system. In 1805 he had the existing network extensively repaired and the following year began to have new canals and ditches dug farther down the Nadadores. The harassed foreman of Tapado appealed to the curate, pointing out that he lacked the laborers necessary to carry out José Melchor's orders.[81] While appreciating the importance of his nephew's project, the curate ordered that routine hacienda activities receive first priority and that work on the irrigation system proceed only when men could be spared.[82]

José Melchor reluctantly accepted this ruling but continued to use every available man to work on the *casco* of Hermanas and on an irrigation system for the new hacienda. He proposed to dig a large canal from the Ojo Caliente to the headquarters, a mile and a half distant. As did everything else at Hermanas, the canal evidenced solid construction, for it was completely lined with masonry. While one crew toiled at the Ojo Caliente, another excavated the large reservoir into which the canal would empty.[83]

Not until the early 1820's would the project be completed, but by 1817, a temporary irrigation ditch enabled José Melchor to plant some fifty acres in maize. Hermanas would eventually eclipse Tapado, but for the remainder of the colonial period, the older hacienda remained the center of the growing agricultural complex. In 1816, for example, José Melchor greatly enlarged the vineyard at Tapado, adding 3,200 new grapevines.[84]

The *hacendado* was simultaneously developing the northern section of the landholding. Soledad underwent the greatest improvement, as it was primarily an agricultural estate. By 1815 the hacienda produced wheat, corn, and sugar cane, and land had been prepared for planting cotton. In addition there was an extensive orchard, and the *mayordomo* was supervising the planting of three thousand new grapevines. Even at the nearby Hacienda de Dolores, used for stock raising, a modest agricultural program was under way.[85]

The increasing emphasis on agriculture began to pay dividends, although recurring drought still caused periods of anxiety. The years 1805–1807 were unusually dry, but thereafter conditions progressively improved until by 1811 even José Melchor was satisfied.[86] That year the June wheat harvest at Tapado was excellent, and the maize crop in October exceeded 1,000 bushels.[87] Agriculture flourished through the summer of 1814, when the wheat harvest produced more than 1,100 bushels of high-quality grain.[88]

But another drought cycle was developing; by the spring of 1816, the Sánchez Navarros again faced the problem of securing enough maize for their peons' rations. Anticipating a crisis, the curate arranged to purchase corn in Saltillo despite its outrageous price. To be doubly certain of an adequate supply, he also investigated the possibility of buying grain in Nuevo León.[89] José Melchor prevailed on his uncle to suspend these negotiations. Having made a careful inventory of the granaries at Tapado, the young *hacendado* felt there was just enough grain to tide them over until January, 1817, when the harvest would be in from the northern haciendas.[90] José Melchor's confidence in the Sánchez Navarros' internal resources proved justified. In January he proudly reported that the maize harvest at Soledad, combined with the remaining stores at Tapado, amounted to more than two thousand bushels, enough for the foreseeable future.[91]

The same pattern repeated itself a year later: the possibility of a temporary shortage by January, 1818, the Sánchez Navarros making arrangements to purchase grain if necessary, and the crisis ending as a result of good harvests at the northern estates. Soledad produced 1,555 bushels of maize, two-thirds of which quickly went to Tapado for rations. In addition, 365 bushels of wheat from Soledad went to Monclova, presumably destined for the Sánchez Navarros' flour mill.[92]

Drought hampered agriculture for the remainder of the decade. The Ojo Caliente, for example, flowed at less than its normal rate much of the time.[93] Yet the Sánchez Navarros managed to operate without undue hardship because the harvests from the northern haciendas offset the reduced yields at the Tapado-Hermanas complex.[94] José Melchor had achieved his goal of making the *latifundio* self-sufficient regarding rations. This was a remarkable accomplishment since agriculture had but a secondary priority.

José Melchor's main concern was always the livestock, particularly the *hacienda de ovejas*. In the decade 1810–1820, with the viceroyalty in the throes of the struggle for independence, the conditions under which José Melchor worked became increasingly unfavorable. Not only did he face the problem of drought, but also he had to contend with encroachment on the *latifundio*: the military made requisitions, and, most ominously, there was a terrifying new wave of Indian depredations.

The sheer magnitude of their operations kept the Sánchez Navarros in business, for they could absorb losses that would have ruined smaller ranchers. There was, for example, the matter of epidemics that occasionally swept the flocks. One in 1805 was so severe that the January lamb crop barely offset the number of animals dead from disease; another in 1814 resulted in the loss of 3,600 sheep during October and November alone.[95] But since revolutionary turmoil deprived the Sánchez Navarros of their accustomed markets outside Coahuila, the *hacienda de ovejas* continued to show a net increase in the years immediately following the outbreak of the rebellion.

The revolution heightened José Melchor's concern for the flocks. On one occasion in 1814 the foreman of Tapado reported that one hundred sheep had perished of thirst before they could be driven to the river.[96] This explanation enraged José Melchor, who held the foreman personally responsible, demanding that he salvage the pelts and fat from the dead animals. José Melchor's anger over the loss of a few sheep was not merely an example of his impatience with incompetent subordinates; it also reflected the *hacendado*'s deep fears for the future. Any loss to the flocks was now magnified in importance by his belief that the Sánchez Navarros' only hope lay in preserving the *hacienda de ovejas* until peace returned to the viceroyalty.[97]

One aspect of the turbulent times was the emergence of a new threat to the Sánchez Navarros' interests—rustlers. At first José Melchor simply ignored them, but by 1816 the inroads they were making on the stock at Tapado forced him to take action. His suspicions centered on a cluster of *vinaterías*, crude distilleries producing the potent liquors *sotol* and *aguardiente*. Established within the southern boundary of the landholding by squatters, these stills attracted a disreputable element; and the *hacendado* became convinced that their clientele consisted mainly of rustlers. Determined to eliminate the *vinaterías*, José Melchor secured the cooperation of the military authorities, who placed a detachment of cavalry at his disposal. In July, 1816, he led the troops in a sweep across the range southeast of Tapado. From José Melchor's point of view the operation was highly successful, for he burned out nine *vinaterías* and in the process discovered cowhides bearing the Sánchez Navarro brand as well as other evidence of criminal activity.[98] This show of force seemingly put an end to the wave of rustling.

Yet the malefactors showed surprising resiliency. Squatters soon established new *vinaterías*, and rustlers resumed their activities. José Melchor again secured the cooperation of the authorities in meeting the threat. Troops were in short supply, but the Sánchez Navarros' relative, Arizpe, the tax collector, went to Tapado as the representative of officialdom; José Melchor detailed a group of *vaqueros* to accompany Arizpe in destroying three new distilleries. The *hacendado* regretted that the press of work prevented him from leading the raids in person. But, in spite of the harsh measures employed against rustlers, a few hardy thieves continued to ply their trade.[99]

José Melchor failed to stamp out rustling, for his adversaries were not only persistent but also imaginative. One time the *hacendado* sent six riders to scour the range for some missing oxen, and in the course of their search the men blundered into a party of eight Indians. Several of the warriors were busily butchering a cow while the rest guarded a herd of stolen Sánchez Navarro horses. Because the *vaqueros* had imprudently left their muskets some distance away so as not to damage the firearms while they searched through heavy brush, they had to race back to retrieve their weapons. One of the men rode on to the *casco* to give the alarm while his companions engaged the Indians. José Melchor immediately dispatched reinforcements, and, in a running fight lasting a day, his men managed to recover the horses and capture two of the Indians, only to discover that they were rustlers in disguise.

Caught red-handed with the meat they had stolen, the rustlers were conducted under guard to Tapado. José Melchor notified the authorities but requested that, instead of sending the prisoners to Monclova for trial, he be permitted to punish them at Tapado by putting them in irons and forcing them to labor in the fields until they had worked off the value of the butchered cow.[100] It is not known whether the authorities agreed, but, given José Melchor's hatred of rustlers and the chronic labor shortage at the hacienda, if his request was in fact granted it may be assumed that the cow became the most valuable animal ever raised in Coahuila.

Besides rustlers, the Sánchez Navarros faced another threat, this time from the authorities themselves. As the revolution wore on, forced loans and military requisitions became the order of the day, much to José Melchor's disgust. In 1814, a detachment of presidial cavalry began seizing cattle, but, as matters developed, only a few head were taken. The foreman of Tapado gleefully reported that the troops proved singularly inept at rounding up the livestock. They spent a week in the attempt—during which time bulls gored three of their horses and the soldiers rode several of their mounts to death—and were unable to catch a single animal. The foreman contemptuously cut out a few head for them, and the mortified troops left with twelve bulls and eight yearlings.[101] Other forced contributions were somewhat less amusing. They included 575 sheep, 85 head of cattle, a quantity of produce, and a sum in cash. The value of the contributions totaled 3,067 pesos, but the only part that really mattered was the 530 pesos paid in cash; natural increase soon offset the loss of the other items.[102]

The whole matter of forced contributions became a real crisis in the spring of 1817. The Spanish exile Javier Mina had organized an expedition to aid the Mexican insurgents, and in April the commandant general of the Interior Provinces received word that part of the rebel expedition had landed at the mouth of the Río Grande. Reacting to this alarming news, the general ordered two-thirds of the troops in Coahuila to concentrate at Laredo without delay. Furthermore, horses and mules throughout the province were to be requisitioned in order to provide remounts and to transport ammunition. In issuing these orders to the commander of the Monclova garrison, Lt. Francisco Adam, the general emphasized that, if any favoritism were shown, Adam would be held personally responsible.

Adam reluctantly sent his friend José Melchor a copy of the order, together with a covering note stating that an officer was on his way to Tapado to collect the livestock. A badly worried José Melchor immediately notified his uncle, the curate. José Miguel, in turn, brought sufficient pressure to bear on Adam to make that officer risk incurring the general's wrath by exempting the Sánchez Navarros' stock.[103] But, in view of the emergency, the governor of Coahuila personally intervened, overruling Adam and demanding that José Melchor send all his livestock to Monclova for the army to select what they needed. The *hacendado* grudgingly began rounding up the animals at Tapado, and his disposition was not improved by learning that the authorities at Santa Rosa were doing the same with the stock at the northern haciendas. The loss of this livestock, whose numbers had already been greatly reduced by Indian raids, would, of course, be a staggering blow to operations throughout the *latifundio*.

With disaster looming, the Sánchez Navarros were saved by a stroke of sheer luck. Word reached Santa Rosa that the report of Mina's landing had been erroneous; the rebels had actually disembarked much farther down the coast of Tamaulipas. Since the Coahuilan troops would not be involved in combatting the invasion, the requisitioning of livestock was halted.[104] Despite this reprieve, the Sánchez Navarros still faced the bleak prospect of trying to carry on their ranching operations under the dual threat of levies by the Spanish authorities and raids by the Indians.

This new wave of depredations was essentially a by-product of the struggle for independence. Except for occasional minor raids, the Indians had been quiescent since the early 1790's.[105] But from 1810 on, with the government concentrating its military forces in the central part of the viceroyalty where the rebellion was the most serious, frontier defenses were necessarily weakened.

Once again the Apaches posed a major threat to the inhabitants of Coahuila. Travel on the roads became extremely dangerous, and strong war parties assembled in the vicinity of Santa Rosa. During the summer of 1814, they raided not only the Hacienda de San Juan de Sabinas but also more distant estates, such as Encinas. Even as far away as Tapado, the foreman began taking extraordinary precautions to protect the *remuda*.[106] But the Indians retained the initiative, and conditions progressively deteriorated. By 1816, José Melchor had to contend with an alarming turnover among his shepherds, many of whom were fleeing in fear of the Apaches.[107] More importantly, the Indians' relentless pressure on the Santa Rosa region forced José Melchor to prepare to evacuate the remaining horses and mules from his Dolores and Soledad haciendas. He arranged with his brother-in-law, José Gerónimo Cacho, to transfer the livestock to Cacho's ranch on the Mesa de Cartujanos, an extensive tableland on the Nuevo León border.[108] But because José Melchor became involved in combatting rustlers and burning out *vinaterías* he delayed the evacuation until it was too late.

The blow that José Melchor was dreading fell in January, 1817. Apaches devastated northern Coahuila with a ferocity unmatched for a generation. Arriving at Soledad to supervise the proposed evacuation, the *hacendado* was greeted with a tale of disaster. Several nights earlier a raiding party had swept through a pasture near the headquarters, stealing thirty-four pack mules as well as other livestock gathered there for safekeeping. At daybreak, the *mayordomo* and seven *vaqueros* set out in pursuit but after following the trail for some distance discovered the tracks of a large war party, whereupon they discreetly withdrew. The Indians not only kept the animals they had stolen but also boldly struck again the next night at Soledad, running off two more herds of José Melchor's stock. Another halfhearted pursuit was mounted, but only the marauders' tracks were found. Writing to inform his uncle of these outrages, José Melchor mentioned that lately the only topics of conversation around Santa Rosa were the daily losses inflicted by the Apaches and the settlers' lament that there was little hope of stemming the tide.

Determined to keep Soledad in operation, José Melchor took personal charge of the hacienda. His immediate concern was that of shipping corn to Tapado for rations. Mule trains had customarily been used for this purpose, but as a result of the depredations only ten pack mules remained at Soledad. Nevertheless, by employing oxcarts and making several round trips, the *hacendado* managed to get the vital grain to its destination without undue delay.[109] He had been surprised and relieved to learn that the oxcarts had not been ambushed on the road. Perhaps this was because the Apaches continued to concentrate on stripping Soledad itself of livestock.

Even with José Melchor personally directing the defense, the Indians scored successes. On the night of January 23, they surrounded the *casco* of Soledad, and, though José Melchor and his men repelled the attack, the nomads made off with a drove of horses. This time the pursuit was more vigorous. The *hacendado* sent a party of *vaqueros* to cut the raiders' probable line of retreat. The ensuing ambush was partially successful; the Indians escaped, but some of the stolen stock was recovered.

With resistance stiffening at Soledad the Indians turned their attention to José Melchor's other hacienda, Dolores. In a night attack, they burned several of the workers' huts, although the peon families sleeping inside managed to escape. The next day, however, the Apaches returned and stole most of the livestock at the hacienda.[110]

By then the focus of José Melchor's concern was elsewhere—the Apaches had been attacking the *hacienda de ovejas*. They swept through the flocks in late January, just as the lambing season was beginning, killing two shepherds and capturing two youths working as lambers. Combined with the other depredations, this attack proved too much even for the resolute José Melchor: he took the unprecedented step of ordering the evacuation of the *hacienda de ovejas*. The imperiled flocks were moved from their location along the Sabinas River: the pregnant ewes were herded to the Hacienda de Encinas where the lambing would take place, and the remainder of the sheep were dispersed to the east of Tapado. Armed guards defended the lambing pastures, but the rest of the shepherds had to shift for themselves. Their only protection was to keep each other in sight and to run for the hills if the alarm were given.[111]

As if to make painfully clear that they dominated the northern part of the province, the Apaches several months later daringly attacked the interim governor of Texas who, accompanied by Lieutenant Adam and other officials, was traveling to Santa Rosa with an escort of sixty presidial troopers. Nor was this all; the Indians murdered several carters on the road north of the beleaguered town.[112] José Melchor continued to strengthen the defenses of the northern haciendas, but he soon had to suspend this activity and race back to Tapado.

In an ominous development, the Apaches were now raiding into central Coahuila, and the curate had summoned José Melchor to the headquarters of the *latifundio* to deal with the situation. The *hacendado* detailed ten armed men to guard the *hacienda de ovejas*, but the measure failed to raise the morale of the terrified shepherds, who frequently sighted Apaches near the flocks. Depredations in the vicinity of Tapado did intensify, with both the Sánchez Navarros and their neighbors the Vázquez Borregos suffering appreciable losses of livestock but surprisingly few casualties. The incursions certainly did not bear out José Melchor's pessimistic prediction that the Indians would soon destroy the haciendas in central Coahuila.[113]

The northern section of the *latifundio* remained under heavy attack, though, and José Melchor traveled with an armed escort back to Soledad to direct operations. He found the northern haciendas literally overrun; not only were war parties frequently sighted on the range but also bands of Indians occupied the sandbars in the Sabinas River and were even moving into the fields at Soledad. According to José Melchor, they flaunted themselves day and night. When some twenty Apaches were discovered calmly picking watermelons and ears of corn at Soledad, it was more than the frustrated *hacendado* could bear. He immediately sent a dozen riders, composed of his escort and *vaqueros* from Dolores, to attack the arrogant tribesmen. The Indians were routed with a loss of four killed, but three of José Melchor's men were mortally wounded.[114]

José Melchor had planned only a brief visit to his haciendas before returning to Tapado, but the situation was so grave that he had to remain for several months. So much livestock had been stolen that the whole routine of operations was breaking down. To rebuild the *remuda* at Soledad he had stock brought in from Dolores, but the Apaches stole the animals almost as soon as they arrived. The distraught *hacendado* then had horses brought all the way from Tapado, with the same result.[115] On one occasion he was even reduced to using his own coach mules to transport a shipment of freight to Santa Rosa.

After each raid, he duly notified the garrison at Santa Rosa, but there was little the troops could do. And even on those infrequent occasions when the cavalry did succeed in recovering stolen herds the *hacendado*'s jubilation was usually brief, for the Indians seemed to take pride in their work and could be counted on to steal the animals back within a matter of days.[116]

Summarizing the Indian invasion during the catastrophic year 1817, the governor of Coahuila stressed the defenseless condition of the inhabitants. Very few of them could afford firearms, and, in any case, the military had already collected most of the weapons in the province for use against the insurgents in central New Spain. Frontier defense therefore rested with the presidial garrisons totaling 400 men. Yet the governor could barely put 200 troops in the field, and only 136 of these were cavalry. Despite these limited resources the army had managed to contain the invasion, preventing the Apaches from penetrating any farther southward than the Hacienda de Tapado.[117]

More significantly, conditions gradually improved after 1817. The struggle for independence was collapsing throughout the viceroyalty, and the government could finally devote serious attention to the embattled northern frontier. The rejuvenated presidial cavalry became somewhat more effective at recovering stolen livestock, a development quite pleasing to José Melchor, who otherwise had nothing but contempt for the military and their exactions. In the fall of 1818, for instance, the cavalry recovered several herds for the *hacendado*, one of them consisting of 215 horses stolen from Tapado.[118]

Matching the military's newly found fighting spirit was the increasing aggressiveness shown by the settlers themselves. Firearms were evidently becoming available in greater quantities because the citizenry took a more active, if uncoordinated, role in combatting depredations. An example of this trend was a series of clashes near Santa Rosa in September, 1819. The running skirmishes involved not only the cavalry, but also some of José Melchor's *vaqueros* and several parties of townspeople. Though each side suffered five killed, it was the Indians, accustomed to raiding with impunity, who broke off the engagement and fled with their enemies in hot pursuit.[119]

Resistance to the Indians was stiffening, but lack of cooperation among the settlers sometimes reduced its effectiveness. The foreman of Tapado notified the curate in September that Indians had stolen José Melchor's prize coach mules; the animals had been recovered, but the Apaches had escaped scot-free despite an excellent opportunity to chastize them. As the foreman and his men were pursuing the fleeing raiders, they encountered the *alcalde* of San Vicente de Arriba at the head of a group of horsemen. While the foreman and the *alcalde* argued about who should command the joint force, the Indians disappeared across the Nadadores.[120]

As the decade drew to a close, the Indian menace was stabilizing.

Raids remained a way of life, and stock continued to be stolen from the *latifundio*, but the incursions lacked the ferocity of earlier years.[121] And, even though they had lost thousands of horses and mules, the Sánchez Navarros could still count themselves fortunate. Since Coahuila had not been a major battleground during the revolutionary war, the family had escaped the destruction visited on *hacendados* nearer the center of the viceroyalty. To mention but a single instance, insurgents in Guanajuato had looted and burned the magnificent Hacienda de San Diego del Jaral, the seat of the Marquis of Jaral de Berrio's *latifundio*. It was a blow from which the Marquis never fully recovered.[122]

The Sánchez Navarros, on the other hand, emerged from the turbulent decade with their landholding relatively intact. None of their *cascos* had suffered appreciable damage, the livestock they had lost could be replaced by natural increase, and, above all, the *hacienda de ovejas* was still intact. But the flocks required shepherds to tend them; and, as long as the Indian menace continued, it aggravated one of the most critical problems the Sánchez Navarros faced—a chronic labor shortage.

3. Labor

The salient feature of the labor system in Coahuila was debt peonage, the practice whereby servants were bound to their masters as long as the former owed the latter money. Because of the sparse population and the often hazardous working conditions in the province, labor was scarce, and peonage constituted the most effective means of ensuring a continuing supply.

But peonage was a system in which workers were largely at the mercy of their employers. Writing in 1766 to the viceroy, the governor denounced the conditions then obtaining in Coahuila. He reported that servants were paid by the month, but in Coahuila a thirty-day month was used instead of the twenty-four–day work month common in most of New Spain. The month, furthermore, consisted of thirty individual days of work; employers often assigned tasks that could not be completed in a single day and then refused to credit workers for this labor. The governor mentioned the case of a servant who had worked for three years but had only ten months' labor credited to his account. Servants received payment in merchandise whose price was fixed at the whim of the employer. Labor was in demand mainly at planting and harvest time—approximately one month in the spring and another in the fall. During the rest of the year there was little work for servants to perform to reduce their indebtedness, although they continued to receive goods on credit. The result was that they incurred debts they could never hope to pay. The governor cited the case of a servant who owed his master more than three hundred pesos.[1] When servants died, not only were their few possessions taken in partial payment, but also their sons, sometimes while still minors, entered the master's service to work off the balance of the debt.

Such was the situation when the Sánchez Navarros began forming their *latifundio* in 1765. Adhering to the accepted practice, they relied primarily on debt peonage as they recruited their servants. The brothers' labor force consisted mainly of agricultural workers who fell into two broad classifications: full-time resident employees and temporary seasonal hands.

In 1765 José Miguel already had some full-time servants bound by peonage, including five muleteers and several peons, as well as the shepherds who tended his flocks. Most of these individuals had been acquired from other *hacendados*. Whenever peons changed masters their indebtedness accompanied them: the new employer simply reimbursed the former master. A certain Hipólito de Alvarado was sent in 1762 from the Hacienda de Carmen to become a muleteer for the Sánchez Navarros; the money he owed at Carmen was entered as the first item in his account with José Miguel. As in other aspects of the Sánchez Navarros' activities, the Monclova store gave the brothers an advantage in securing peons from neighboring *hacendados*. When a Vázquez Borrego shepherd took service under José Miguel in 1762, for instance, Fernando Vázquez Borrego requested that the sum the man owed the Vázquez Borregos be credited against what the latter owed the curate at the store.[2]

The resident labor force increased as the Sánchez Navarros' ranching operations expanded. Sometimes the brothers hired fugitives from other haciendas, accepting responsibility for the peons' debts to their former masters. But this practice occasionally resulted in disputes between the employers over how much a peon actually owed.[3] During the first two decades of the *latifundio*'s existence many of the resident workers seem to have been either fugitives or persons trying to work off debts incurred in Monclova. There was no lack of opportunity for people to become debtors of the Sánchez Navarros: through credit purchases at the store, small sums borrowed from the curate, or religious fees owed to him.[4]

By the 1790's the Sánchez Navarros were actively soliciting resident workers. Writing from Monterrey in 1793, José Miguel complained that peons could not be secured, though he had instructed his contacts in several cities to hire anyone available. He had done likewise regarding shepherds, ordering that as many as possible be signed on regardless of the amounts owed to their present masters. The curate himself was in touch with the Marquis of Aguayo concerning the hiring of fugitives from that *latifundio*.[5]

More than a decade later, the brothers' business agent in Saltillo was recruiting workers in that city. He dispatched two peons and their families to Tapado in September, 1804, together with an account of the money he had advanced to the men. In 1806, the agent was again carrying out the curate's instructions to secure shepherds. He reported that some were available, but their present masters demanded payment of their debts before allowing the men to take service under the Sánchez Navarros. The agent, knowing little about the shepherds in question, hesitated to accept financial responsibility for them. A business associate of the Sánchez Navarros in Saltillo agreed to act as guarantor while the men went to Tapado for a trial period.[6]

In succeeding years, part of the resident labor force continued to be made up of impoverished individuals who begged the curate for work or for loans, which they guaranteed with their labor. There were also peons who simply presented themselves at Monclova or at Tapado seeking employment. In 1813, these persons included a group of ten shepherds who arrived from Patos; they had left that hacienda because their rations had been reduced. Some of the Sánchez Navarros' property acquisitions constituted yet another source of resident workers. In the course of foreclosing on the late Juan Ignacio de Arizpe's estate in 1818, José Melchor acquired the debts of ten peons who worked for Arizpe.[7]

The Sánchez Navarros also used debts as a means of securing temporary manpower for the *latifundio*. People owing small amounts at the store performed odd jobs, such as assisting the muleteers or, as happened during the drought in 1802, digging a well at Tapado.[8]

The primary need for temporary labor, however, was during the lambing and shearing seasons. For years José Miguel had used his influence to arrange for Tlaxcalans from the settlements around Monclova to go to the Aguayo *latifundio* as shearers.[9] Once the curate himself became a rancher, he engaged the Tlaxcalans to shear Sánchez Navarro sheep.

José Miguel worked through the heads of the Tlaxcalan settlements, such as the villages of San Francisco de Coahuila and Boca de Leones, as well as the Misión de San Miguel de Aguayo. When he sent word of the date on which shearing was scheduled, crews were assembled at these communities and dispatched to Tapado. The shearers received payment in cash, but many of them were also working off debts incurred during the year. In August, 1774, twenty-five Tlaxcalans from San Francisco de Coahuila and the Misión de San Miguel de Aguayo had debts ranging from twelve pesos to five reals, the average being slightly less than four pesos a man. The Sánchez Navarros kept a special ledger at the store to record the indebtedness of shearers, who included persons, not necessarily Tlaxcalans, from the settlements of Nadadores, San Vicente, and Candela. From time to time, the brothers wrote to the local authorities requesting that debtors in those localities be forced to serve as shearers.[10] The number of shearers obtained through these practices varied from season to season. At least twenty-five individuals conducted the August, 1774, shearing, but fewer than twenty worked in August, 1784. In succeeding decades the number ranged from thirty to forty-five.[11]

The Sánchez Navarros recruited extra hands during the lambing season as well as for shearing. In fact, some of the shearers returned to act as lambers.[12] There were differences, though: whereas shearing was conducted mainly with temporary personnel, many of the lambers were resident laborers. In addition, more youths participated in lambing than in shearing. There is no record of wages paid to the temporary lambers. The demand for lambers depended on the number of ewes scheduled to give birth, so the number of people involved fluctuated more widely than during the shearing seasons.

There is no indication whether any of them were temporary personnel, but twenty-two lambers proved more than adequate in January, 1780. Seasonal workers did assist in 1784. Ten of the hired lambers were sent home in January when fewer ewes than anticipated gave birth. The October season was more productive: ten persons went to the pastures initially, followed by two groups of temporary workers, some of them recruited in San Buenaventura. In January, 1786, the lambers numbered twenty-seven, including nine from Nadadores. The January, 1787, season was worked by eighteen men and boys from Tapado assisted by a group of hired hands; for the October season the Sánchez Navarros recruited some forty hired lambers. The season in June, 1790, required only six boys to supplement the workers at Tapado. In January, 1792, however, when a large lamb crop was expected, Manuel Francisco became disturbed because only four persons had arrived from San Buenaventura. According to the *hacendado*, the rest had appealed to the local *alcalde*, claiming that they were not debtors. Manuel Francisco promptly wrote to that official in rebuttal, and he also had the countryside scoured for temporary help.[13]

No major change occurred in the practice of securing temporary lambers when José Melchor managed the *latifundio*. In June, 1811, he dispatched two groups of lambers to reinforce the resident workers already at the pastures. During the October, 1812, season, twenty-six hired hands went to assist the ten lambers sent there initially, and the foreman of Tapado was trying to secure still more men. A year later the lambing crew consisted of thirteen men and sixteen boys. In October, 1814, the foreman sent a group of ten boys to the pastures, and he planned to send another ten within a few days. In November, 1815, an unspecified number of boys went to the lambing. Six youths formed the initial party in April, 1818, and another contingent of temporary lambers joined them shortly afterward. Fourteen men began the January, 1819, season, but the October lambing suffered from a shortage of manpower. Because of the danger of Indian raids, the Sánchez Navarros failed to recruit any youths to act as lambers.[14]

Temporary help at shearing and lambing time was a perennial requirement on the *latifundio*. By the 1780's, however, seasonal help was needed in agriculture, although ranching always had priority when it came to apportioning the work force. The demand for harvesters became especially acute when the acreage devoted to wheat expanded. The Sánchez Navarros had difficulty in securing enough farm workers as early as 1785, when José Miguel tried to hire some harvesters from the Hacienda de Sardinas. In subsequent years, the Sánchez Navarros usually obtained seasonal hands from the Tlaxcalan communities near Monclova, but rarely in the numbers they would have liked. The harvesting crew generally consisted of some ten to twelve men.[15]

The family's urban workers, like those on the *latifundio*, included both resident servants and temporary laborers. The resident servants were mainly Negro and mulatto slaves. Slavery existed on a minor scale in Coahuila; the most heavily populated part of the province—Saltillo and its environs—contained only eighteen male and thirty-five female slaves in 1785. The slaves were usually household servants of one kind or another. On occasion they were even permitted to seek new masters; in 1762, for instance, several Negroes approached Fernando Vázquez Borrego—with their master's consent—and asked the *hacendado* to purchase them, which he did.

Buying a slave represented a substantial investment. When the *hacendado* Francisco Flores de Abrego died in 1772, his possessions included a seven-year-old female slave valued at 100 pesos, as well as another female, age unspecified, worth 50 pesos.[16] José Miguel's and Manuel Francisco's slaves were still more expensive. The curate bought a fifteen-year-old household servant in 1763 for 200 pesos. The youth was guaranteed to have no criminal record and to be sound of wind and limb. Manuel Francisco paid 150 pesos in 1779 for a thirteen-year-old mulatto servant girl, whom the seller certified to be healthy. The *hacendado* acquired additional slaves, for he subsequently referred to several young Negro and mulatto slaves he owned. Furthermore, in 1802 he mentioned that two of his mulattoes had died during an epidemic in Santa Rosa, leaving him with only three. José Miguel also continued to have household slaves for the remainder of the colonial period.[17]

References to other types of resident urban workers are scarce. José

Melchor became the new employer of an unspecified number of laborers in 1813 when he purchased their debts, together with the establishment in Monclova where they worked. Two years later, because of frequent robberies in Monclova, he assigned a permanent night watchman to guard the family's properties in that city. By 1816, the Sánchez Navarros also had a clerk in Monclova. Besides assisting the cashier at the store, the clerk acted as secretary to José Miguel, who was then eighty-six years old.[18]

Although slowed by his age, the curate remained active. Among his interests was the Monclova parish church, which was constructed largely at his expense. The work had been continuing intermittently for decades, and it was in connection with this project that the Sánchez Navarros employed some of their temporary urban labor. The small crew of day laborers secured locally was supplemented by skilled craftsmen, most of them from Saltillo. These artisans included several masons and a master bellmaker, who arrived in 1797 to cast the copper bells the curate had selected for the church. From 1800 through 1805, the Sánchez Navarros kept another crew of a dozen men busy with several building projects designed to improve some of the family's Monclova properties. When these projects were completed, the men joined the crew working on the church.[19]

In contrast to the situation of the urban workers, there was a definite organizational structure for the labor force on the *latifundio*. Large sheep ranches in northern New Spain were organized along similar lines, and the main elements of a typical staff were the *administrador*, *mayordomos*, *caporales*, *vaqueros*, and shepherds. The *administrador* occupied the apex of the hierarchy of employees. Ranking below him were the *mayordomos* who managed the haciendas composing the landholding. Each *mayordomo* issued orders to one or more *caporales*, or foremen, who were responsible for the livestock. A *caporal* in turn supervised several subforemen, often called *vaqueros*. A *vaquero* usually had charge of three shepherds and their flocks.[20]

The Sánchez Navarros conformed to the broad outlines of this organizational structure, but with notable variations. The most significant, of course, was the absence of an *administrador*. By filling this crucial post themselves, first Manuel Francisco and then José Melchor protected the family's interests much more zealously than a hired manager would have done.

The *hacienda de ovejas*, furthermore, had a permanent staff of its own that accompanied and controlled the flocks wherever they might be on the *latifundio*. Like haciendas that were geographical entities, the *hacienda de ovejas* was run by a *mayordomo*. His principal assistant was the *sobresaliente*, a scout who not only selected pastures and checked waterholes but also helped to supervise the lambing and prepare reports. The position of *sobresaliente* existed on the Sánchez Navarro *latifundio* as early as 1771.[21] The rest of the *mayordomo's* immediate staff consisted of several assistants called simply *ayudantes*. Besides carrying out whatever duties the *mayordomo* might assign, each *ayudante* directed a group of mounted overseers who supervised the shepherds. These overseers were called *bacieros* rather than *vaqueros*; on the Sánchez Navarro *latifundio* the latter term referred exclusively to cowboys. The use of the term *baciero*, incidentally, was not peculiar to the Sánchez Navarros, for it was employed on other Coahuilan *latifundios* as well.[22] The Sánchez Navarros' *bacieros* generally had charge of three flocks each, but sometimes the ratio was smaller. When sheep were being fattened for slaughter at Tapado or for market, there might be a *baciero* for every two flocks, or even one per flock. Though the *hacienda de ovejas* was self-contained, it was not autonomous; the *mayordomo* reported to his superior, the foreman of Tapado.

Next to the Sánchez Navarros themselves, the foreman was the most important individual on the *latifundio*. His title, that of *caporal*, does not adequately convey the authority of his position, which in some respects approached that of an *administrador*. During the infrequent absences of Manuel Francisco and José Melchor, it was the foreman who directed the day-to-day operations. Normally, however, his duties were to run Tapado and to supervise the *hacienda de ovejas*. When Hermanas was founded in the nineteenth century, it also came within the foreman's sphere of responsibility.

Acting as his own *mayordomo*, the foreman ran Tapado with the assistance of two overseers. One of them was in charge of the *vaqueros* tending the hacienda's cattle and horses, while the other had responsibility for the *cuadrillas*, or gangs, of peons engaged in agriculture. There were also several assistant overseers, whose duties encompassed the pursuit and capture of fugitive peons.

The staff at Tapado expanded over the years to include various specialists, whom the foreman himself supervised. Among them was the clerk who operated the *tienda de raya*, or hacienda store, and handled the workers' accounts. At one time or another, Tapado also boasted a tanner, a master soapmaker, a blacksmith, and a tailor who made some of the cheap clothing worn by the servants.[23] The *remudero*, or wrangler, and the coachman likewise performed jobs that raised them above the level of the field hands. The half-dozen muleteers formed yet another group of specialists. Although they transported merchandise for the store, the muleteers spent so much of their time in activities connected with the *latifundio* that they may properly be listed among the personnel at Tapado. One muleteer, for example, had the unenviable assignment of making weekly trips across the Indian-infested rangeland to take provisions to the shepherds. Finally, the group of armed *vaqueros* whose function was not to tend cattle but to protect the Sánchez Navarros and their property from the Indians may also be considered specialists of a sort.

Hermanas had a *mayordomo* who reported to the foreman of Tapado.[24] Since Hermanas was an agricultural estate, the labor force consisted entirely of field hands. The *mayordomo* was technically in charge of Hermanas, but his authority seems to have been limited to agricultural activities. The foreman of Tapado not only directed the various construction projects at Hermanas but also made frequent inspections of that estate.

The personnel at the northern haciendas theoretically did not come under the foreman's jurisdiction. Because Soledad and Dolores belonged first to Manuel Francisco and then to José Melchor, the *mayordomo* of Soledad, who was in charge of both estates, reported directly to those *hacendados*. In practice, however, the haciendas and their personnel formed an integral part of the *latifundio*, and the Sánchez Navarros readily transferred *vaqueros* and peons from Soledad whenever workers were needed at Tapado.

To cope with manpower shortages, the family had no qualms about disregarding the organizational structure to shift personnel not only between haciendas but also from job to job. Manuel Francisco sent a contingent of workers and their families from Dolores to Tapado in 1786, and the following year another group of peons went to help with spring planting at Tapado. In 1820, shepherds were being shuttled between the *hacienda de ovejas* and Dolores. On several occasions it even became necessary to strip a *casco* of its workers so they could assist with the lambing. When sufficient hired hands were lacking in January, 1792, Manuel Francisco sent every employee at Soledad and Dolores, except the *mayordomo*, to the lambing pastures. A similar situation occurred during the October, 1819, lambing, when the *mayordomo* was the only one left at Hermanas. There were also transfers of personnel from the flocks to the fields. In 1785, the Sánchez Navarros had a temporary—and rare—surplus of shepherds; the excess herders were promptly dispatched to the fields at Tapado. During José Melchor's personnel reorganization in 1813, he assigned one of the overseers from the *hacienda de ovejas* to be the *mayordomo* of Hermanas; the action led to complaints that the man knew nothing about agriculture.[25]

Since the Sánchez Navarros controlled their labor force through debt peonage, working conditions were determined to a large extent by the operation of this system. Though the available records are fragmentary, it is quite evident that the salaries paid did not constitute a living wage. In the 1760's, the best-paid muleteer in the Sánchez Navarros' employ made ten pesos a month. Other muleteers received from four to seven pesos, while a *baciero*'s wages were seven pesos. One of the peons received a monthly salary of two pesos, and another peon, working on a temporary basis, made two reals a day. This salary scale conformed to the wages paid elsewhere in the region. Writing to José Miguel in 1764, an individual in Santa Rosa bemoaned the fact that he was having to pay a servant three reals a day. Five years later the Sánchez Navarros hired a fugitive from a hacienda in Nuevo León, where the man had been making six pesos a month.[26]

Wages rose little during the 1770's. The shearers were paid on a piecework basis, but other temporary workers got between two and four reals a day. Of the resident employees, the *baciero* still made seven pesos a month, a stable boy received three pesos, and one of the muleteers drew six pesos.[27] In general, the wage scale on the Sánchez Navarro *latifundio* was comparable to that prevailing elsewhere in New Spain.[28]

At the turn of the century, laborers working for the Sánchez Navarros in Monclova made three reals a day, while skilled artisans got from six reals to one peso. The workers drew their pay once a week. A few of these men were fugitives, and, when their former employers could locate them, arrangements were made to deduct a portion of their wages. One such case occurred in 1808. The mason at the Hacienda de Santa María near Saltillo fled to Monclova, where he found employment working on the parish church. The *administrador* of the hacienda notified the Sánchez Navarros that the man owed thirty-nine pesos and requested that part of his wages be withheld until the debt were liquidated. The *administrador* added that, if the mason objected, the Sánchez Navarros should have him imprisoned until "he vomits the balance." The chances of the mason's producing the balance while in jail were infinitesimal; in 1813, a prisoner in Monclova appealed to José Miguel for help, stating that in the jail workhouse he received one real a day, which barely kept body and soul together.[29]

Wages for laborers, at least in the Saltillo area, improved slightly in 1815, when the prevailing rate was five reals a day. It must be noted, however, that this was during a labor shortage. The normal urban wage probably remained about three reals a day.[30]

The only reference to wages on the *latifundio* after 1800 is an account José Melchor prepared in 1820–1821 in connection with the Elizondo lawsuit. The *hacendado* listed among his expenses the wages paid to the servants who accompanied him on trips to San Juan de Sabinas. According to José Melchor, he paid the members of his escort one peso a day, while the women taken along as cooks received four reals daily on one trip and two reals on another. These wages seem exaggerated: not only were the servants already in the Sánchez Navarros' employ, but also the losing party would bear the costs of the lawsuit; and José Melchor confidently expected the Elizondos to lose.[31] Though rural wages did not increase appreciably over the level of the

1760's, the Sánchez Navarros at least paid in cash, unlike those *hacendados* who used metal tokens redeemable only at the *tienda de raya*.[32]

In the case of agricultural workers, *hacendados* traditionally used a weekly ration of corn or wheat to supplement—and to justify—the meager wages they paid. The amount and type of foodstuffs depended, of course, on the individual *hacendado*. The proprietor of the Hacienda de la Iguana, for example, in the 1760's gave each peon slightly less than a peck of corn a week. On the Aguayo *latifundio*, the weekly ration in 1807 was a peck of corn and three pounds of meat per adult. Some *hacendados*, such as the Vázquez Borregos, provided salt and soap every week in addition to the corn ration.[33]

As a general rule the Sánchez Navarros supplied nothing but grain to their servants. In 1764, some shepherds, presumably the heads of families, received nearly three bushels of corn a week. The standard ration, however, was two pecks of corn per adult per week, and temporary workers drew the same rations as did the resident laborers.[34] The muleteers fared somewhat better than did most other employees, for they enjoyed a more varied ration. On one occasion in 1786, for example, the men taking a pack train from Monclova each received three pecks of beans, and they were to share ten cones of brown sugar, one and one-half pecks of corn, and seven bushels of flour.[35] Sunday was the day for issuing rations at the *cascos*; on the same day a muleteer left Tapado with loads of tortillas for the shepherds on the range.

Even with the ration and with free housing in the form of a hut at one of the *cascos*, it was impossible for a worker, especially a man with a family, to live on his salary. Not only did he have to buy whatever manufactured articles he needed, but also part of his income usually went for foodstuffs to supplement the ration. A worker's salary had little purchasing power at the Sánchez Navarro store, as the account of the muleteer making ten pesos a month in the 1760's shows (see table 2). This individual was the highest-paid worker for whom records exist. The plight of most servants more closely approximated that of one Nicolás Mendieta, whose salary in the 1760's was only four pesos a month.[36]

TABLE 2

A Muleteer's Monthly Purchasing Power in the 1760's

	Pesos	Reals
1 *almud* (6.88 dry quarts) of beans		4
1 *almud* of salt	1	
1 *arroba* (25 pounds) of flour		6
1 pound of sugar		3
1 pound of cacao		7
1 ounce of cinnamon	1	
1 *fanega* (2.58 bushels) of corn	2	
1 lamb	1	
1 bunch of tobacco	1	
1 hat	1	4
	10	
or		
1 pair of buckskin shoes		6
1 yard of Brittany linen	1	
1 yard of Rouen linen	1	
1 yard of cotton cloth from Puebla		5
2 pairs of cotton hose	1	
2 yards of plush	6	
	10	3

SOURCE: SNP (2064).

Debt peonage was much more important on the Sánchez Navarro *latifundio*, and, by extension, elsewhere in the North than it was on many haciendas in the central plateau.[37] The only way the Sánchez Navarros' resident workers could make ends meet was by going into debt—which, of course, was the object of the peonage system. As is indicated by some of the above items, workers did not confine themselves to essentials when purchasing goods on credit. Since they would be in debt anyway, they enjoyed at least a few amenities to brighten their otherwise drab existence. By making available such merchandise as imported linen, the Sánchez Navarros presumably hoped to hold a labor force that would be reasonably contented while its members remained securely in debt.

The servants made their purchases at the Tapado *tienda de raya,* which after its establishment in 1780 replaced the Monclova store as headquarters for supplying the *latifundio*. Peons at the northern haciendas placed their orders with the *mayordomo* of Soledad, who then ordered the merchandise from Tapado. The majority of the goods shipped to the *latifundio* from the store in Monclova consisted of clothing and coarse textiles.[38] The hacienda tailor formed another link in the chain binding workers to the land. If the servants wished, the tailor would make them articles of clothing, his fee being added to their accounts. Judging from earlier records, the tailor's services were expensive; in the 1760's it cost one of the muleteers two pesos to have a pair of plush trousers made, and the same amount for a vest.[39]

Religion, the main solace of the peons, was also a most effective means of keeping them in debt. Every *hacendado* maintained a ledger, called a *cuadrante*, in which he entered the sacramental fees incurred by his servants. The fees represented an immediate charge against the *hacendado*, who periodically reimbursed the priest performing the services. The *hacendados* ultimately passed the fees on to their workers by transferring the amounts from the *cuadrante* to the individual peon's account.

As curate of Monclova from 1755 to 1790, José Miguel ministered to the peons from various landholdings: the Hacienda de Sardinas, the Aguayo Cuatrociénegas and Carmen haciendas, the Vázquez Borrego estates of Encinas and El Alamo, and, of course, the Sánchez Navarro *latifundio*. The curate derived several advantages from his position. First, he received a continuing income from the other *hacendados*: between July, 1773, and March, 1775, for instance, he made 286 pesos—including his yearly honorarium of 50 pesos—for ministering to the Aguayo haciendas alone.[40] Furthermore, when attending to the spiritual needs of his own workers, José Miguel saved himself most of the immediate outlay for clerical fees. Still another advantage was that, when a peon fled the *latifundio*, José Miguel, in contrast to other *hacendados*, suffered only a small monetary loss for whatever sacramental fees the servant owed.

The only fees affecting José Miguel in such cases were those that he himself did not receive as curate. The principal charge in this category was a burial tax levied to help finance the building of the parish church in Monclova. This tax amounted to two pesos, six reals for an ordinary burial and four pesos for a more elaborate service, an *entierro mayor*. Baptisms also involved a fee of four reals for the sacristan and between three reals and one peso, four reals for the cantor. All other clerical fees went to José Miguel. The curate charged two pesos, two reals for an ordinary burial service and six pesos for an *entierro mayor*. Baptisms were two pesos each. Marriages cost eight pesos, plus three pesos for the notary's fee. Not surprisingly, the notary was José Miguel.

The curate's earnings were not limited merely to his fees. From the Monclova store he supplied his parishioners with a variety of items used in religious services, such as material for shrouds at four reals a yard. If the bereaved relatives so wished, José Miguel would also have the shroud made, for a charge of four reals. Rope for securing the shroud cost one real. The candles required for burials, marriages, and vigils sold for five reals each. Lastly, the store carried a stock of items, such as fireworks, which the faithful purchased for religious holidays and other festive occasions.[41]

With the exception of mass, the most frequently performed services were baptisms and burials. The peons were prolific, but there was a high rate of infant mortality. Epidemics and Indian raids also took their toll among the servants. The *cuadrante* for Tapado from February 23, 1791, to November 1, 1794, shows that during this period there were sixty baptisms, thirty-one burials, mostly of infants, but only thirteen marriages.[42] The cost of these services constituted a heavy financial burden for the peons involved.

The combination of religious and secular debts made it all but impossible for resident peons to liquidate their accounts, as the case of Nicolás Mendieta illustrates. With a salary of 4 pesos a month, he owed the Sánchez Navarros 60 pesos in August, 1764. When his account was adjusted two years later, the debt had declined to only 22 pesos. Furthermore, Mendieta had received a raise, to 5 pesos a month. By the next adjustment of the account fourteen months later, however, his indebtedness had reached 87 pesos—the equivalent of his salary for the next seventeen months.[43] Although Mendieta's situation was in fact hopeless, on paper at least he was better off than some of the Sánchez Navarros' other peons, whose debts ranged up to 244, 320, and even 400 pesos.[44]

Debt peonage was important in the operation of haciendas, but the practice was by no means limited to *hacendados*. Even missionaries used debts as a means of controlling labor. The friar in charge of the Misión de San Francisco Vizarrón, which had seventy-nine impoverished converts, wrote an indignant letter to José Miguel in 1802 protesting the forcible removal of a member of his flock by the curate's agents. The man had been seized because he had guaranteed with his person the debt of a brother who had subsequently fled the Sánchez Navarros' service. The friar, anxious to protect the interests of the mission, wanted José Miguel either to return the man or to credit the mission for the amount the captive owed that establishment. He enclosed an itemized account showing that, after the man's labor had been deducted, he owed seven pesos, five reals.[45]

Peonage was theoretically a foolproof system. Debts being legally enforceable, a servant lived out his days bound to the land. Death provided an escape, but oftentimes it doomed his sons to a similar existence as they futilely tried to work off their father's unpaid balance and the debts they themselves were incurring. Although inherited peonage was illegal in the eighteenth century, it was nevertheless used in Coahuila; and the Sánchez Navarros took full advantage of the practice.[46]

The family also used other techniques to control their laborers. The overseers scrupulously recorded all *fallas*, or days of work missed, and workers' salaries were docked accordingly. Peons also needed permission from the overseers in order to leave the *latifundio* for any reason, such as going to Monclova to get married. The practice of keeping the servants' families at the *cascos* discouraged peons from fleeing, but it also produced complaints among the workers that their families were being held as hostages—as, in fact, they were. The irons and stocks with which Tapado was equipped further discouraged attempts to flee the landholding.[47] Apart from the physical measures, the Sánchez Navarros exerted psychological pressure on their workers through José Miguel, since he was both the peons' employer and their religious confessor.

Nevertheless, in practice, debt peonage was far from foolproof. Runaway peons constituted a perennial drain on the labor force. The Sánchez Navarros, in common with other landowners, never knew from one day to the next how many of their servants had deserted overnight; and the family had to devote considerable energy to the pursuit and apprehension of fugitives.

Since shepherds made up most of the resident labor force, they naturally presented the greatest problem. The shepherds were inclined to desert because, isolated and unarmed, they were easy prey for raiding Apaches; moreover, working on the open range, they had the best opportunity to flee. A shepherd would simply abandon his flock and strike out across the range on foot. Occasionally a man succeeded in escaping with his entire family.[48] Manuel Francisco was resigned to the situation, accepting it as one of the problems inherent in ranching. He notified the curate in 1792 that some of the shepherds had fled, while others had not reported for work, but he observed that, since absenteeism "is their profession, there is no cause for alarm."[49]

The paternalism characterizing the hacienda system makes it difficult to ascertain the jobs many of the fugitives held. Since the Sánchez Navarros and their overseers knew most of the workers by name, they often identified deserters by phrases such as "Polito, the son of Angela," or "one-eyed Contreras," omitting any reference to the individual's job.[50] Besides shepherds, the fugitives included muleteers, field hands, and at least one mounted watchman.[51]

The majority of deserters enjoyed their liberty only a short time. The difficulty they faced was not so much in effecting their escape as in avoiding capture. Though *hacendados* sometimes hired runaway peons, there was considerable cooperation among the landowners in returning one another's fugitives.[52] Many deserters from the Sánchez Navarros' haciendas sought employment on the Aguayo *latifundio*. The *administrador* at Patos, who was José Miguel's nephew by marriage, was particularly helpful. He would accommodate the men, but, upon receiving word that they were escapees, he would imprison them in the *obraje* awaiting the curate's pleasure.[53] The *administrador* also cooperated in tracking down fugitives reported to be at other landholdings; in 1804, he was attempting to secure the return of Sánchez Navarro deserters from the Hacienda de Ramos, in San Luis Potosí. Through this grapevine among *hacendados* the curate on other occasions succeeded in locating fugitives at haciendas in the Colonia de Nuevo Santander and the Nuevo Reino de León.[54]

A deserter's chances of remaining at liberty were slim even if he fled to an urban area, for *hacendados* had the help of the authorities in apprehending runaway peons. The Sánchez Navarros received co-operation not only from Coahuilan officials, but also from the governors of Texas. Fugitives sometimes crossed the 250 miles of brush country to San Antonio de Béxar in the vain hope of escaping their debts. The governor, either on his own initiative or upon notification by the Sánchez Navarros, would jail the deserters pending the arrival of the pursuing overseers from Tapado. In this manner, small groups of peons were apprehended in 1786 and 1787.[55] A similar incident occurred in 1802. José Miguel's agents arrived in San Antonio armed with a letter to the governor, who was a personal friend of the curate. The governor subsequently informed José Miguel that five fugitives had been located. Only two were dispatched to Tapado in shackles, however; the others had raised the cash to pay their debts. In the case of two of the fugitives, their present employers reimbursed the curate, while the third deserter persuaded a prostitute to pay his debt. According to the governor, the "wretched woman" disposed of all her gold and silver trinkets to raise the necessary eighty-eight pesos. The governor considered the man hardly worth this sacrifice, for besides being lazy he was half-blind.[56]

Some of the Sánchez Navarros' peons headed for Monterrey instead of San Antonio, but they, too, were usually caught. While José Miguel was residing in Monterrey from 1791 to 1795, he personally directed the search for fugitives in that city and in neighboring communities. After the curate's return to Monclova, one of his nephews who was a priest in Monterrey handled this chore. Though most deserters were seized in the Northeast, a few managed to flee into the central region of the viceroyalty. José Miguel had a long reach, however. The curate would contact one of his business associates who would in turn secure the assistance of the local authorities in running the fugitives to earth. In 1802, for instance, a merchant in the city of San Miguel el Grande, located 440 miles from Tapado, reported that he had written to the chief of police in a nearby village, and that the official would spare no effort to capture two deserters from Tapado rumored to be in the area.[57]

Captured deserters could count themselves fortunate if the only penalty they suffered was imprisonment, for both Manuel Francisco and José Melchor were harsh disciplinarians. Prisoners were marched back to Tapado in chains and upon reaching the *casco* were put in stocks while their punishment was decided. Since the Sánchez Navarros were anxious for every peon to earn his keep, offenders worked in the fields in irons and were locked up at night, measures applied both to fugitives and to other servants who had been derelict in their duties.[58]

José Miguel was interested in maintaining discipline, but he also used his influence to moderate the punishments that Manuel Francisco and José Melchor meted out. In 1793, for example, one of the family's slaves walked all the way to Monterrey to seek the curate's protection. José Miguel interceded on the man's behalf, writing a letter to Manuel Francisco that, although phrased as an appeal, in effect instructed him to treat the slave more humanely.[59]

The curate had even more reason to intervene when José Melchor began operating the landholding, for in his desire to increase efficiency the *hacendado* imposed severe punishments on the workers. Despite a warning from Arizpe, the tax collector, that the governor was becoming incensed at José Melchor's treatment of the peons, the *hacendado* remained unmoved. Matters came to a head in August, 1802, when the governor ordered José Melchor's arrest after a peon had been severely beaten. The *hacendado* surrendered himself at Monclova, where he was placed under house arrest while the authorities investigated the case. Though the curate was furious with José Melchor, he nevertheless began working to secure his nephew's release. José Miguel instructed Arizpe to propose that charges be dropped in return for the Sánchez Navarros' agreement to pay the court costs and to write off the debt owed by the beaten peon, who was to be banished from the *latifundio*. When both the judge and the peon agreed to these terms, José Melchor, who had been under arrest for three days, regained his freedom. The *hacendado* postponed his departure in order to take leave of the local dignitaries who had visited him during his confinement.[60]

José Melchor's arrest produced little change in his attitude toward the workers. In December, 1802, the curate received a warning to restrain his nephew because the governor was still disturbed by the punishments employed at Tapado. The curate tried to ameliorate the lot of the servants by pardoning some of them for various offenses.[61] His interference led to growing friction between himself and José Melchor, who referred to the peons as "those malevolent servants who are fraudulently earning my money without my being able to remedy the situation."[62] For several months in 1809, relations between the curate and his nephew deteriorated to the point that José Melchor reported through the cashier at the store rather than directly to José Miguel. The *hacendado* complained about the disorganization at Tapado, which he attributed to the fact that José Miguel accepted the servants' excuses at face value instead of seeking the truth. José Melchor declared himself unable to operate the estate effectively under these conditions; he pointed out that, if the peons were not disciplined, the hacienda would fail, and the curate would undoubtedly blame him for its failure.[63]

The *hacendado* finally made his point, and in succeeding years was permitted to run Tapado as he saw fit; his relationship with José Miguel improved accordingly. Besides reorganizing the labor force, José Melchor personally dealt with recalcitrant peons on occasion. Once when he was berating the wrangler for his negligence, the latter responded in an insolent manner, whereupon José Melchor seized a handy oak limb in order to thrash the servant. Instead of submitting, the wrangler grappled for possession of the limb. After a bloody scuffle, the *hacendado* succeeded in overpowering his adversary and gave him a beating "in proportion to his effrontery." The battered servant's troubles were by no means over, for José Melchor then transferred him to the fields, where he would have less chance to shirk his duties.[64]

José Melchor's constant frustrations regarding the peons stemmed from the fact that the *hacendado* was trying to operate efficiently what was inherently an inefficient labor system. The number of permanent employees on the *latifundio* was certainly not unmanageable; in 1814 there were probably some two hundred men in all.[65] But the peons, bound to the land, had little incentive other than fear. The fundamental weakness of debt peonage was that both *hacendado* and peon were trapped in a vicious circle in which the peon pretended to work and the master pretended to pay him.[66]

4. *Latifundio* Production

José Miguel's object in speculating with the tithe livestock was to build a flock of his own in order to enter the sheep trade, one of the principal forms of commercial activity in northern New Spain. *Hacendados* in Nueva Vizcaya, Coahuila, and the Nuevo Reino de León annually dispatched large flocks to market in the central part of the viceroyalty. Ranchers in some sections of Nueva Vizcaya also found markets closer to home by supplying mining centers, such as Parral.[1] Since there was little mining in Coahuila and Nuevo León, sheepmen in those provinces sent nearly all of their production to the south. Of 100,000 sheep in Nuevo León in 1740, only some 4,000 were consumed locally; the remainder were destined for Mexico City. In Coahuila the Marquis of Aguayo overshadowed all others exporting to the capital; in 1783, for example, he marketed 19,000 head.[2]

The curate quickly established himself in the sheep business. Beginning in 1762, he made annual sales to José de Lanzagorta, a leading merchant in San Miguel el Grande. Upon Lanzagorta's death in 1764, his nephew Andrés Vicente de Urizar, head of a commercial house in Mexico City, became José Miguel's buyer.[3] No cash changed hands in livestock transactions. Through their annual sales, the Sánchez Navarros amassed credits with commercial houses, drawing against these accounts by means of *libranzas*, or drafts. In return for acting as the brothers' bankers, the mercantile establishments paid no interest on the funds they held. In January, 1775, the brothers had 10,550 pesos on deposit with Urizar, which indicates the lucrative nature of the all-important Mexico City market.[4]

The Sánchez Navarros' secondary outlet remained San Miguel el Grande, where in the 1780's their buyer was Domingo Narciso de Allende, a prominent Spanish merchant and *hacendado*.[5] Manuel Francisco sold him 2,052 slaughter ewes in 1783 at five reals a head and the following year supplied another 1,713 slaughter ewes at five reals, plus 1,217 goats at twelve reals.

The credits to Manuel Francisco's account from these transactions included reimbursement for the money and supplies furnished to Allende's trail crews going to Coahuila to receive the animals.[6] In all of the Sánchez Navarros' livestock sales, it was the buyer who assumed the risks of delivery. The brothers' responsibility ended when the flocks were turned over to the buyer's trail crew at the Hacienda de Anhelo. To ensure the safe arrival of the sheep at Anhelo, the Sánchez Navarros provided several armed guards for each flock.

Livestock transactions were arranged by mail, with the curate handling the vital Mexico City account. He and Urizar customarily began negotiating early in the year. Replying to an inquiry from the buyer, José Miguel sounded a pessimistic note in January, 1785; he stated that at the moment he could not even estimate the number of marketable sheep he would have, much less reach an agreement on their sale.[7] Negotiations continued throughout the spring. José Miguel finally set a price of twenty and one-half reals a head, which Urizar considered outrageous. After reminding the curate that he had been the Sánchez Navarros' buyer in good times and in bad for over twenty years, Urizar stated his case. First, the curate's sheep had already been sheared, which lowered their market value. Second, there were still on the market sheep left over from the previous year. Last, José Miguel's asking price was out of line with what buyers were currently offering.[8]

The curate remained adamant, and Urizar capitulated. He agreed to pay twenty and one-half reals for two-year-old sheep and to defray the costs of delivery. The merchant still considered the price excessive; he mentioned that the Mexico City firm of Miro had bought the flocks from the Río Florido region in Nueva Vizcaya at nineteen reals, and these sheep produced the finest mutton available. Urizar himself had been purchasing flocks at eighteen reals, while other merchants were obtaining unsheared two-year-olds at twenty reals. He reiterated that José Miguel had received an excellent price considering that the curate's sheep were not first-quality animals, that they had been sheared, and that the costs of delivery would necessarily be high.

Urizar accepted his defeat with good grace, candidly admitting that he had paid José Miguel's price in order to keep his business. Though Urizar would make only a small profit that year, on several occasions in the past he had obtained the curate's sheep at an advantageous price. He had also been counting on José Miguel's flocks all along and had already assembled drovers to receive the animals.

By the terms of the agreement José Miguel would deliver 8,000 to 9,000 sheep at the Hacienda de Anhelo no later than February 15, 1786, provided it rained and there was adequate grass and water along the road to Mexico City.[9] Even if José Miguel delivered only 8,000 head, he would still make 20,500 pesos from this transaction, the main sale for 1785. Manuel Francisco, who handled the sales to Allende in San Miguel el Grande, contributed an additional 3,618 pesos to the 1785 livestock revenues by selling 1,001 slaughter ewes at 5 reals and 1,995 goats at 12 reals.[10]

Manuel Francisco's sales to Allende fell drastically in 1786; he supplied only 1,228 slaughter ewes at 5 reals, for a mere 767 pesos. José Miguel, however, continued to get an excellent 21 reals a head from Urizar in 1786. The following year, Urizar grudgingly paid the same price but took only 2,000 sheep, for which the curate received 5,125 pesos.[11] The bottom had dropped out of the sheep market.

The demand for mutton had increased sharply in the mid-1780's as the result of a catastrophe: heavy frosts in 1784 destroyed the maize and bean crops in a wide area of central New Spain, producing a famine in which an estimated 300,000 persons died of starvation and related causes.[12] Sheepmen profited from the situation; but, by the end of 1786, agricultural conditions were returning to normal, and sheep became a glut on the market. José Miguel's situation at this time was especially uncomfortable, for, as a speculation, he had purchased several thousand tithe sheep; now he was unable to resell them. The curate's attempts to find a buyer shed some light on market conditions in general.

José Miguel had originally arranged the sale of the tithe flocks to the *administrador* of the Aguayo *latifundio*, who planned to resell them in central New Spain. But the *administrador* reneged on the deal early in 1787 because of the ruinously low prices being offered. He cited the case of sheep that in 1784 and 1785 had brought ten reals a head in Saltillo but were currently selling for five. The *administrador* pointed out that the market in San Miguel el Grande had also collapsed. In 1785, when the market was still rising, the leading merchants in San Miguel had unwisely committed themselves to pay a specified price for sheep to be delivered in 1786 and 1787. With the market now dropping, the merchants were cutting their own losses by arbitrarily discounting a percentage of the previously agreed price.[13]

The merchants to whom the *administrador* referred were Francisco Lanzagorta, Domingo de Unzaga, and Domingo Narciso de Allende, whose firms dominated commerce in San Miguel. Late in 1787 a group of irate sheepmen from Saltillo and Monterrey filed suit against these firms over the prices paid for their livestock in 1786–1787.[14] This lawsuit corroborates the *administrador*'s allegations regarding price cutting.

The San Miguel firms of Lanzagorta, Unzaga, and Allende could take concerted action because they were closely linked to each other as well as to prominent sheep buyers in Mexico City.[15] Controlling the Mexico City market were the commercial houses of Bassoco, Urizar, Yermo, Berrio, and Miro, which shared the *abasto*, or privilege of supplying meat to the capital.[16] The relationship between these groups is illustrated by the circumstances following the death of Domingo Narciso de Allende, who had been the Sánchez Navarros' buyer in San Miguel for over a decade. When Allende died in 1787, his mercantile establishment was managed for a few months by his executor José María de Unzaga, and then by Allende's nephew Domingo de Berrio.[17] There was, as is apparent, a close bond between the Allendes and the Unzagas; through Domingo de Berrio, they were also linked with the Berrios in Mexico City. Moreover, the San Miguel merchant family of Lanzagorta was related to the Mexico City businessman Urizar.

It was to Urizar that the curate turned in his efforts to sell the tithe sheep in 1787. But Urizar refused to purchase them in a falling market; the bitterness arising from his refusal led José Miguel to sever his relationship with Urizar, ending a mutually profitable association that had spanned twenty-three years.

José Miguel needed a buyer in Mexico City not only because of his break with Urizar but also because he stubbornly continued buying tithe sheep in hopes that the market would recover. In 1788, the curate started dealing with Antonio de Bassoco, a Spaniard who was one of the most powerful merchants in the capital. Bassoco had come to New Spain at an early age under the patronage of his uncle, the Marquis of Castañiza. Through the latter's protection and through his own abilities, Bassoco had risen swiftly in commerce. Following his marriage to his cousin María Teresa de Castañiza, who brought him a considerable dowry, Bassoco had expanded his activities, becoming a mining magnate and a *hacendado* as well as a merchant, and holding several posts in the government.[18]

The curate's livestock dealings with Bassoco began inauspiciously. Because of the saturated market, the merchant would accept no sheep in 1788. The following year, when Bassoco showed some interest in making a purchase, José Miguel overplayed his hand. Having concluded no sales for the last two years, the curate was anxious to receive the best possible price, and he prolonged the negotiations. Bassoco became impatient and had little difficulty in finding another supplier. In fact, sheep were so plentiful that, as of September, the end of the buying season, even the Marquis of Aguayo had failed to sell the flocks from one of his haciendas.[19]

The Mexico City market seemed even more dismal in 1790. José Miguel, desperate to conclude a sale, decided to approach other buyers besides Bassoco. The curate had a representative in the capital, his nephew the priest José Domingo de Letona, who made the rounds of all the commercial houses except that of Urizar. Letona was unsuccessful, explaining that each firm hesitated to be first to quote a price; they were all waiting until the end of the summer before committing themselves.[20]

Despite Letona's discouraging report, 1790 proved to be a turning point, for the Mexico City market began to make a gradual recovery. Much to José Miguel's relief, when the commercial houses placed their orders in the fall of 1790, Bassoco finally bought some of his sheep. But there is no reference to the price paid, the number of animals involved, or whether they were tithe sheep or those raised by the Sánchez Navarros themselves. This is also the case for 1791, when Bassoco again purchased a flock from the curate.

The Mexico City market remained a source of concern for the Sánchez Navarros. In discussing their prospects for 1792, Manuel Francisco informed his brother that some 8,500 two- and three-year-old sheep would be ready for shipment to the capital in the fall; José Miguel could therefore begin to negotiate their sale.[21] When the curate offered the sheep to Bassoco, the latter was less than enthusiastic, stating that in view of what prime unsheared animals were bringing he could offer only thirteen reals a head. And the only reason he would take the flock was so that José Miguel would have a buyer. Bassoco hoped the curate could sell the sheep elsewhere, though he conceded that finding another buyer in Mexico City was most unlikely.[22]

The Sánchez Navarros discussed Bassoco's offer at length. José Miguel confirmed the buyer's remarks concerning the overabundance of sheep. Writing to Manuel Francisco from Monterrey, the curate reported that sheepmen in Nuevo León had been unable to market their flocks in Mexico City. Commenting further on the sheep trade in Monterrey, he mentioned that in Nuevo León, unlike Coahuila, no distinction was made regarding the age of animals, which were classified simply as sheep and goats, male and female. Sheep of all ages were currently selling in Monterrey for whatever they would bring, *hacendados* wishing only to relieve themselves of having to care for the stock. Unable to resist a bargain, José Miguel himself had even bought two hundred head, the most expensive at eight reals.[23] Yet purchasing sheep was a luxury, especially since the Sánchez Navarros had made only one sale so far in 1792: 2,500 slaughter ewes to the firm of Allende, which had continued making annual purchases despite the slump in the market.

Since it was imperative to conclude a sale in Mexico City, José Miguel accepted Bassoco's offer. The curate advised Bassoco to receive the 8,500 sheep at Anhelo in September, as the latter had been doing since 1790.[24] The 1792 sale set a pattern for the next few years (as shown in table 3), with Bassoco taking a flock of two-year-olds annually but only so the curate would have a buyer.

There had been some difficulty in selling the 1795 flock. For some reason, Bassoco decided not to buy the sheep, but his nephew and business associate, Domingo Castañiza, began negotiating with José Miguel. Castañiza inquired as to the price, number, and quality of the animals, offering to pay cash if they were still for sale. The curate's nephew, the priest Letona, acted as intermediary in the discussions. According to Letona, there was no question of Castañiza's ability to pay in cash: besides the money Castañiza had made in the firm of Bassoco and the dowry he had received from his wife, Castañiza was the heir to the wealthy Marquisate of Castañiza.[25] The deal was presumably concluded, because, from this time on, the Sánchez Navarros had business dealings directly with Castañiza.

The circumstances of the 1797 sale are obscure. In September, the Sánchez Navarros delivered 8,833 two-year-old sheep at Anhelo to the Marquis of Aguayo's trail crew. But Aguayo was not purchasing

TABLE 3
Sheep Sales to Antonio de Bassoco

Year	Number	Price (Reals)	Total (Pesos)
1792	8,500	13	13,812
1793	10,000	13	16,250
1794	8,129	13	13,209
1795			
1796	6,980	16	13,960

SOURCE: SNP (3508); José Miguel SN's account with Bassoco, December 4, 1793–September 7, 1810, MCSN.

the flock; his men were merely driving the sheep to Mexico City for delivery.[26] Although neither the buyer nor the selling price were mentioned, it seems likely that the flock went to Bassoco.

The Sánchez Navarros' secondary outlet, the firm of Allende, continued its yearly purchases into the nineteenth century. The brothers supplied 1,040 slaughter ewes in 1801 and 1,891 ewes the following year. In 1803 the curate notified the firm that he could provide no sheep because of severe losses resulting from the disastrous rains in Coahuila in 1802. As late as 1806, though, the San Miguel firm was purchasing Sánchez Navarro ewes at five and one-half reals, the prevailing price for the last five years.[27]

In the meantime, important developments had been occurring in Mexico City. For one thing, the sheep trade had fully recovered by 1800 from the slump of the late 1780's. For another, José Miguel had again changed buyers. In 1800 he began selling to Gabriel de Yermo, head of another large commercial house. Yermo was both a merchant and a *hacendado*. A Spaniard by birth, he had emigrated to New Spain where he married his cousin, María Josefa Yermo. She had inherited from her father two opulent sugar-producing haciendas in the valley of Cuernavaca. Besides spending vast sums to improve these properties, Yermo enlarged his holdings by purchasing two more haciendas in the same area.[28]

José Miguel's dealings with Yermo were profitable, for there was an upward trend in the price of sheep, as shown in table 4. Yermo, in fact, experienced considerable difficulty in meeting the growing demand for mutton in the capital.[29]

The market for wool, though less lucrative than the sheep trade, had remained steadier through the years. The wool clip from the semiannual shearings at Tapado constituted the Sánchez Navarros' secondary source of income from the *latifundio*. Following the August shearing, the brothers' pack trains arrived at Tapado to move the wool to market. The muleteers trampled the freshly shorn wool to reduce its bulk, packed it into large fiber sacks, and loaded it onto the mules, which carried an average of three hundred pounds each.

The principal market for Coahuilan wool was Saltillo, whose annual fair was famous throughout New Spain. Saltillo owed its com-

TABLE 4
Sheep Sales to Gabriel de Yermo

Year	Number	Price (Reals)	Total (Pesos)
1800	9,208	22½	25,897
1801	9,134	20½	23,405
1802[a]			
1803[b]	1,941	20	4,852
	5,280	21½	14,192
1804	5,767	18½	12,975
1805	7,117	19	16,902
1806	5,658	22	15,559
1807	4,466	22½	12,560
1808	8,265	24	24,975
1809	5,782	26½	19,152

SOURCE: SNP (2249); (2251); (96); (2677); (3551); (2250); (2248).
[a] There was no sale because of the losses caused by torrential rains in Coahuila.
[b] Two flocks were sold to Yermo.

mercial prominence mainly to its location astride the trade routes linking the central plateau with Coahuila, Texas, Nuevo León, and a large section of Nueva Vizcaya. The fair, held in the last week of September, briefly transformed the placid provincial city into a bustling metropolis. Merchants and peddlers from throughout the viceroyalty congregated to exchange their finished products for wheat and woolen blankets from Saltillo, wine from Parras, and livestock, wool, and hides from Coahuila and Nuevo León. Since the few inns were soon crowded to capacity, the municipal authorities erected temporary huts near the parish church to accommodate the influx of visitors. Many came to the fair seeking excitement rather than business opportunities, and celebrations matched the frantic pace of the commercial activity. The fiestas, bullfights, cockfights, and horse races held during the fair provided one of the few social outlets for the inhabitants of the northeastern provinces.[30]

The Sánchez Navarros sent about half of the August wool clip to Saltillo as quickly as possible, for sale at the opening of the fair. The

remainder was stored at Tapado and went to Saltillo according to demand, as did the production from the spring shearing. Sales were
handled by the brothers' business agent, who not only managed their
warehouse but also advanced money and supplies to the trail crews
going to Anhelo. In keeping with the Sánchez Navarros' policy of
employing relatives whenever feasible, they had first a brother, then a
nephew, as their Saltillo representative from 1775 to 1801, when they
finally had to hire an outsider.

Wool sales followed a pattern that remained essentially unchanged
for decades. Small amounts were sold at retail to weavers in Saltillo,
but the bulk of the Sánchez Navarros' production was bought by middlemen for resale in central New Spain. Wool was handled by the
arroba, a unit of twenty-five pounds (see table 5). The brothers' principal buyer was one Manuel Carrillo, who from 1790 through 1805
purchased four pack trains of wool a year for resale in San Miguel and
Querétaro.[31]

The Sánchez Navarros rarely shipped wool directly to those cities,
even though it brought a higher price there than in Saltillo.[32] The
brothers were content with the smaller profit margin because they thus
avoided the problems involved in moving wool to markets in the central plateau. One of the gravest difficulties was a recurring shortage of
muleteers. For example, a merchant who bought nineteen thousand
pounds of wool from the Sánchez Navarros in September, 1786, still
had not been able to remove it from Saltillo by February, 1787, for
lack of transport.[33] And sometimes, when muleteers were available,
there were insufficient sacks in which to pack the wool for shipment.[34]

Only once did the Sánchez Navarros make a direct shipment to San
Miguel, one of the leading textile centers in the viceroyalty.[35] The
curate arranged the sale of the entire March, 1806, wool clip—some
25,000 pounds—to the firm of Allende. The firm not only agreed to
provide pack trains to transport the cargo from Saltillo to San Miguel
but also accepted the risks of delivery. In this instance, as often happened, the shipment was delayed by a shortage of sacks in Saltillo. The
muleteer even proposed that, instead of repacking the cargo at Saltillo,
it continue on to its destination in the same sacks in which it had been
packed at Tapado. The Sánchez Navarros' Saltillo representative in-

TABLE 5
Wool Sales through Saltillo

Date	Wool Clip (Pounds)	Shipments to Saltillo	Sales	Price per Arroba (Reals)	Total (Pesos)
August, 1774	32,875	18,050			
August, 1785		19,675			
March, 1786		20,500			
August, 1786	30,100	19,775	19,775	22	2,175
February, 1788			14,125		
May, 1792				25	
1801[a]			10,635	20–24	1,098
February, 1802		19,275		20	1,926
May, 1802				14–21	
August, 1802				16–21	1,246
1803[a]	40,580	40,580	40,580	19–24	4,086
March, 1805		20,000			
March, 1806	28,550	28,550	28,550		
March, 1809			16,250		
August, 1809		20,700			

SOURCE: SNP (2505); (1946); (2686); (3421); (1889); (3063); (3508); (1682); (3404); (845); (1021); (1637); (1702); (2100); (2102); (972); (739); (1841); (1152).
[a] The amounts of wool given for 1801 and 1803 represent a consolidated figure from the available data.

dignantly refused, emphasizing that at Tapado the sacks were more valuable than the wool they contained.[36]

Manuel Carrillo, the Sánchez Navarros' buyer in Saltillo, protested vehemently against the 1806 sale to the firm of Allende. Reminding the curate of their long association, Carrillo asked for preferential treatment. He offered to pay cash, to receive the wool at Monclova if necessary, and to buy the entire wool clip in the future, as long as the price was equitable. If José Miguel could not sell him the entire production, Carrillo asked to receive half of each future shearing. Carrillo's desperation arose from his having counted on receiving the Sánchez Navarros' wool as he had in the past; he had not dealt with other suppliers, and now his mules were without cargo. The merchant offered to pay up to twenty reals for the wool, merely to be able to dispatch his idle pack trains. The matter was finally resolved when José Miguel agreed to sell Carrillo whatever wool remained after the 25,000-pound order for San Miguel had been filled.[37]

In succeeding years the curate dealt with other merchants besides Carrillo. One was Román de Letona, the Sánchez Navarros' nephew who operated pack trains between Saltillo and the center of the viceroyalty. His kinship with Letona notwithstanding, José Miguel ordered that the August, 1809, clip be sold to the highest bidder. Letona protested that he had already counted on shipping the wool to Querétaro. He offered to pay cash for the current wool clip, as well as that produced at Tapado in the future.[38] Judging by the demand for the Sánchez Navarros' wool, the market for this product underwent a rise in the early nineteenth century comparable to that for sheep.

Livestock and wool accounted for most of the Sánchez Navarros' revenues, but the family also dealt in such commodities as maize and brown sugar; and early in the nineteenth century they were also developing a market in Saltillo for cotton.[39] Information on these ancillary activities is so fragmentary that no clear pattern emerges.

There are a little more data on the sale of the meat and other products resulting from the annual slaughter at Tapado. Most of the mutton was retailed in Monclova and surrounding communities. The tallow and soap not needed at Tapado were shipped to the Monclova store for sale, and, in the nineteenth century, to Saltillo as well. The hides were usually sent to Monclova or Saltillo for tanning, though on occasion hides were sold to the firm of Allende.[40]

The *latifundio*, which produced only a part of the Sánchez Navarros' revenues, returned a comfortable income. Manuel Francisco estimated in January, 1785, that the total income from the flocks during 1783–1784 had been 56,000 pesos. The total expenses had been 17,000 pesos, leaving a net profit of 39,000. Since José Miguel considered the expenses entirely too high, his brother promised to reduce them as much as possible in the future.[41] Whatever economies Manuel Francisco effected were in all probability more than offset by the decline in the sheep market during the late 1780's.

The extant documents do not permit a complete analysis of the costs of operation. A major expense, however, was the cash outlay at shearing time, which averaged about 1,000 pesos a year.[42] Another expense was the *alcabala*, a sales and turnover tax on products shipped to market. Records exist only for the *alcabala* paid on some livestock transactions between 1779 and 1801, when 3,920 pesos were incurred in taxes.[43] Beginning in 1791, furthermore, the Sánchez Navarros' operating expenses increased. José Miguel's ecclesiastical promotion and transfer to Monterrey ended the brothers' relative advantage in the payment of sacramental fees. They were now on an equal footing with other *hacendados*, having to pay the new Monclova parish priest for performing religious services for their peons. From February, 1791, to November, 1794, his fees totaled some 455 pesos. Though information for subsequent years is scanty, these fees remained a regular charge against the *latifundio*.[44] In addition, the Sánchez Navarros had to start paying the tithe after 1795. Like other *hacendados*, they sometimes delivered the commodities to the collectors, while on other occasions they simply turned in their local cash value.[45]

Even with increased costs the Sánchez Navarros profited handsomely from the *latifundio*, especially during the first decade of the nineteenth century. With the growing demand for sheep and wool, the curate and his nephew José Melchor could anticipate an indefinite period of prosperity. Their expectations were unrealized, for Hidalgo's insurrection broke out in September, 1810.

The uprising shattered the traditional pattern of trade between Coahuila and the central plateau. As the conflict intensified, trade routes were cut; in January, 1811, the rebels occupied Saltillo and Monclova, bringing business activity to a standstill. The capture of Hidalgo and his principal associates in March, 1811, restored royalist control in Coahuila, but warfare in the center of the viceroyalty kept commerce at a depressed level.

By the summer of 1811, the wool in the Sánchez Navarros' Saltillo warehouse had spoiled for lack of buyers.[46] Insurgent activity during the next few years made the roads south of Saltillo hazardous, and business suffered accordingly. Nonetheless, the Sánchez Navarros continued to ship hides and wool to Saltillo. Commenting on the wool trade in 1814, José Melchor lamented the low price being offered in

Saltillo. He had refused to sell any of the wool in the warehouse because buyers offered "practically nothing" for it. Even in San Luis Potosí, wool brought only sixteen to eighteen reals. José Melchor predicted that prices would drop even further because of the revolution.[47]

But by the end of 1815, the rebellion was in decline. Pack trains could again operate between Saltillo and San Luis Potosí in reasonable safety, although the market for wool was slow to recover. The production from Tapado was sold to Román de Letona and his brother José María, who was also a wool merchant. The Letona brothers resold the wool in San Luis Potosí, where its price was only slightly higher than in Saltillo. Since they operated on a slim profit margin, the Letonas necessarily had to offer a low price—fourteen reals—for the wool clip from Tapado, delivered at Saltillo.[48] This price was not to the Sánchez Navarros' liking, but, counting themselves fortunate even to have a regular buyer, they accepted.

In 1816, shipments from Tapado totaled 22,525 pounds through July; the August shearing produced an additional forty mule loads. More than 38,400 pounds, including 29,375 from the August shearing, went to Saltillo in 1817. A pack train transported thirty mule loads in the summer of 1818, returning to begin hauling the August wool clip of 29,575 pounds. The only record of shipments in 1819 is for a train of thirty mules, which carried 9,325 pounds to Saltillo in October.[49] During the decade of the struggle for independence, the Sánchez Navarros' earnings from wool fell off while their costs of production remained about the same, but at least they had a market for their wool.

The sheep trade, by contrast, had collapsed. The outbreak of the revolution prevented delivery of the flock in 1810, and, for the remainder of the decade, it was impossible to resume shipments to central New Spain. Unwilling to accept the risks involved in moving these flocks to market, buyers in the capital preferred to deal with *hacendados* much closer to Mexico City. The Sánchez Navarros were reduced to selling what few sheep they could in regional markets while awaiting the return of peace to the viceroyalty.

They were confined mainly to participating in the *abastos* of Monclova, Saltillo, and Monterrey. Saltillo was the best market: in October, 1814, for example, a flock of two thousand sheep was dispatched from Tapado. Shipments to Saltillo continued through 1819, with the Letona brothers acting as the family's representatives. The Letonas periodically requested a flock of one thousand head, which they slaughtered a few at a time according to local demand.[50] But, for the Sánchez Navarros, participation in a regional market hardly compensated for the loss of a national one.

5. Commerce

The Sánchez Navarros' commercial activities explain in large measure the family's success in building and operating the *latifundio*. Capital resulting from various business ventures not only made possible the acquisition of the land itself but also enabled the Sánchez Navarros to withstand periods of adversity in their ranching operations. Furthermore, commerce complemented ranching in that the Sánchez Navarros purchased large amounts of trade goods from the firms to whom they sold livestock.

The general store in Monclova was the headquarters of what developed into a commercial empire. By 1762, when José Miguel became involved with the tithe, the store was functioning efficiently under the direction of José Gregorio, his brother and junior partner.[1] The Sánchez Navarros' principal customer in the early 1760's was Francisco de Mata, *mayordomo* of the Aguayo Hacienda de Carmen, west of Monclova. The distance between Patos, the seat of the Aguayo *latifundio*, and Carmen often made it more practical to supply that hacienda from Monclova. The Sánchez Navarros received this business because of the close friendship between Mata and the curate José Miguel.[2] Such items as salt, paper, tobacco, shoes, candy, and soap were sent to Carmen, but the bulk of the merchandise consisted of cheap textiles that the Sánchez Navarros had imported from the central part of New Spain. The same pattern held true for the goods they sold to other haciendas in the vicinity, among them the Vázquez Borrego estates of Encinas and El Alamo, although on occasion such items as chocolate were also supplied.[3] The basis of the Sánchez Navarros' operation was credit: *hacendados* and other customers periodically came to the store to settle their accounts, while smaller merchants in such places as Santa Rosa also began ordering merchandise on credit.[4]

The system of debt peonage accounted for much of the business done at the store, since a great deal of the merchandise sold was ordered by *hacendados* for their peons. Francisco de Mata, for example, would either place the orders himself or send his peons into Monclova with a note specifying the amount of credit they were to receive.[5] The account books were periodically adjusted, with the *hacendados* paying the Sánchez Navarros and entering the corresponding amounts on their peons' accounts.

The same procedure was followed for the soldiers of the Monclova garrison. The troops and their families bought goods on credit for religious ceremonies, and they also incurred debts with José Miguel for sacramental fees. In fact, on one occasion the governor complained that he owed the curate a considerable sum resulting from these services, and José Miguel was demanding payment in cash rather than in trade goods, as had always been customary.[6]

In this connection, José Gregorio increased the Sánchez Navarros' share of the commerce in Coahuila by engaging in presidial supply. Prior to 1772 the troops were paid in goods whose purchase was centralized in the hands of the presidio commanders. Theoretically, the commanders could get a better price from merchants than could the individual soldiers, though in practice the officers frequently engaged in profiteering at the expense of their men.[7] When Captain Manuel Rodríguez, commander of the Río Grande presidio, solicited bids in 1769 for supplying the garrison, it was José Gregorio who secured the contract; the fact that Rodríguez was a relative of the Sánchez Navarros undoubtedly helped.[8] The merchant provided foodstuffs, horses, clothing, and whatever else the soldiers and their families required. Since the supplies were provided on credit, Rodríguez wrote to the viceroy asking that José Gregorio be reimbursed in Mexico City from the presidio's annual appropriation of some ten thousand pesos. The viceroy agreed. Several months later Rodríguez recommended to the viceroy that commerce between Río Grande and Monclova be fomented by providing military escorts for merchants wishing to engage in this trade. The viceroy accepted the suggestion, issuing the necessary order to the governor of Coahuila.[9] It is unlikely that José Gregorio failed to take advantage of these escorts.

Having established the new line of trade with Río Grande, José Gregorio traveled to Mexico City late in 1770 to arrange various business affairs. While there, he secured for himself appointment as the Coahuilan administrator of the royal tobacco monopoly, opening yet another avenue of commerce. He returned to Monclova early in 1771, and among the customers for his tobacco was the garrison at Río Grande, to whom he supplied five hundred pounds of unprocessed leaf that year.[10]

The Sánchez Navarros' highly successful partnership was disrupted by José Gregorio's death in 1774. A revealing picture of José Gregorio and his contribution to the family enterprises is provided by the inventory of his estate.[11] The merchant had been a bachelor who evidently prided himself on being well dressed, well armed, and well mounted. He possessed an extensive wardrobe that included an assortment of elegant riding apparel; he had a shotgun, a brace of pistols, a rapier, a saber, a cutlass, and a dagger, all richly inlaid with silver; and he owned more than one hundred horses, plus a variety of riding equipment. José Gregorio had few other personal possessions. The only books he owned were the account books from the store, around which the merchant's life had revolved. He had occupied a sparsely furnished parlor and bedroom in the building housing the store, although he also owned the house next door. At the time of his death he had been enlarging the store because the original facilities, including a back room and a small warehouse, had become inadequate for the stock on hand.

The inventory of the store is particularly interesting since it shows both the selection of merchandise available and its wholesale value in Monclova.[12] Considering the frontier condition of northern New Spain at this time, it is surprising that there existed a demand for some of the goods. The store stocked dried shrimp, as well as cacao from Caracas. There were also imported textiles, such as fine linens from Brittany, Rouen, and Brabant; lace from Flanders; ribbon from Spain and France; Italian velvet; English woolens; bombazine from Spain and China; and cloth from Ypres and Prussia. Among the articles of clothing were stockings from Italy, Persia, and China. There were even several fine kimonos. The most valuable items were a twenty-one–piece silver service and 3,035 pesos' worth of silver leaf. The majority of the merchandise was much more commonplace. There was a large stock of cheap textiles and clothing, mainly from Puebla, as well as 1,088 pairs of various kinds of footwear. In addition, religious primers, stationery, foodstuffs and spices, hardware, weapons and riding equipment, household utensils, and such miscellaneous items as fireworks were carried in stock. The value of the merchandise totaled 19,871 pesos.

Most of José Gregorio's sales had been made on a credit basis, and thus the greatest part of his estate consisted of accounts receivable. These were kept in a set of five ledgers whose entries provide insight into the nature and volume of the business he had been transacting. José Gregorio had been supplying the missions in Coahuila, probably because of José Miguel's clerical connections, and one ledger contained the accounts of the missionary fathers. The thirteen missionaries listed owed amounts ranging from 247 pesos to 1,378, with four of them owing more than 1,000 pesos each. The total amount of their debts was 8,632 pesos.

Another ledger had the accounts of a number of citizens of Monclova, as well as a few from Río Grande. The social standing of these customers was indicated by the fact that before twenty-six of the eighty names the title of "Don" or "Doña" was omitted; those who fell into the inferior social classification included the midwife, a master carpenter, and two tailors. Only one of these accounts exceeded 1,000 pesos, and the total indebtedness was 4,574 pesos.

The three remaining ledgers contained José Gregorio's most important accounts. Not only did various local *hacendados* owe him considerable sums, but so did the leading royal officials in the province. The governor, Jacobo de Ugarte y Loyola, owed 5,377 pesos; the governor's lieutenant, José de Castilla y Terán, 2,079; the commander of the Río Grande presidio, 7,499; and the commander at Santa Rosa, 518. The largest single account was that of Andrés de Urizar, the Mexico City merchant, who owed 10,547 pesos. In addition, various relatives of the Sánchez Navarros owed some 2,200 pesos. The accounts receivable in these three ledgers totaled 66,216 pesos.

Miscellaneous items further increased José Gregorio's assets, but there were a number of charges against the estate. The expenses connected with the simple funeral of José Gregorio, who was buried wearing the habit of a Franciscan, were 39 pesos. In his will the merchant had made a series of pious bequests: 4,000 pesos to endow in José Miguel's favor a chaplaincy, 1,000 pesos to help build the new church in Monclova, 200 pesos to be distributed among the poor, and 756 pesos for masses to be said for his soul, those of his relatives, and the souls in purgatory. The debts outstanding connected with his business affairs included 7,079 pesos to the royal treasury for the tobacco he had sold and 4,095 to businessmen in Saltillo and San Miguel. But José Gregorio's principal creditor was his own brother, José Miguel. The two had maintained a separate account, and the balance showed 13,663 pesos payable to the curate.

Furthermore, the merchant had stipulated that his twenty-eight best mules, valued at 520 pesos, were to go to José Miguel. The remainder of his livestock went to Manuel Francisco, as did his clothing, weapons, and riding equipment, plus 1,500 pesos in cash. Another 3,308 pesos were to be divided among the other brothers and sisters, most of whom still resided in Saltillo. Unfortunately, the last pages of the inventory are missing, making it impossible to establish with accuracy the net amount of José Gregorio's estate. It can be determined that at least 38,478 pesos were charged against the estate, leaving net assets of something under 66,238 pesos.

Manuel Francisco and José Miguel received most of José Gregorio's assets. Of the 38,000-odd pesos charged against the estate, they received 20,737. Moreover, the merchant had bequeathed his net assets to these two brothers, one-third going to Manuel Francisco and two-thirds to José Miguel.[13] The latter's share included all the real property. The bulk of José Gregorio's estate was merely redistributed among his two brothers, preventing dissipation through inheritance of the family's growing properties—a prime factor in the Sánchez Navarros' rise to power.

His brothers made a satisfactory adjustment to José Gregorio's death, and Manuel Francisco took over management of the store in addition to operating the *latifundio*. Although he spent most of his time at the landholding, the brothers' commercial activities continued with little disruption; the cashier at the store handled routine transactions, and José Miguel kept track of matters during the absences of Manuel Francisco.[14]

The Sánchez Navarros remained active in presidial supply despite a change in the regulations governing the garrisons. In an effort to eliminate profiteering, commanders were ordered in 1772 to disassociate themselves from the purchase of supplies. Instead, garrisons would be provisioned by a noncommissioned paymaster elected by the troops. The paymaster was to obtain the necessary supplies and sell them to the men at cost plus 2 percent to cover his expenses. In practice, however, some paymasters dealt with particular merchants instead of seeking the lowest prices, and profiteering continued.[15] The paymaster at Santa Rosa wrote to the Sánchez Navarros in 1776, asking to borrow two thousand or three thousand pesos, as he had done previously, in order to purchase supplies for a forthcoming campaign. It would have been remarkable indeed if these supplies were purchased anywhere but at the Sánchez Navarro store. The brothers also enjoyed an advantage regarding the Río Grande presidio, whose commander, their relative, remained heavily in debt to them.[16]

Their aggressive business practices won for them a commercial position in Monclova bordering on monopoly, as Father Morfi noted when he passed through that capital in 1777. Although there were three or four other merchants in town, they barely managed to stay in business. According to Morfi, customers either paid the curate's price for merchandise or did without, and they paid for their purchases with grain and sheep whose value was fixed at the curate's whim. Morfi concluded his comments by stating that these commodities were shipped outside Coahuila; in this manner José Miguel had acquired a considerable fortune and various haciendas that would, if the province were pacified or more heavily populated, constitute a truly magnificent heritage.[17]

The monopoly in Monclova reflected the situation in the principal cities of New Spain, where a handful of powerful mercantile houses dominated business. Over the years the Sánchez Navarros had developed close ties with several of these firms in San Miguel and Mexico City. Business was normally transacted through correspondence, but from time to time it became necessary to arrange matters in person. Manuel Francisco performed this essential task.

Although badly needed at the *latifundio*, in 1777 he went on a business trip to Mexico City, where he remained for nearly three months. Manuel Francisco not only conferred with Urizar, the sheep buyer, but also reviewed his account with Captain Francisco Antonio de Rábago, another prominent merchant in the capital. There is no indication that Rábago dealt in livestock, but Manuel Francisco had been doing considerable business with his firm. When the two men settled their account in October, 1777, Manuel Francisco had a balance of some 13,800 pesos. He withdrew the entire amount in coin but kept the account open by simultaneously borrowing 1,500 pesos from his business associate.

Their relationship continued for a decade, with Rábago sending periodic shipments of merchandise to Monclova. The goods were mainly textiles and clothing but included books, household decorations, gunpowder, and a set of equipment for a flour mill. There were also several consignments of tobacco destined for the missionary fathers in Coahuila. The Sánchez Navarros continued to supply the missions and received payment by having the funds appropriated in Mexico City for the missions transferred to the account Manuel Francisco maintained with Rábago; in 1777, for instance, the appropriation was 3,600 pesos, while in 1780 it totaled 6,460. Manuel Francisco occasionally made other deposits into this account, and the next time it was adjusted, in September, 1787, he still had a respectable balance of some 9,460 pesos.[18]

The Sánchez Navarros maintained their connection with the firms in Mexico City and San Miguel, but in the early 1780's the brothers suffered a setback in Coahuila by losing their share of the presidial supply business. The paymaster system had proved unsatisfactory, and by 1781 the government adopted a new method for provisioning the frontier presidios: using designated merchants on a contract basis. The governor took bids from the only two merchants in the province whom he considered capable of fulfilling the contract. They were Manuel Francisco Sánchez Navarro and Francisco Yermo. The latter, who had been in business in Santa Rosa for over twenty years, was probably a relative of the Mexico City merchant Gabriel de Yermo, whose firm shipped goods by pack train all the way to Santa Rosa.

After comparing the two bids, the governor recommended in 1782 that Yermo's be accepted, for Manuel Francisco had made demands the governor considered unreasonable: a guaranteed profit of 19 percent, military escorts for his pack trains, and fifteen thousand pesos a year in working capital from the tobacco monopoly. Yermo began supplying the presidios in 1784, but the private contract system proved as unsatisfactory as had its predecessors.[19]

In the meantime, the Sánchez Navarros had been strengthening their commercial organization by recruiting personnel. By far the most important addition was their nephew José Domingo de Letona who, at José Miguel's expense, was studying at the famous Jesuit seminary of San Ildefonso in Mexico City. Letona acted as the Sánchez Navarros' confidential agent beginning in 1784 while he was still a student. Initially his duties consisted of transmitting the news of the day and of purchasing books on religious subjects for José Miguel, but by 1785 Letona was representing the Sánchez Navarros in litigation over land in Coahuila.[20] Following his ordination in 1787, Letona remained in Mexico City, where he played a vital role in handling the family's business affairs.

The brothers also strengthened the Monclova end of the network in 1784 by appointing a nephew by marriage, Francisco Castellano, as cashier of the store.[21] Castellano was much more than a cashier, for in effect he ran the store besides discharging a variety of additional duties, such as managing José Miguel's real estate holdings in Monclova. Manuel Francisco was thus able to concentrate on the *latifundio*. By the mid-1780's, the Sánchez Navarros had trusted members of the family representing their interests in Mexico City and Monclova as well as in Saltillo, where their brother José Antonio had been their agent for a decade.

Management of the commercial operations had improved, but there remained another problem, one that was insoluble. The unreliability of pack trains in moving the heavy volume of merchandise northward along the route from Mexico City, through San Miguel and Saltillo, to Monclova frequently hindered the flow of commerce. The last leg of the journey normally presented little difficulty, as the Sánchez Navarros operated their own pack trains between Monclova and Saltillo. Getting the merchandise to Saltillo was another matter. Businessmen relied mainly on self-employed muleteers; when conditions were unsatisfactory, the muleteers simply refused to travel. Two factors usually determined their willingness to venture into the inhospitable northern region of the viceroyalty. The first was the price of corn; when the grain was expensive, the men could not provision themselves and still make a profit. Second, their departures were governed by the availability of forage along the road. Arranging transport was difficult under the best of conditions; in the mid-1780's, it sometimes became impossible, due partly to the catastrophic crop failure and famine that began in 1784.

José Miguel ordered a shipment of footwear and hats from Urizar in December, 1784. The goods had not left Mexico City as of May, 1785, and Urizar notified the curate that the chances of their being sent in the near future were slim. The price of corn had soared, and drought had blighted the vegetation along the trail north. Urizar could find no muleteers willing to undertake the journey, even at double the usual freight rate. He commented that he himself was experiencing the same frustrations as José Miguel; the previous year's wool clip from Urizar's hacienda was still awaiting transport to Mexico City. Urizar hoped that by July the summer rains would revive the vegetation enough for mule trains to operate.[22]

While awaiting the resumption of freight service, Urizar kept José

Miguel abreast of business conditions in Mexico City, passing along the welcome news that the price of dry goods had dropped considerably and should decline even further. The curate evidently placed additional orders with Urizar in light of this information, for in July, when muleteers once again became available, the Mexico City merchant sent him a substantial shipment of goods, followed by another in September.[23]

The second shipment did not reach Monclova until March, 1786, and similar delays marked the northward progress of other cargoes. For example, on December 16, 1785, the Mexico City firm of Bassoco dispatched a shipment consigned to the San Miguel firm of Allende, which was to forward the merchandise on to Saltillo. Despite assurances that the goods would reach Saltillo no later than February 20, 1786, the cargo had not yet left San Miguel on February 1. The firm of Allende assured José Miguel that shipment would be made that week, but they mentioned that the muleteer had agreed to transport the goods only as far as the Hacienda de Bocas, in San Luis Potosí. The manager of that hacienda had offered to transship the cargo to Saltillo, where it should arrive some time in March.[24] But during the spring the price of corn continued to rise, and by April pack trains suspended operations, bringing commerce between the central and northern regions of New Spain to a standstill. The Sánchez Navarros' cargo was still stranded at the Hacienda de Bocas at the end of July.[25]

The rhythm of commerce resumed during the following month, and goods began moving to Saltillo at relatively frequent intervals. Not only was the cargo that had been delayed for so long at Bocas finally delivered, but, in August and September, Urizar dispatched two more loads of dry goods. These included six bolts of linen cloth, each containing some thirty yards of material, plus bolts of baize, silk serge, fine Brittany linen, and coarse cotton cloth from Puebla. Moreover, cargoes continued to arrive at Saltillo through February, 1787, containing such items as cacao, olive oil, and white woolen cloth from Querétaro.[26]

After this short interlude, transportation was again sporadic: in March, 1787, Urizar could no longer find pack trains for Saltillo.

The muleteers preferred to make the more comfortable and more profitable journey between Mexico City and Acapulco. Urizar again had to inform the curate that until the rains came there was not the slightest hope of resuming shipments.[27] This became possible late in May, and Urizar sent the curate twelve loads of merchandise valued at some 2,950 pesos. Although Urizar could arrange transport only as far as the mining community of Charcas in San Luis Potosí, on this occasion the goods reached Saltillo without undue delay. The Sánchez Navarros sent their own pack train to Charcas to receive the shipment when it arrived there at the end of June.[28]

This was the last shipment from Urizar, and 1787 also marked the last time the Sánchez Navarros sold him livestock. Because of Urizar's refusal to purchase the tithe sheep, José Miguel decided to end his relationship with the Mexico City merchant. In fact, the curate had already begun to liquidate the account. Between 1783 and 1785 he had withdrawn 28,000 pesos, transferring the funds to the other mercantile houses with whom the Sánchez Navarros traded.[29] And in December, 1787, Manuel Francisco arrived in Mexico City to close out the Urizar account. The merchant was so anxious to retain what the brothers still had on deposit that he even offered to pay interest, but to no avail. José Miguel had instructed Manuel Francisco to collect every peso Urizar owed, ". . . for if you, being on the scene, do not collect, who is going to get it from him later?"[30]

Manuel Francisco also collected his 9,460-peso balance from Francisco Antonio de Rábago, thus completing the shift in the Sánchez Navarros' Mexico City trading pattern: in the future they would deal principally with the firms of Bassoco and Yermo. Besides settling financial matters, Manuel Francisco made various purchases; José Miguel continued to send him instructions, including a last-minute reminder not to forget a supply of sheepshears, of which there never seemed to be enough. While Manuel Francisco transacted his business in Mexico City, he had dispatched a nephew to Veracruz to buy a large stock of merchandise. Upon the latter's return to the capital, they set out by coach for Coahuila in February, 1788.[31]

On his way back through San Miguel, the hacendado placed a substantial order, totaling some 5,150 pesos, with the firm of Allende.

The volume of trade with this mercantile house had been expanding notably during the last few years. Besides textiles from Querétaro and from San Miguel itself, the firm of Allende supplied most of the shoes and other leather goods for the Monclova store. The Sánchez Navarros themselves provided the raw materials for this trade by sending cargoes of goatskins to the San Miguel concern.[32]

Their ability to do so had been considerably enhanced by José Miguel's reassuming the administration of the tithe in 1785. The curate used the same techniques that had proved so profitable during his earlier tenure, and this time he derived an additional benefit in the form of ecclesiastical preferment. In 1790 he was promoted to canon of the cathedral chapter in Monterrey.[33] This honor was, in all probability, bestowed in recognition of his years of service in administering the tithe in Coahuila. Leaving his agents to continue managing the tithe in that province, José Miguel departed for Monterrey in January, 1791. Among his new duties was that of reviewing the tithe accounts for the entire diocese.[34]

Besides attending to his ecclesiastical duties, the curate found time to conduct a bit of business on the side. From time to time he loaned money to individuals at 5 percent annual interest, and he also became a property owner in Monterrey. In 1794 José Miguel paid 6,500 pesos for a fifteen-room mansion on the east side of the plaza a few doors south of the cathedral. The two-story mansion was one of the most imposing in the city—it had been the residence of the last two governors of Nuevo León.[35]

Yet the curate had bought the property as an investment rather than as his own residence. Having achieved recognition in the Church, he decided to retire to Monclova and devote himself to his private affairs. The bishop was most reluctant to accept José Miguel's resignation, and the latter had to resubmit his application. The case went all the way to Madrid, where in 1795 the crown finally approved his retirement.[36] The curate was now free to concentrate on managing his increasingly complex commercial affairs.

Throughout the 1790's he maintained the connection with the firm of Allende, although the volume of goods purchased gradually declined; the largest shipment during this period was in August, 1795, and was worth 2,472 pesos. Most of the merchandise consisted of textiles from Querétaro, but orders for sheepshears, knives, and other types of ironware were filled in San Miguel itself. Whenever items were not available locally, the House of Allende relied on its connections in Mexico City: the head of the firm, Domingo de Berrio y Zavala, was related to Juan Antonio de Zavala, a prominent merchant in the capital.[37]

The Sánchez Navarros had strong business connections of their own in Mexico City, principally the mercantile house of Bassoco. That establishment supplied some of the goods going to Coahuila, but its primary role was as banker and financial clearinghouse.[38] To illustrate, between 1788 and 1793, José Miguel amassed credits with Bassoco totaling 88,971 pesos. But, as of 1794, he had withdrawn nearly half, having a balance of 48,480. Subsequent credits earned by selling sheep to Bassoco were more than offset by José Miguel's continued heavy withdrawals, only a small part of which went to pay for merchandise. Besides a number of drafts for miscellaneous purposes, the curate in 1795 wrote one for 14,000 pesos in favor of the Count of la Cortina.[39] This draft may have represented a loan to the count, for the Sánchez Navarros were investing an increasing amount of the money held for them by Bassoco.

The trend toward making their capital more productive had begun in 1784 when the curate invested two thousand pesos, in Manuel Francisco's name, in the Mexico City *consulado*, or guild of merchant importers. The money was for investment in the Royal Philippine Company, and in 1786 Manuel Francisco himself deposited another one thousand pesos in the *consulado* for this purpose.[40] The volume of investment increased markedly in the 1790's. José Miguel deposited twenty thousand pesos at interest in the *consulado* in 1798, earmarked for the construction of a toll road between the capital and Veracruz. He also made loans at 5 percent annual interest to individuals, a Saltillo merchant family receiving four thousand pesos and the Marquis of Aguayo borrowing sixteen thousand.[41] Having the haughty Marquis as one of his debtors must have given José Miguel great satisfaction.

At the turn of the century José Miguel could take considerable pride in the commercial empire he had built. Yet he had no intention of resting on his laurels, for a program to improve the family's Monclova properties began in the fall of 1800. Work was started on a new residence for the curate and a new store, both located on the plaza near the parish church. The disastrous flood in 1802 delayed completion of these projects, but it also caused José Miguel to rebuild the flour mill on a more substantial scale. Besides the improvements made at Monclova, the Sánchez Navarros renovated their warehouse in Saltillo.[42]

In the early years of the new century local commerce followed the established pattern. The Sánchez Navarros bought agricultural commodities from the region around Monclova and supplied that area with merchandise from their general store. They did a brisk trade in wine, brandy, and vinegar that they brought in from the Aguayo *latifundio*. The Hacienda de Parras, along with the Hacienda de Cedros in Zacatecas, was one of the largest producers of liquor in the entire viceroyalty.[43]

The center of the brothers' regional commerce was Saltillo, their principal market for wool. A new pattern was developing with the Sánchez Navarros having greater amounts of their wool and skins processed in Saltillo rather than in San Miguel. Each year their Saltillo business agent arranged for local artisans to weave a gross of sarapes, another of blankets, and a hundred yards of coarse woolen cloth, all destined for the peons on the *latifundio*. He also handled the sheepskins and goatskins, averaging between one thousand and fifteen hundred a year, which were tanned into chamois and cordovan leather.[44]

During this same period the annual Saltillo fair, the leading commercial event in northern New Spain, was becoming a lackluster affair. The decline resulted in large measure from a sharp increase in the price of manufactured goods, which in turn reflected Spain's involvement in European wars. Arranging the shipment of goods for the forthcoming fair, the Sánchez Navarros' nephew in Mexico City wrote in the summer of 1799 that he was "scandalized" by the high prices he had been forced to pay. Prices at the 1800 fair were little better. Manuel Francisco complained that the fair was greatly below par; he had bought only a few goods while experiencing difficulty in selling the wool clip from Tapado.[45]

Though the fair was undoubtedly declining, Manuel Francisco's complaints must be kept in perspective. Writing to José Miguel in 1801, he again lamented the high prices prevailing at the fair and the lack of customers for the Sánchez Navarros' wool and cotton. He mentioned, however, that three pack trains had just departed for Monclova carrying most of his purchases: twenty-six mule loads of crockery from Michoacán, for which he paid some 3,000 pesos; another 3,702 pesos' worth of merchandise for the Monclova store, including twenty mule loads of soap and six of *metates*, or concave stones for grinding corn; and 1,673 pesos of goods for the peons at Tapado. Among the items in the latter shipment were a dozen pairs of cheap shoes, a 100-yard bolt of blue baize from Mexico City, a coil of rope from Puebla, eight dozen shawls, four dozen knives, several crates of hats, some earthenware from Guadalajara, and ninety pounds of chocolate. So, despite his complaints, Manuel Francisco had managed to purchase some 8,300 pesos' worth of merchandise at the 1801 fair.[46]

The Saltillo fair continued at a depressed level during the next few years. Manuel Francisco reported in 1803 that, with the fair about to commence, few people had arrived from central New Spain, and it was felt that the current drought would discourage attendance from the center of the viceroyalty. The few traveling merchants who braved the discomforts of the trail to Saltillo were able to sell their wares at exorbitant prices. The following year the fair got off to an indifferent start, according to the Sánchez Navarros' Saltillo agent who was trying to fill their orders for merchandise.[47]

In the Sánchez Navarros' dealings with firms outside Coahuila, there were some elements of continuity and others of notable change as the nineteenth century opened. The long-standing connection with the firm of Allende continued for a time, but the amount of business transacted steadily decreased.[48] By the end of 1806 the connection between the Sánchez Navarros and the San Miguel firm ceased altogether, ending an association that had spanned a third of a century.

Significant changes were also occurring in the brothers' trade with the Mexico City commercial establishments. The last recorded shipment from Bassoco was in the summer of 1799, though that firm continued to handle many of the Sánchez Navarros' financial transactions. The brothers were transferring most of their commercial activities to the house of Gabriel de Yermo. Partly through their sales of sheep they amassed substantial credits with Yermo beginning in 1800. By January, 1806, José Miguel's credits had ascended to some 98,460 pesos, against which he wrote drafts for some 40,738.[49] Not only did the curate still have a balance of 57,722 pesos, but also part of the money he had withdrawn was used to finance a new line of trade with Oaxaca.

This venture had its inception when the Sánchez Navarros' nephew and business agent in Mexico City, the priest José Domingo de Letona, was promoted in 1799 to the Oaxaca cathedral chapter. In November, 1800, José Miguel established a special account with Yermo's firm to finance Letona's stay in Oaxaca. Some of the funds came from the curate's own account with Yermo, but most of the money consisted of the interest from several of José Miguel's investments.[50] Letona took charge of purchasing thousands of pesos' worth of coarse cotton textiles in Oaxaca for clothing the Sánchez Navarros' peons.[51] Several shipments were made, but this promising venture was cut short by Letona's transfer to an ecclesiastical post in Mexico City at the end of 1802. He did arrange for a shipment in 1804, but this was the last time the Sánchez Navarros had merchandise brought directly from Oaxaca.[52]

The bulk of their goods came from Mexico City, where Letona had resumed his role as the brothers' confidential business agent. He dealt mainly with the firm of Yermo, which supplied the merchandise and handled the financing. Transporting the cargoes to Saltillo again became extremely difficult in the early 1800's because of the drought afflicting northern New Spain.[53] On one occasion in 1802 the Sánchez Navarros' agent in Saltillo even had to send pack mules as far as Cedral in San Luis Potosí to receive a shipment from the capital.

Although commerce had settled into a routine and goods were moving northward as rapidly as could be expected, José Miguel's financial affairs became progressively more complicated. Even though retired, the curate continued to receive part of his income from the Church; in 1802, for instance, when the tithe revenues from the Bishopric of Linares were distributed, his share exceeded 7,000 pesos. Furthermore, José Miguel's investments were returning a steady 5 percent annual interest—1,000 pesos on the funds deposited in the *consulado*, 500 on the 10,000 pesos still owed by the Marquis of Aguayo, and 400 on loans to several Saltillo merchants. The curate had also rented out the mansion in Monterrey for 355 pesos a year.[54]

An increasing portion of this income as well as that derived from ranching and commerce was being invested in loans. Those secured by mortgages on property in Coahuila, such as the 12,300 pesos lent to Juan Ignacio de Arizpe and the 15,000-peso loan to the Vázquez Borregos, have already been discussed. There was, of course, an element of risk involved in making loans to individuals. Sometimes it proved impossible to secure repayment, as in the case of Jacobo de Ugarte y Loyola, governor of Coahuila from 1769 to 1777. He owed the Sánchez Navarros some 5,380 pesos in 1775, and in 1801 José Miguel was still trying to collect. Unfortunately, Ugarte had assets of approximately 6,000 pesos and debts totaling more than 20,000.[55] Whenever possible, therefore, José Miguel required real estate as collateral, but when this was not feasible the curate would accept chattels as security. He loaned the governor of Nuevo León, Simón de Herrera, 3,000 pesos in 1802, secured by a lien on five hundred brood mares and a general lien against all of Herrera's present and future property. The curate also made money available to relatives, such as his nephew the priest Rafael Trinidad Ramos Arizpe, who borrowed 1,000 pesos at interest in 1801, and to employees, such as his Saltillo agent José Camacho, who did likewise in 1802.[56]

José Miguel conducted these financial operations despite a mounting threat to his widespread interests. As part of the crown's policy of restricting the power of the Church, legal discrimination against clerics was increasing. In 1799 Letona had notified the curate of a recent change in the law—henceforth clerics could bequeath only such property as they had inherited from their fathers. Because of the new restriction José Miguel began transferring considerable sums from his Mexico City accounts to Manuel Francisco. In 1803, for example, he wrote his brother a 25,000-peso draft against Bassoco as well as 49,000 pesos in drafts against Yermo. Manuel Francisco was engaging in financial operations of his own. When failing health prevented him from making a business trip to Mexico City in 1804, he sent the Sánchez Navarros' nephew, Juan Ignacio de Arizpe, in his place. Arizpe delivered to Yermo fifty-five bars of silver belonging to Manuel Francisco. Yermo then turned the bullion in at the mint and credited the *hacendado*'s account with the proceeds.[57] Manuel Francisco's death in February, 1805, abruptly halted the process of building up his Mexico City balances.

The *hacendado*'s death also precipitated a bitter family quarrel over the distribution of his estate, a dispute that sheds some light on the nature of the Sánchez Navarros' financial arrangements. The estate could not legally be divided until a detailed inventory of Manuel Francisco's property had been prepared, so the crucial question was to determine exactly what had belonged to him. The family split into two factions on this issue. On one side were José Miguel, who was the executor and the guardian of his late brother's children, and José Melchor, the eldest son and principal heir. Opposing them were the rest of Manuel Francisco's heirs.[58] The *hacendado*'s land was not in dispute, having been willed to José Melchor; it was the remainder of Manuel Francisco's assets that was at issue. The curate and his nephew were determined to conserve what Manuel Francisco had amassed, while the other heirs understandably wanted all the money to which they felt entitled. Having decided to make José Melchor his sole heir, the curate claimed for himself as many of Manuel Francisco's assets as possible, for in this way he could eventually pass them on undivided to José Melchor. The curate undoubtedly planned to circumvent the recent legal restrictions applying to the clergy.

Because of complicated financial transactions between himself and Manuel Francisco, José Miguel had considerable difficulty in establishing his right to some of the property in Manuel Francisco's name. For one thing, there was disagreement over who actually owned the Sánchez Navarros' store. After José Gregorio's death in 1774, Manuel Francisco had received his one-third interest in the store in cash, leaving José Miguel as sole owner. Subsequently, however, he and the curate had drawn up an agreement to operate the store as a company, with Manuel Francisco having title to the establishment but José Miguel supplying most of the capital.[59] Moreover, in their financial dealings, each of the two brothers had maintained separate accounts with the mercantile houses in San Miguel and Mexico City; they had also maintained an account with each other. Embroiling matters even further was the fact that the curate's transfers of funds to his brother had sometimes been based simply on oral agreements between the two men. José Miguel now asserted that he had merely loaned this money to Manuel Francisco; the latter's heirs demanded that the funds be included as part of the *hacendado*'s estate.

A small fortune was at stake. Besides the 2,000 pesos invested in the Royal Philippine Company and the 74,000 he had transferred to Manuel Francisco in 1803, the curate had previously put another 93,000 pesos in his brother's name. Most of the 93,000 pesos was held by Bassoco, the remainder by Yermo. Since the transaction rested only on an oral agreement between the brothers, José Miguel was badly worried about being able to prove that he had really loaned the 93,000 to Manuel Francisco so the latter could invest it and enjoy the income. The curate sought the advice of his nephew, the priest José Domingo de Letona. Letona, who had a doctorate in law, replied that the matter was an extremely delicate one, turning on whether or not a donation had been involved. All doubt, he asserted, would be eliminated if, at the time of the transfer or later, José Miguel had stated in the presence of witnesses that he was only loaning the money. Another way of validating the curate's claim would be if Manuel Francisco had entered the original 93,000 pesos, as well as the money subsequently transferred to him, in the account he had maintained with José Miguel. Letona advised the curate, in any case, to enter these amounts now on his own copy of the account and present the account as a legitimate debt owed by the deceased, since all debts would have to be paid before the heirs could receive the remainder of the estate.[60]

José Miguel was already taking measures to retain part of the money in Manuel Francisco's name. The *hacendado* had not cashed several of the drafts written in his favor in 1803. José Miguel now stopped payment on these instruments, thus retaining 50,000 of the 74,000 pesos he had transferred to his brother in 1803.[61] And, acting on Letona's advice, José Miguel pressed his claim for the rest of the funds in Manuel Francisco's name. Despite the outraged objections of all the heirs except José Melchor, the curate evidently succeeded in retaining the bulk of this money as well as control of the store. By December, 1805, the inventory of the estate was nearing completion, and in June of the following year the schedules were being prepared so it could be distributed. The final sum apportioned among the heirs is not known, but, presumably as part of the settlement, José Miguel ceded to them the 2,000 pesos invested in the Philippine Company, the value of an unspecified amount of silver bullion, and at least 7,760 pesos in cash.[62] The curate continued as guardian of Manuel Francisco's children until 1809, when he resigned in favor of José Melchor, who had come of age.[63] The two men had acted ruthlessly but they achieved their goal of preventing the dissipation of Manuel Francisco's property. The family's long-range interests had been protected.

The confusion following the *hacendado*'s demise forced José Miguel to reexamine his own financial position. He had become uneasy regarding the ten thousand pesos that the Marquis of Aguayo still owed; on the curate's instructions, Letona attempted to call in the loan on the pretext that the money was needed to help settle Manuel Francisco's estate. Aguayo professed to be greatly distressed by this lack of confidence in his ability to repay. The matter was smoothed over when José Miguel reluctantly allowed the Marquis to continue paying interest until the end of 1805, when Aguayo agreed to repay the principal.[64]

The curate was also considering whether to reinvest the funds in the several accounts with Bassoco and Yermo. Between them the merchants held nearly 140,000 pesos of Sánchez Navarro money, most of it being in Bassoco's hands. Letona suggested that, if it could be done tactfully, the curate should withdraw this money and invest it at interest, pointing out that the 7,000 pesos it would produce annually at 5 percent were currently being lost. José Miguel hesitated, not wishing to risk offending the two Mexico City merchants.

Writing from the vantage point of the capital, Letona urged his uncle in stronger terms to withdraw the funds and loan them at interest. He reiterated that at present José Miguel received no return on this capital and, more important, the curate risked losing everything if the firms should fail. To support his argument Letona stated that bankruptcies were not uncommon among mercantile houses, as shown by the failure of the firm of Vertiz, which had been considered the strongest establishment in the entire viceroyalty. Should Yermo and Bassoco fail, the curate's position as a creditor would be precarious. Since his funds were not secured by a legal instrument, other creditors would have preference. For this reason, Letona explained, he had suggested that, if José Miguel were determined to leave some of the money with Bassoco and Yermo, he should at least protect himself by requiring the merchants to borrow it at interest under a formal agreement and to secure the loans by mortgages on some of their rural properties.[65] Heeding this advice, the curate began withdrawing some of the money in order to invest it in Coahuila.

Real estate remained the safest form of investment. Even so, it was becoming increasingly advisable to avoid *bienes de obras pías*—those properties bearing ecclesiastical mortgages. The crown desperately needed funds, and properties in which the Church had an interest became the target of harsh laws designed to raise revenue.[66] In advising his uncle, Letona stressed that no one in Mexico City would currently invest in *bienes de obras pías* for fear of what might happen to this type of real estate.[67]

José Miguel's involvement with rural properties often resulted from loans he had made. In 1805, for instance, he acquired a claim on a hacienda in Nuevo León upon the death of its owner, Juan Manuel Mexía. The latter, an attorney in Monterrey, had performed legal services for José Miguel, and the curate had granted him an interest-free loan of four thousand pesos, which had not been repaid by the time of Mexía's death. As one of his principal creditors, José Miguel thus had the opportunity to claim the hacienda, located near the settlement of Boca de Leones, as well as a house Mexía had owned in that village. In this instance, however, the curate declined to accept real estate to satisfy a debt. Both the *casco* of the hacienda and the house in Boca de Leones had been virtually demolished by the disastrous flood of 1802, so José Miguel instructed his nephew in Monterrey to press for a cash settlement from Mexía's estate.[68] By contrast, as a result of the ten thousand pesos he loaned at interest to Ignacio Elizondo in 1808, José Miguel acquired a claim against the Hacienda de San Juan de Sabinas. As we have seen, the curate and his nephew José Melchor were anything but reluctant to accept that hacienda in settlement of Elizondo's debt.

The curate's urban real estate became rather more diversified. Not only did he rent out some of his considerable holdings in Monclova, but also by 1806, his Saltillo properties included several rental houses. He also owned two houses in the village of Candela, where the local priest, who happened to be one of his nephews, looked after his interests. For years another nephew, also a priest, managed the curate's mansion in Monterrey. Although the bishop became interested in the structure for use as a college, private individuals continued renting it through 1815.[69]

The Sánchez Navarros' regional commerce followed the established pattern. They still dealt in tithe produce, though on a much smaller scale than in past decades. On occasion they also bought such commodities as cotton from small producers for resale at Saltillo.[70] The store in Monclova continued to function as the wholesale supplier for merchants in villages around the capital. Among the more unusual items brought in from Saltillo were a pack train loaded with forty chests of gunpowder, in 1806, and a shipment of eighteen hundred gilded tacks, in 1809.[71]

The family imported a much greater peso volume of merchandise through Saltillo in the years immediately preceding the struggle for independence. José Miguel drew heavily on his Mexico City accounts to finance these operations. In June, 1806, he had a balance of 57,726 pesos with Yermo; despite substantial credits from sheep sales, this balance had dropped to 7,181 pesos by May, 1810. His account with Bassoco showed a similar decline, from 38,670 pesos in August, 1806, to 11,131 in September, 1810. Of course, not all the withdrawals went to finance trade, but much of the money was used in this manner. Even in cases where the reason for withdrawals was unspecified, as when José Miguel had 2,000 pesos in gold coins brought from Mexico City in 1806, or when he wrote drafts for 12,000 pesos in José Melchor's favor in 1806–1807, it is likely that the funds were for the Sánchez Navarros' commercial ventures.[72]

The renewed emphasis on commerce reflected an attempt to lay in a stock of merchandise before prices rose any higher. With Spain embroiled in the Napoleonic wars, the flow of European goods to the viceroyalty was declining, and prices in Veracruz and Mexico City soared.[73] José Miguel bought merchandise on an unprecedented scale —a single shipment of textiles from Puebla and Mexico City in 1808 totaled 17,297 pesos. And in the spring of 1810 he authorized his nephew Letona to spend another 20,000 pesos on trade goods.[74] It was just as well, for in the fall of 1810 the outbreak of the revolutionary war wrecked the commercial network that José Miguel had so painstakingly built over the preceding four decades.

The swiftly spreading insurrection paralyzed trade throughout much of the viceroyalty, especially between the northern and central regions of the country. The Sánchez Navarros were not immediately affected, because they could buy quantities of the merchandise already in Saltillo for the 1810 fair. But during the following year they increasingly felt the impact of being cut off from their Mexico City source of supply.

The family confronted the problem with their customary resourcefulness. They began by strengthening the management of the Monclova store, firing the relative in charge and replacing him in May, 1811, with a more dynamic kinsman, José Alejandro Sánchez. The latter, José Melchor's second cousin and the curate's nephew, had been discharging minor assignments in the business since 1809.[75] Sánchez now spent much of his time scouring the region for merchandise. Despite the ever-present danger of guerrilla bands, Sánchez's buying trips took him as far afield as San Luis Potosí. With José Melchor providing 2,500 pesos to finance the trip, Sánchez laid in a stock of goods that included four crates of cigarettes.[76]

Yet this type of operation was at best a stopgap, so José Melchor and his cousin conceived a much more ambitious venture. Because it was impossible to transport goods overland from Mexico City, they decided to run a large shipment up the coast from Veracruz. Sánchez set out in May, 1812, for Tampico, where he embarked together with several merchants from Chihuahua and Monterrey engaged in similar undertakings.

Arranging the financing for an operation of this magnitude posed a major problem in itself. Besides the danger of transporting large sums, there was the difficulty of getting the cash in the first place. New Spain's financial structure was collapsing, and merchants were desperately short of working capital. But because of their monetary resources and familial connections the Sánchez Navarros managed to surmount these obstacles.

In order to meet his sailing deadline, Sánchez had needed a substantial sum on short notice. He obtained it from the cathedral chapter in Monterrey, which obligingly advanced him twelve thousand pesos. It so happened that the chapter treasurer, Mariano José Monzón, was the curate's nephew who for years had been the Sánchez Navarros' representative in Monterrey. The cathedral chapter was duly reimbursed, for José Melchor gathered together twelve thousand pesos in coin, concealed it in one of his pack trains, and sent it safely to Monterrey. On Monzón's instructions the mule train then proceeded toward the coast to await the arrival of Sánchez and the cargo.[77]

In the meantime, he had arrived at Veracruz and was in the midst of a three-week buying spree. Textiles and clothing comprised the majority of his purchases, but he also bought sundries, hardware, paper, coffee, crockery, a crate of windowpanes, and eighty-four iron bars. His total bill came to 18,823 pesos, which he paid partly in cash and partly in promissory notes payable at Tampico. By June 18, the cargo was on board two schooners bound for that port.[78] Not so Sánchez; he was bedridden, a victim of the pestilential climate of Veracruz. The vessels reached Tampico on June 24, and the pack train was waiting a few miles north at Altamira to receive the cargo. Having regained his health, Sánchez himself reached Altamira on July 8. While awaiting a second mule train from Monclova to finish transporting the original cargo, Sánchez employed his time in Altamira profitably by purchasing another 6,528 pesos' worth of goods, consisting mainly of 2,400 lengths of cloth from Oaxaca.[79] Thus when

Sánchez finally started the four-hundred–mile trip back to Monclova he could congratulate himself on having restocked the store with 25,350 pesos' worth of goods.

Emboldened by this coup, Sánchez repeated the operation on his own the next year. Unfortunately, he went to the well once too often. He purchased a huge stock of goods on consignment for merchants throughout northern New Spain only to find himself caught in a deepening depression. By 1814 he was committed for 71,262 pesos but had been able to collect only 3,000 from his buyers. To compound his troubles, his taxes were in arrears, and when he tried to make partial payment with a draft the royal treasurer in Saltillo rejected the instrument, demanding cash. Facing imminent ruin, Sánchez resigned as manager of the Monclova store to salvage what he could from his own enterprises.[80]

As the case of Sánchez illustrates, business conditions had deteriorated to the point that, even if merchandise could physically be transported to Coahuila, people could no longer buy it. Confirming the extent of the depression was José Melchor's painful decision in 1814 to close down the Monclova store. In the face of continuing revolution and a shrinking economy the *hacendado* felt that the Sánchez Navarros' only hope lay in retrenchment.[81]

Among the factors contributing to José Melchor's decision were increased taxes. To combat the insurrection the government had more than doubled the *alcabala*, ordinarily 2 percent of the value of merchandise; there was now a one-third surcharge on the *alcabala* plus another 2 percent collected as a convoy tax. The taxes, moreover, were levied both when goods arrived in Monclova and, if they were subsequently shipped elsewhere, at the final destination as well.[82] Furthermore, local authorities collected taxes of their own. Officials in Saltillo charged pack trains stopping over in that city three pesos for each day they remained, in addition to collecting two reals per mule load of merchandise.[83]

Besides being taxed, pack mules were subject to confiscation by the military. José Melchor indignantly reported to the curate in 1814 that this was being widely practiced on the roads leading into Saltillo and Monterrey. According to the *hacendado*, the troops not only were seizing mules but were also stripping the muleteers of whatever weapons they might have; if the latter resisted, they were impressed into the army on the spot. José Melchor sourly observed that the military always caused more damage than did hostile Indians.[84]

His antipathy toward the military stemmed not only from their exactions on commerce and their indifferent success in fighting Indians, but also from the forced loans that the army was collecting. To replenish the subtreasuries in the face of a critical shortage of cash, the commandant general of the Eastern Interior Provinces had ordered in 1813 that the wealthiest citizens were to deliver two-thirds of their cash to the treasury, which would then issue receipts for their protection. As was to be expected, the Sánchez Navarros fell into this privileged category; and, as was to be expected, neither José Melchor nor the curate intended to deliver a single peso more than they absolutely had to.

By a singular piece of ill-luck, José Melchor's assets were a matter of record. In connection with another project, he had in 1813 certified his net worth to be 85,000 pesos, and the declaration had been made within a matter of days before the commandant general's order was issued.[85] Ever since, the *hacendado* had been pleading poverty, explaining that his assets were in land, livestock, and commercial drafts but that he had very little cash. The curate had yet to declare his own assets, and he took his time in doing so. In June, 1814, he was still preparing a statement of his net worth, and José Melchor, who was assisting him, took pains to undervalue his uncle's property.[86] There is no indication of the total amount the Sánchez Navarros ultimately delivered under this loan, but it must have been considerably less than the required two-thirds. They could count on receiving at least a sympathetic hearing from the royal treasurer in Saltillo, since he was their relative by marriage.

As successive forced loans were levied on the citizens of Coahuila, the Sánchez Navarros had to part with more of their liquid assets. For instance, the contribution that José Melchor delivered to the military in January, 1815, included 530 pesos in jealously hoarded cash.[87] And, because the religious establishment was also being squeezed for money, José Miguel found himself being taxed in his capacity as a cleric. Needing funds for his troops, the commandant general imposed a forced loan on the Monterrey cathedral chapter in 1815 but with scant success, receiving only 1,180 pesos. He continued to press the chapter, which in 1816 imposed contributions on the ecclesiastics in the diocese. As the leading cleric in Coahuila, José Miguel was assessed 3,569 pesos. Despite his appeals citing the personal expenses he had been incurring in building the Monclova church, the curate had to pay. José Melchor suggested that this be done by a draft on the family's Saltillo agent in order to conserve what cash they still had in Monclova.[88]

The curate could derive some small comfort from learning that forced loans against the Church were much heavier in Mexico City. The priest Letona wrote him of cases in which nunneries had been forced to sell even their furniture to meet their quotas. Though the clergy in the northeastern provinces fared considerably better, the cathedral chapter in Monterrey was still assessed 50,000 pesos, of which they had delivered 36,000 by February, 1818. The following year José Miguel petitioned the bishop for the return of his 3,569 pesos, but the prelate declared himself to be without authority to grant the request.[89]

The revolution had dealt a decisive blow to the Sánchez Navarros' relations with the Mexico City mercantile houses. By 1816, when insurgent activity was declining, many firms in the capital were no longer in any condition to transact business; the financial system centered on Mexico City had collapsed. Letona informed José Miguel that virtually no drafts were being honored there. Letona himself had recently returned half a dozen drafts to Oaxaca because he had been unable to cash them.[90]

The Sánchez Navarros were extremely fortunate in that they escaped the full effect of the collapse, since the curate had withdrawn most of his funds from Mexico City prior to the outbreak of the rebellion. At that time his deposits in the capital consisted of 20,000 pesos invested in the *consulado*, 11,131 held by Bassoco, and 7,181 in Yermo's hands.

José Miguel subsequently empowered Letona to draw against the

Bassoco account, which by then had decreased to some ten thousand pesos. Letona withdrew seven thousand, using some of the money to cash small drafts the curate occasionally wrote in favor of other relatives. The arrangement proved to be a fortunate one because the House of Bassoco fell on hard times. Antonio de Bassoco, who had been elevated to the title of Count of Bassoco in 1811, died in November, 1814. But as of 1817 Letona informed the curate that he doubted whether the Bassocos could deliver the three thousand pesos they still owed José Miguel, even though on paper the Bassoco family was worth over three million pesos. Nevertheless, the House of Bassoco's financial condition did improve to some extent, for two years later Letona was able to collect the balance.[91] But the outlook for recovering the curate's other deposits in the capital remained gloomy.

Letona had done what he could to manage the curate's affairs in Mexico City, but he himself had been ruined by the financial crash. Apologizing for his inability to assist some of the family's needy relatives, the priest explained that he could not collect any of the money owed to him from various business ventures. Letona's departure in 1818 to assume a position in the Valladolid cathedral chapter severed one of the Sánchez Navarros' last links with Mexico City.[92]

Thus, during the revolutionary decade the Sánchez Navarros were forced to retrench into Coahuila. Yet their situation was not so bleak as it might appear. Regional commerce was beginning to revive by 1816, and José Melchor reopened the Monclova store under the management of Juan José de Cárdenas, who was an employee rather than a relative.[93] José Melchor attended the Saltillo fair that year, reporting a reasonably good selection of merchandise from Spain but a shortage of some articles produced in the viceroyalty itself. Textiles, plus a few shawls and kerchiefs, comprised the bulk of the *hacendado*'s purchases, which totaled only some 3,612 pesos. This sum included a 12 percent surcharge added to the price of merchandise to compensate for the depreciation of the currency resulting from the revolution.[94] The *hacendado* sometimes supplemented his purchases by acquiring a few items from San Luis Potosí. The trickle of goods going to Monclova included 675 pounds of cacao, four mule loads of sugar, and 1,600 yards of cloth.[95] But San Luis Potosí remained the limit of the Sánchez Navarros' commercial radius.

Their financial operations were likewise curtailed. They did make a few loans to relatives, among them José Melchor's brother, who received 6,000 pesos, and the *hacendado*'s cousin, the priest José Miguel Ecay Múzquiz, who borrowed 1,370. The principal beneficiary of the curate's bounty, however, was his nephew Juan Ignacio de Arizpe, the Monclova tax collector, who received some 7,190 pesos in cash and in credit.[96]

These familial transactions were the exception, for in general the Sánchez Navarros were calling in loans as part of their policy of retrenchment. Occasionally a note was paid on schedule, as in 1813 when the Saltillo merchant José Miguel Lobo Guerrero finished repaying 12,000 pesos he had borrowed five years earlier. By contrast, some accounts receivable were dead letters; in 1818, legal proceedings still dragged on at Guadalajara concerning the estate of Jacobo de Ugarte y Loyola, against whom the Sánchez Navarros had a claim dating back to 1775.[97] Nevertheless, by pressing their various claims José Miguel and José Melchor did manage to collect some 5,250 pesos owed to them.[98] And when debtors could not raise the cash, as was usually the case because of the times, the Sánchez Navarros tried to secure a fresh acknowledgment of the indebtedness in order to strengthen any future legal action. They obtained such acknowledgments for 6,830 pesos of the money they had outstanding.[99]

Furthermore, during the decade 1810–1820 the Sánchez Navarros continued to acquire property in Monclova, and in several instances they took real estate in settlement of debts. José Melchor paid 6,000 pesos in 1813 for a house together with an adjoining *obraje* and its equipment. The purchase price, incidentally, included the debts of the workers at the *obraje*.[100] Another piece of real estate passed into the *hacendado*'s hands as the result of a business failure. In 1816 he put up 1,300 pesos to finance a local merchant who proposed to bring in goods from San Luis Potosí. As collateral, José Melchor secured a mortgage on his partner's house. The venture ultimately failed, and in 1819 the *hacendado* received title to the house. Though the deed listed a purchase price of 500 pesos, in all probability that was merely the balance outstanding on his original investment.[101]

The Sánchez Navarros' Monclova holdings increased significantly in 1820. The curate received title to the property that his nephew and debtor Juan Ignacio de Arizpe had mortgaged in 1801. This block of real estate consisted of a store, four houses, and two flour mills. Besides the mills and their equipment, the walled compound in which they were located contained an orchard and a rudimentary smelter.[102] That same year José Melchor acquired another house, at a bargain price. The *hacendado* offered to buy the property for 239 pesos, two-thirds of its market value. The owners, unable to raise the 170 pesos they owed him, had no choice but to accept. José Melchor paid them 69 pesos and took possession.[103]

The *hacendado* was also improving some of his Monclova properties. In the spring of 1820 he began constructing a commercial establishment containing several warehouses built around a patio. A portico covered three sides of the patio, the other side opening onto an extensive walled corral, for José Melchor planned to use part of the structure as an abattoir.[104]

This new venture reflected a return of business confidence, which in turn reflected the progressive pacification of the viceroyalty. By 1820 it appeared that the struggle for independence had failed, and, as legitimate authority was reestablished throughout most of New Spain, businessmen were becoming cautiously optimistic. The Sánchez Navarros had come through the revolutionary decade in surprisingly good condition. Though they had suffered serious commercial reverses, they had escaped the full effects of the Mexico City financial crash. Moreover, they were in a position to rebuild, for now they were more firmly entrenched than ever in Coahuila.

6. Politics

The struggle for independence plunged the Sánchez Navarros into the mainstream of politics, thereby breaking a pattern that had prevailed for decades. Except for one instance in 1790 when Manuel Francisco served as justice of the peace in Santa Rosa, they had shunned overt participation in political life.[1] Secure in their economic power and in José Miguel's prestige as the leading cleric in Coahuila, the family had traditionally preferred to work behind the scenes.

In addition to their personal friendship with local officials, the Sánchez Navarros could rely on two relatives who occupied public posts. One was Juan Ignacio de Arizpe who, besides being tax collector at Monclova for some thirty years, was interim governor of Coahuila from August, 1805, through July, 1807.[2] The other relative was Manuel Royüela, a Spaniard born in 1759 into a family of *hidalgos*.[3] As a young man, he held the post of secretary to the warden of the fortress at Acapulco, and, when in 1792 the crown established a branch treasury in Saltillo to facilitate paying the troops in the four northeastern provinces, Royüela received the appointment as treasurer. The Spaniard's services were evidently satisfactory, for in 1794 he received the Order of Charles III.[4] Royüela became a member of the Sánchez Navarro family by marrying Manuel Francisco's daughter María Josefa around 1798.[5]

Though they preferred to concentrate on their business enterprises, the Sánchez Navarros nevertheless had a lively interest in politics. Through his extensive network of correspondents, José Miguel knew what was happening not only in the viceroyalty but, especially after the French invasion of Spain in 1808, in the Peninsula as well. As for José Melchor, he was avid to learn whatever he could about the United States. The *hacendado*'s curiosity was described by Lt. Zebulon Pike, who stopped at Tapado in 1807 while being escorted under guard to the border of New Spain. The two men got along well together, and José Melchor exhibited a seemingly insatiable thirst for knowledge about American laws and institutions.[6] The *hacendado*'s interest in public affairs eventually became more than academic, for he broke with family tradition by accepting public office. In January, 1810, he became the *alcalde* of Monclova.[7]

Yet José Melchor's real involvement in politics began in the fall of that fateful year. He was in Saltillo for the fair when news reached that city on September 22 of Father Hidalgo's uprising on the sixteenth in the region of San Miguel el Grande. Saltillo was crowded with thousands of visitors, and José Melchor, apprehensive that the local authorities might be unable to preserve order in view of the sensational news, took it upon himself to act. He sent a message to Monclova urging the governor of Coahuila, Lt. Col. Antonio Cordero, to march to Saltillo and take control of the situation.[8]

Having received a similar dispatch from the Saltillo authorities, the governor began assembling the presidial troops and mobilizing the militia. Cordero designated Saltillo as the assembly point, but, because of the distances involved, it took him several months to concentrate his forces. Meanwhile, Saltillo was kept in turmoil by disturbing reports of Hidalgo's military triumphs. Anxiety increased when in November a large caravan of refugees arrived. Many of them were mine operators from Cedral, Matehuala, and Catorce; since the roads to the south had been cut, they were bringing their bullion for safekeeping in the Saltillo treasury. The refugees also brought the alarming news that the city of San Luis Potosí had fallen to the rebels and that one of Hidalgo's subordinates was preparing to march on Saltillo itself. To defend the city, Cordero ordered his troops

to concentrate at the strategically located Hacienda de Aguanueva sixteen miles to the south. During November and December, Cordero,
with the assistance of the royal treasurer Manuel Royüela, worked feverishly to arm and equip the units streaming into the royalist camp.

Cordero had some seven hundred troops and six cannon at Aguanueva by the beginning of January, 1811, when the long-dreaded insurgent horde made its appearance. The rebels, commanded by Gen.
Mariano Jiménez, numbered between seven and eight thousand and
boasted an artillery train of sixteen cannon. The two forces sighted
each other at Aguanueva on January 7, 1811. Cordero began deploy-
ing his troops, but the royalists, unnerved by the overwhelming su-
periority of the enemy, deserted en masse to the insurgents without
firing a shot. The hapless governor fled, a mob of rebels and ex-
royalists at his heels. Run to earth a few miles north of Saltillo, he
was delivered to the insurgent commander Jiménez, who treated him
with consideration.[9]

Jiménez made a triumphal entry into Saltillo on January 8. Besides
sending units to occupy Parras and Monterrey, Jiménez detached five
hundred men under Brig. Pedro de Aranda, whom he appointed governor, to seize Monclova. The capital of Coahuila was in Aranda's
hands by January 18. Hearing rumors that some royalists contemplated falling back into Texas to continue resistance, Aranda marched
to the Presidio de Río Grande early in February. While there he
learned that a coup by Hidalgo's sympathizers in San Antonio on
January 22 had already delivered Texas to the insurgents.[10]

It had taken the rebels less than a month to capture the northeastern provinces. Nonetheless, as royalist sympathizers in Coahuila recovered from the succession of disasters that had befallen their cause,
they began to organize a counterrevolution. Acting independently at
first, various groups and individuals soon joined in a single, well-
planned conspiracy.

One of the chief plotters was Manuel Royüela. As a precaution
against an insurgent victory, he had loaded the bullion and records in
the Saltillo treasury on pack mules. Within hours after the royalist
debacle at Aguanueva, Royüela, his family, and the treasure of nearly
300,000 pesos were on the road to Monclova with a small military

escort. Royüela hoped to reach San Antonio, which, as far as he knew, was still held by the government. At the Presidio de Río Grande, however, most of Royüela's escort mutinied. Assisted by the townspeople, the mutineers on January 16, 1811, shot down the only four men who remained loyal to the treasurer, seized the pack train, and imprisoned Royüela together with his wife and six young children.

Royüela was still in jail at Río Grande when the insurgent governor Aranda arrived there early in February. Aranda, an elderly alcoholic, was generous and trusting by nature. He treated Royüela kindly, even permitting him to have visitors. One of them was the retired militia captain Ignacio Elizondo, who owned half of the Hacienda de San Juan de Sabinas.[11]

Elizondo's role in these events was as mysterious as it was to be decisive. He has gone down in Mexican history as a traitor. The accounts of his participation in the revolution usually allege that he was recalled to active service in 1810, that he was the first officer to desert at Aguanueva on January 7, 1811, that Jiménez promoted him to lieutenant colonel in the insurgent army, but that, disgruntled because his petition for further promotion was rejected, Elizondo again switched his allegiance, returning to the royalist side.[12] Yet, since Elizondo's name does not appear on the roster of the royalist officers at Aguanueva, this interpretation is open to question.[13] On the other hand, a captured insurgent subsequently referred to Jiménez's having issued orders for the disposition of some three hundred bars of silver that Elizondo seized at Río Grande, part of the treasure from Saltillo.[14] It would appear, therefore, that whatever treachery Elizondo committed occurred at Río Grande, not at Aguanueva.

In any case, by the time Elizondo began visiting the imprisoned Royüela in February, 1811, he was a confirmed royalist. The two men held several conversations in which Elizondo commiserated with the treasurer and lamented the current state of affairs in the viceroyalty. Having decided that Royüela could be trusted, Elizondo made a startling disclosure on February 17, confiding to Royüela that he and a few friends planned a counterrevolutionary coup to seize the Presidio de Río Grande. Though delighted to learn of Elizondo's intentions, the treasurer vehemently objected to the plan. Royüela argued that at best it would achieve a local victory and result only in the capture of the rebel governor Aranda and a few of his aides. The treasurer prevailed on Elizondo to postpone any action, in hopes of being able to strike a more meaningful blow.[15]

Elizondo's original objective in plotting the seizure of the presidio had been not only to capture Aranda but also to liberate the royalists imprisoned there. Besides Royüela, these included the governor of Texas, Lt. Col. Manuel Salcedo, and the military commandant of that province, Lt. Col. Simón de Herrera. The two had been captured in San Antonio and, together with nine junior officers, had been marched in shackles to Río Grande, their ultimate destination being the rebel headquarters in Saltillo.

It was Aranda who obligingly solved the problem of freeing the royalists. Because the situation in Texas was under control, he returned to Monclova late in February, taking along the prisoners from Río Grande. In Monclova several prominent citizens offered to make themselves personally responsible for the prisoners. Perhaps to curry favor with his new subjects, the insurgent governor readily agreed, stipulating only that the royalists be restricted to the settlement of Santa Rosa and its environs. Royüela was taken to Santa Rosa itself; Salcedo and Herrera were dispatched to the nearby Hacienda de San Juan de Sabinas, for Ignacio Elizondo was one of the guarantors.[16] The other guarantors were the Sánchez Navarros.

While Royüela and Elizondo had been plotting at Río Grande, the Sánchez Navarros had been plotting at Monclova. José Melchor took the lead in working for the reestablishment of royal authority. He evidently made little effort to hide his contempt for Aranda and the other rebels, and he repeatedly shunned the governor. Moreover, although the Sánchez Navarros had lost their markets because of the rebellion, José Melchor refused to sell livestock and supplies to the insurgent garrison.[17] In view of the *hacendado*'s thinly disguised hostility, the most reasonable explanation for Aranda's willingness to parole the captured Spaniards into his custody is that the governor was trying to ingratiate himself with the powerful Sánchez Navarros.

Assisted by his brother the curate's namesake, by the curate himself, and by Juan Ignacio de Arizpe, José Melchor spent much of his time sounding out the local citizens to determine who could be counted on when the time came. Aranda's blunder in paroling the prisoners greatly facilitated the *hacendado*'s task, for it enabled the plotters in Monclova to cooperate with those in Santa Rosa.

Furthermore, the course of events in the viceroyalty was now running in the conspirators' favor. Hidalgo's uprising had taken the government by surprise, and during September and October, 1810, the insurgents seemed irresistible. Their initial momentum carried them to the outskirts of Mexico City. But by the beginning of November this momentum was spent. The reorganized royalists inflicted several defeats on Hidalgo's forces, which fell back to Guadalajara. With the rebellion in decline, Hidalgo and his principal subordinate Ignacio Allende, son of the Sánchez Navarros' old business associate in San Miguel, decided to gamble on one decisive battle. This engagement, fought at the Bridge of Calderón near Guadalajara on January 17, 1811, resulted in a crushing defeat for the rebels.

Leading the remnants of their shattered forces, Hidalgo and Allende retreated northward to Saltillo. On the way the two rebel chieftains quarreled violently. Allende, disgusted with Hidalgo's leadership, assumed command himself. Hidalgo was reduced to a mere figurehead and became a virtual prisoner of his former subordinate. Allende reached Saltillo on February 24; Hidalgo arrived a few days later and was quartered in treasurer Royüela's house. The insurgent leaders realized that Saltillo afforded only a temporary refuge, for royalist columns were advancing from San Luis Potosí, Zacatecas, and Durango. The rebels therefore decided to retreat to Texas where they hoped to secure aid from the United States and keep the rebellion alive.[18] The customary route from Saltillo to Texas was by the road through Monclova.

Now that the leaders of the insurrection were within striking distance, the plotters in Monclova were determined to ensure that the rebels would take this road. Late in February a series of meetings was held at José Melchor's house in Monclova. The *hacendado* and his brother conferred secretly with three other royalist sympathizers: Lt. Rafael del Valle, Lt. José de Rábago, and the Baron de Bastrop. Del

Valle was a militia officer. Rábago had been a member of the presidial forces but had ostensibly gone over to the rebels—Governor Aranda had promoted him to lieutenant colonel and had even placed him in command of the Monclova garrison. The Baron de Bastrop was a Dutch soldier of fortune who had left the employ of Frederick the Great to take service under the king of Spain. He obtained a grant of land in Louisiana but, when that province passed from Spain to France in 1800, Bastrop moved to Texas, where he had resided until the outbreak of the revolution.[19]

At the meetings it was decided to send Bastrop, at José Melchor's expense, to Saltillo as a spy. The Dutchman was given an extremely difficult assignment: to observe and report on the strength and military dispositions of the rebels, to gain the insurgent leaders' confidence by passing himself off as a fervent supporter of their cause, to use his influence to prevent the transfer of the paroled royalist officers to Saltillo where they faced execution, and to encourage the insurgent generals to travel to Texas with the smallest possible escort.

Bastrop left for Saltillo at the beginning of March. A few days later the royalist cabal in Monclova sent another spy, also at José Melchor's expense, to join the baron. Sebastián Rodríguez was a Spanish settler, a surveyor by profession, to whom the Sánchez Navarros had loaned money on occasion. Rodríguez was a nonentity, but under the present circumstances he was useful because before the revolution he had been a personal friend of Ignacio Allende and also of Mariano Abasolo, another of the rebel generals in Saltillo. His pretext for traveling to the insurgent headquarters was to secure amnesty from his old friends.

The two agents carried out their mission brilliantly. Rodríguez renewed his friendship with Allende and Abasolo, who gave him a warm welcome. The Baron de Bastrop was also well received, for the rebels were anxious to acquire information from him about the United States. Professing to be well acquainted with the road to Texas, Bastrop and Rodríguez volunteered their services as guides for the insurgent army. Allende gratefully accepted their offer, and the two spies were included in the rebels' most secret deliberations. The agents took full advantage of this stroke of fortune. Not only did they dissuade the insurgents from transferring the paroled royalists to Saltillo but they also convinced Allende and Jiménez to order the withdrawal of 150 men from the Monclova garrison. These troops were supposed to be sent to Baján, where the largest well on the road between Saltillo and Monclova was located.[20] In their retreat across this arid region the rebels would have no choice but to camp at Baján, and it was there that the royalist conspirators planned to strike.

Receiving word from their spies in Saltillo that the insurgents would begin their retreat to Texas on March 17, José Melchor and his associates moved swiftly. The *hacendado* made available the Sánchez Navarros' considerable economic resources to finance the impending counterrevolution. Leaving Lieutenant Rábago in Monclova to continue subverting the rebel garrison, José Melchor himself departed to work out details with the royalist officers, who were then residing at his house in Santa Rosa. While en route to Santa Rosa he stopped at the Hacienda de Encinas to enlist the support of the Vázquez Borregos. The owner of Encinas, Macario Vázquez Borrego, readily joined the conspiracy for he harbored a grudge against the insurgent governor. On his way to Río Grande in February, Aranda had stopped at Encinas and, being overly fond of celebrations, had ordered a fiesta to be held in his honor. During the festivities the governor became so intoxicated that he was on the verge of having his artillery demolish Vázquez Borrego's house.[21]

His work at Encinas completed, José Melchor went on to Santa Rosa where the royalists formulated their plan of attack. The counterrevolution was to unfold in two stages. First, the conspirators would seize Monclova, preventing any news of its recapture from reaching the approaching rebel army. The insurgents would then be ambushed at Baján as they confidently traveled toward Monclova. As a precaution in case the plan miscarried, José Melchor and his brother provided weapons, mounts, and provisions so that the paroled royalist officials could escape from Santa Rosa, make their way through the mountains, and reach the government lines in Nueva Vizcaya.[22] The Sánchez Navarro brothers dispatched Ignacio Elizondo to Monclova to lead the attack; they themselves prudently remained at Santa Rosa to await developments.

Elizondo reached Monclova on March 17, the day the rebel column

set out from Saltillo. After conferring secretly with local royalist sympathizers—among them the garrison commander Lieutenant Rábago,
the *hacendado* Macario Vázquez Borrego, and the Sánchez Navarros'
cashier Faustino Castellano—Elizondo decided to strike that very
night. Aided by dissident members of the garrison, the royalists occupied the hospital, barracks, and governor's palace with little difficulty.
Governor Aranda, however, was not in the palace: following his customary practice, he was wandering through the streets with a group
of his officers as drinking companions. One of the conspirators had
been detailed to follow the group. Showing considerable initiative, he
lured the governor and his companions to a house on the edge of
town, where he plied them with brandy and conversation. By the
time Elizondo arrived with ten soldiers to apprehend the governor,
Aranda was barely conscious, and his officers were in no condition to
offer resistance. Once the befuddled insurgents had been securely
imprisoned in the barracks, Elizondo and his associates spent the rest
of the night sending dispatches to their co-conspirators in Santa Rosa
and to the military headquarters in Chihuahua. They also sent mes-
sengers to the settlements and haciendas around Monclova ordering a
concentration of the men and supplies needed to implement the second phase of the plan.

At daybreak on March 18, the townspeople of Monclova were
combing the surrounding countryside for any insurgents who might
have eluded capture the previous night; thus, the Monclovans succeeded in preventing news of Elizondo's coup from reaching Saltillo.
During the afternoon, groups of armed riders from the neighboring
haciendas began arriving in Monclova. Atanacio Vázquez Borrego,
Macario's brother, rode in from Encinas with ten *vaqueros*, Elizondo's brother Nicolás brought eight more, and still other bands kept
arriving throughout the afternoon. One group of riders came from
Tapado, where the Sánchez Navarros' foreman had been assembling
horses, cattle, and provisions for use by the growing royalist force,
now encamped a short distance south of Monclova.[23]

José Melchor and the other conspirators, waiting anxiously at Santa
Rosa, left for Monclova as soon as they received word of its recapture.
Now that almost all the royalists were congregated in the capital, they

organized a provisional government on March 21. Lieutenant Colonel Herrera, as the senior officer present, became the acting governor, with Lieutenant Colonel Salcedo as his assistant. A twelve-man Committee of Public Safety was also formed, with Herrera as its head. The committee members included Juan Ignacio de Arizpe, José Melchor, and the curate.

While the royalists were reestablishing Spanish authority in Monclova, the second phase of the conspiracy was proceeding according to plan. Elizondo remained in command of the striking force, which had swelled to more than two hundred soldiers and settlers. By midmorning on March 20, he had them encamped about two miles southeast of Baján, at a point where the road curved around a low hill. Besides stationing pickets on the road, Elizondo decided to send scouts that night to reconnoiter the insurgent camp.

Having left a detachment to hold Saltillo, the rebel chieftains and more than one thousand of their followers had been marching slowly north for the last four days, blissfully unaware not only that Monclova was in enemy hands, but also that royalists had seized San Antonio on March 1. As the insurgents made their way across the dusty plain, they resembled a column of refugees more than a military force. The straggling caravan consisted of groups of soldiers and civilians in coaches, on horseback, and on foot, traveling interspersed among the artillery and baggage trains. On the night of March 20, the rebel bivouacs extended for some fifteen miles along the road, with the advance elements only ten miles from the royalists waiting at Baján.

Elizondo's scouts easily penetrated the loosely guarded insurgent lines under cover of darkness, and their report on the enemy's disorganized condition greatly heartened the outnumbered royalists. Growing more confident of victory, Elizondo nevertheless employed a stratagem. He had one of his subordinates, a turncoat rebel officer from the Monclova garrison, write to General Jiménez assuring the latter that the force of 150 insurgents was guarding Baján as ordered.

The courier who delivered the letter, at dawn on March 21, further deceived the unsuspecting Jiménez. In response to the general's questions about the situation in Monclova, the courier replied that a warm welcome had been prepared for the insurgents, complete with triumphal arches and with the townspeople lining the streets to cheer their arrival. Satisfied that all was well, Jiménez then inquired about the availability of water at Baján. The astute courier gravely informed him that there was barely enough for the insurgent multitude. He suggested that the rebels reach Baján at intervals, to facilitate the drawing of water from the well. He urged, moreover, that the insurgent chieftains be in the first contingent, so they could drink their fill and be on their way to Monclova without undue delay. Jiménez considered these to be excellent suggestions, and the rebels arranged their order of march accordingly.

Their minds on the water at Baján, the parched rebels got under way on the morning of March 21 without troubling to post outriders or an advance guard. The courier unobtrusively dropped out of the column and galloped across the hills to report to Elizondo. The excited royalists now made their final preparations. Three hundred lengths of rope were stockpiled for binding prisoners. Four men were assigned to this task, while others were detailed to guard the captives as well as the pack trains known to be transporting the rebel treasury. There was even a priest to take charge of the camp followers and clerics in the enemy column. Elizondo deployed the bulk of his command along both sides of the road, ostensibly as an honor guard. Since the road curved around a hill, the royalists would be able to deal with each rebel contingent without alerting those still approaching.

The plan worked almost to perfection, for the unsuspecting rebels were indeed taken piecemeal. In most cases they were too astonished to resist and were quickly hustled away to be bound, after which they were marched off to Baján. The few recalcitrant insurgents were shot down in their tracks. The fifth coach to roll into the ambush contained Generals Allende and Jiménez, who were identified for the royalists by an officer captured earlier. When ordered to surrender in the name of the king, Allende opened fire with his pistol; the answering fusillade cut down Allende's son and one of his aides. Jiménez alighted from the coach, asking indignantly whether this was any way to welcome a general. One of the royalists dryly replied that he really did not know, but that Jiménez could check with Elizondo if he liked.

With the capture of Allende and Jiménez, the royalists had accomplished a vital part of their mission. They now waited impatiently for Hidalgo to fall into their hands. Several more coaches arrived, in one of which were riding the exultant Baron de Bastrop and Sebastián Rodríguez. Hidalgo, however, was not in the coach assigned to him. The worried royalists finally sighted the priest, mounted on horseback, approaching at the head of a unit of forty soldiers. Waiting until they had marched between the royalist files, one of Elizondo's subordinates demanded their surrender. Hidalgo reached for a pistol but desisted when he realized the futility of resistance. As for the soldiers, they had deserted to the rebels at Aguanueva; when offered the choice of remaining loyal to Hidalgo and becoming prisoners or returning to their allegiance and keeping their weapons, they promptly joined the royalists.

As the afternoon wore on, groups of rebels fell into the ambush so frequently that additional men had to be assigned to help bind them. When the supply of ropes was exhausted Elizondo's men resorted to using bridles. By late afternoon over six hundred captives had been taken, and it was decided to send two-thirds of them under guard to Monclova. At this point the officer in charge of the prisoners received a dispatch from Elizondo notifying him that an insurgent artillery unit refused to surrender and was threatening to open fire. The royalist officer ordered his men to begin slitting prisoners' throats the moment they heard cannon fire. Hidalgo, horrified by this prospect, ordered the artillerymen to surrender.

As dusk fell, the royalists herded the rest of their prisoners to Baján. Elizondo and his followers found it difficult even now to grasp the magnitude of their victory. Besides the rebel chieftains, they had taken nearly one thousand prisoners, twenty-four cannon, vast stores of military supplies and equipment, and over one million pesos in coin and bars of silver. Only the rebel rear guard had escaped, and they were fleeing in disarray back to Saltillo.

Early the next morning, March 22, 1811, the camp was the scene of furious activity. The rank-and-file prisoners were roped together, the rebel leaders and other notables were loaded aboard coaches, the treasure was put aboard pack mules, and the whole procession started for Monclova.[24] As the courier had assured Jiménez, the townspeople lined the streets to witness the arrival of the insurgent army.

The Committee of Public Safety began disposing of the prisoners. On March 25, the rebel leaders were sent in chains to Chihuahua, the military headquarters for northern New Spain. There Hidalgo, Allende, and Jiménez, among others, were shot by a firing squad. Several hundred of the lesser prisoners were shot in Monclova itself. Some of the remaining officers were condemned to presidial service in Nuevo Santander. The rest, along with the rank-and-file prisoners, were technically freed but were assigned to labor in haciendas and mines throughout Coahuila.[25]

José Miguel was considerably embarrassed to learn that among the insurgents captured at Baján were two of his nephews. One was José María de Letona, whom the curate had put through law school in Mexico City. After taking his degree Letona had returned to Saltillo, trying his hand at several business ventures with indifferent success. Restless and frustrated, he had joined the rebels at Saltillo in hopes of improving his situation. According to one account, Letona served as the judge advocate in the insurgent column smashed at Baján. An official list of the captives, however, referred to him simply as being "without employment."[26]

The other nephew was José Juan Sánchez Navarro, also a native of Saltillo. The curate had sent him to Mexico City for an education, but José Juan, an adventurous youth, had abandoned school for a military career. He had joined Hidalgo at the outbreak of the rebellion and had fought in all the major battles. Though still in his teens, he had risen to the rank of captain and was one of Allende's aides. José Juan was reportedly among those condemned to be shot but was spared through the influence of his uncle the curate.[27]

Though many of the prisoners were shot, it is possible that neither Letona nor José Juan was considered important enough to warrant execution. Yet the curate probably did exert his influence on their behalf, for he subsequently used his contacts in Mexico City to help secure amnesty for yet another nephew involved in the rebellion. Melchor Múzquiz, born in Santa Rosa, had been sent at the curate's expense to study at San Ildefonso in Mexico City. In 1810, he became an insurgent and fought in Veracruz and Michoacán, attaining the rank of colonel before his capture by government forces. Múzquiz finally received a pardon in 1817, going on to become a prominent general and politician after independence.[28] The town of Santa Rosa was renamed in his honor. Letona and José Juan likewise were to have distinguished careers, the former serving as governor of Coahuila and the latter as military commandant of that state.

The high offices these ex-insurgent relatives eventually attained redounded to the benefit of the Sánchez Navarros, for, despite their political differences, the members of the clan had a highly developed sense of family loyalty. When José Domingo de Letona, like José Miguel a staunch royalist, was trying in 1816 to secure the pardon for Melchor Múzquiz, he assured the curate that "I will do everything I can for him, as I would for any of our other relatives."[29] The priest Letona spent the revolutionary decade in Mexico City where, as a well-connected member of the hierarchy, he was invaluable in securing favors for the Sánchez Navarros.[30]

The Sánchez Navarros were certainly in a position to ask favors. Like other *hacendados*, such as their business associate Gabriel de Yermo who raised one thousand cavalry from among his own retainers, they had amply demonstrated their loyalty to the crown.[31] José Miguel, José Melchor, and the curate's namesake were basking in the prestige gained from their prominent role in the counterrevolution. From his headquarters in Chihuahua, the commandant general of the Interior Provinces, Nemesio Salcedo, wrote José Miguel a flattering letter on April 8, 1811. He mentioned that Lieutenant Colonel Herrera had apprised him of the Sánchez Navarros' services, and General Salcedo graciously thanked the curate for having supplied the royalist force in Coahuila and for having made a general offer to provide whatever was necessary to ensure the success of the counterrevolution. The general stated his intention of informing the Spanish government so the Sánchez Navarros could be suitably rewarded. As a mark of his own appreciation for their "conspicuous merit," Salcedo commissioned José Melchor and his brother as captains in the militia. The following day Salcedo wrote another letter thanking the curate for securing the parole of the general's nephew, Lt. Col. Manuel Salcedo, the governor of Texas.[32]

Manuel Salcedo and José Melchor had become friends during the former's internment at Santa Rosa. The *hacendado* now availed himself of this friendship, as well as his long-standing acquaintance with Lieutenant Colonel Herrera, in an effort to obtain a title of nobility. José Melchor outlined the project in a letter to Salcedo in May, 1811. He mentioned that Herrera had already submitted an official report of José Melchor's services and was exerting his influence on the *hacendado's* behalf. Salcedo was to do likewise. José Melchor wanted the title to be based on the surname Sánchez Navarro, and he proposed entailing his Hacienda de Dolores; he was determined to bestow honor, as well as wealth, on his descendants. The documentation to support José Melchor's petition was being prepared by Miguel de Vargas Machuca, the Sánchez Navarros' lawyer, who resided in Catorce.[33]

José Melchor's project developed favorably through the spring of 1812. Herrera and Salcedo, both of them now back in San Antonio, continued to give it their enthusiastic support. Herrera suggested that José Melchor request the title of Marquis of the House of Sánchez Navarro, "a surname well known as illustrious in Spain." The *hacendado's* two friends read the documents being assembled to support the petition, and they urged that additional affidavits be prepared before submitting the petition to Commandant General Salcedo, who had agreed to recommend its approval.[34]

By the summer, the lawyer Vargas Machuca had all the necessary documentation except a certified statement of José Melchor's net worth. Such a statement was essential, since one of the requirements for obtaining a title of nobility was that the recipient be wealthy enough to maintain the title with dignity. In his instructions to the *hacendado*, Vargas Machuca stressed the importance of claiming as large a fortune as possible. The statement was to be certified by the governor of Coahuila and by the *alcalde* of Santa Rosa, but, if they should balk at accepting José Melchor's own estimate of his worth, Vargas Machuca suggested that their affidavits be suppressed and replaced by those of more cooperative citizens of Santa Rosa.[35] As it developed, early in

1813 these two officials duly certified José Melchor's wealth to be 85,000 pesos. This statement, together with documents setting forth José Melchor's paternal and maternal lineage and his services during the revolution, supported the *hacendado*'s petition.[36] The papers began their tortuous journey through the various levels of Spanish bureaucracy in 1813, but José Melchor was destined to remain a commoner, for, when Mexico gained her independence in 1821, the title had not yet been granted.

The *hacendado*'s eventual disappointment in failing to become a grandee was perhaps exceeded by that of his brother-in-law Manuel Royüela, who did receive a reward for his revolutionary services only to have it cancelled. In 1812, Commandant General Salcedo notified the government of Royüela's role in the counterrevolution so the treasurer could receive proper recognition.[37] Royüela, meanwhile, had been working feverishly at the task of reorganizing the pillaged Saltillo treasury. Laboring under the enormous handicap created by the loss of his records at Río Grande in 1811, the treasurer's health broke, and in 1813 he requested retirement. Instead, he was promoted. The Spanish Cortes, or parliament, in September, 1813, created a new intendancy, whose seat was Saltillo, comprising the four northeastern provinces. In April, 1814, the Spanish regency notified the viceroy of New Spain that the appointment as intendant had been conferred on Royüela, who would draw a yearly salary of four thousand pesos plus a six-hundred-peso allowance for expenses.[38]

Whatever elation the treasurer may have felt was short-lived. The despotic Ferdinand VII, who had been restored to the Spanish throne, decreed that all appointments made by the Cortes after March 28, 1814, were null. In compliance the viceroy cancelled Royüela's appointment, and the new intendancy was never established.[39]

To add to Royüela's troubles, his superiors in the Mexico City treasury began questioning him about irregularities in his accounts. The treasurer spent the next several years attempting to answer these charges, arguing that his records were still incomplete as a result of the revolution.[40] The strain proved too great, and, in 1816, Royüela became seriously ill. The following year he again requested retirement.

With the priest José Domingo de Letona expediting the petition, Royüela's request was finally granted in 1818. The treasurer died in Mexico City in April, 1819.[41]

It has been stated that the abortive Saltillo intendancy was created at the insistence of José Miguel Ramos Arizpe, the Coahuilan deputy to the Spanish Cortes.[42] Ramos Arizpe, a native of Coahuila, was another of José Miguel's nephews. He had studied at the seminary in Guadalajara, had been ordained in Mexico City in 1803, and had been studying law at the University of Mexico at the time of his election to the Cortes in 1810.[43] In the parliament Ramos Arizpe was a vigorous champion of local and provincial autonomy; one example of this was a comprehensive report he presented in 1811 on the condition of the Eastern Interior Provinces.[44] Through his efforts, the liberal 1812 Spanish constitution provided for popularly elected provincial deputations to function as local legislatures in New Spain.[45] The deputations were established in 1814 but were suppressed that same year when Ferdinand VII abolished the 1812 constitution. Ramos Arizpe, along with other liberal deputies to the Cortes, suffered imprisonment in Spain until a revolt in 1820 forced Ferdinand to reestablish the constitution. In 1822, Ramos Arizpe returned to Mexico, where he quickly became a prominent public figure.

Several of the Sánchez Navarros were involved in the elections for the provincial deputation established in 1814 for the Eastern Interior Provinces. The family's influence in Coahuila had been reinforced by the appointment of José Ignacio Sánchez Navarro as acting curate of Monclova. A native of Saltillo, he was the brother of the future general José Juan Sánchez Navarro. Their uncle José Miguel had paid for José Ignacio's education in Mexico City, where he was ordained in 1809. The priest's two-year tenure at Monclova was followed in 1816 by his transfer to a parish in Nuevo León; in 1819, he became curate of Saltillo, taking an active part in local politics.[46]

As a preliminary to voting on Coahuilan representatives to the provincial deputation, an election was held in Monclova in February, 1814, for a new municipal council consisting of two magistrates, twelve aldermen, and two syndics. Among the aldermen were José Melchor, his brother, their cousin Faustino Castellano, and another cousin, Víctor Blanco.[47] Under the municipal council's supervision, the process of choosing deputies to the provincial deputation got under way. Election was indirect, involving three steps. First, parish electors would be chosen. They in turn would cast their ballots for district electors. Finally, the three district electors, from Monclova, Saltillo, and Parras, would vote for two Coahuilan delegates to the provincial deputation.

Among the five parish electors chosen for Monclova were José Melchor, his brother, and their cousin the priest José Ignacio. When the Monclova parish electors met to vote on a district elector, there resulted a three-way tie between José Melchor, José Ignacio, and an individual from San Buenaventura. The flip of a coin settled the deadlock; José Ignacio became the district elector. In this capacity he then helped to elect José Melchor on March 21, 1814, as one of the two representatives from Coahuila.[48]

José Melchor found his tenure as a member of the provincial deputation disagreeable, for both personal and political reasons. The deputation met in Monterrey, and the *hacendado* planned to occupy José Miguel's mansion in that city, but the house was being rented by another of José Miguel's nephews, who adamantly refused to vacate the premises, citing the rights of tenants under the law.[49] José Melchor had to find less comfortable lodgings.

Carrying out his public duties, he made two speeches presenting a somber picture of the situation in Coahuila. José Melchor expounded at length on the depressed condition of ranching, arguing that the requisitions and forced loans being levied by the government were hastening the ruin of his fellow Coahuilans. His second speech was in a similar vein, except that the *hacendado* focused on the current status of mining. Potentially valuable silver deposits existed near Santa Rosa but were not being exploited, partly because of a shortage of laborers. José Melchor contended that the necessary workers could easily be secured if only the authorities would cooperate with mine owners by impressing the numerous vagabonds in the province.[50]

The *hacendado* grew increasingly dissatisfied with the provincial deputation, mainly because that body had little real power to alleviate the situation in Coahuila. By the end of June, José Melchor had decided to request a leave of absence. Not only was he concerned about his own enterprises, but he also was worried about his health, which had been affected by the sweltering summer heat of Monterrey.[51] Before departing for Monclova he delivered a final speech urging the deputation to provide relief for the suffering citizens of Coahuila. As matters developed, within a short time his colleagues were also homeward bound. The viceroy, implementing Ferdinand VII's order, dissolved the provincial deputation in August, 1814.[52]

Thereafter the Sánchez Navarros confined themselves to local politics, maintaining their influence in Coahuila. In 1815, for instance, José Melchor served another term as *alcalde* of Monclova. His cousin Faustino Castellano was a magistrate in that city in 1820, the same year in which José Melchor's brother again became *alcalde* of Santa Rosa.[53]

But in 1820 there occurred a dramatic change in the political life of New Spain. Ferdinand VII was forced to reestablish the Spanish constitution, and one result was the revival of the provincial deputations. When elections were held in March, 1821, to choose deputies for the biennium 1822–1823, José Melchor again became a member of the provincial deputation for the Eastern Interior Provinces.[54] More important than the elections themselves was the climate in which they took place. On February 24, 1821, the royalist Gen. Agustín de Iturbide had promulgated the Plan of Iguala, which called for the independence of New Spain but without the social and economic reforms for which Father Hidalgo and his followers had fought. The Plan was calculated to appeal especially to the powerful, ambitious, but hitherto staunchly royalist creole element, such as the Sánchez Navarros, who had been horrified by the egalitarian aims and racial violence of the initial struggle for independence.

In Coahuila, as elsewhere in the viceroyalty, copies of the Plan were circulated surreptitiously, and it soon became public knowledge that Iturbide's movement was rapidly gaining support. By June, rumors were flying in Monclova that Saltillo and Monterrey were on the verge of proclaiming their adherence to the Plan. Not to be outdone, some of the leading citizens of Monclova began plotting similar action. The conspirators included José Melchor and his cousin Víctor

Blanco, who was the *alcalde*. They resolved to effect a coup on the night of July 5, seizing the public buildings and if possible persuading the governor to swear allegiance to the Plan of Iguala. In any event the conspirators intended to assemble the garrison and the townspeople and proclaim independence.

The coup miscarried, for at the last minute one of the plotters, not mentioned by name, lost his nerve and informed the authorities. In desperation the rest of the conspirators immediately sent an emissary to persuade the governor to declare independence anyway. The two men were still debating the matter when, at dawn on July 6, a courier arrived with an urgent dispatch for the governor. The message was from Gen. Joaquín de Arredondo, the commandant general of the Eastern Interior Provinces, notifying the governor that, on July 2, Arredondo himself had led the city of Monterrey in joining the Plan of Iguala; Arredondo urged the governor to follow suit.[55]

Influencing Arredondo's decision to espouse the Plan was the fact that the garrison and citizenry of Saltillo had already done so on July 1. Several of José Melchor's cousins had played prominent roles in the events at Saltillo. The ex-insurgent José Juan Sánchez Navarro, at the time a lieutenant of militia, was among the military leaders of the coup, while Román de Letona, the muleteer and wool merchant, helped to finance it. José Ignacio Sánchez Navarro, the curate of Saltillo, was instrumental in persuading his fellow clerics to support the independence movement. Finally, Ignacio Arizpe and the former insurgent José María de Letona were members of the provisional junta that took power in Saltillo.[56]

The issue in Monclova was thus happily resolved. The governor summoned the citizens, had the dispatch read to them, and everyone swore allegiance to the Plan. They then retired to the parish church for a Te Deum, after which the Monclovans gave themselves over to celebrating the independence of Mexico.[57]

One of the most prominent Monclovans did not live to witness this momentous event. José Miguel Sánchez Navarro had died on April 18, at the age of ninety-one. The curate's body lay in state for several days in the parish church, on whose construction and adornment he had spent more than sixty thousand pesos of his own money. On

April 23, five priests officiated at his funeral, the most elaborate in the history of the capital. José Miguel was buried in a crypt beneath the east transept of the church.[58]

His monument was the *latifundio* he had built. Yet the vast amount of land the curate had owned formed but a small part of his wealth. The Hacienda de Tapado, for instance, covered some 314,509 acres, but the land itself was valued at only 3,450 pesos. The aggregate value of José Miguel's estate, on the other hand, exceeded 240,000 pesos.[59]

As specified in the curate's will, his sole beneficiary was José Melchor. The wealth that the Sánchez Navarros had been generating for more than six decades was finally concentrated in the hands of a single individual. José Melchor, moreover, was a man with a mission. Haunted by the fear that he would die at an early age, he was determined to leave his young children a secure inheritance.[60] With the wealth and power now at his command, José Melchor was in a position to achieve this goal.

PART TWO

THE NATIONAL PERIOD (1822–1867)

7. The Family and the Land

Independence proved disappointing for Mexico. The mood of optimism that pervaded the country in 1821 quickly evaporated in the face of some unpleasant realities. The antagonisms between social and economic classes, political factions, and vested interest groups made the establishment of orderly government extremely difficult. The fifty years after independence were characterized by a dizzying turnover at the executive and ministerial levels.[1]

The country got off to a wobbly start as a monarchy. Gen. Agustín de Iturbide, who had engineered the final movement for independence, contrived his own election as Emperor Agustín I in May, 1822. His brief and unhappy reign lasted until the following spring when he was overthrown by a republican revolution. With the adoption of a republican system, the question then became whether to have a centralist republic dominated by the national government or to maintain a federal republic permitting considerable state autonomy. For decades Mexican politics would turn on this fundamental issue. Other factors contributing to the endemic political instability were a bitter dispute regarding the position of the Church in society, the domination of political life by an irresponsible army, the chronic bankruptcy of the government, and a faltering national economy. *Hacendados*, who had been anticipating an era of peace and prosperity, found themselves caught up in the turmoil and had to conduct business as best they could while trying to avoid being crushed in the factional struggle.

This then was the milieu in which José Melchor strove to preserve the Sánchez Navarros' elite position. Ill health and the overwhelming burden of administering the family's economic empire made it imperative that he find a capable assistant. Ordinarily he could have counted on a close relative, such as his brother José Miguel or half-brother Manuel; but apparently neither inspired much confidence, and José Melchor kept them on the periphery of family affairs as ranchers on a modest scale. As far as his immediate family went, there was little that his wife, Apolonia, and daughter, María Vicenta, could do, while sons Carlos and Jacobo were still in grammar school in 1822.

The solution seemed to be a son-in-law. A suitor appeared in the person of Rafael Delgado, an ambitious young businessman from San Luis Potosí. Well educated by the standards of the times—he had studied Latin, philosophy, and law—Delgado had dabbled briefly in politics before becoming a wool merchant and one of José Melchor's principal buyers. In addition, Delgado frequently discharged important commissions for José Melchor, who soon came to regard him as an acceptable candidate for his daughter's hand.[2] Apolonia had serious reservations about Delgado, whose unctuous letters to the Sánchez Navarros suggest that he was attracted by more than María Vicenta's charm. Despite Apolonia's misgivings, the wedding took place in the spring of 1824 and was not only a memorable social event in Monclova but also one that assured the fortune of young Delgado, who enthusiastically assumed the role of right hand to his new father-in-law.

Besides assisting José Melchor in legal disputes and commercial transactions, one of Delgado's chief duties was to supervise the education of Carlos and Jacobo.[3] The boys' schooling had always been a matter of keen interest to José Melchor, but now the *hacendado* was developing a sense of urgency. With his health breaking under the strain of his responsibilities, José Melchor's goal was to survive long enough to see his sons take over the *latifundio*, and he was determined that they be educated gentlemen when that time came.

Delgado's task was a trying one. Neither Carlos nor Jacobo had a scholarly nature, but, of the two, Jacobo presented the greater problem. "Jacobo has been neglecting his studies, for he prefers to watch the masons in company with the barber," was typical of Delgado's reports to José Melchor.[4] Gradually, though, Delgado was able to motivate the boys in their studies. By the fall of 1825, they had exhausted the limited educational facilities in Monclova, which consisted of two grammar schools supported by the pupils' parents, and José Melchor was making plans to send them to secondary school in San Luis Potosí.[5] Delgado could take satisfaction in the job he had done, for, while supervising the boys' studies, he had also won their friendship. Delgado needed all the friends he could make, because his position within the family was rapidly deteriorating.

Relationships in general had become increasingly abrasive. José Melchor spent much of his time at the northern haciendas, where he was often in bed for weeks at a time with a painful stomach disorder. His wife, Apolonia, complained that he was driving himself to an early grave, reiterating that she was much more concerned about his health than about the business interests, which had become his overriding concern.[6] The friction between these two contributed to their mutual irritation with Delgado. José Melchor came to resent what he considered an overly aggressive attitude on Delgado's part. The latter heatedly denied any intention of being inordinately ambitious and implored José Melchor to explain what he was doing wrong. As for the *hacendado*'s complaints about being overworked, Delgado contended that it was José Melchor's own fault; Delgado was anxious to help, but José Melchor kept him at arm's length. Perhaps most pathetically, the distraught Delgado complained that José Melchor refused to call him "son."[7] Neither, for that matter, did Apolonia. She had never liked Delgado, and, in 1825 when Vicenta became ill, probably with tuberculosis, Apolonia was convinced that somehow it must be Delgado's fault. Even though doctors were brought from Monterrey to assist the local physician in Monclova, Vicenta became worse. As a last resort, Delgado considered taking her to Mexico City for treatment but abandoned the idea when it became apparent that she could not survive the trip.[8] When Vicenta died on May 24, 1826, Delgado's prospects died with her.

Vicenta's death precipitated a family crisis. Apolonia could no longer endure the sight of Delgado and insisted that he leave Monclova immediately after the funeral. The funeral itself, conducted with "all the pomp possible," was marred by José Melchor's absence. Apolonia, not unnaturally, was deeply hurt that her husband would allow his business affairs to take precedence over paying his last respects to their only daughter.[9]

With matters at this awkward juncture, José Melchor soon rid himself of Delgado by sending him on an assignment away from Coahuila. In the summer of 1826 Delgado traveled with Carlos and Jacobo to San Luis Potosí, where he installed the boys in school. From there he went on to Guadalajara to represent José Melchor in an important lawsuit. But by the end of that year the *hacendado* no longer required Delgado's services. Relations between the two men had become severely strained, but Delgado, evidently lacking the wit to realize that he was not wanted, enthusiastically made plans to rejoin the Sánchez Navarros.[10] The latter must have made their attitude painfully explicit, and as a parting sop José Melchor used his influence to secure his son-in-law a minor government post in Saltillo.[11] Delgado clung tenaciously to the remnants of his ties with the Sánchez Navarros; having lost the friendship of José Melchor and Apolonia, he assiduously cultivated the affection of Carlos and Jacobo, who were still in school in San Luis Potosí.

José Melchor's interest in his sons' education continued unabated. The *hacendado* tried to impart to the boys his own capacity for pursuing a goal with single-minded determination, insisting that they complete their education as rapidly as possible. To encourage them, he ensured that they led a spartan existence. Instead of giving them an allowance, which might lead to frivolous activities, he had a relative of Delgado's provide them with occasional luxuries, such as fruit and candy, while from time to time the *hacendado* sent them gifts, such as piggy banks, to encourage frugality.[12]

In their loneliness the boys turned increasingly to their brother-in-law, Delgado, for whom they had developed a genuine affection. Apolonia put a stop to this, however, when she visited her sons in San Luis Potosí during the summer of 1827. She had always been suspicious about Delgado, and, now that she was in his native city, she had a perfect opportunity to investigate his background. Apolonia communicated her findings to José Melchor in a series of blistering letters. She opened by berating the *hacendado* for having married Vicenta to such a scoundrel. "Many persons have asked me what we were thinking about when we consented to his marrying our daughter . . . I know that all your hopes were founded on the ability and good faith of this man . . . ," who turned out to be an unscrupulous liar. "Do you remember when you asked him the size of his family and he replied that there were only two elderly aunts? Well, so far I've met half of San Luis Potosí who are related to him—*including two daughters!*" Nor was this all; according to Apolonia, Delgado had secured fraudulent credentials in order to be admitted to the bar in Guadalajara.[13]

José Melchor's reply, which unfortunately has not been preserved, merely increased Apolonia's wrath: "I tell you that ever since Delgado left my house I never permitted the boys to visit him, much less associate with relatives of his, because I've already told you that they are nothing but riffraff." As for the personal items Delgado had left behind in Monclova, "don't bother to send him the rags still in our possession—let him send for them so he'll have to pay the freight."[14]

Having gotten Delgado out of her system, Apolonia discussed José Melchor's forthcoming visit to see their sons before the latter entered school again in the fall. On this his second trip outside Coahuila, the *hacendado* traveled in style, using the more elaborate of his two coaches, taking four mule loads of baggage, and having five armed outriders for protection on the road.[15] When he and Apolonia returned to Coahuila at the end of 1827, both the *hacendado*'s health and his spirits had been restored by the pleasant interlude in San Luis Potosí. He plunged into the management of his affairs with renewed vigor, causing Apolonia to complain because he spent months at a time away from home on business.[16] Occasionally, even José Melchor managed to relax for a brief period, usually in Saltillo, where he could enjoy the company of his cronies while attending the cockfights and sharpening his game of billiards.[17]

But he always remained vitally interested in the academic progress of his sons. One of their instructors regretted that he could not report favorably on their progress, speculating that perhaps they had been "surprised" by Latin. However, a more encouraging report came from another faculty member, who pointed out that his colleague's opinion was based solely on the boys' performance in mathematics and Latin. Carlos and Jacobo were also taking sketching, French, and Spanish; after an initial period of difficulty, they were doing much better in all subjects. To inspire them to greater effort, Apolonia sent a copy of *Don Quixote*, and José Melchor also dispatched a selection of books.[18]

Though they set no records, the boys at least managed to remain in school, and each year their father sent a crew of servants to bring them back to spend their vacations on the *latifundio*.[19] He undoubtedly impressed on Carlos and Jacobo that someday the vast domain would all be theirs and reiterated his demand that they apply themselves scholastically.

In the meantime José Melchor continued to drive himself mercilessly in order to preserve their inheritance. By 1830 his health had again deteriorated seriously. Writing to Apolonia to report temporary improvement in his condition, he nevertheless stressed to her that "I intend to die like the draft bullock that continues in the traces as long as he has any vigor left; as long as I have breath I'll do likewise with my interests because I realize that no one is determined to safeguard and increase them unless it be the owner himself, who has created and nurtured them."[20] Apolonia tartly replied: "I'm sorry that you are in poor health, but there's nothing I can do about it. I realize that no one can give you orders, but you persist in preferring your work to your health, which is more precious than any business interests can ever be."[21]

Unable to reason with José Melchor, Apolonia vented her frustration on Carlos and Jacobo. When they wrote asking permission to sell their books before coming home for vacation in 1830, they received the full blast of her displeasure. Not only did she order them to bring their books, but she also administered a stinging rebuke for their mediocre scholastic record. After threatening to bring them back to Monclova to work as field hands, she added: "You'll remember me once you find yourselves dressed in coarse clothing performing the tasks of a servant because you've thrown away the career we've made available to you. This is all I have to say. Wait until your father tells you what he thinks. It will be in person as soon as he meets you in Saltillo."[22] Apparently José Melchor decided to give them a taste of working in some menial capacity, for by March, 1831, Apolonia was remonstrating with him for having retarded the boys' careers for so long by keeping them in Monclova, which had become hateful to them.[23]

As a result of this episode, the boys settled down to their studies. In 1831 José Melchor enrolled them in a preparatory school in Mexico City; in due course they would enter the College of San Ildefonso to study law. To maintain close supervision over the boys, the *hacendado* arranged for their lodging in the home of his cousin, the priest José Ignacio Sánchez Navarro. José Melchor made ample provision for his sons, sending the priest a draft for one thousand pesos to cover expenses, including the meals the housekeeper took to the boys at school and the cost of a new wardrobe for them. As young gentlemen of fashion, Carlos and Jacobo wore black moleskin trousers at school, while for social occasions their trousers were of fine black or blue wool, or of white corduroy.[24]

The boys, especially Carlos, reveled in the excitement of living in the nation's capital, and their letters home reflected a keen interest in the political events of the day.[25] Life in Mexico City could be exciting on other counts; in 1833 a devastating cholera epidemic swept the metropolis, claiming thousands of lives. Although the boys had a bad scare when their cook fell ill, they managed to avoid contracting the dread disease.[26]

José Melchor was not so fortunate. The epidemic spread across much of the country, taking its toll in both Saltillo and Monclova. The *hacendado* became critically ill, and he was taken to Saltillo for treatment.[27] While he was convalescing there, Apolonia suggested that they take an extended trip to Mexico City to visit their sons.[28] Perhaps because of his weakened condition, José Melchor agreed. Though he probably grumbled about neglecting his business interests, the *hacendado* thoroughly enjoyed the months he spent in the capital in 1834. In fact, no sooner did he return to Coahuila than he began making plans for another trip the following year, "to revisit my old haunts."[29] Worn out by illness and hard work, José Melchor had at last decided to take life a bit easier. In May, 1835, he again set out for Mexico City, escorted by eight servants armed with six muskets and carbines, two pistols, a sword, and a saber.[30]

This visit to the capital failed to have the same therapeutic effect as José Melchor's earlier sojourn. After his return to Coahuila in October, he devoted less and less time to his affairs, for his health was failing rapidly.[31] In the spring of 1836 it was time to send for Jacobo, as the elder son, to be at his father's bedside. Ironically, when José Melchor died at Santa Rosa in June, 1836, the burden of making the arrangements for his unpretentious funeral fell on Jacobo because Apolonia was away at Saltillo on business.[32]

The strong-willed Apolonia, who over the years had tried to lighten José Melchor's burden by handling some of his routine affairs, had been forced to assume much of the responsibility for managing the *latifundio* during her husband's final illness. Whereas José Melchor does not fit the stereotyped view of the Mexican *hacendado*, neither does Apolonia conform to the picture of the *hacendado*'s pampered wife whose sheltered existence revolved around social activities and childbearing. Apolonia's character was as strong as that of her formidable husband. In the period of adjustment following his death, she played an important role in ensuring a smooth transition as Carlos and Jacobo assumed the direction of the family's empire; she thus accomplished José Melchor's goal of leaving his sons a secure inheritance.

The inheritance was truly magnificent. Not only had José Melchor managed to preserve what the family had amassed in the colonial period, but also, since 1821, he had nearly doubled the size of the *latifundio*. Virtually all the expansion had resulted from successful foreclosures, no mean feat considering the condition of the legal system—if the colonial system had been ponderous and exasperating, it was a model of efficiency compared with the legal process following independence.

In most of José Melchor's court battles the issue was perfectly clear: he was simply trying to collect legitimate debts. This was the case in his suit against the Vázquez Borregos, who had owed the Sánchez Navarros fifteen thousand pesos since 1819. The Vázquez Borregos were unable to afford an expensive legal struggle to prevent foreclosure on their *latifundio*, and this fact, rather than the justice of José Melchor's cause, proved to be the decisive element in the case. The *hacendado*'s lawyer in Monterrey, who happened to be his cousin, pressed the suit and in 1824 obtained the necessary judgment.[33] The capitulation of the Vázquez Borregos added another name to the growing list of *hacendados* who had discovered to their sorrow that the limited social mobility existing in Coàhuila included downward mobility; ruined *hacendados* like the Vázquez Borregos subsequently reappeared as renters or as foremen working for their more successful rivals, usually the Sánchez Navarros.

Unlike previous instances of foreclosure, the Sánchez Navarros did not obtain title to the Vázquez Borregos' haciendas of El Alamo and Encinas. José Melchor had to share El Alamo with a business associate, Francisco Vidaurri, who had a minority interest in that estate through kinship with the Vázquez Borregos. Subsequently, however, José Melchor acquired Vidaurri's claim.[34] The management of Encinas was taken over by a committee of creditors, but José Melchor as chief creditor dominated the committee, installing one of his brothers-in-law to head the group.[35] Despite the lack of a clear title, the Sánchez Navarros had gained firm control over yet another 700,000 acres of Coahuilan rangeland.

An indication of how the Vázquez Borregos might have thwarted José Melchor had they possessed some capital is provided by examining the resistance of the Elizondo family, the most resolute adversaries the *hacendado* ever encountered. The Elizondos' legal position was untenable, there being no question about their inability to repay the ten thousand pesos borrowed from the Sánchez Navarros in 1808. Nevertheless, as they struggled to prevent José Melchor from foreclosing on their half of the Hacienda de San Juan de Sabinas, the Elizondos demonstrated a remarkable talent for legal obfuscation.

For example, they used the tactic of repeatedly changing the legal guardian of the minor Elizondos; since each change entailed prolonged formalities, the lawsuit came to a standstill for more than a year. The exasperated José Melchor finally demanded that the *alcalde* of Santa Rosa, the official most directly concerned in the case, do something. That worthy, who was the brother of one of José Melchor's *mayordomos*, took it upon himself to appoint a guardian despite the Elizondos' angry protests.[36] The latter promptly appealed to the Audiencia of Guadalajara, but in the meantime the case could proceed.

By April, 1822, victory was within José Melchor's grasp. His representative in Santa Rosa wrote that the sympathetic *alcalde* was ready to issue the foreclosure judgment, adding that should the *hacendado*'s presence be required "I'll send you a strong horse in strictest secrecy as you've instructed."[37] On May 2, the *alcalde* formally awarded the property to José Melchor, giving the Elizondos exactly twelve days to vacate the hacienda.[38]

José Melchor's representative, Francisco Vidaurri, immediately informed him of the judgment and the Elizondos' reaction to it. According to Vidaurri, their faces turned "deathly pale as they heard the *alcalde* read his decision." One of the Elizondos was so upset that he actually vomited, perhaps, Vidaurri chortled, because his stomach "refuses to keep down another man's fare." When the Elizondos furiously protested, the *alcalde* demanded they show proper respect for the law and the authorities, threatening to jail them for contempt if they so much as dared to sit down in his presence. The Elizondos stormed out of the office in an extremely ugly mood, fulminating against José Melchor and everyone connected with him. The atmosphere was so tense that the *alcalde* prudently scurried home to avoid meeting the armed Elizondos on the street. Vidaurri himself was getting out of town, for fear of receiving a musket ball through an open window some night. His pretext for leaving was a hunting trip, to which he invited a number of heavily armed friends and relatives.

Vidaurri urged José Melchor to remain in Monclova and on no account make any trips through the countryside. The *hacendado*'s presence in Monclova was also essential so he could use his influence with the governor in case the *alcalde* of Santa Rosa had to call for help in controlling the Elizondos. Vidaurri explained that the local garrison was useless. The troops' pay was so far in arrears that their captain had in desperation disarmed his men and had given them all a leave of absence to find jobs in order to support themselves.[39]

The Elizondos had no intention of admitting defeat, but instead of resorting to violence they adopted subtler tactics, allying themselves with another group of José Melchor's enemies. Since 1817 the *hacendado* had been engaged in a lawsuit against José María Echais and his partner, José Antonio Quirós, the curate of Santa Rosa, over a tract near the headwaters of the Sabinas River. This suit was pending in the Audiencia of Guadalajara, as was the Elizondos' appeal. The Elizondos and the Echais-Quirós faction sensibly decided to present a united front against the *hacendado*, with Echais emerging as the leader of the coalition.

Since the *alcalde* of Santa Rosa was a partisan of José Melchor, the Elizondos and their allies decided on a bold stroke. They scraped together all the cash they could lay hands on—3,500 pesos—and in May, 1822, dispatched a delegation to Mexico City. They planned to use the money to gain the favor of Gen. Agustín de Iturbide, hoping that he would use his considerable influence to have the Audiencia of Guadalajara rule in their favor.[40]

While his associates were intriguing in Mexico City, Echais continued to file petitions with the *alcalde* of Santa Rosa, who promptly informed José Melchor of their contents and requested his instructions.[41] We do not know what success Echais's friends had with Iturbide, but it can be established that in November, 1822, the Audiencia ruled that the Elizondos had not been allowed to exhaust all legal recourse and therefore the award of San Juan de Sabinas to José Melchor had been premature.[42] The *hacendado*'s reaction may be imagined.

Even worse news was in the offing. When Iturbide's empire collapsed in the spring of 1823, the judicial system fell into greater confusion. José Melchor's informant in Guadalajara passed along the news that the Audiencia had suspended action on all cases involving parties who were not residents of the state of Jalisco.[43] When in due course the tribunal resumed deliberation on these cases, José Melchor suffered a serious setback. On October 3, 1823, the Audiencia not only restored to the Elizondos their water rights but also ordered José Melchor and his brother to rebuild the Elizondos' dam destroyed in 1819, as well as to pay damages and all the costs arising from the subsequent litigation.[44]

Encouraged by this turn of events, the Elizondos began pressing their other suit to recover possession of San Juan de Sabinas. They delivered five thousand pesos to the Santa Rosa *alcalde* as partial payment of their debt and demanded to be reinstated while they paid off the balance. That official, however, required them to make payment in full; when they were unable to do so, he again awarded the hacienda to José Melchor.[45] The Elizondos immediately began preparing another appeal.

After years of frustration, José Melchor was developing a philosophical attitude toward the Elizondo affair, commenting in 1824 that "from all indications the Elizondos are still causing trouble and will continue to do so until the Day of Judgment."[46] By now the *hacendado* confined himself to plotting strategy and securing expert legal counsel, for he left the actual conduct of the dispute to Delgado. Through the summer of 1825, Delgado presented petitions to the Santa Rosa authorities and kept track of the rapidly mounting expenses connected with the litigation.[47] The following year, since no conclusion was discernible despite the blizzard of legal documentation, José Melchor decided to send Delgado to Guadalajara.[48]

Once there, Delgado reported that no end was in sight, expenses were continuing to mount, and nothing favorable could be expected from the Audiencia.[49] That tribunal had taken the position that the Elizondos were entitled to the prospective profits from San Juan de Sabinas ever since 1822, when José Melchor had taken possession of the hacienda. This ruling caused the Sánchez Navarros' lawyer to protest to the court in exasperation that not only José Melchor but also "the next three generations of Sánchez Navarros will all be dead and buried before the family can collect a cent of the money owed to them."[50]

Since the Audiencia was a dead end, José Melchor began thinking of having the lawsuits transferred to a more sympathetic court, but no other tribunal had the requisite jurisdiction. The obvious solution, therefore, was to create such a court. This resourceful suggestion came from the *hacendado*'s lawyer in Monterrey, who advised him that his only chance of winning was if the Coahuilan legislature could be persuaded to establish a supreme court for that state as quickly as possible.[51] This was a project José Melchor could get his teeth into, and he launched an intensive lobbying campaign in the fall of 1826.

He spent months in Saltillo with his political cronies, busily enlisting support for the measure. By November he was elatedly informing his friends that the legislature was about to act on the matter.[52] The *hacendado* deplored the fact that he had been forced to neglect all his other interests and go to this length in order to secure justice, but justice he was grimly determined to have.[53] As a means of exerting pressure he mobilized his partisans in Monclova and Santa Rosa to have the municipal councils in those towns petition the legislature for the speedy creation of the court.[54] In June, 1827, the legislature provided for the establishment of the tribunal, which thus came into being partly to serve José Melchor's special interest.[55]

His adversaries were unaccountably slow to grasp the implications of this development; nearly a month later they were still celebrating José Melchor's apparent defeat before the Audiencia of Guadalajara.[56] The celebrating stopped abruptly when it became known that the cases would be transferred to Coahuila. From this point on, matters moved swiftly to a conclusion—relatively speaking.

Faced with inevitable defeat once the Coahuilan supreme court took up the pending cases, the Elizondos now tried to salvage what they could by adopting a conciliatory attitude toward José Melchor. He had no objection to letting them try. In September, 1827, he and Echais appeared before the *alcalde* in Saltillo and declared that since both parties were tired of the delays and costs involved in their dispute they requested that a board of arbiters be formed to settle the matter. Despite the parties' eagerness to end their quarrel, it took until April, 1828, merely to designate the arbiters, fulfill the legal formalities, and establish the board.[57]

From José Melchor's point of view the delay, though irritating, proved eminently worthwhile because the board was decisively loaded in his favor. Each party had named one member, and they had agreed on a third arbiter to be used in the event of discord, as seemed likely. The third judge, from whose decision there was no appeal, was in José Melchor's pocket: he was a close political associate of the *hacendado*.[58]

Once the parties presented their evidence, there was certainly no lack of discord. The Elizondos' strategy was to secure enough compensation for the prospective profits lost at San Juan de Sabinas to enable them to pay off what they owed on the hacienda itself. According to their figures, between 1822 and 1828 they would have realized the staggering sum of 102,400 pesos. José Melchor, on the other hand, argued that in this period the hacienda had actually returned a profit of exactly 351 pesos![59]

With matters deadlocked, the third arbiter came into play. Not surprisingly, he accepted José Melchor's figures. By the arbiter's computations, the Elizondos owed José Melchor a total of 22,631 pesos and had a counterclaim against the *hacendado* for only 7,117. The judge therefore ruled that José Melchor's waiving of the balance of 15,514 pesos would amply compensate the Elizondos for whatever damages they had suffered. He ordered that José Melchor be formally awarded possession of San Juan de Sabinas, once and for all.[60]

When the *alcalde* of Santa Rosa performed this action on June 3, 1829, the Sánchez Navarros not only added another 117,000 acres to their *latifundio* but also successfully concluded ten years of frustrating litigation, the bitterest court battle in the family's history. As for the Elizondos, José Melchor could take satisfaction from having achieved his goal of breaking them, for they soon slid into obscurity. Like the mills of the gods, the Sánchez Navarros ground slowly but they ground exceedingly fine.

Having elected to stand with the Elizondos, their allies Echais and Quirós fell with them. In 1828 José Melchor was preparing his case against the two partners for trial in the Coahuilan supreme court, and his sympathizers in Santa Rosa were simultaneously waging a campaign to discredit the curate Quirós. The latter's position was made so uncomfortable that he was forced to resign. With Quirós having lost his position of influence in the community, his and Echais's chances of withstanding José Melchor's legal onslaught diminished visibly.[61] And on April 2, 1829, the *hacendado* wrote a jubilant letter to Apolonia informing her that he had won the lawsuit. Not only was José Melchor confirmed in his possession of the land near the headwaters of the Sabinas, but also his opponents were ordered to pay damages and costs.[62]

In the amount of satisfaction it gave José Melchor, this victory rivaled even his triumph over the Elizondos. True, he had added to the *latifundio* more than twenty thousand acres comprising the Hacienda de la Purísima del Nacimiento, which Quirós and Echais had founded on the right bank of the Sabinas,[63] but what really mattered was that he now controlled the headwaters of the river. As José Melchor explained to his wife, while the source of the Sabinas remained in the hands of rival *hacendados*, the Sánchez Navarro estates of Soledad and San Juan de Sabinas suffered from a water shortage so acute as to make them relatively worthless.[64] The situation had now been corrected.

Even while embroiled in major land disputes, José Melchor had not disdained to acquire small properties whenever possible. For some time he had coveted the water rights at the modest Hacienda de San Andrés on the Sabinas River near Santa Rosa. In a series of purchases between 1827 and 1837, the Sánchez Navarros managed to acquire twenty-three of the hacienda's thirty days' water rights, plus most of its nine thousand acres, for 1,282 pesos.[65] In 1829, José Melchor snapped up at public auction for 375 pesos a nearby farm known as El Realito, consisting of one hundred acres and three days' water rights.[66] That same year he accepted two days' water rights at the Hacienda de San José del Oro near Monclova in settlement of a petty lawsuit.[67] Similarly, in 1831 and 1834 he took two days and fourteen hours of water rights at the Estancia de los Flores near Monclova as payment for debts totaling 366 pesos.[68] No property was too insignificant to escape José Melchor's attention: in 1829 he paid a widow 25 pesos for one-third of her one-tenth interest in the grazing land at a ranch near Santa Rosa.[69]

It may not be entirely coincidental that the majority of small-scale acquisitions took place during and after 1829. José Melchor's success against his major rivals probably induced some of the smaller property owners to sell in order to avoid a similar fate. The infrequency of these minor purchases compared with those in the colonial period reflects no lessening in the Sánchez Navarros' craving for land, but simply the fact that it was becoming more difficult to find smallholders who had not already sold out to the family.

As a result of José Melchor's determined efforts, by the time of his death in 1836 the sprawling *latifundio* covered more than 1,650,-000 acres. More significantly, the Sánchez Navarros enjoyed a near monopoly over the water in the Sabinas and the Nadadores, the only two rivers of any consequence in arid Coahuila.

Upon José Melchor's death, management of the *latifundio* became more than ever a family enterprise, for the *hacendado* bequeathed his property jointly to Apolonia and their two sons. Jacobo, the elder, automatically became the head of the family, and in keeping with his new responsibilities remained in Coahuila to manage the landholding. He may not have been too reluctant to abandon the study of law, since he had never shown marked enthusiasm for the discipline. As for Carlos, he remained in law school for two cogent reasons: he preferred the cosmopolitan atmosphere of Mexico City, and, as an attorney in the capital, he could materially advance the family's interests.[70]

Carlos's contribution was not long in coming. He received his law degree in 1838, and in 1840 the twenty-four–year–old attorney negotiated a business deal that utterly eclipsed all of the family's previous land acquisitions.[71] In a fitting climax to the drive for land that had characterized the Sánchez Navarros for generations, Carlos enabled the family to achieve their greatest coup by purchasing the entire Marquisate of Aguayo, thereby attaining the premier position among Mexican *hacendados*.

The recent history of the Marquisate had been turbulent.[72] It will be remembered that on the eve of independence the Marquis of Aguayo was virtually bankrupt. In 1820, however, he managed to escape his numerous creditors by dying. His eldest son, José María Valdivielso, thus inherited not only the title and *latifundio* but also a crushing burden of litigation and debt.

Entailment was the obstacle frustrating the swarm of creditors, since it prevented them from foreclosing on the Aguayo properties. The chief creditor, the socially prominent politician Francisco Manuel Sánchez de Tagle,[73] even brought suit in the Audiencia of Mexico to prevent the new Marquis from taking possession of the Aguayo estates. Sánchez de Tagle based his action on a decree abolishing entailment issued by the Spanish Cortes in 1820.[74] The Marquis, for his part, argued that the decree had never been promulgated in Mexico and hence did not apply. The Audiencia upheld the Marquis. Undaunted by his failure in the courts, Sánchez de Tagle tried another tack. Being an influential member of the Mexican Constituent Congress, he decided to use that body to achieve his objectives. Amid charges that he suborned some of his colleagues and ran roughshod over the opposition, Sánchez de Tagle conducted an intensive campaign in congress, which declared in 1823 that the Spanish decree on entailment had been valid in Mexico since the date of its issuance.[75] Apparently this momentous law, theoretically making possible a more equitable system of land tenure, was enacted primarily to serve Sánchez de Tagle's special interest and only incidentally on its merits as a socially desirable measure.

With congress having cleared the way, the Marquis of Aguayo's creditors could finally act. The law permitted Aguayo to keep half of his properties, and his creditors quickly moved to acquire the remainder.[76] But while the case was still threading its way through the labyrinth of the courts a new element entered the picture.

Latin America held a strong attraction for British investors in the heady decade of the 1820's, but the boom proved to be of short duration and was accompanied by heavy capital losses.[77] Mexico was one of the principal fields of activity during this wave of investment hysteria. Though much of the British capital flowed into government bonds and the mining industry, there seemed to be a wide range of attractive opportunities awaiting only the application of British money and technology. Reflecting this optimistic mood, even the prestigious London firm of Baring Brothers and Company, which followed a conservative policy in its Latin American investments,[78] decided to take a flier by purchasing the Marquisate of Aguayo in conjunction with another British firm, Staples and Company, which was based in Mexico City. Aguayo's creditors were delighted, since what they wanted was their money, not a group of unproductive haciendas located hundreds of miles from Mexico City. As for the Marquis, he, too, was receptive to the British overtures. The loss of social status in ceasing to be the country's foremost *hacendado* was more than offset by shedding the problem of administering his half of the *latifundio* and by receiving enough ready cash to live comfortably in Mexico City.

After prolonged negotiations, the parties reached agreement. In September, 1825, the British firms purchased the Marquisate on installments.[79] Despite its history of mismanagement, the *latifundio*, now operated as the "Parras State and Company," was still a desirable property.[80] When the British prepared inventories in 1826, they valued the landholding at 1,026,250 pesos, compared with an 1815 valuation of 1,172,383. Moreover, as of 1828 the Marquisate encompassed sixty-six settlements with a total population of 9,185.[81] The British went to work with brisk efficiency to capitalize on these assets.

The very success of the English firms proved disastrous for them. Fearful of growing British influence in Mexico, congress in 1828 enacted legislation specifically prohibiting foreigners from acquiring rural property. Not content with providing for the future, congress made this an ex post facto law and anulled the sale of the Marquisate to Baring Brothers and Staples.[82]

In the face of this catastrophe, the parties to the original sale held a series of stormy meetings in an effort to salvage their respective interests. The Marquis had received only about half of the 350,000 pesos owed to him and was now threatening a suit to regain possession of his part of the *latifundio*. The companies' agents were demanding the return of the 367,000 pesos they had invested toward the purchase price of the Marquisate and in developing the property. The committee of creditors was trying desperately to placate both other parties and find some manner of circumventing the recent law. Spurred by the fear of costly and interminable litigation, the parties reached a settlement in September, 1828. In a complicated extralegal arrangement, the Marquis sold his interest to the creditors, who then leased the landholding to the British companies.[83]

By means of this legal subterfuge, the British firms continued operations, though with understandably diminished enthusiasm. As general manager they installed Dr. James Grant, an urbane Scottish adventurer who was a naturalized citizen of Mexico.[84] Besides administering the Marquisate, Grant had to contend with the local authorities in both Coahuila and Zacatecas. Sometimes these matters involved projects to improve the landholding, such as his persuading the Coahuilan legislature in 1830 to approve construction of a highway between Saltillo and Parras. On other occasions his relations with officialdom were less cordial, as when Zacatecas imposed a forced loan on the Hacienda de Bonanza in 1833.[85]

This was a minor crisis, however, compared with what happened in Coahuila the following year—a reform-minded Federalist administration expropriated the Marquisate itself. The justification for this drastic measure was that the landholding's very existence retarded the development of the state. Furthermore, because of the extralegal nature of the committee of creditors and the various transactions into which it had entered, not only had the national laws of 1823 and 1828 been brazenly flouted, but also Coahuila had been systematically cheated of vital tax revenue. The state now proposed to divide the Marquisate into at least thirty parcels and sell them to individuals. From the proceeds Coahuila would collect all taxes in arrears plus whatever fine the state courts imposed on the committee of creditors for fraud. The creditors would receive whatever might be left. Under these conditions, expropriation was tantamount to confiscation.

It would seem that the thrust of the expropriation legislation was not to effect widespread agrarian reform but rather to create a more broadly based Mexican *hacendado* element in Coahuila. The valuations given the proposed parcels effectively placed them beyond the reach of the peasantry, but *hacendados* and would-be *hacendados* could acquire property advantageously at public auction while congratulating themselves for striking a blow against British economic imperialism.

Whether this was in fact the legislature's intention soon ceased to matter. The British chargé d'affaires delivered a formal protest, and the Mexican government ordered a suspension of all expropriation proceedings while congress resolved the matter. On March 21, 1835, that body promulgated its decision: the Coahuilan decree had been unconstitutional.[86]

The British companies thus retained the Marquisate, but they lost the services of their ambitious general manager Dr. Grant. Having become well established in Coahuila, the Scotsman went into business for himself, became deeply involved in local politics as a Federalist, and was killed while fighting for the independence of Texas in 1836.[87] The British firms failed to find an adequate replacement for Grant, a factor contributing to their growing disenchantment with the Marquisate. Their opportunity to extricate themselves came when Carlos Sánchez Navarro offered to buy the *latifundio*. Recognizing a bargain when he saw one, the young attorney boldly decided to commit the family fortune in order to acquire the Marquisate.

His negotiations reached fruition on November 13, 1840. Acting for himself, his mother, and his brother, Carlos bought out the committee of creditors for 206,000 pesos. He purchased the British companies' interest for an additional 120,000. The latter sum would be paid in installments, and as security Carlos agreed to give Baring a mortgage on the Sánchez Navarro landholding.[88]

It had taken the Sánchez Navarros exactly seventy-five years to build their *latifundio* to a size that made any ranch in the United States seem slightly ridiculous by comparison. The famous King Ranch in Texas, for instance, covered 1,065,000 acres, the Maxwell Ranch in New Mexico 1,714,764, while the largest American ranch, the XIT in Texas, comprised 3,050,000.[89] Among Mexican landholdings, one of the most extensive was that amassed by Gen. Luis Terrazas in Chihuahua, encompassing 5,019,776 acres.[90]

All of these properties would have fit comfortably within the boundaries of the Sánchez Navarro empire; on paper it now embraced some 16,500,000 acres, or roughly 25,780 square miles—an area larger than Connecticut, Massachusetts, New Jersey, Rhode Island, and Delaware combined. But it should be stressed that the above-mentioned acreage is merely what can be reconstructed from the available documentation and is therefore a conservative figure. Rural properties were generally much larger than the deeds specified. For example, the Hacienda de San Lorenzo de la Laguna, comprising the westernmost part of the Marquisate, contained 982,104 acres according to the land titles but in fact covered nearly 2,200,000.[91] In view of this factor, the Sánchez Navarro holdings were probably a fourth to a third larger than the documentation would indicate.

This empire, however, rested on a precarious foundation, for the family stood to lose everything should they fail to pay off the mortgage to Baring. Having undertaken the gigantic gamble, they had no intention of losing. Even while Carlos was negotiating for the Marquisate, Jacobo continued to expand the family's holdings in Coahuila by purchasing small rural properties.[92] Once the deal for the Marquisate had been closed, the Sánchez Navarros necessarily concentrated on the problem of integrating this landholding with their other estates.

Taking possession of the Marquisate went smoothly enough, for here the Sánchez Navarros enjoyed the cooperation of the national government. The minister of war ordered the military authorities to assist Carlos in the transfer, stressing the administration's belief that any delay would be detrimental to the committee of creditors and could also lead to diplomatic representations from Great Britain. To ensure that the transfer went off without a hitch, Carlos even made one of his infrequent visits to Coahuila, spending several months there in 1841.[93]

As if to compensate for the lack of difficulty in transferring the Marquisate, a major controversy arose over the *alcabala* attendant on its sale. The state of Coahuila, chronically starved for revenue, seemed determined that this time someone would finally pay the sales tax on the Marquisate. The state authorities demanded that the Sánchez Navarros pay. The latter insisted that it was the sellers' obligation to do so, but the committee of creditors adamantly refused. In frustration, the state appealed to the national government for assistance. By early 1842 the affair had become acrimonious, and the parties involved were exerting all the political influence they could muster in Mexico City.

The state authorities sent a writ to Mexico City for Carlos to show cause why he should not pay, and the ministry of war authorized the commandant general in Coahuila to attach the family's properties for nonpayment of taxes. The general temporized, pointing out that the Sánchez Navarros had the law on their side. The ministry soon amended the order, allowing the general to use his own discretion. In the meantime, the writ had disappeared somewhere within the bureaucracy in Mexico City, where it remained for several months without Carlos's being summoned to make any statements.[94] He was, nevertheless, preparing his defense, stressing the committee of creditors' obligation to pay the *alcabala*. The Mexico City authorities finally returned the writ to Coahuila unanswered, much to the consternation of the state officials. Although the latter sporadically manifested their annoyance, the affair gradually died down.

It ended in October, 1843, under circumstances indicating that the committee of creditors had powerful allies in the national government. The president of the republic ruled that the sale of the Marquisate was not subject to the *alcabala*, but that 34,000 pesos in salaries and expenses of the committee, as well as 22,000 pesos in revenues owed on the Marquisate, were. The tax on these items—3,560 pesos—would be deducted from a bond of 4,000 pesos that Carlos had posted.[95] The Sánchez Navarros thus achieved a partial victory, while the real loser was, as usual, the state of Coahuila.

The dispute over the *alcabala* had been fomented in part by some of the Sánchez Navarros' rivals in Coahuila who were anxious to buy sections of the Marquisate. The Aguirre family in particular coveted a large tract of land between Saltillo and Parras.[96] When the Sánchez Navarros declined to sell, the Aguirres began exerting pressure. Rafael Aguirre filed a claim to a strip of land on the boundary of the Marquisate, thereby involving the Sánchez Navarros in an unwanted lawsuit at a time when they were already fighting similar claims before magistrates in the towns of Viesca and Mazapil.[97] By virtue of his friendship with the governor of Coahuila, Aguirre quickly gained possession of the lands in question. He continued to use his influence with that official to create difficulties for the Sánchez Navarros at every opportunity.[98]

While Jacobo was trying to fight off the family's enemies in Coahuila, Carlos wrestled in Mexico City with a host of financial problems, primarily that of retiring the debt owed to Baring Brothers. At times Carlos was on the verge of despair, as when he wrote in 1843 complaining bitterly that Jacobo's last letter "was a mortal blow to me, because, when I was counting on your sending the money you had promised, you completely forgot, since you don't suffer the torments that I undergo."[99]

Despite continued interest from other Coahuilan *hacendados* in buying sections of the Marquisate, the hard-pressed Sánchez Navarros stubbornly refused to sell.[100] Moreover, they battled to recover the land awarded to the Aguirres. Complicating this controversy was an element often present in land disputes: the area in question, in this case 43,360 acres, had not been surveyed—only a visual estimate had been made. Hopelessly deadlocked, in 1845 the parties resorted to the time-honored expedient of arranging a compromise out of court. They divided the disputed rangeland, but the Sánchez Navarros lost two minor *cascos* contained therein; San Antonio del Jaral went to José María Aguirre, while the smaller complex of Ciénega Grande passed into the hands of Rafael Aguirre. In arranging this settlement, the Sánchez Navarro brothers had once again drawn on their relatives for assistance. Representing them was a second cousin, Juan Nepomuceno de Arizpe, a rising young Saltillo attorney.[101] With litigation constituting a way of life, Arizpe's talents were in constant demand by the family.

Yet, to all outward appearances, the Sánchez Navarros' position in Coahuila seemed secure and untroubled. An American observer, Capt. George W. Hughes, wrote in 1846: "More than half the whole State of Coahuila belongs to the two brothers Sanchez, who also own some thirty thousand peons. Several of their vast estates are managed by stewards, while the remainder are rented. Their principal town residence is in Saltillo, but their favorite country seat is the magnificent hacienda of Patos. This powerful family, together with their relations, the Blancos, the Yvarros [*sic*], and the Zuloagos [*sic*], own nearly the entire state and its population."[102] Undoubtedly, Hughes would have been quite surprised to learn of the atmosphere of crisis in which the Sánchez Navarro brothers habitually worked. Nevertheless, the family's position was basically sound, and they would have won their gamble concerning the Marquisate had it not been for the Mexican War.

The outbreak of that conflict in May, 1846, plunged the Sánchez Navarros' affairs into confusion. Among other arrangements, Jacobo took his mother, Apolonia, to live with Carlos and his family in Mexico City, where she would be out of the way of the fighting. Jacobo kept his own family with him on the *latifundio*. By the end of 1846, American forces had occupied northeastern Mexico, and the Sánchez Navarros were experiencing increasing difficulty in conducting business. As during the revolutionary war, the circulation of bills of exchange between Coahuila and Mexico City presented an especially vexing problem. Each time Carlos was able to arrange the transfer of funds to Mexico City, he felt he had won another reprieve in his struggle to meet the mortgage payments as well as the rest of the family's heavy financial commitments.[103]

In spite of Carlos's best efforts, he was losing this critical struggle. As the war ground on, business conditions deteriorated, and by September, 1847, when the American army battered its way into Mexico City, the economy was in shambles. Badly overextended and facing the loss of their entire landholding for failure to make the mortgage payments, the Sánchez Navarros grimly reassessed their position. Matters were so serious that Jacobo made one of his rare journeys to Mexico City, late in 1847, to confer with his brother and mother.[104] As a result of these discussions, the family regretfully decided that their only recourse for raising capital quickly was to sell portions of the Marquisate.

Fortunately, other Coahuilan *hacendados* had continued to show interest in the landholding even during the war, and with the restoration of peace in February, 1848, their interest quickened. As early as June of the previous year, one of these individuals, Leonardo Zuloaga, had begun sounding out Jacobo regarding the possibility of acquiring the westernmost part of the Marquisate.[105]

Zuloaga, a wealthy Basque, was a man of enterprise and vision. Emigrating to Mexico in the 1820's, he had purchased the Hacienda de Santa Ana de los Hornos, originally part of the *latifundio* belonging to the Jesuit College of Parras. Around 1830, Zuloaga further advanced his fortunes by marrying a seventeen-year-old heiress, Luisa Ibarra, a distant relative of the Sánchez Navarros. Her dowry consisted of a hereditary interest in her family's Hacienda de San Lorenzo de Parras. Zuloaga soon bought out the other heirs and added this valuable estate to his Hacienda de Hornos.[106] Over the years the Basque developed a dream, nothing less than acquiring the whole Laguna region, the inhospitable southwestern part of Coahuila. Whereas others viewed the Laguna as being an immense expanse of grazing land notable for fierce dust storms and even fiercer nomadic tribes, Zuloaga became convinced that with irrigation much of the land could be transformed into a rich agricultural area. In 1847 he began to implement his plans by forming a partnership with one Juan Ignacio Jiménez and, more to the point, by negotiating with the Sánchez Navarros to buy that portion of the Marquisate located in the Laguna.

Zuloaga's offer came at the right moment. The Sánchez Navarros discussed his proposal while they were all together in Mexico City; when Jacobo returned to Coahuila early in 1848, it had been decided that he should close the deal with Zuloaga. The transaction involved a considerable block of land: the Hacienda de San Lorenzo de la Laguna.

Though it had a large and populous *casco* situated on the right bank of the Nazas,[107] and though the hacienda was enormous, San Lorenzo de la Laguna had several drawbacks. For one thing, most of its acreage was arid or semiarid, suitable only for grazing. Also, the hacienda was extremely vulnerable to Indian depredations and by 1848 had suffered heavy losses. For these reasons the Sánchez Navarros made relatively little from its sale. Jacobo executed the sales contract with Zuloaga and Jiménez at Saltillo on April 24, 1848. The purchase price of eighty thousand pesos was to be paid in installments, from December, 1850, through December, 1854.[108]

Having acquired the necessary land, Zuloaga and Jiménez proceeded with their ambitious irrigation project. Zuloaga, who was to remain a power in the region for years, laid the basis for the Laguna's spectacular development late in the century as one of Mexico's wealthiest agricultural districts.[109]

While Zuloaga was pursuing his irrigation schemes, the Sánchez

Navarros divested themselves of another hacienda in order to raise working capital. In 1848 they sold to their archrival Rafael Aguirre one of the choicest properties in the Marquisate, the Hacienda del Rosario, on the outskirts of Parras.[110] The estate produced large amounts of maize and even greater quantities of wheat, which was ground into flour on the premises. But Rosario's chief glory, as it is even today, was its wine and brandy, of which some ten thousand gallons were produced annually. Accounting for the hacienda's remarkable fertility was its superior water supply—a series of springs whose flow was carefully channeled through an extensive irrigation network. Whether Rafael Aguirre paid 130,000 pesos for Rosario as a contemporary traveler reported or 148,000 as a modern authority states,[111] it is readily apparent why the Sánchez Navarros realized so much more from the sale of this hacienda, which covered only 190,800 acres, than they did from selling San Lorenzo de la Laguna. Water, and not merely land, remained the key to wealth in Coahuila.

The sale of Rosario relieved the Sánchez Navarros of their most pressing financial worry, for with part of the proceeds they finished paying off the mortgage to Baring Brothers in 1850 and once again owned their *latifundio* free and clear.[112] The family's position improved even more once Zuloaga and Jiménez began paying the installments on San Lorenzo de la Laguna at the end of 1850.[113]

Having survived a series of crises, early in 1851 the Sánchez Navarros once again met in Mexico City to plan for the future. During the reunion several family and business matters were settled. Apolonia chose to return with Jacobo to live in Coahuila, where she felt most comfortable. Carlos, on the other hand, was making preparations for an extended trip to Europe, where he was to spend the next several years. With regard to their business affairs, even though the Sánchez Navarros now enjoyed substantial liquid assets they were determined to be absolutely certain of having abundant working capital, so they decided to sell yet another hacienda.

They accepted a certain Bruno Lozano's offer for the Hacienda de Aguanueva, a few miles south of Saltillo. During the Mexican War, the *casco* at Aguanueva had been burned by retreating American troops on the eve of the decisive battle of Buenavista in February,

1847. But by the end of that year extensive repairs were under way at the headquarters complex.[114] Besides having a brand new *casco*, Aguanueva's major selling point was that the hacienda consisted of 117,000 well-watered acres advantageously located on the highway between Saltillo and San Luis Potosí. For these reasons the Sánchez Navarros got a handsome price—135,000 pesos—when Lozano purchased the estate in 1852.[115]

Though the family had failed to retain the Marquisate intact, they had nevertheless done rather well for themselves. By selling San Lorenzo de la Laguna, Rosario, and Aguanueva they had made 363,000 pesos—more than they had originally paid for the entire Marquisate. Furthermore, even without these three haciendas, the Sánchez Navarro landholding still exceeded fifteen million acres.

Compared with this eventful decade of land transfers, the family's other real estate dealings were anticlimactic. In 1851, they relinquished a small tract to the national government. The authorities devised a scheme to resettle fugitive Indians from the United States, mainly Kickapoos, in return for their help in combating the devastating raids of the Comanches and Apaches. The Kickapoos were relocated on 17,353 acres at the Hacienda de Nacimiento, near the headwaters of the Sabinas.[116] In the absence of documentary evidence, one may only speculate as to the family's reasons for not contesting the government's action, but, as will appear, the likeliest explanation is that the Sánchez Navarros received compensation in the form of political favors.

A few years later the family again came under pressure to divest themselves of a part of their holdings. This time it was the governor, Santiago Vidaurri, who was doing the persuading. Vidaurri emerged in 1855 as the strong man of northeastern Mexico; in 1856 he brazenly annexed Coahuila to neighboring Nuevo León, installed himself as governor of the combined state, and openly defied the national government to do anything about it.[117] The Liberal regime in Mexico City was having enough trouble simply trying to remain in power, so, after considerable backing and filling, the government acquiesced to Vidaurri's *fait accompli*. For the next decade the Northeast was to be his political fief. In short, Vidaurri was a dangerous man with whom to trifle—yet the Sánchez Navarros succeeded in trifling with him for years.

The affair had its roots in the fact that Vidaurri's ancestors had settled in Coahuila, where by intermarriage in the eighteenth century they had acquired an interest in the Vázquez Borrego family's *latifundio*. Later the Sánchez Navarros had gained control of the Vázquez Borrego landholding, including the Hacienda del Alamo. Now that Santiago Vidaurri had attained a position of power undreamed of by his forebears, he yearned to give the Vidaurri name the luster that only landed wealth could confer. Therefore, in 1857, he suggested that Carlos and Jacobo might be willing to sell him El Alamo.

The brothers found themselves in an extremely awkward position: they were Vidaurri's political enemies and had no intention of selling him a single acre. There ensued an exchange of flowery correspondence in which, while continually assuring Vidaurri of their most distinguished compliments, the Sánchez Navarros managed to prolong the negotiations through a series of pretexts. These usually revolved around the necessity for both Carlos and Jacobo to be together in order to close the deal and the seeming inability of the brothers to be at the same place at the same time. But, when by 1860 Vidaurri finally started to lose patience, the Sánchez Navarros agreed to sell forthwith.[118] They still had one ploy left, however. Before El Alamo could be sold the brothers had to prepare detailed inventories of all their properties owned in common, for they planned to divide their holdings. This procedure naturally took time, and as late as October, 1861, El Alamo still formed part of the Sánchez Navarro *latifundio*.[119]

The division of property between the brothers did in fact occur in December, 1862, but it proved to be largely meaningless. By then the French Intervention was at hand, and all of Mexico was swept into the maelstrom of foreign invasion and civil war. The *latifundio* remained essentially intact until the Sánchez Navarros' political activities, originally so instrumental in building the landholding, led the family to disaster.

8. Ranching

The mechanics of ranching remained essentially unchanged after Mexican independence, but there occurred significant innovations in the administration of the *latifundio*. As we have seen, upon the curate's death in 1821 José Melchor assumed the long-range direction of the landholding in addition to supervising its daily activities. While the fusion of these roles was a natural development, and certainly one in keeping with José Melchor's passion for efficiency and detail, the result was less than satisfactory.

The problem lay in the weakness of the managerial structure. In the colonial period the *latifundio* had functioned as well as it did precisely because the formulation of policy and its implementation had been kept separate. The curate had insisted on making the important decisions himself, relying on trusted kinsmen—first Manuel Francisco and then José Melchor—to carry them out.

Now that José Melchor was trying to run everything himself, he found it increasingly difficult to keep the family's affairs in perspective. With such important matters as the Elizondo litigation requiring his constant attention, the *hacendado* nevertheless spent an inordinate amount of time supervising routine *latifundio* activities, in effect acting as his own *administrador*. In the decade of the 1820's, his frequent trips back and forth across the landholding indicated not only his desire to keep abreast of developments but also a deterioration in the administrative structure.

The lines of authority established in the colonial period became blurred even at the lower levels. José Melchor really had only one subordinate on whom he could rely implicitly—Manuel Castellano, who had been *mayordomo* of the Tapado-Hermanas complex since 1813. Managing these two haciendas was a full-time job in itself, but Castellano was now saddled with additional duties, such as supervising the flocks and periodically counting the *hacienda de ovejas*.[1] Moreover, when in 1824 José Melchor decided to develop a section of the *latifundio* east of Monclova by establishing a cattle ranch called the Estancia de la Mota, Castellano also had to manage this new *casco*.[2]

With Castellano trying to do the work of three men, the opposite situation obtained at the northern complex of haciendas—Soledad and its satellite estates Dolores and San Juan de Sabinas—where three individuals proved incapable of doing the work of one good man. The *mayordomo* of Soledad in the early 1820's was clearly incompetent, as evidenced by complaints from one of the overseers that he could not direct the flocks out on the range because the *mayordomo* refused to provide him with a horse.[3] As a stopgap solution to this annoying situation, José Melchor relied on one of his brothers-in-law, Nicolás Beráin, who lived in Santa Rosa, and on Francisco Vidaurri, who was handling some of the *hacendado*'s affairs in that town, to assist the *mayordomo*. But there was no clear-cut division of responsibilities; on occasion it was Vidaurri rather than the *mayordomo* who conducted the annual roundup.[4]

Operations at Dolores and Soledad remained in a state of confusion, largely because of constant bickering among José Melchor's three subordinates about who was responsible for doing what.[5] Finally, in the summer of 1824, José Melchor was able to take time from his other affairs and make an extended visit to Soledad. Infuriated by the slipshod administration he found, the *hacendado* decided to clean house. In what must have been a spectacular display of his fiery temper, he dismissed the *mayordomo*, relieved his brother-in-law and his business agent, and took charge himself.[6] It was several months before he could find a new *mayordomo*, but thereafter the northern haciendas began to operate more efficiently.[7]

An important factor in the improving administrative situation was the addition in 1828 of a clerk to the staff at Soledad.[8] His main function was the preparation of weekly reports for José Melchor. These, together with similar reports that the faithful Castellano had been submitting all along from Hermanas, now enabled the *hacendado* to stay abreast of the general condition of the *latifundio*. Because José Melchor seldom remained in one spot for long, the reports usually went to the Monclova store to be read by his wife, Apolonia.

Her involvement in José Melchor's business affairs was gradual and stemmed directly from the failure of their son-in-law Rafael Delgado to become the kind of assistant the *hacendado* so urgently needed. Besides helping José Melchor in his legal battles, Delgado tried to oversee some of the ranching operations, but his background as a wool broker hardly fitted him for this task.[9] As he became disenchanted with Delgado, José Melchor relied on Apolonia to handle some of the family's routine affairs, and, after the final break with Delgado, Apolonia evolved into José Melchor's business confidant and adviser.

Perhaps Apolonia's enthusiasm for her new role reflected her desire to share at least this part of José Melchor's life, since she did not get to see much of him in person. Whatever the reason, Apolonia proved to have an aptitude for business, to which she brought a shrewd common-sense approach and a jealous regard for the family's interests. By 1828 she was serving as the clearinghouse for information concerning the landholding. As reports flowed in from Soledad and Hermanas, she read and digested them, then forwarded the pertinent data to José Melchor wherever he happened to be.[10] José Melchor's confidence in his wife's judgment grew to the point that she was soon making many of the routine decisions, merely informing José Melchor of the action taken.[11] She was, however, extremely careful about phrasing her letters tactfully to avoid wounding José Melchor's ego.

One indication of the position she carved out for herself is that, when José Melchor was away on business trips, the *mayordomos* reported directly to Apolonia, for on these occasions it was she who ran the *latifundio*.[12] The few times that both the Sánchez Navarros were away on trips, orders went through Apolonia's assistant, Juan José de Cárdenas, the family's storekeeper in Monclova.[13]

This reorganized administrative structure relieved José Melchor of part of his burden, enabling him to devote more time to his favorite occupation, that of trying to supervise every detail of the *latifundio*'s operation. In the 1830's he visited his properties frequently, but more in the capacity of an inspector general than to cope with crises, as had been the case in the preceding decade.

Despite the improvement in management, there remained enough instances of incompetence to keep the *hacendado* in a state of frustration. In one of his letters to Apolonia he raged that nothing was accomplished unless he were there to supervise, for otherwise his employees spent their time in idle conversation: a year ago he had ordered the construction of some corrals at the Hacienda de Nacimiento and to date nothing had been done. Nor would anything be accomplished in the near future, for he lacked the time to oversee the project in person.[14] And, even when things were done, they were often not to the *hacendado*'s liking, as when he disgustedly informed his wife of the progress on painting the interior of the main house at Hermanas. The painter had thoroughly botched the job, leaving the gilt trim looking "as though he had applied it with his heels."[15]

Determined to make ranching operations as efficient as possible, José Melchor spent hours poring over the accounts maintained at the various *cascos*. No detail was too insignificant to escape his attention; writing to Apolonia from Hermanas concerning the fees due the clergy, he mentioned that in checking the records he had discovered that he had been charged for one burial too many and was making a note of this eight-peso error.[16] Though he controlled a vast economic empire, José Melchor was not one to be cheated out of eight pesos if he could help it.

This obsession with protecting the family's interests finally undermined José Melchor's health, causing his premature death in 1836. The *latifundio*, however, continued to function reasonably well under his successor, his elder son Jacobo, for, while the latter was gaining the experience necessary for directing an enterprise of such magnitude, he could rely on the invaluable assistance of Castellano, Cárdenas, and, especially, Apolonia. Castellano assumed supervision of all ranching operations, acting as the *administrador*. Cárdenas served as the clearinghouse for information and represented the family in their dealings with local officialdom.[17] The intelligence of Apolonia, the imperious matriarch, was behind the whole operation. Jacobo made good use of his period of apprenticeship, becoming sufficiently well versed in ranching matters to cope with the difficulties that arose in 1840 when his brother, Carlos, purchased the Marquisate of Aguayo.

Jacobo's immediate concern was reorganizing the administrative structure, for at one stroke the *latifundio* had increased nearly eightfold in size. He sensibly decided to adapt the family's original landholding to the managerial practices used on the Marquisate; to do otherwise would have been a case of the tail wagging the dog.

The Marquisate may not have been the most efficiently run enterprise in Mexico, but it did have an elaborate administrative structure, a consequence partly of the British companies' efforts to introduce sound business practices but mainly the result of the sheer size of the landholding, which was organized into thirty-one large geographical units. The main headquarters were at Patos, while the Rosario and Bonanza haciendas constituted regional headquarters for the western and southern sections. Under these three centers were grouped the remaining nine haciendas as well as the nineteen sections used primarily for rangeland.[18] Besides these major units, many of the haciendas included their own subordinate ranchos.

The organization of the supervisory personnel was conventional enough. The *administrador*, assisted by a staff of clerks, directed operations from Patos. He transmitted his instructions verbally to the *mayordomo* of Patos and by letter to the *mayordomos* at each of the other haciendas. They in turn issued orders to their own foremen and overseers who dealt directly with the labor force. The *mayordomos* of Rosario and Bonanza, however, had the additional duty of supervising the industrial activities carried on at those *cascos*—winemaking at Rosario and silver mining at Bonanza. In each case the *mayordomo* had a foreman for the technicians involved. With regard to the flocks, there was a completely separate chain of command. The sheepherders and *bacieros* were under their own *mayordomo* who reported directly to the *administrador*.

The Marquisate was thus characterized by numerous supervisory personnel working within a rigid structure that had clearly defined lines of authority. Nonetheless, in broad outline this structure resembled that already existing on the Sánchez Navarro *latifundio*, the difference being one of degree rather than kind.

On the other hand, the purchase of the Marquisate produced a radical change in the Sánchez Navarros' system of accounting. The family had traditionally employed a generally effective but informal method—inventories were taken, livestock was counted, and so on, but neither a prescribed manner nor a regular schedule was observed.[19] As the *latifundio* expanded in the early nineteenth century, the inadequacies of this system had become increasingly apparent; the acquisition of the Marquisate made it imperative for the Sánchez Navarros to develop a better procedure for keeping track of ranching operations.

Fortunately the solution was at hand, because a minutely detailed accounting system was already in use on the Marquisate. The *administrador* rarely stirred from Patos, relying on a systematic inflow of data from across the landholding. Some of it came through frequent letters from subordinates, but this correspondence merely complemented the information in a series of standardized reports. From the various subdivisions, detailed reports went each month to Patos. There they were added to those for Patos itself, and the *administrador* had at his disposal a presumably accurate picture of conditions throughout the landholding.

Each *mayordomo* prepared a report on the last day of the month. Since sheep raising was the principal activity, the reports dealt mainly with the status of the flocks, which had been carefully counted a day or two earlier. The excerpt in table 6 illustrates the standard format. Oftentimes the "Explanation" included a detailed accounting of the sale, transfer, or slaughter of sheep, as well as a listing of saddle stock, tools and implements, weapons, and days worked by each shepherd. In addition, whenever there was a change in *mayordomos* a comprehensive inventory was made of the hacienda involved.

TABLE 6
Sheep at the Hacienda de Hermanas, November 1, 1847

Types of Sheep (By Flocks)	Shepherds	Living on This Day	Died	Lost
Rams	2	2,000	10	
Prime ewes	10	19,869	220	12
Yearling rams	2	5,685	43	10
Lamb crops of April and May	2	5,980	60	4
Lamb crop of October	8	6,527		
Old sheep	1	336	13	
Rams	3	5,246	30	9
Lame and bell sheep	2	415	90	22
Unweaned lambs		6,629	245	
Total	30	52,687	711	57

Comparison

Sheep living on October 1	46,826
Increase during October	6,629
Should be	53,455
Sheep living on November 1	52,687
Difference	768

Explanation

Sheep that died	466
Sheep that were lost	57
Unweaned lambs that died	245
Total	768

SOURCE: Harris, *The Sánchez Navarros*, pp. 25–26.

This meticulous accounting system, combined with the personal attention to their properties for which the Sánchez Navarros were noted, meant that from 1840 on there was a marked improvement in the administration of the sprawling *latifundio*. The point of departure in this new order was the information contained in the inventories and reports prepared in connection with the sale of the Marquisate.[20] Even as Carlos and Jacobo were familiarizing themselves with their new acquisition, they were able to keep up with developments because they retained the administrative structure in its entirety, and the flow of reports to Patos continued without interruption. In fact the flow increased, for one of the most significant changes the brothers made was to extend the accounting system to the family's original *latifundio*, which now became merely the northern division of the expanded landholding. The Hacienda de Hermanas was designated as the regional headquarters, occupying an administrative position equal to that of Rosario and Bonanza.

Hermanas was the logical choice not only because it had been the seat of the old *latifundio* but also because by the 1840's its *casco* had become one of the finest in Coahuila, constituting a fitting memorial to José Melchor and the effort he had lavished on building Hermanas.[21] Though it was certainly an impressive estate, and one whose main house eventually boasted twenty-one rooms,[22] the fact that Hermanas was now but a subheadquarters served to underline the dramatic shift southward in the *latifundio*'s center of gravity after 1840. Whereas Tapado was the hacienda intimately associated with the curate, and Hermanas the one favored by José Melchor, it was Patos that held a special attraction for Carlos and Jacobo.

Located some thirty miles west of Saltillo, the *casco* of Patos nestled in a valley whose natural fertility had been enhanced by an intricate irrigation network. Dominating the complex of stuccoed adobe buildings was the main house, a quadrangle with sides one hundred yards long. At its southeast and northwest corners rose fortified towers from which enfilading fire—including that from an *esmeril*, or small piece of ordnance, mounted on a swivel—could sweep the walls. The entrance to the structure was through a passageway barred by massive iron-studded oak gates. Across a tree-shaded plaza was the chapel, a much more pretentious building than those usually found on northern haciendas. Its two-story walls were surmounted by a square bell tower over the main door. Extending out from the plaza along dirt streets were the lesser structures—tenements for the peons, granaries and warehouses, stables, and the hacienda mill.[23]

Such was the seat of the consolidated *latifundio*. The mere fact that Patos was their country home visually demonstrated the wealth and power that the third generation of Sánchez Navarro *hacendados* enjoyed. By 1866, when its resident population numbered some two thousand, Patos was one of the most splendid haciendas, not only in Coahuila but in all of Mexico.[24]

The ranching operations that Jacobo directed from Patos did not encompass all the territory within the boundaries of the *latifundio*. One of the most notable developments since the time of independence was the practice of renting out an increasing portion of the family's properties. This trend was basically a function of size; as their holdings expanded, it became impossible for the Sánchez Navarros to make productive use of everything they owned, and rentals at least brought in some revenue. Another consideration was that in many instances the tenants constituted the first line of defense against Indian depredations.

As in so many other aspects of ranching, the year 1840 was the watershed in the Sánchez Navarros' rentals. Prior to that year the family's leases fell into two broad categories: water rights and moderately sized parcels of land. Most of the rights were to water from the Monclova River, which humble farmers needed to irrigate their wheatfields. The number of farmers involved totaled about a score, only one of whom received as much as four days of water a month, at the rate of twenty-four pesos a day; the rest could afford an average of only a day to a day and a half per month. Leases were for one year and were ordinarily renewed as a matter of course. Even though the business of water rights was a modest operation, the Sánchez Navarros fully expected the lessees to meet their contractual obligations; whenever a farmer fell behind in his payments, he was promptly taken to court.[25] If he had no assets, the Sánchez Navarros were quite amenable to his working off the debt as a peon on one of their haciendas. The family displayed the same attitude toward those who rented land from them.

These leases took various forms. For example, at the Hacienda de San Juan de Sabinas in the early 1820's, the Sánchez Navarros' tenants included not only a few small farmers but also the Elizondos, who were allowed to stay on pending final judicial disposition of the hacienda.[26] This situation was atypical, for tenants were usually smallholders interested in renting a farm near Monclova or perhaps a tract on the eastern ranges of the *latifundio* near Candela. Sometimes the Sánchez Navarros accepted payment in kind—maize from farmers and sheep or goats from ranchers. In other instances payment was made in labor: when the family was assessed for road repairs, for example, the tenants performed this chore.[27]

In rangeland management, there was an interesting innovation. After years of battling those enterprising individuals who persisted in establishing *vinaterías*, José Melchor decided in the 1820's to reach an accommodation with them. He began renting them the maguey plants on specified sections of the range so they could distill *aguardiente* and *mescal* in peace. At least fifteen persons availed themselves of José Melchor's new policy, agreeing to pay one barrel of liquor every four months.[28] This arrangement solved the nagging problem of trespassing but created a new one. Even though the *hacendado* appointed an agent to supervise the distilleries and collect the rent, some of the tenants fell behind in their payments, resulting in petty legal squabbles.[29] It is questionable, therefore, whether in the years up to 1840 the benefits of renting offset the nuisance of having to deal with the tenantry.

This was definitely not the case after the Sánchez Navarros acquired the Marquisate. Various properties were already rented out, and Jacobo simply assumed the direction of this activity. First, however, he had to prove himself as a landlord. Many of the minor tenants—especially those working small parcels on the Hacienda de San Lorenzo de la Laguna—bitterly resented their current situation and, since Jacobo was an unknown quantity, decided to take his measure by going on a rent strike. Much of their boldness stemmed from the fact that they had the support of the local authorities in such towns as Mapimí, who saw an opportunity to break the Marquisate's domination over the inhabitants of the Laguna region. When in 1841 Jacobo dispatched an agent, one José Benito Noguera, to collect rents and renew leases, the latter returned a shaken man. Noguera reported having been met with almost universal hostility on his rounds; on one occasion he had narrowly escaped being lynched. The substance of Noguera's report was that the prevailing attitude toward Jacobo was one of open contempt.[30]

If the Laguneros thought they could intimidate Jacobo they were very much mistaken, for the *hacendado* quickly put an end to this nonsense. Precisely how he did it remains unclear, but in all likelihood he threatened to secure the assistance of the military, who had been ordered to facilitate the transfer of the Marquisate to the Sánchez Navarros. In any case, the rent strike soon collapsed and the inhabitants of the Laguna were brought to heel. Having demonstrated that he would tolerate no insubordination, Jacobo thereafter enjoyed a gratifying degree of deference from his tenants.

This pleasant state of affairs resulted not only from Jacobo's show of firmness but also because he passed along to others many of the problems involved in rentals. Continuing the traditional practice on the Marquisate, Jacobo leased out entire estates. This system had several advantages over that used on the old Sánchez Navarro *latifundio*. For one thing, rental fees were much higher. For another, Jacobo ordinarily dealt only with the principal lessees, who were relatively few in number. Each of them in turn sublet parcels, so it was they who had to cope with trying to collect rent from a multitude of small farmers and ranchers. Last, it was possible to prorate among the principal lessees their share of the property taxes imposed on the *latifundio*.[31] -

Despite the fragmentary nature of the surviving records, it is possible to identify some of the haciendas the Sánchez Navarros rented out. Aguanueva, with its subordinate rancho, Encarnación, was one. Its tenants included Eduardo González, the lieutenant governor of Coahuila, from 1847 until its sale in 1852. González's yearly payment of 2,500 pesos included the use of 10,000 sheep with which Jacobo stocked the hacienda.[32] This practice of furnishing livestock to tenants was not at all uncommon and was consonant with the Sánchez Navarros' policy of minimizing their risks by making others responsible for safeguarding part of the family's property.[33] Besides Aguanueva, other estates leased out included Buenavista and Hedionda Grande, Aguadulce and its subdivision San Juan del Retiro, La Ventura, Anhelo and La Joya, San Juan de Sabinas, and Encinas.[34]

Finally, there was the matter of water. Already dominating the rivers in the north, the Sánchez Navarros gained control of much of Coahuila's remaining water resources when they bought the Marquisate, and Jacobo was pleased to rent water rights to those less fortunate. These lessees ran the gamut from sharecroppers at Patos to the citizens of Parras, where from 1840 to 1848 the Sánchez Navarros controlled three-fourths of that town's water supply through their ownership of the Hacienda del Rosario.[35]

It was just as well that large sections of the landholding were under lease, for Jacobo had quite enough to do in operating the remainder. With the exception of the improved accounting system, ranching procedures had not changed materially since colonial times. Sheep were the mainstay of the consolidated *latifundio*, and the operations cycle still centered around the lambing and shearing seasons. What had changed, and changed drastically, was the number of sheep the Sánchez Navarros owned. Scanty documentation makes it impossible to reconstruct the size of the flocks between 1822 and 1840, but there appears to have been a marked decline in the 1820's, when the semiannual lamb crops averaged only some four thousand head a season, followed by a gradual recovery during the next decade, when the lambs averaged close to ten thousand head a season.[36] Whatever the size of the flocks by 1840, there is no question but that they increased enormously with the acquisition of the Marquisate.

The flocks were now so huge that it was impractical to keep them all together in the *hacienda de ovejas*. Consequently, Jacobo established what were in effect three *haciendas de ovejas*: the first was based on Hermanas and roamed the old Sánchez Navarro *latifundio*; the second, centered on Patos, grazed in the southern part of the expanded landholding; the third, the *hacienda de ovejas* proper, used the western ranges, including those on the huge Hacienda de Santa Catalina del Alamo in Durango, where the Sánchez Navarros had acquired grazing rights in the 1840's.[37]

The surviving monthly reports give some indication of the scale on which the Sánchez Navarros now engaged in ranching: besides the three main flocks, they had thousands of additional head at San Lorenzo de la Laguna, San Juan del Retiro, and the Rancho de San Antonio (see tables 7 and 8).

By the late 1840's there was no question about the Sánchez Navarros' right to consider themselves sheep barons. Their flocks on March 31, 1847, totaled a staggering 218,988 sheep and 18,857 goats. In January and February, 1848—the period for which the most complete records exist—the number of their sheep averaged 196,000, and their goats 19,600. These of course are merely the verifiable figures. If one considers the flocks at haciendas whose records have not survived, as well as sheep rented out, it seems reasonable to speculate that in the late 1840's the Sánchez Navarros' flocks probably numbered 250,000 head. For example, the total of 218,988 sheep on March 31, 1847, does not include any report from San Lorenzo de la Laguna. If there were already some 20,000 head there, as was reported a few months later, then the total in March, 1847, approached 240,000. Besides the flocks, the Sánchez Navarros owned large herds of cattle, horses, and mules, normally kept at the Punta de Santa Elena and at Hedionda Grande.

Quantity rather than quality was the basis of their whole operation. Despite the impressive number of livestock, the Sánchez Navarros frequently had difficulty assembling enough prime animals to meet their marketing commitments, a situation attributable in part to the inferior strain of sheep they produced—the same scrubby type as in colonial times. This is not to say that Carlos and Jacobo were blissfully unaware of the problem: from his vantage point in Mexico City, Carlos kept abreast of the competition, and as early as 1849 he wrote to Jacobo that some of the other leading *hacendados* were importing superior Merino sheep from Great Britain. Carlos dolefully predicted that within a few years the Sánchez Navarros' wool would be considered "the worst there is."[38] Not until the 1860's, however, is there any record of the brothers trying to upgrade their stock by introducing Merinos, and even then it was on a minor scale with a flock of some fifteen hundred kept at Patos.[39]

The reason was rather simple. Given the conditions under which the Sánchez Navarros carried on their ranching operations, it had been pointless to make the considerable investment required to improve the flocks. It still seemed, as in the colonial period, that whatever livestock escaped Indian depredations was destined to perish by drought. For the northern frontier at least, Indians and drought are a more nearly valid explanation of the traditional nature of ranching than is the usual picture of an indolent *hacendado* class.

The Indian menace had always been one of the grim facts of life in

TABLE 7
Sheep of All Types at Patos, Hermanas, and the *Hacienda de Ovejas*

Date	Patos	Hermanas	Hacienda de Ovejas
1847			
March	63,707	59,734	58,969
April	63,151	48,195	56,132
September	76,881	46,826	45,533
October	74,496	52,687	49,093
1848			
January	67,289	52,699	24,422
February	64,948	51,580	27,829
April	63,658	43,046	41,180
May	66,732	46,269	45,377
July	61,476		42,476
August	59,299		41,200
1849			
November	53,279	38,470	15,267
December	51,180	37,663	16,443
1850			
March	42,630	49,125	19,681
April	41,925	48,490	18,724
May	39,603	50,525	18,079
June		49,730	17,626
September	41,821	39,222	17,017
October	43,262	38,384	16,235
December	38,665		
1851			
January	36,153	39,435	14,493
February	33,803	45,204	11,373
March	34,653	44,030	19,823
April	32,101	42,305	11,820
May	27,719	44,789	11,001
June	25,373	45,026	10,430
July	23,174	43,210	10,081
August	22,864	41,521	9,819
1857			
April	4,315		
October		34,419	

Date	Patos	Hermanas	*Hacienda de Ovejas*
1861			
October		38,994	
1862			
March	1,543		
1863			
March		35,841	

SOURCE: Harris, *The Sánchez Navarros*, pp. 27–28, 56–57, and:
Patos: SNP (3078), (3617), (3637), (3622), (3618), (3624), (2399), (3077), (3076), (3308), (2511), (2288), (2169), (682), (617), (2312), (3170), (2923), (2614).
Hermanas: (3078), (3617), (3637), (3622), (3624), (2389), (2404), (3076), (725), (527), (2290), (664), (639), (623), (2313), (3168), (2889), (2887).
Ovejas: (3078), (3617), (3637), (3622), (3618), (3624), (2391), (3077), (2415), (3076), (2507), (2279), (2173), (649), (614), (2323), (3174).

Coahuila, but after independence the depredations increased decade by decade, reaching a bloody climax at mid-century when the Indians overran the state.

Immediately after independence the tribesmen were relatively quiescent, for the Lipan Apaches signed a peace treaty in Mexico City in 1822.[40] This interlude lasted all of a year, after which the Lipans again made their presence felt. Striking from their strongholds in the Santa Rosa Mountains, they spread terror across northern Coahuila.[41] On occasion their war parties were strong enough to keep the Hacienda de Hermanas under virtual siege.[42] Formidable as they were, the Lipans posed only a secondary threat, for the Comanches rapidly overshadowed them as the scourge of the frontier.

By 1825, José Melchor was deeply concerned not only about his properties, but also about his personal safety and that of his family. The *hacendado* reported that the area around Santa Rosa was infested with Comanches, who were frequently sighted from the *cascos* of San Juan de Sabinas and Soledad. He scolded Apolonia for having left the safety of Monclova to attend a fiesta in a nearby village. The roads were so dangerous that José Melchor even curtailed the number of

TABLE 8

Sheep and Goats at San Lorenzo de la Laguna, San Juan del Retiro, and the Rancho de San Antonio

Date	San Lorenzo Sheep	San Juan Sheep	Rancho de San Antonio Goats	Sheep
1847				
March		26,948	18,857	9,630
April		26,033	19,303	4,427
September		22,256	17,869	3,434
October		23,685	21,191	2,559
1848				
January	22,162	26,378	18,771	4,019
February	20,380	25,968	18,417	4,491
April		23,858	17,913	6,086
May		24,946	20,340	6,001
July		22,962	20,108	3,286
August		22,411	19,894	3,194
1849				
October			21,790	541
November	23,009		21,704	530
December	31,112		21,489	1,309
1850				
March	30,554		22,109	19,554
April	32,647		21,438	18,841
May	31,769		21,912	
June	31,112		21,677	
September	26,724		18,879	
October	31,287		23,440	
December			22,742	
1851				
January	25,071		20,745	
February			20,230	
March			19,554	
April			18,841	
May			19,048	
June			18,672	
July			18,478	
August			18,327	

Date	San Lorenzo Sheep	San Juan Sheep	Rancho de San Antonio Goats	Sheep
1857				
April			29,651	
1862				
January			43,033	
February			42,400	
March			46,776	
April			45,528	
May			44,786	
June			43,831	

SOURCE:

San Lorenzo de la Laguna: SNP (3637), (3624), (2389), (2404), (3076), (725), (527).

San Juan del Retiro: (3078), (3617), (3637), (3622), (3618).

Rancho de San Antonio: (3078), (3617), (3637), (3622), (3618), (796), (3624), (2174), (2393), (3077), (2403), (3076), (3325), (2506), (2280), (654), (619), (2322), (3169), (2923), (2630), (2614), (1586), (1588), (906).

letters he wrote, so as not to jeopardize the lives of the peons who would have to deliver them.[43]

At the same time, he was demanding that the authorities do something about the Indians. Replying to the *hacendado*'s indignant letters, his cousin Víctor Blanco, who happened to be the governor of Coahuila, assured him in 1826 that both the national and state governments planned to take vigorous action.[44] Yet because of political turmoil and a lack of resources the government could accomplish little. The raids continued, and José Melchor reiterated his demands that the authorities provide some relief.[45] In 1830, for example, the *hacendado* sent a proposal for combatting the Indians to a friend who was one of the congressmen from Coahuila. The latter brought the recommendation to the president's attention but was not very sanguine about its prospects, judging from the government's past performance.[46]

His pessimism proved amply justified, for the Indians continued to make life in rural Coahuila quite exciting in the 1830's. A trip by road was still not to be undertaken lightly; when in 1832 Apolonia went in the family coach from Monclova to Hermanas, José Melchor insisted on providing an escort of eight heavily armed *vaqueros*. As in the colonial era, the Sánchez Navarros maintained a small group of riders to guard the *cascos*, but these retainers were not available to protect the citizenry in general. The state government in 1837 raised a force of "volunteers" to screen the trails most frequented by the Indians. The Sánchez Navarros' quota for this project was three riders, who were to be well armed, mounted, and supplied. Apolonia haughtily notified the *alcalde* of Monclova that she had no intention whatsoever of complying. All her people were needed to protect the *latifundio*.[47]

This lack of cooperation with the authorities hampered defensive measures at a time when the Comanches were already making large-scale incursions. Facing increasing pressure from the westward advance of settlement in Texas from 1836 on, the Comanches compensated by stepping up their depredations into northeastern Mexico, where rich plunder was available for the taking.[48] They raided into Mexico each September, following the so-called Comanche Trail, which crossed the Río Grande near the old Presidio de San Carlos.[49] After their forays, which sometimes reached as far south as Zacatecas and San Luis Potosí, the Comanches wintered at the Laguna de Jaco, deep within the forbidding Bolsón de Mapimí.[50] These dread marauders now poured into Coahuila by the thousands.

The four presidial companies in the state proved incapable of repelling the invasion.[51] These units had been neglected for years; their ranks were filled with vagrants, felons, and other undesirables; and the demoralized troops showed a marked disinclination to challenge a fierce and mobile enemy. The brunt of the struggle was borne by the citizens themselves who fought desperately to defend their homes. An ominous new pattern developed, for places that even in the colonial period were considered safe from the Indians now came under attack.

December, 1840, marked the beginning of the most terrible incursions in recent history. One war party of some four hundred Comanches swept down from the north, passing within a few miles of Monclova and devastating the villages and farms to the west of that city. A hurriedly assembled force of volunteers managed to drive them off and took up the pursuit as the Indians raced for Saltillo, plundering and killing along the way. The Comanches reached the very outskirts of the capital, whose inhabitants from the governor on down turned out to give battle. In the ensuing combat Saltillo was saved, but the raiders left a smoking trail of destruction all the way to the Hacienda de Bonanza before doubling back to the Río Grande. In this single foray, which lasted about a month, the Comanches killed an estimated three hundred persons and took some sixty captives, though in their retreat the Indians lost most of the three thousand horses they had stolen.[52]

Nor was this all; in 1841 the town of Parras also came under attack. The Indians fought their way in as far as the cemetery, killing eleven townspeople before being repulsed. Numbering about two hundred, the tribesmen ravaged the region between Parras and Mapimí, inflicting more than seventy casualties on the Mexicans, burning ranches, and running off large herds of livestock.[53]

These raids, together with minor incursions throughout the state, left the Coahuilans reeling, especially when they contemplated what lay in store when the Comanches returned. Carlos in Mexico City reflected the prevailing view, writing to his brother in June, 1842, "I fear that the incursions to date, committed by such a small number of Indians, will turn out to be like last year, merely the prelude to greater and greater tragedy."[54] He was right.

By November, the region southwest of Saltillo swarmed with Comanches, and Patos itself faced imminent attack. Apolonia sent out a frantic appeal for additional ammunition to defend the *casco*. For once the army reacted swiftly, perhaps because the colonel commanding the relief column was her cousin José Juan Sánchez Navarro, the onetime insurgent, who had since become a redoubtable Indian fighter.[55] José Juan immediately dispatched two hundred cartridges to Patos and assured Apolonia that he would be there soon with seventy troops, "unless on the way I have the good fortune to encounter the savages."[56]

While nervously awaiting José Juan's arrival, the *mayordomo* of Patos sent a report on the crisis to Jacobo, who was at the Hacienda de Bonanza. Unable to defend the entire *casco* for lack of weapons, the *mayordomo* had concentrated the few available firearms in the main house and the chapel. The peon families had been ordered to take refuge in these strongpoints; the signal of an impending attack was the ringing of the chapel bell and the beating of a drum in the plaza. The *mayordomo* planned to have families from outlying ranches take refuge at Patos, and he had already ordered the shepherds to abandon their flocks and take to the hills. He ended by reporting that Apolonia was in a much better mood since she had received Jacobo's promise not to leave the safety of Bonanza.[57]

As it turned out, José Juan's column reached Patos ahead of the Comanches, who retreated westward toward the Bolsón de Mapimí. Within a few days the commandant general of Coahuila assembled at Patos a force of three hundred soldiers and volunteers and set out in lukewarm pursuit. Most of his remounts were requisitioned Sánchez Navarro horses, few of which the family ever saw again.[58]

Patos was an island of security compared with the northern haciendas. Nacimiento, San Juan de Sabinas, and Soledad remained favorite targets of the Comanches, whose raids were so devastating that by 1846 the entire district around Santa Rosa was paralyzed economically. The Sánchez Navarros in fact had to abandon the Hacienda de Nacimiento.[59]

Affording some consolation in the midst of this terrifying situation was the fact that the Indians were also overrunning neighboring states. In a monumental display of arrogance a band of two hundred Comanches penetrated the very city of Durango in August, 1847, calmly parading through the streets for hours before withdrawing unmolested.[60] In their own struggle against the nomads, the Coahuilans received assistance from an improbable source—the United States Army.

Along with the rest of the Northeast, Coahuila had been occupied in the fall of 1846, and on occasion American troops participated in combatting incursions. One such clash occurred in May, 1847, at the Ibarra family's Hacienda del Pozo west of Parras, where an American detachment inflicted a stinging defeat on Lipan Apaches confidently returning from a successful raid.[61] Of more direct benefit to the Sánchez Navarros, the deployment of American troops around Aguanueva not only prevented a powerful Comanche band from raiding that hacienda but also provided increased security for the whole southeastern section of the *latifundio*.[62] Thus, when the Mexican War ended, the Sánchez Navarros viewed the Americans' departure with mixed emotions. Though they hated the Americans as foreign invaders, still the latter's presence had been advantageous in some ways, not the least being their role in fighting the Indians.

The Coahuilans needed all the help they could get.[63] The postwar period constitutes a dreary chronicle of death and destruction at the hands of the marauders, whose incursions became more terrible each year. The climax came in 1851, when, according to the Mexican government, more than three thousand Comanches and Lipans inundated the state.[64] Even Jacobo, who had devoted his adult life to the *latifundio*, was losing heart. Discussing the condition of the livestock, specifically the losses caused by Indian raids and the concomitant shortage of labor, he wrote in February, 1851: "This evil has no remedy, nor is there hope of its ever being remedied. It is imperative to proceed with the idea of disposing of the livestock, and to do it in the speediest possible manner."[65]

The main topic of conversation continued to be the latest Indian outrages,[66] and subsequent events only confirmed Jacobo in his judgment. The Hacienda de Hermanas was repeatedly attacked; four of its personnel were killed during a single week in March.[67] The embattled *mayordomo*, Francisco Beráin, fully shared the attitude of his counterparts in the southwestern United States that "the only good Indian is a dead Indian." Commenting on the news that a delegation of eighteen Comanches had reportedly gone to Monterrey to negotiate a peace treaty, he expressed the fervent hope that "the peace they find be at the end of a rope, as we would then have eighteen fewer enemies."[68] Most of Beráin's fellow citizens would undoubtedly have concurred.

Despite his desperate situation, the *mayordomo* managed to retain a wry sense of humor. Reporting on the casualties at Hermanas he mentioned that the *casco* was beginning to resemble a hospital, adding, "If I do not become an accomplished surgeon it will be due to my own ineptitude, not to a lack of patients on whom to practice."[69] Yet the supply of potential victims was shrinking. As Comanche raids continued unabated, the shepherds became so terrified that they were abandoning not only their flocks but even their own families. The Comanches were so bold that war parties laden with loot brazenly passed by the *casco* of Hermanas in broad daylight, defying anyone to impede their journey back to the Río Grande.[70]

No help was forthcoming from the *administrador* of the *latifundio*, Quirino Benavente. He was already deluged with frantic appeals pouring into Patos from the other *mayordomos*.[71] During a single day in July they reported the deaths of one overseer, three shepherds, and three peons, plus another peon taken captive. And all this was in addition to the relentless raids on the horse herds in the vicinity of Patos.[72]

The following year brought some relief, for only 2,000 warriors pillaged Coahuila in 1852.[73] According to the Mexican government's official figures, in the period between 1848 and 1857 alone, the Indians killed 229 Coahuilans, wounded 128, and captured 82.[74] Though depredations gradually diminished in intensity, they remained the most unpleasant aspect of life in Coahuila through the mid-1860's.[75]

The Indians could raid the *latifundio* with impunity because Jacobo made little effort to protect his estates.[76] Even had he tried to conduct a vigorous defense, this would have been a formidable—probably an impossible—undertaking for several reasons. One was the sheer size of the landholding. Another was Jacobo's understandable reluctance to arm the peons, who might then entertain thoughts of revolt. A third was that, as we shall see, Jacobo was complying with the policy of the national government. The peons, especially the shepherds scattered across the ranges, thus remained at the mercy of the Indians.

Firearms were normally kept at the *cascos* under the control of the administrative personnel. Even so, the *cascos* certainly did not boast arsenals by any stretch of the imagination. In 1857, for example, Patos had thirty-six muskets, four pistols, and seven daggers; Hermanas had one *esmeril*, three rifles, twenty-four muskets, twenty bayonets, and one double-barreled shotgun—with a broken stock.[77] From the foregoing, it may be concluded that the chief protection for the inhabitants of the *latifundio* was the Virgin of Guadalupe.

Since the Sánchez Navarros were unable to cope with the incursions, they necessarily looked to the government to defend their properties. Yet neither the central government nor the state authorities could provide much relief, particularly in the aftermath of the disastrous Mexican War. Efforts to protect the northern frontier ranged from the establishment of military colonies and the reorganization of the militia to the desperate expedient of offering bounties for Indian scalps and prisoners.[78] But at the same time the national government's distrust of the citizenry largely negated these measures: to forestall revolutions, the government disarmed the inhabitants of northern Mexico.[79]

The northerners' feeling that they had callously been abandoned by the central government was expressed by the *administrador*, Quirino Benavente. Commenting in 1851 on a report that the Coahuilan legislature contemplated paying bounties for Indian scalps, Benavente sarcastically wrote, "If the legislature resolves to decree that 25 pesos be paid for every scalp, I swear I will grant each member of the legislature a plenary indulgence as soon as I am ordained, and it matters little that the legislators be excommunicated by those profound politicians in Mexico City who, preoccupied with their European theories, know nothing of the necessities which unfortunately must be adopted by our northern states."[80]

A few examples suffice to illustrate the futility of relying solely on the military to contain the Indians. The Saltillo national guard, 200 men organized into eight infantry companies, was described in 1849 as lacking both uniforms and weapons.[81] In 1849 and 1850, the Coahuilan legislature authorized the formation of a 150-man flying column. Besides being too small to pose a serious threat to the Comanches, the unit's effectiveness was doubtful; its ranks were to be filled, as were those of the presidial forces, with the scum of society.[82] In 1851, the state government ambitiously undertook a military campaign against the Indians' stronghold, the Bolsón de Mapimí. The project occasioned prolonged and acrimonious debate in the legislature over the tactics to be employed and the amount each municipality would contribute. Although the total sum involved was only 2,500 pesos, the town of Parras obstinately refused to participate, alleging that its assessment of 500 pesos was exorbitant and that the proposed campaign would benefit other towns more than Parras. Matters reached the point that the legislature had the *alcalde* of Parras arrested and the town's contribution doubled by way of punishment. When the military campaign belatedly got under way the results were meager; the tribesmen remained firmly in control of the Bolsón.[83]

Because neither the Sánchez Navarros nor the government could protect the family's domains, the only recourse was to seek compensation for the tremendous losses suffered. The Sánchez Navarros found a possible solution to their problem in Article XI of the Treaty of Guadalupe Hidalgo, in which the United States had accepted responsibility for Indian incursions into Mexico.[84] In conjunction with a number of other northern landowners, the Sánchez Navarros prepared claims against the United States. Jacobo instructed his cousin and lawyer, Juan N. de Arizpe, not to be conservative in estimating losses from 1848 on, as "it is important that the total amount of the claim I plan to file be from 300,000 to 500,000 pesos." Moreover, Jacobo pointedly reminded Arizpe that *all* losses had been caused by "Comanches from the tribes that inhabit the territory of the United States."[85] Jacobo, sometimes together with Carlos, filed several claims over the next few years, but while the cases were still pending a new complication arose.

In 1853 the United States and Mexico signed the Gadsden Treaty, by which the United States paid Mexico $10 million for a strip of territory along the border and for release from all liability for Indian incursions as imposed by Article XI of the earlier treaty.[86] The Sánchez Navarros could therefore hope to collect only for those depredations committed between 1848 and 1853. Nevertheless, the brothers cannot be accused of timidity in estimating their losses, as shown in table 9. The value of the livestock, the indebtedness of the slain workers, the miscellaneous property stolen or destroyed, plus 12 percent annual interest brought the aggregate amount of the Sánchez Navarros' claims to a respectable $865,165.89.[87]

To deal with matters of this nature, the two governments established a mixed Claims Commission in 1868. Among the claims presented by Mexico were 366 for Indian depredations totaling more

TABLE 9

Indian Depredations Claims

July, 1848–August, 1853

Personnel killed
        43 peons
        98 shepherds
Livestock stolen or killed
        12,918 horses
        2,106 mules
        100 burros
        204,212 sheep
        2,080 goats
        111,867 cattle
        1,230 unspecified animals

SOURCE: NA, Mexican Docket, Memorials accompanying Claims 129c, 726, 727, 728, and 729.

than $31 million.[88] Not until 1874 were these claims disposed of, and even then they were not considered on their merits. Rather, the claim of *Rafael Aguirre* v. *The United States* was used as a test case.[89] The commission disallowed it on the ground that the Gadsden Treaty had released the United States retroactively from liability for Indian depredations; the remaining 365 claims were then dismissed.[90]

The Sánchez Navarros thus never collected a cent for their alleged losses, which appear to have been exaggerated. To take a single instance, Jacobo stated that in March, 1849, he had concluded a deal to sell "80,000 head of sheep and swine" kept at Hedionda Grande and the Punta de Santa Elena, but, when the livestock was inspected, it was found that Indians had slaughtered 68,000 of the sheep.[91] Killing that many animals between July, 1848, and March, 1849, would have been exhausting work even for the Comanches. Furthermore, the Sánchez Navarros claimed to have lost 95,000 sheep at Hermanas between July, 1848, and September, 1851. The available monthly reports, admittedly incomplete, show a total of 12,530 sheep dead and 4,462 missing. Even assuming that all of the latter perished, the total is only

16,992. Another check is that for the year 1851, which was disastrous for ranching, there are reports for Hermanas covering eight of the twelve months, and they list 11,220 sheep dead and 2,950 missing. Viewing the whole matter realistically, it would have been remarkable indeed had the Sánchez Navarros not inflated their considerable losses, since the financial burden of the United States government was not one of their principal concerns.

The livestock enumerated in the Sánchez Navarros' Indian depredations claims quite probably included thousands of animals killed by drought, that other scourge of northern ranchers. Coahuila underwent serious droughts in 1823, 1826–1828, 1847, and 1863, but these were overshadowed by the great drought of 1851.[92] As early as February, the tenor of the reports reaching Patos was one of apprehension, for the drought was already exacting a heavy toll.[93] During the spring, livestock losses mounted sharply as the range continued to scorch under a pitiless sun.[94] The harassed Francisco Beráin at Hermanas was moved to declare, "The sheep are taking days off my life; if it's not Indians it's drought."[95] Despite some scattered rainfall, the drought intensified with the approach of summer, and Juan N. de Arizpe wrote in despair to Jacobo, "The drought is killing us; if it doesn't rain soon we're going to lose everything."[96] At Hermanas the tank at the hot springs, which ordinarily filled in one night, now took two days and nights to replenish. In desperation Beráin suspended most operations and moved the flocks to the Sabinas River, which still carried a trickle of water.[97]

It was Arizpe who perhaps best described the situation. Recounting the severe losses already suffered on the *latifundio*, he added: "I fear they will be much heavier next year if, by misfortune, heaven does not aid us with some rain. Believe me, one cannot ride out on the range, for not only does it feel as though fire is falling from the sky, but one is moved by the pitiful condition of the stock, which can find nothing to eat. The small amount of maize planted is at the point of dying, and everything indicates even worse misery in the future."[98] Jacobo could take some small comfort in the thought that other *hacendados* shared his plight, for the drought extended as far south as the city of San Luis Potosí.[99]

There is no question but that the 1851 drought made appreciable inroads on the Sánchez Navarros' flocks and herds. It can be verified that some 21,000 sheep and 4,000 goats died, in addition to the 3,400 sheep and 300 goats listed as missing, but the total was much greater, taking into account gaps in the existing records and livestock at those haciendas whose records have disappeared. Nor were the prospects for 1852 encouraging: Jacobo mentioned in the fall of 1851 that the scant rainfall had partially restored some of the ranges, but with the approach of winter the young grass would probably be killed by the first freeze, leaving the range in even worse condition for the coming year.[100]

With Coahuila subject to periodic droughts, the importance of irrigation to agriculture cannot be overstated. The Sánchez Navarros continually strove to expand the irrigation networks at their haciendas. During the 1851 drought, for instance, the *administrador* took advantage of the low water level to overhaul the network of canals at Patos and to construct a new dam.[101] Much of this backbreaking work was still performed, as in the colonial period, by peons using shovels, but there had been a growing trend toward using blasting powder on irrigation projects. The most elaborate networks were at the northern haciendas of Soledad and San Juan de Sabinas, at Patos, and at the Tapado-Hermanas complex. In 1846, Hermanas had an estimated one thousand acres under cultivation, while there was "considerable cultivation" in the vicinity of Tapado.[102] While they owned Rosario and San Lorenzo de la Laguna, the Sánchez Navarros also relied heavily on irrigation at those estates. The extent to which irrigation was practiced often provoked comment by travelers passing through the *latifundio*.[103] As with other aspects of agriculture, however, a lack of data prevents the precise reconstruction of the irrigation system.

Agriculture still centered around the production of maize for the peons' rations and wheat, the principal cash crop. There was some diversification: at the haciendas of Soledad, San Juan de Sabinas, and Hermanas, cotton and sugar cane were raised extensively on a commercial basis; and some barley was grown at Hermanas and Patos. In further contrast to colonial times, there was increased emphasis on the raising of fruits and vegetables for local consumption; seeds and cuttings were periodically brought from Mexico City to improve the orchards.

Distribution of agricultural commodities within the *latifundio* centered around Hermanas and Patos. The northern haciendas shipped their production to Hermanas, retaining only enough maize for rations. Occasionally, as in 1828, crop failures at Soledad and San Juan de Sabinas forced a reversal of this procedure, with Hermanas providing maize rations for the other two estates. Patos, on the other hand, was the clearinghouse for the remainder of the landholding. The wheat from San Lorenzo de la Laguna and Rosario went to Patos, where a quantity of it was ground into flour, the surplus being shipped on to Saltillo for milling. Patos also received the maize production from Castaño and Castañuela. In turn Patos provided the rations for those estates where agriculture was not emphasized, such as Hedionda Grande, the Punta de Santa Elena, and Bonanza. Yet, despite the trend toward diversification and increased production, the primary objective in agriculture remained the same as in the colonial period: ensuring that the *latifundio* was self-sufficient in foodstuffs.

The Sánchez Navarros labored mightily for generations to achieve this objective; in the end they failed, not because such traditional problems as Indian depredations, drought, or the chronic labor shortage overwhelmed them, but because it was impossible to insulate the *latifundio* from the political convulsions that wracked Mexico in the nineteenth century. Because Coahuila was usually on the periphery of the turmoil, for decades the Sánchez Navarros escaped much of the destruction endured by *hacendados* in central Mexico. Occasionally the army would demand supplies, as in 1836 when maize was requisitioned at Hermanas during Santa Anna's ill-fated Texas campaign.[104] Even though payment was problematical, these exactions were more of a nuisance than a threat to the family's interests. A more serious situation arose during the Mexican War, but here again the Sánchez Navarros were relatively fortunate. The United States Army requisitioned large amounts of supplies, but these were generally paid for in cash. The only real damage to the *latifundio* was the burning of Aguanueva in 1847, and the Sánchez Navarros rebuilt that *casco* in short order.

Not until 1855 did the family's luck begin to run out. This occurred during the revolution of Ayutla, which finally ended Santa Anna's dominance of Mexican politics. Forces loyal to Santiago Vidaurri, who had come out in support of the revolution, descended like locusts on the *latifundio*, helping themselves to remounts and supplies and levying forced loans in the name of the cause.[105]

Jacobo protested indignantly to Vidaurri in 1856 that the perpetrators of these outrages all claimed to be acting under Vidaurri's orders. Now that the latter was in control of the state government, Jacobo expected to be reimbursed; and he presented a substantial claim for damages. Vidaurri disavowed responsibility, blandly suggesting that in any case the total might perhaps be exaggerated.[106] There ensued a bitter correspondence between the two men, in which Jacobo haughtily requested that his claim be returned, as he was not accustomed to having his word questioned. With relations badly strained, Carlos intervened to effect a reconciliation of sorts, persuading Vidaurri in 1857 to acknowledge a reduced claim and recommend to the national government that it be paid.[107] Perhaps not coincidentally, about this time Vidaurri broached the subject of purchasing the Hacienda del Alamo from the Sánchez Navarros.

Despite outwardly correct relations with Vidaurri, the Sánchez Navarros' ranching interests continued to suffer while he remained as governor. Some of the brothers' tenants were harassed by the authorities, forced loans were the order of the day, and rustling increased significantly. In fact, rustling took on political overtones, for Jacobo was convinced that Vidaurri protected the malefactors, some of whom were his own kinsmen and partisans. By 1860, according to Jacobo, the incessant robberies had "ruined" the Sánchez Navarros' northern haciendas.[108] Furthermore, in 1861 the state government seized the haciendas of Nacimiento and Encinas for alleged nonpayment of taxes, and when this pressure proved insufficient Hermanas was seized the following year.[109]

This was merely a portent of what was to come, for the French Intervention was now under way, and it sealed the doom of the *latifundio*. By 1864, Coahuila had become one of the battlegrounds in the desperate struggle pitting the republican supporters of President Juárez against the French and their Imperialist allies. During the next two years the *latifundio* was thoroughly pillaged in the course of the savage guerrilla warfare that raged across the state. For example, a retreating republican column that looted Hermanas in 1864 stripped the hacienda of livestock and grain, and destroyed all the orchards and standing crops. The hacienda never recovered.[110]

As the conflict intensified, other *cascos* were likewise plundered. A sizeable band of guerrillas occupied Bonanza early in 1866, and it may be presumed that they made off with everything that was not nailed down.[111] Patos was spared until relatively late in the war, partly because the French maintained troops there on various occasions, but, as the invaders were forced back into central Mexico in 1866, its turn came too.[112] By 1867 the Sánchez Navarro *latifundio* had been reduced to a shambles.

9. Labor

Nowhere in the wide range of the Sánchez Navarros' activities did independence produce less change than in the labor system they employed. In fact, considering labor practices from the peons' point of view, the changes that did occur were, with few exceptions, for the worse. Working conditions became more hazardous as Indian depredations intensified, and workers now had less legal protection against abuse. During the colonial period royal officials had tried, often ineffectually, to curb the more flagrant abuses, but, with the governmental instability that characterized Mexico after 1821, the authorities did little to prevent the exploitation of peons by their masters. Debt peonage remained the core of the labor system, becoming even more firmly entrenched not only in Coahuila but also elsewhere in the country.

As in the viceregal period, the Sánchez Navarros relied heavily on this practice in securing their labor force. The majority of new resident workers came in 1840 with the purchase of the Marquisate of Aguayo, since the Sánchez Navarros acquired the debts of these individuals as part of the transaction. Usually, however, new laborers were peons from other landholdings who were merely seeking a change of master.[1] In addition, sons trying to work off the debts their fathers had incurred comprised another source of labor.[2] And there were always destitute individuals not yet entrapped by peonage who asked for work.[3] But there were never enough laborers, and it became necessary from time to time actively to recruit peons and even to transfer a few of the family's urban employees to the *latifundio*.[4]

The chronic manpower shortage was particularly acute in the 1820's, when *latifundio* administration was in a state of flux. During the prolonged litigation over San Juan de Sabinas, the Elizondos' resident labor force of 150 peons dwindled to exactly seven, the remainder having drifted away in the midst of the confusion.[5] In order to operate San Juan, José Melchor had to transfer a score of peons from the Tapado-Hermanas complex, which in turn increased the problems at those haciendas, where the *mayordomo* was already complaining that the shepherds and *bacieros* he had were less than proficient.[6] Since the flocks continued to have the highest priority for laborers, the *mayordomo* at times found himself with as few as seven peons to cultivate the crops and work on improvements.[7] The labor crisis at Hermanas lasted from 1824 through 1826, with the *mayordomo* bemoaning both the lack of workers and the incompetence of the few on hand. Even when additional resident laborers became available, they could not always be used in the most efficient manner. In 1827, for instance, crows descended on the cornfields at Tapado in such numbers that for two weeks the *mayordomo* had to assign an overseer and ten peons to act exclusively as scarecrows, and for weeks afterward he had to keep two men on horseback and one on foot in the fields to chase away the birds.[8]

The scarcity of labor hindered both agricultural and ranching operations for the remainder of the decade: wheat harvesting had to be postponed for lack of hands, and inexperienced peons had to be transferred to the flocks to serve as shepherds. On occasion the *mayordomo* of Hermanas was so short-handed that he had no trustworthy subordinates available to send in pursuit of fugitives.[9]

The labor situation gradually improved in the 1830's, although sometimes it was still necessary to shift employees from job to job. One time the *mayordomo* of Hermanas had to use several *vaqueros* to help grind sugar cane and an overseer to drive the oxcart hauling wood for the kettles where the cane juice was being boiled.[10] Undoubtedly these worthies were mortified at having to perform tasks ordinarily handled by lowly peons.

Although the great majority of the Sánchez Navarros' resident employees were either shepherds or agricultural workers, there were also groups of *vaqueros* tending herds of cattle and horses. These men enjoyed a certain status, since they formed the Sánchez Navarros' personal escort whenever needed. Furthermore, they cut a dashing figure. In the words of one observer:

Fancy to yourself a rather light-colored Indian, dressed in a pair of leather unmentionables, without suspenders, buttoning from the knee downwards, which are usually left open in warm weather for comfort, and to exhibit the white drawers underneath; a common cotton shirt, often wanting; a red sash tied tightly around the waist; a pair of sandals on his feet, and enormous iron spurs on heel; with a heavy conical felt hat (that would almost resist a sabre cut) on head, and a long iron-pointed aspen goad in hand, and you have a perfect picture of the ranchero, or rather vachero [*sic*]. Mounted on a spirited pony, with a lasso at his saddle-bow, he is no mean adversary for a single man to encounter. He rides well and fearlessly, and throws the lasso with unerring aim. It is a beautiful sight to see him with his red blanket (worn as a poncho in cold weather) streaming in the wind, his head bent eagerly forward, and lasso whirling in circles high in air, riding down some refractory animal that he seldom fails to catch, at the first throw, by the neck or hind foot, bringing him violently to the ground.[11]

The other specialists on the *latifundio* prior to 1840 were perhaps less colorful but more useful. As the seat of the original landholding, Hermanas had an *obraje*, manned by two weavers. The hacienda also had a carpenter, a stonemason, a blacksmith, an expert in growing sugar cane, and a clerk—as did Soledad.[12] The carpenter and stonemason did quite a bit of traveling, for their services were frequently required at the other *cascos*.

The Sánchez Navarros' recurring problem was not that of securing specialists but rather of getting sufficient unskilled and semiskilled labor to make the expanding *latifundio* operate smoothly. The breakthrough came in 1840, when along with the Marquisate they acquired a number of badly needed shepherds and peons. It was now possible to shift enough workers to staff the undermanned northern division of the consolidated landholding. The clearest picture that emerges regarding the size of the labor force and the variety of job classifications is for the 1840's and 1850's, precisely the period when the *latifundio* was at its height.

Taking the shepherds first, the distribution shown in table 10 obtained. In accordance with traditional practice, one *baciero* normally supervised three shepherds, though the ratio was sometimes two to one, or occasionally even one to one. With regard to supervisory personnel, the *hacienda de ovejas* had its own *mayordomo*, assisted by a *sobresaliente*. The flock at Hermanas, on the other hand, was managed by one of the regular overseers assigned to that hacienda. Again it should be stressed that the extant reports give an incomplete picture, for the number of shepherds at several important haciendas, such as Bonanza, is unavailable.

After 1840, crews of *vaqueros* were maintained at various points on the landholding. At mid-century a *caporal* assisted by a *caudillo* directed from fifteen to eighteen *vaqueros* at Hedionda Grande, while another *caporal* and *caudillo* were in charge of some dozen *vaqueros* at the Punta de Santa Elena.

Turning to the agricultural laborers, the most complete figures are for 1846 but still represent only an estimate (see table 11). Caution is indicated in attempting to generalize on the proportion of peons in each of these resident populations, however. Whereas at Hermanas it seems to have been nearly half, the opposite was the case at San Lorenzo de la Laguna. In 1847 there were an estimated one thousand persons living around that hacienda, yet only some sixty were resident peons, indicating that most of that labor force was seasonal or casual in nature, many inhabitants being renters or sharecroppers.[13]

The most detailed breakdown of a resident work force is for Patos, in 1855. The *administrador* was assisted by the *mayordomo* and a staff of four: a wrangler, a *ranchero* or quartermaster who dispensed the servants' rations, and two overseers to supervise the agricultural workers. In addition there was a *caporal* to supervise the score of *vaqueros* and *bacieros* permanently assigned to Patos. The field hands averaged

TABLE 10
Distribution of Shepherds

	Hacienda de Ovejas Shepherds[a]	Hermanas Shepherds[b]	Patos	San Lorenzo de la Laguna Shepherds	San Juan del Retiro Shepherds	Rancho de San Antonio Goatherds	Shepherds
1847							
April	50		47 *bacieros* & shepherds		23	34	19
October	49	30	50 *bacieros* & shepherds		23	37	6
1848			*bacieros*				
February		32	37		25	31	11
April				15			
May	42	28	36		22	33	14
August	45[c]				22	27	9
1849							
November						36	
December						32	
1850							
January		30		19			
April	21	26	23	23		35	
May	21					34	
June	21	25		18		32	
October	19	21	66	16		41	
1851							
January		20	20	13		30	
February	14	26	19			30	
March	23	28	20			29	
April	16	26	19				
May	17	28	18			42	
June	16	25	16			36	
July	16	24	15			36	
August	16	24	14				

SOURCE: See tables 7 and 8.
[a] These figures include one *mayordomo* and one *sobresaliente*.
[b] These figures include one *ayudante*.
[c] Twenty-three shepherds were transferred to Patos.

TABLE 11
Resident Population, 1846

Hermanas	over 300
Tapado	approximately 100
Las Adjuntas	approximately 500
Estancia de los Flores	approximately 200
Castaño	approximately 350
Castañuela	over 200
Aguanueva	200–300
Buenavista	approximately 100
Rancho de la Encantada	approximately 50
San Juan de la Vaquería	100–200
La Florida	300–500
Patos	800–1,000

SOURCE: Hughes, *Memoir*, p. 25; Davis, *Autobiography*, p. 108; Gregg, *Diary*, I, 270–272, 286, 306–307.

between 100 and 120 in number. Other employees included six men at the grist mill, one at the *obraje*, eight watchmen, three gardeners, one gatekeeper, one water carrier, one soapmaker, one scarecrow, a sacristan, eight household servants, and a blacksmith.[14] The latter was one of the busiest individuals on the premises, since his tasks ranged from repairing muskets and making machetes and sheepshears to fashioning decorative wrought iron bars and gratings. Some of the employees doubled as musicians, for the Sánchez Navarros maintained a band of sorts at the hacienda.[15] By 1866, when the resident population of Patos had increased to some 2,000, the number of field hands was probably around 250. By then, however, the turmoil resulting from the French Intervention had produced a serious labor shortage at some of the other haciendas.[16]

It may be concluded that the total number of full-time resident employees for the entire *latifundio* at its height numbered some 1,000 to 1,500, a figure that includes an unspecified number of miners working at Bonanza.[17] Statements by travelers, such as one made in 1846 that the Sánchez Navarros "own some thirty thousand peons,"[18] can be discounted simply because the logistics involved in feeding and

clothing that many peons and their families would have been insuperable, to say nothing of the enormous amount of capital that would
have been tied up in their debts. This exaggerated image of the Sánchez Navarros' resident labor force may have resulted in part from
the inclusion of those peons on estates that the family had leased out.
A more likely explanation is that travelers simply assumed that all
the laborers they observed were resident employees, whereas in fact
many of them were only seasonal hands.

A partial solution to the chronic manpower shortage was still the
use of seasonal help, especially at lambing, shearing, and harvest
times.[19] Up to 1840 this temporary help came from the settlements
around Monclova and Santa Rosa, often reluctantly, for many persons
were working off small debts incurred during the year.[20] More often
than not, the Sánchez Navarros had to appeal to the local authorities
for assistance in forcing these petty debtors to discharge their obligations.[21] Once the Sánchez Navarros acquired the Marquisate, their
sources of temporary labor increased considerably because they could
now recruit in such places as Saltillo, Parras, and the Laguna region.

The practice of searching the countryside for youths to assist with
the lambing continued while José Melchor directed the *latifundio*.
During the 1820's, however, fewer lambers were used than in the
colonial period, which not only indicates the scarcity of labor but also
reinforces the impression that the Sánchez Navarros' flocks suffered a
decline in that decade.[22] With the easing of the labor situation after
1840, the majority of lambers were resident employees sent out from
the various *cascos*.[23]

Over the years the Sánchez Navarros lessened their dependence on
seasonal help at lambing time, but the need for temporary manpower
at the shearing and harvest seasons increased. As in the colonial period, many of the shearers were from Tlaxcalan settlements. But by the
1840's there was a trend toward professionalism among these shearers.
The Sánchez Navarros' agent in Saltillo negotiated with the leader
of a crew, who agreed to have his men at specified haciendas at designated times and to work for an agreed-upon wage.[24] Nevertheless,
the colonial practice of recruiting groups of relatively unskilled individuals to serve as shearers still persisted, although it was gradually

declining. As an example, in 1845 Tlaxcalans from the Saltillo area balked at going to Patos as shearers because Jacobo offered them only a cash wage but no rations. The *hacendado's* Saltillo agent urged him to begin the shearing with locally available labor, for then the Tlaxcalans would quickly agree to Jacobo's terms; and, once they had arrived at Patos, he could do as he pleased with them.[25]

The most important of the remaining seasonal laborers were those employed at harvest time. Unfortunately, beyond the fact that it was difficult to secure enough of them in the 1820's, and that they continued to be used into the 1860's, little data are available.[26] The only specific reference to the size of these crews is for 1848, when twenty-nine men were cutting wheat and another eight were harvesting barley at Hedionda Grande.[27] The paucity of data is particularly exasperating, for, given the expansion of agriculture, harvesters were not only a perennial requirement but also constituted the majority of all seasonal laborers used on the *latifundio*.

With regard to urban employees, in the 1820's the Sánchez Navarros maintained a staff of some dozen household servants in Monclova. As late as 1825 three of the maids were slaves, but this ended by 1829 when Mexico abolished slavery.[28] The three women probably continued in Apolonia's service, although there was a frequent turnover in maids, for Apolonia was an exacting mistress. She was constantly annoyed by the stupidity of the Monclova serving girls and finally began recruiting them in Saltillo.[29] Besides the maids, there were several *mozos* to perform a variety of menial tasks. Since no particular skill was necessary, these men were usually peons sent in from one of the haciendas, as when José Melchor dispatched a replacement for "the perverse coyote Antonio," who had had the poor judgment to be impudent to Apolonia.[30] The coach crew, consisting of a coachman, an assistant, and a postillion, comprised the rest of the household staff.[31] Other urban employees in the 1820's and 1830's included a storekeeper, clerk, and night watchman in Monclova and a storekeeper in Santa Rosa.[32]

This urban labor force subsequently increased in various areas. As of 1841, the family cotton gin in Monclova, managed by the Sánchez Navarros' cousin Miguel Blanco, employed eleven full-time laborers.[33]

Moreover, by then the Sánchez Navarros also had a hired business agent in Saltillo, and by 1850 they had another in Mexico City.[34] At the capital Carlos maintained his own staff of household servants; the surviving records do not provide a numerical breakdown, but there seem to have been at least half a dozen servants, which would have been in keeping with Carlos's elegant style of living.[35]

Information regarding the salaries of urban employees is fragmentary. In the 1820's, the prevailing wage for maids was between three and four pesos a month, in addition to room and board.[36] The same scale obtained for the *mozos* and coach crew, though the latter were given a peso or two in lieu of rations when they were on the road.[37] Workmen at the Monclova cotton gin made six pesos a month and drew a ration of two pecks of corn per week.[38] The most highly paid of the family's urban employees seems to have been Juan F. de Puyade, their Mexico City agent, who in the 1850's was making fifty-eight pesos a month.[39]

A clearer picture emerges regarding the wages of agricultural laborers. Temporary hands were paid in cash, and sometimes they received rations in addition. Harvesters, for example, were paid by the day, making from three to four reals, but whatever foodstuffs they received were deducted from their wages.[40] In the case of shearers, their pay was on a piecework basis, with not inconsiderable sums of cash being involved; in 1824, fifty shearers at Tapado made a total of 280 pesos, while the totals were 220 pesos in 1830, and 500 in 1833.[41] As we have seen, shearers later began demanding a ration over and above their cash wage, but there is no evidence that they succeeded.[42] Lambers, on the other hand, did receive a ration. Since most of the lambers in the 1820's and 1830's were youths, their pay was a pittance, but they also drew one peck of corn a week.[43] The prevailing wage for day laborers varied between three and four reals, with the workers drawing their pay at the end of the week.[44]

As for the resident peons, their condition elicited sympathetic comment from several travelers. One, writing in 1846, stated: "The poor peon lives in a miserable mud hovel or reed hut (sometimes built of cornstalks, thatched with grass). He is allowed a peck of corn a week for his subsistence, and a small monthly pay for his clothes;

but as all his purchases are made from his master . . ."[45] The situation
had not materially improved twenty years later, for another observer
wrote in 1866: "Poor Mozos! When they have unjust and illiberal
masters, their condition is pitiable indeed. With a legal claim for $5
per month and two pecks of corn per week, they are 'de facto' slaves.
Suppose their wages not paid; if they complain the Patron can order
them & their families to leave the hacienda in twenty four hours.
Without money, food, or clothing, what can they do."[46]

An examination of practices on the *latifundio* reveals that the wage
and ration scale for resident workers was more complex than the
standard five pesos a month and two pecks of corn a week. There
were two basic wage scales for shepherds and goatherds: five pesos a
month and two pecks a week for experienced men and three pesos
and one peck for novices.[47] Yet there were numerous exceptions; one
man might receive three pesos and two pecks, another five pesos and
one and one-half pecks, while yet another got five pesos and two and
one-half pecks. There is one instance of two men being hired as
shepherds at eight pesos a month, but they received no ration.[48] In
contrast to the colonial epoch, *bacieros* and shepherds also received a
flour ration of six pecks a month when they were on the range.[49]
Furthermore, employees were permitted to slaughter a certain number
of sheep a month from their flocks as part of their rations: a *mayordomo* was allowed six sheep, a *sobresaliente* five, and the rest of the
hands averaged two animals per man.[50] Any additional flour, sheep,
or other foodstuffs were charged to the individual's account at the
hacienda store.[51]

Rations were provided under a different system for the trail crews
driving flocks to market. There is only one instance of a crew having
been issued supplies; in 1851 the foreman of a drive received twenty-
five pounds of flour.[52] The usual procedure was to provide cash in
lieu of rations; the trail boss received at Patos anywhere from thirty
to forty-four pesos, depending on the size of the crew. For the drive
to Mexico City the trail boss was given ten pesos; *bacieros*, four pesos;
and shepherds, two.[53] At the capital the Sánchez Navarros' business
agent not only provided funds for the return trip but also advanced
spending money so the crew could sample the delights of the metrop-

olis. Normally each *baciero* got three pesos on which to subsist in the capital and nine for the journey back to Coahuila. In addition, he received fifteen pesos in pocket money. For shepherds the amounts were two, six, and ten pesos respectively. The cash advances were reported to the *administrador* at Patos, who ensured that they were duly entered on each man's account.[54]

Wage scales for *vaqueros* were similar to those for the shepherds. The *vaquero*'s salary was five pesos a month and two pecks of corn per week, though here again there were numerous exceptions, presumably based on experience, with some of the men receiving only one and one-half pecks, and a few being paid only four pesos. The weekly ration for a *caporal* varied between five and six pecks, while that for his assistant, the *caudillo*, was three. Furthermore, on the first day of each month a steer was slaughtered for each crew of *vaqueros*.[55] Additional foodstuffs were of course available on credit.[56] Like the shepherds, *vaqueros* received cash instead of rations while on cattle drives. The crews, composed of a *caporal* and four or five *vaqueros*, were given a total of thirty-five pesos for subsistence on each drive.[57] While in Mexico City the *caporal* received an advance of twenty pesos, plus five pesos for rations on the trip home, on the basis of twenty days at two reals a day. Each *vaquero* received fifteen pesos on account and five pesos for rations.[58] Compared with shepherds, *vaqueros* were somewhat better off in regard to salary, but their ration was considerably less.

Both groups, however, generally fared better than did the ordinary peon. There is one instance of a peon earning seven pesos a month plus two pecks a week, and another case of a man making five pesos a month, but the usual range was four pesos and one and one-half pecks or less. Some peons made three pesos and one peck, others two pesos and either one or two pecks. The most extreme case was that of a scarecrow, whose monthly wage was two reals, plus one peck a week.[59] Although this was an appallingly low wage, it should be kept in mind that salaries were really irrelevant, since laborers rarely saw the pesos they were theoretically earning. In a few instances a peon received a peso for rations when he was on the road performing some mission, such as delivering a letter.[60] As with the other classes of resident employees, if peons desired food over and above their ration it was charged to their account. The single exception to this procedure occurred in 1834 at Tapado, when the *mayordomo* distributed some overripe watermelons free to the workers.[61] Every other item was entered on the books. To cite an example, from time to time a steer was slaughtered, and the value of the beef that each peon received was carefully recorded.[62] Sometimes it was not even necessary to slaughter a steer, as is indicated by a "List of the meat from an ox that died in the fields and was distributed to the servants."[63]

There were also some miscellaneous employees. One was the man who collected the rent from the Sánchez Navarros' tenants who operated *vinaterías*. His salary was one-third of all the liquor he collected; in 1826 its market value was 101 pesos, making his earnings slightly less than 3 pesos a month.[64] Perhaps the most unlikely of all the family's employees was a schoolteacher, hired in 1851 at the Punta de Santa Elena. His wages were 4 pesos a month and one and one-half pecks of corn a week, fully the equivalent of what an able-bodied peon made.[65]

Quite obviously a nominal wage of three, four, or five pesos a month did not go very far in terms of purchasing power, nor was it intended to, since each *casco* had its *tienda de raya*. As was the case with wages, the prices charged at hacienda stores were largely meaningless because they were set by the *hacendado*, who charged whatever he pleased. In 1828, for instance, the clerk at Soledad pointed out to José Melchor that the corn, beans, and chile he had been supplying to the peons at that store had no price, and he asked what amounts to enter on the books.[66] José Melchor's instructions have not survived, but table 12 shows representative examples of purchasing power.

Further reducing the purchasing power of the nominal wage was the practice of recording the *fallas*, or days of work missed by each laborer, and making the appropriate deductions from his salary.[67] Also, whenever a man lost an implement, an item of equipment, or an animal, its value was charged to his account. One man, who in May, 1851, lost a mule and was charged thirty pesos for it, had in effect just spent most of his next year's salary.[68] This practice applied not

TABLE 12
Peons' Purchasing Power

	Pesos	Reals
A peon earning 3 pesos in 1847 could buy:		
1 machete	2	
1 goat	1	4
	3	4
Someone whose wage was 5 pesos in 1862 could afford:		
1 pound of chocolate		4
1 yard of coarse frieze		2
1 bottle of white wine		3
1 *almud* (6.88 dry quarts) of beans		3
1 *fanega* (2.58 bushels) of corn	3	4
	5	2
In 1863 a wage of 4 pesos purchased:		
1 pair of buckskin shoes	1	
1 straw sombrero	1	4
1 bunch of chile		6
1 yard of muslin		3
1 cheap *rebozo*		6
	4	3

SOURCE: SNP (3617), (2225), (2887).

only to peons but also to the supervisory personnel; in 1850 the *mayordomo* of the *hacienda de ovejas* had also been charged for a mule, which he had traded to a passing American for a double-barrelled shotgun.[69]

The net result was indebtedness, in most instances a hopeless indebtedness. This situation prevailed despite attempts by the Coahuilan legislature, operating under the theory that there existed an oral contract between employer and employee, to ameliorate the lot of the peons. A law passed in 1828 carefully specified the conditions under which debts could be incurred, and it prohibited debts from exceeding the yearly earnings of servants except in the case of illness. The following year another law forbade keeping one account for two or more peons even though they might be father and son. Employers were also required to withhold a third of each worker's wage in order to liquidate the latter's indebtedness, except in the event of illness or other emergency. Furthermore, peons were to be charged only the fair market price for foodstuffs supplied to them on account.[70] Laudable as this legislation may have been, the evidence clearly shows its utter futility.

The simple fact that the *hacendado* kept the books constituted the insuperable obstacle to any peon working his way out of debt. True, each servant was periodically shown his account, and a notation was entered that it had been "adjusted to his entire satisfaction."[71] But since the illiterate peon had to accept his master's word as to what was owed, this traditional practice of a file of peons humbly shuffling hat in hand through the *tienda de raya* as the clerk read off their indebtedness was an empty ritual.

As was the practice elsewhere in Mexico, the only way a peon legally left the Sánchez Navarros' service was by being allowed to find another master, in which case the new employer reimbursed the Sánchez Navarros for the man's indebtedness. That sum became the initial entry in the peon's new account.[72] Of course, the procedure operated in reverse when the Sánchez Navarros hired a worker from another hacienda. A peon might improve his situation by finding a more agreeable master, but his debts accompanied him wherever he went.

Despite the good intentions of the Coahuilan legislature, these debts not infrequently exceeded a worker's annual salary. It will be remembered that the majority of peons earned from 3 to 5 pesos a month, or from 36 to 72 pesos a year. Yet there are instances of peons owing amounts ranging from 54 to 137 pesos.[73] There seems to have been a policy, however, of maintaining the peons' debts at something under 50 pesos whenever possible. From a business point of view this made good sense, for the worker was still securely bound to the land, yet the Sánchez Navarros did not have an inordinate amount of capital invested in him. Moreover, in 1856 the Sánchez Navarros, along with other *hacendados*, received a scare when a Liberal national government announced a policy of having the authorities intervene to regulate the oral contracts and the accounts affecting peons. Jacobo even cautioned the *administrador* at Patos to keep the servants' indebtedness down until the government's policy was clarified.[74]

Jacobo's fears proved groundless, for, as had so often happened, the new regime's good intentions had little practical effect on the debt peonage system. The aggregate book value of the workers' indebtedness to the Sánchez Navarros remained a substantial sum. In 1860, debts for the resident peons at Bonanza totaled 577 pesos and by 1861 had ascended to 833. That same year the workers at Hermanas and Soledad owed 7,164 pesos.[75] Figures for Patos are not available, but, since that hacienda had by far the largest resident population on the *latifundio*, the total indebtedness probably exceeded that of all the other *cascos* combined.

As in the colonial period, a sizeable part of the workers' indebtedness resulted from religious fees. The *cuadrante*, the ledger recording what peons owed for sacramental fees, continued in use in the 1820's and 1830's, but by the middle of the century a more efficient bookkeeping system had been worked out.[76] Whenever a baptism, marriage, burial, or memorial mass was required, the interested peon approached the *administrador*, who issued him a voucher good for the particular fees involved. The peon presented the voucher to the local priest, who then performed the ceremony. Periodically, the priest delivered batches of these vouchers to the *administrador*, who reimbursed the cleric and entered the sums on each peon's account.[77]

Religion remained a vital part of the peonage system not only because of the debts incurred but also because of the powerful moral influence of the priest in maintaining a docile labor force. Some fifty years later, in fact, the author of a handbook for hacienda managers stressed the benefits of a close alliance between the *administrador* and the resident priest: the chapel bell could be used to regulate the lives of the peons, conditioned to unquestioning obedience, and from his pulpit the priest could influence them in ways not available to the *administrador*.[78] Patos was a prime example of such an alliance. For the decade prior to 1851 the resident priest was one of the Sánchez Navarros' relatives, Juan E. Beráin, a brother of Apolonia.[79] Ill health forced Beráin's retirement, but it may be speculated that his successors rarely placed the interests of their parishioners above those of the Sánchez Navarro family.

Though the religious system unquestionably operated to the Sánchez Navarros' advantage, there is considerable evidence that at the same time they were genuinely concerned about the spiritual welfare of their employees. In the 1820's, religious facilities on the *latifundio* were limited. Tapado was the only *casco* with a usable chapel, and even Tapado lacked a resident priest. Arrangements were therefore made for the curate of Monclova periodically to visit Tapado to say mass and hear confessions. So that none of the workers missed this opportunity, even the shepherds were brought in from the *hacienda de ovejas* in shifts.[80] José Melchor's concern with religion—and with improving his properties—was manifested in 1833 when he petitioned the bishop for permission to construct chapels at Soledad, Hermanas, and San Juan de Sabinas. The *hacendado* also requested that in the meantime the bishop allow mass and the other sacraments to be performed in the living rooms of the main houses at these *cascos*. The requests were granted, and the bishop also authorized the interment of peons at the cemeteries of these haciendas so that burial parties would not be exposed to Indian attacks on the roads.[81]

The acquisition of the Marquisate brought with it impressive chapels at Rosario and Patos, but it was still necessary on occasion to dispatch a priest to the outlying sections of the landholding to say mass.[82] Patos, which by 1849 ranked as a vice-parish under the curate of the town of Parras, was the focal point of religious activity on the landholding.[83] Ordinarily the workday ended with the priest leading the faithful in evening prayers, but this routine was varied several times a year by major celebrations, among them Holy Week, which served to brighten the lives of the peons.[84]

The solace of religion was particularly welcome whenever epidemics struck the residents of the *latifundio*, for with medical facilities virtually nonexistent the only recourse was prayer. There occurred a virulent epidemic of measles in 1825, which ravaged not only Coahuila but also Monterrey and even cities as distant as San Luis Potosí.[85] Throughout the summer and fall the *mayordomo* of Hermanas dolefully reported the progressive incapacitation of his already inadequate labor force; in November he wrote that within the space of three days the hacienda carpenter and two of his best peons had perished from measles.[86] Another epidemic struck Hermanas in the fall of 1829. The disease is not specified, but the *mayordomo* lamented that most of his people were ill.[87] Four years later the deadly wave of cholera that swept over Mexico took its toll on the *latifundio*. As we have seen, José Melchor nearly died of the disease, but at that he was more fortunate than many of his employees. An indication of the inroads that cholera made on the labor force is a report that in a single week an overseer and five peons had died at the Hacienda de Nacimiento and two more peons at Soledad.[88] The situation seems to have improved in subsequent years, for the only other reference to epidemics is in 1851, when many of the inhabitants of Patos were ill from an unspecified malady.[89]

Besides burying the casualties of epidemics, the priests officiated at the last rites of those who died by violence. The overwhelming majority of these were shepherds and peons slain by Indians, but sometimes the deceased had been the victim of a crime.

The incidents of crime that occurred among the resident employees were generally affairs of passion, in which heated words quickly resulted in the drawing of knives and machetes. An especially trouble-prone individual was one Leocadio Tavares, who in 1825 was an overseer at Tapado. In an argument with a subordinate, he made his point by slashing the latter on the wrist. The local justice of the peace handled the matter routinely, ruling that Tavares had acted in self-defense. A few months later, however, the magistrate in Monclova reopened the case, found Tavares guilty, and imposed a staggering fine of two hundred pesos. When Tavares was unable to pay, he was jailed. At this point the Sánchez Navarros, who needed Tavares's services, petitioned the governor for the prisoner's release on the ground that the magistrate had merely acted out of greed for the fees he could collect.[90] Their intervention was evidently successful, for we next hear of Tavares in 1826, again in connection with a brawl. This time he became involved in a violent argument with the *sobresaliente* at Hermanas over the latter's negligence in performing his duties. The dispute was settled with knives, and Tavares came out decidedly the loser, suffering critical stab wounds.[91] Quarrels of this type occasionally resulted in a death, but the usual outcome was a couple of wounded laborers, as when a *baciero* and a shepherd slashed each other repeatedly in an argument over a cigarette.[92]

Most crimes among the inhabitants of the *latifundio* were dealt with internally, for the important *cascos* had a resident police delegate. Though responsible to their administrative superiors, these agents also took orders from the Sánchez Navarros. In 1847, for example, the lieutenant governor of Coahuila wrote to his cousin Jacobo in this connection. On Jacobo's orders the agent at Patos had arrested three suspicious-looking individuals, remitting two of them to Saltillo and incarcerating the third. The lieutenant governor informed Jacobo that the two in Saltillo were indeed fugitives from justice but that their companion was innocent. He therefore requested that the *hacendado* notify the police delegate to set the man free.[93]

These police officials spent much of their time dealing with fugitives, though the great majority of peons stoically accepted their lot in life. Aside from their indebtedness, an intangible but powerful factor keeping them bound to the *latifundio* was their feeling for the land.[94] Despite the docility of the labor force as a whole, absenteeism and desertion remained an insoluble problem. Many peons worked for short, irregular periods during a month even knowing their wages would be reduced accordingly; since they were already hopelessly in debt it really did not matter.

Manuel Castellano, the *mayordomo* of Hermanas and Tapado, complained repeatedly to José Melchor that such-and-such peons "have either deserted or are hiding from me."[95] In most cases the delinquent workers had merely taken a few days off—whether because of illness or accident, overindulgence in fiery *mescal*, or simple malingering— and they eventually returned to work. Yet this chronic absenteeism seriously impaired the efficient operation of the *latifundio*, for it was by no means uncommon for a peon to miss a good part of the month.[96] As a concrete example, the rate of absenteeism at Patos from August 1 through December 30, 1855, approached 20 percent.[97]

Without attempting to generalize from limited data, it seems clear

that chronic absenteeism was one of the major problems confronting
the administrative personnel. This in turn helps to explain—but not
to justify—the harsh measures used to control the labor force. Workers
and their families had to secure permission to leave a *casco* for any
reason. Moreover, at each of the *cascos* there was a jail of sorts,
usually a stoutly built room, for holding recalcitrant peons. In addition, the *cascos* were well supplied with stocks, fetters, and irons.[98]

Corporal punishment was an accepted part of hacienda life. In fact,
it had legal sanction. The same legislature that in 1828–1829 had
tried to ameliorate debt peonage had prohibited whipping as a means
of disciplining peons but had empowered *hacendados*, *administradores*, or *mayordomos* to punish delinquent peons by imprisoning
them for a period of up to four days, or putting them in shackles
for an equal period of time. If these measures proved insufficient,
the employer could seek assistance from the nearest magistrate, who
could punish the unruly peon with shackles "or other correctional
punishment to make him do his duty."[99]

The degree to which corporal punishment was employed depended
on the *mayordomo* involved. In a class by himself, as far as brutality
went, was Atanacio Muñoz, *mayordomo* of Soledad in 1828. The
Muñoz affair is interesting not merely as an instance of an overseer
mistreating his peons, but because it sheds light on the relations between *hacendados* and local officialdom. The *alcalde* of Santa Rosa in
1828 was Melitón Castellano, brother of the *mayordomo* of Hermanas
and a staunch partisan of José Melchor. In January, Castellano wrote
to the *hacendado* that three peons from Soledad had come to Santa
Rosa to lodge complaints against Muñoz for beatings he had given
them. Castellano assured José Melchor that he would put an end to
this abuse so that the peons would remain on the hacienda where they
belonged.[100] Castellano spoke repeatedly with the *mayordomo*, urging
him to moderate his punishments, but to no avail. Since whipping was
illegal, Muñoz used a club, which he wielded with enthusiasm. By
March there were four more accusations, and José Melchor was informed that Muñoz was frightening away the peons at Soledad because
"he doesn't treat them like a Christian." The *hacendado* was urged to
write to Muñoz.[101]

Whether José Melchor reprimanded the *mayordomo* is not known, but in any case the situation worsened, for, in April, Castellano had to write an apologetic letter to José Melchor. He pointed out that from the time he had taken office he had been receiving complaints from the peons at Soledad that the *mayordomo* was beating them unmercifully. For some time Castellano had simply ignored the workers' pleas, but there had recently occurred an incident that had forced him to act.

The *mayordomo* had become irritated with a peon for using profanity in his presence, and Muñoz had manifested his displeasure by clubbing the hapless servant almost to death. Several weeks later, when the peon had recovered sufficiently, he had hobbled to Santa Rosa to swear out a complaint and seek compensation. As luck would have it, one of José Melchor's political enemies was passing the time of day with the *alcalde* Castellano when the peon entered the office and described the incident. Castellano found himself in the awkward position of having to take some kind of action in the matter. He decided to send for the *mayordomo*, who readily admitted having administered what he felt was a richly deserved beating. Castellano fined Muñoz a token six pesos, whereupon the case was closed. Castellano ended his letter by reiterating that, had it not been for the presence of José Melchor's enemy, he would have ignored this complaint as he had the previous ones, but that he had to be careful, for his own political foes wanted to prove that Castellano was subservient to José Melchor.[102]

There should have been little doubt in anyone's mind on that score. While he had been ignoring the plight of the peons at Soledad, Castellano had been zealously protecting the workers at the Hacienda de Nacimiento, whose owner chanced to be one of José Melchor's principal adversaries—José Antonio Quirós, the curate of Santa Rosa. José Melchor was then engaged in the bitter legal struggle with Quirós for possession of the hacienda, and Castellano was using his official position to harass the curate at every opportunity. Even though a priest, Quirós had no qualms about mistreating his own peons, in this respect rivaling even the *mayordomo* of Soledad. Ostensibly outraged by this situation, Castellano had gone to Nacimiento and had personally burned the stocks. A few weeks later Castellano gleefully reported to José Melchor that, because of the curate's brutality, every peon at Nacimiento had fled.[103] It is doubtful whether Castellano was co-operating with Quirós in tracking them down. As for the infamous Muñoz, he was soon replaced as *mayordomo* of Soledad, presumably not because of his treatment of the peons but because his continued presence was becoming a political liability for José Melchor.

It is hardly surprising that peons would flee from haciendas operated by the likes of Quirós and Muñoz. These men serve to illustrate one of the ironies of the labor system: when carried to extremes, the very measures designed to keep the work force under control had precisely the opposite effect. Yet cruelty on the part of the administrative personnel was by no means the only reason for desertion. Indian war parties provided a powerful incentive, especially for the isolated and defenseless shepherds, who could expect an agonizing and lingering death if captured. In addition, some of the peons who deserted did so in the hope of escaping their debts and being able to make a fresh start elsewhere. Occasionally desertion was the direct result of some romantic attachment. Deserters were of both sexes, all ages, varying degrees of physical fitness; the jobs they abandoned were varied as well.

Shepherds made up a good proportion of the fugitives; of the 101 cases of desertion for which documentation exists, shepherds are mentioned specifically in 37, and in all likelihood some of the other fugitives were also shepherds. The standard pattern was for a man simply to abandon his flock and strike out across the range. The overseers in charge of each major flock could count on losing several men in this way each month.[104] Although the herders tended to flee alone or in pairs, on rare occasions a man managed to escape with his entire family, usually just before he was due to return to his post at the flocks.[105] Trail crews also deserted. On one occasion both of the shepherds assigned to a flock about to depart for Mexico City deserted, leaving only the *baciero*; on another, the temptations of the capital proved irresistible to the *baciero* and one of the shepherds from a recently delivered flock, and they absconded.[106] One wonders, in fact, why more of them did not drop from sight in the teeming metropolis rather than return to Coahuila.

Field hands constituted a sizeable number of the fugitives.[107] Though their job was not so hazardous as that of the shepherds, they were subject to stricter discipline, being more closely supervised by the overseers. Among the more notable cases of desertion was that of a one-armed peon who simply abandoned the oxcart he was driving to Hermanas; five of the six oxen perished in their traces, so the *mayordomo* promptly added eighteen pesos to the fugitive's account.[108] Another peon fled because he had lost a yoke of oxen for which he was responsible.[109] On at least one occasion desertion resulted from collusion between servants; in 1824 the weaver at Hermanas, who doubled as the hacienda jailer, helped an elderly shepherd to escape. The repercussions of this incident are not known, but they must have been unpleasant, for the weaver himself subsequently deserted.[110] Neither age nor physical condition was a deterrent, as evidenced by an elderly cripple who hobbled away from Hermanas in 1833.[111] A particular problem for the administrative personnel was the habitual deserter: for example, the *mayordomo* of Tapado in 1825 reported in disgust that "Simón del Castillo has run away again; where, I don't know."[112]

The women also proved fleet of foot. Besides those who accompanied their husbands in flight, others deserted because of more casual romantic liaisons. A case in point was the wife of one Francisco Alvarez, a peon at Tapado in 1824. She ran off with a certain Juan José Zamora, but the latter evidently did not fulfill her expectations, for she soon returned and gave herself up.[113] Then there was Josefa Martínez, a maid of Apolonia, who one night in 1828 slipped away from the Sánchez Navarros' home in Monclova. As Apolonia indignantly described the incident to José Melchor: "Good riddance! At least she didn't bring into the house at an indecent hour the pair of scoundrels who I've learned came to pick her up."[114]

Though desertion was prevalent, the fugitives ran a considerable risk, at least technically. The 1829 Coahuilan statute on peonage provided that servants who fled owing money or because they had lost property entrusted to them would be treated as thieves.[115] It is hardly necessary to mention that the authorities generally cooperated in tracking down fugitives.[116]

There existed a set procedure, one involving a certain amount of inconvenience and expense on the employer's part. The latter could, upon payment of a three-peso fee, obtain from the nearest *alcalde* a document known as an *exhorto*, a type of warrant not unlike that employed in connection with runaway slaves in the United States.[117] The following is an example of an *exhorto*:

June 20, 1828   Santa Rosa
Melitón Castellano, sole constitutional *Alcalde* of this Valley and its jurisdiction:
To you the constitutional *Alcaldes* and other gentlemen entrusted with the administration of justice where this my writ should be presented and its execution requested I make known [that]: on June 3, from the Hacienda de Soledad of this jurisdiction, [there] fled María Josefa Robles, wife of Martín Rodríguez, accompanied by two sons of hers—Gregorio Valle and Domingo, both servants at Soledad and having a monetary debt; and having received a report that they were headed for the Town of Candela, and that Manuel Tabares is guiding them—on behalf of the Executive Power of the State I exhort and require you, and on mine I entreat, pray, and request, that upon presentation of this you carry it out by having the four above named searched for. If they are apprehended, deliver them to the bearer.

Melitón Castellano
witness   Juan Martínez
witness   Pedro Vidaurri[118]

Even while the *exhorto* was being prepared, the employer was of course trying to get a lead as to the fugitive's probable destination. In many cases this presented little difficulty. Deserters rarely fled west or north because of the ever-present menace of Indians around the Bolsón de Mapimí and along the Río Grande. Instead, the runaways generally tried to reach sanctuary in Nuevo León or else in Saltillo, from where they could make their way into the interior of the country. But in the inbred communities and rural settlements of northern Mexico any stranger was conspicuous, and the local authorities acted on the presumption that if he were shabbily dressed he must be a fugitive. Unless he had a convincing explanation for his presence, the stranger might well find himself detained on suspicion. For this reason it was unnecessary to include a detailed physical description in the *exhorto*. Cooperation by the authorities greatly facilitated the functioning of the traditional grapevine that existed among *hacendados*.

The process of finding fugitives and bringing them back depended not so much on officialdom as on agents of the aggrieved *hacendado*. If a pursuit could be mounted quickly enough, the deserter was simply captured, taken back to the *casco*, and that was that. On the other hand, if the peon had gotten a good start, the *hacendado* gave the *exhorto* to one or two of his overseers, ensured that they were well supplied with fetters, and sent them on their way.

Sometimes a servant did succeed in making good his escape. For example, when her maid deserted, the furious Apolonia immediately secured an *exhorto* and sent two other servants pounding down the Saltillo road after the maid and her disreputable companions. Only then did Apolonia notify José Melchor, who happened to be in Saltillo, to spread the alarm in that city. Apolonia made it emphatically clear that what she wanted was not the maid, but the thirty-three pesos the latter owed her, besides the three pesos the *exhorto* had cost. Nevertheless, after a few days Apolonia's agents returned empty-handed.[119] In another case, a peon from Tapado eluded pursuit for seven years before he made the mistake of returning to visit his wife one night and was seized.[120] A few runaway peons, deciding that since they were likely to be judged as thieves anyway they might as well become thieves, either stole livestock singlehandedly or joined one of the bands of rustlers operating in Coahuila.[121]

Despite the instances of servants remaining at large, most of the time man-hunting expeditions were successful. Some of the overseers spent a great deal of their time hunting fugitives; no sooner had they returned with one group of prisoners than they were dispatched on a new mission.[122] Occasionally the person whom they escorted back to the *casco* was not a fugitive at all, but rather a peon who had been given permission to seek a new master but had been unsuccessful;

some solicitous local official had jailed the man to forestall any notions of desertion and had notified the Sánchez Navarros to send someone for him.[123]

In the matter of desertion, one gets the impression that in many instances there was about it an underlying element resembling sportsmanship. Peons were expected to desert, and they in turn expected eventually to be caught; whatever interlude of freedom they enjoyed provided a welcome change from the monotony of their existence. Locating a fugitive was the important thing. Once this had been accomplished, bringing him back to the *latifundio* was a routine task that could be performed by whoever happened to be available, for the vast majority of fugitives offered no resistance whatsoever.

A certain Dionisio Beltrán, for instance, deserted in 1824 and made his way to Saltillo, where a muleteer from Monclova recognized him and informed the Sánchez Navarros. Beltrán managed to leave the city in time to avoid apprehension and for the next six years remained at liberty. Through the *hacendados'* informal intelligence network, however, he was eventually traced in 1830 to the mining town of Nieves, in Zacatecas. The same muleteer, who was going to Zacatecas anyway, offered to stop by Nieves on his return trip and bring the fugitive back. Apolonia advised José Melchor of this so he could provide the muleteer with the requisite documents—an *exhorto* and a copy of the fugitive's account. Thus the muleteer could return either with the peon or with the money owed, in the event the fugitive's present employer wished to keep him.[124]

The fate of a recaptured deserter varied. At one extreme, a man might escape punishment altogether, as happened to an overseer, one Quintero, who deserted in 1824. Once Quintero had been apprehended, the *mayordomo* of Tapado sent him to face José Melchor's wrath but took advantage of the occasion to have Quintero escort Carlos and Jacobo, then mere boys, to Monclova—hardly the course one would expect with regard to a recaptured fugitive.[125] Most escapees were less fortunate. The severity of their punishment was in proportion to the inconvenience they had caused. At the very least a deserter could count on being jailed for several days at the *casco*. If his offense had been more serious, such as that of the oxcart driver whose animals had been left to perish, he would not only be imprisoned but also be put in irons. If the deserter had really been bothersome, as in the case of the peon who had remained at large for seven years before being taken while visiting his wife, he was not only imprisoned in irons but also had to spend the days working in the fields in shackles.[126]

With the growth of the *latifundio* and the attendant increase in the number of workers, the latter tended to become mere ciphers. As the element of paternalism declined, treatment of deserters became harsher. But in part this development resulted from the personality of Quirino Benavente, *administrador* of the landholding from the early 1840's until 1852. Benavente was a man of violent temper who had no patience with peons who were derelict in their duty. He firmly believed in physical punishment regardless of the strictures of the law.[127]

Thus, despite the various legal attempts to ameliorate debt servitude, in practice the lot of the labor force continued to depend not on the law but on the employer. For example, in 1864 an *hacendado* wrote to the *administrador* at Patos thanking him for returning two deserters. With reference to one of the peons he wrote, "If you want me to send him back to work for you I will, but what I'd like for us to do is to have him soundly thrashed and put in shackles until he rots, since what he owes you is lost in any case, the same as the 50 pesos he owes me here."[128] Laws to protect peons continued to appear from time to time. As late as 1868, a Liberal regime in Coahuila enacted legislation that in many respects was depressingly similar to that passed by the Liberals back in 1828.[129] But the peon's life remained the same as it had been in the colonial period: miserable.

10. *Latifundio* Production

After independence the Sánchez Navarros began the arduous task of reestablishing the traditional markets for their sheep and wool. In 1822 the outlook was bleak. Not only had the colonial pattern of commerce between Coahuila and central Mexico been shattered, but also business activity in Coahuila itself was in the doldrums, reflecting the political uncertainty of the day. Also, commerce suffered from the continuation of archaic colonial restrictions, such as the *alcabala*, internal customs houses, and a variety of official forms that had to be filled out with great care to avoid delays, fines, or even the confiscation of merchandise.[1]

Having lost a national market for sheep, the best José Melchor could do was concentrate on regional outlets, and even here prospects were disheartening. In 1823 there was a marked reluctance on the part of Saltillo buyers to pay more than a ruinous twelve reals a head for prime sheep, and then on the condition that delivery be made at Saltillo. José Melchor's agent indignantly refused to entertain such a contemptible offer.[2] Nor did José Melchor himself have much luck in finding a buyer farther afield; in 1824 he offered three to four thousand sheep at twenty reals to a Durango businessman. The latter replied that he well understood José Melchor's asking a high price in order to recoup recent losses from Indian depredations, but he politely refused the offer, pointing out that sheep were currently selling for less than twenty reals in Mexico City.[3] José Melchor grudgingly resigned himself to the fact that Saltillo remained the only market. He finally closed a deal, in 1825, for five hundred sheep at sixteen reals. The Saltillo buyer even paid the one thousand pesos in advance, but, when his agent went to the *latifundio* to receive the flock, the animals were so scrawny that he wanted no part of them; the money had to be returned.[4]

After this series of rebuffs, business picked up a bit in 1826. Though he sold a trifling flock of 260 animals to an outsider, José Melchor had to fall back on his family connections; his main dealings were once again with José María and Román de Letona, his cousins in Saltillo who had been buying Sánchez Navarro mutton and wool in the years preceding independence. The *hacendado* sold José María 2,000 sheep at 16 reals, with delivery to be made at the *latifundio*. Half the purchase price was paid on delivery, the remainder when Letona had been able to dispose of the animals. José María's family loyalty exceeded his business acumen, for months later he still had hundreds of the sheep on his hands, and even trying to dispose of them at 12 reals he could find no takers.[5]

Though Saltillo remained José Melchor's primary market, by 1826 the sheep trade in northern Mexico was showing signs of reviving, and he quickly undertook to establish another outlet, in San Luis Potosí. The *hacendado*'s efforts were partially successful. A buyer in San Luis decided to take four thousand sheep at fourteen reals as a speculation; much of northern Mexico was suffering from drought, and he hoped to resell the sheep immediately in Mexico City in case northern *hacendados* had to begin dumping their flocks and consequently glutting the market in the capital.[6] Another of José Melchor's proposals—that of supplying part of the sheep for the *abasto* in San Luis Potosí—failed. The mercantile house he approached rejected his price in view of the fact that there were already thousands of sheep on hand awaiting slaughter.[7] Nevertheless, José Melchor's perseverence in trying to penetrate the San Luis market paid off on another occasion, for at the end of 1826 he transacted a rather lucrative bit of business with a buyer in that city. Referring to the two- and three-year-old sheep he had at Tapado, José Melchor mentioned that he was retailing them at twenty-four reals and those he sold by the flock brought twenty, but, because this buyer was a friend, the *hacendado* was prepared to sell him the four thousand head he had requested at only eighteen reals, on the condition that delivery be made at the *latifundio*.[8] This nine-thousand-peso transaction was at least faintly reminiscent of the booming sheep trade during the first decade of the century.

Within Coahuila itself business activity was also quickening. The same Saltillo buyer who in 1825 had rejected José Melchor's sheep was purchasing flocks regularly three years later. True, the flocks were small—two of six hundred head each and one of five hundred—but at 16 reals they produced 3,400 pesos of badly needed income.[9] Nor was this all; another Saltillo merchant also purchased a flock of five hundred, presumably at the same price.[10] Moreover, an interesting situation was developing at the other end of the state, at the Presidio de Río Grande, whose commander, Domingo de Ugartechea, was a friend and political ally of José Melchor. Ugartechea complained that Río Grande was without a doubt the dreariest place imaginable, but the drabness of his surroundings in no way dulled the officer's eye for business. He wrote to José Melchor that foodstuffs, especially meat, were very scarce, and, if the *hacendado* were agreeable, Ugartechea would buy small flocks from him to slaughter at Río Grande, adding disarmingly that "one has to supplement one's salary."[11] José Melchor began supplying flocks of fifty animals at 16 reals.[12] Obviously the principal benefit to the *hacendado* was in terms not of income but of good will; among other things, Ugartechea kept a sharp eye out for stolen Sánchez Navarro livestock.

Over the next few years José Melchor managed to sell greater numbers of sheep in Coahuila, but there was no corresponding rise in the price per animal, a situation due to an unsteady market and also to the inferior quality of the *hacendado*'s product. In 1830, for example, out of a flock of 300 sold to a merchant in Santa Rosa, 184 were rejected as unfit.[13] Still, under the circumstances, José Melchor did rather well that year, for he developed yet another outlet, at Parras. One merchant offered sixteen reals a head for a flock of 200 animals, specifying that if he could have them on credit for three months, he was prepared to purchase another 200 head.[14]

This was a minor transaction compared with José Melchor's main sale at Parras in 1830, to the ubiquitous James Grant, the sometime *administrador* of the Marquisate of Aguayo. The ambitious Scotsman was well established in the Parras area, and, having decided to go into business for himself, the sheep trade was among the ventures that caught his fancy. José Melchor sold Grant, with whom he was on excellent terms, 5,310 three-year-olds at 14 reals, with Grant incurring the risks of delivery. The transaction proved mutually satisfactory: José Melchor made 9,292 pesos, and Grant was eager to purchase a similar flock in 1831.[15]

Though Grant's price was less than José Melchor would have liked, this market nevertheless proved to be something of a godsend, for the *hacendado* suffered a serious setback in San Luis Potosí in 1830. The overabundance of sheep in that city precluded the shipment of a sizeable flock—only 1,450 head were sent. Furthermore, José Melchor's agent experienced considerable difficulty in disposing of them. He had to settle for a paltry 12 reals, which produced only 2,300 pesos.[16]

Despite such vicissitudes, José Melchor retained a share of the regional markets in northern Mexico. And, although the evidence is inconclusive, it is likely that on his last trip to Mexico City in 1835 the *hacendado* negotiated a contract with one of the metropolitan mercantile houses to supply sheep for the *abasto*; in December, 1836, a flock of Sánchez Navarro sheep was driven from Monclova via the city of San Miguel Allende to the capital.[17] After a lapse of a quarter century, the family had recaptured a portion of the lucrative national market.

The family's representative in the capital was Carlos, who in 1836 was only twenty years old and still in law school but who already displayed the business ability that would culminate in the purchase of the Marquisate four years later. The extent to which the Sánchez Navarros participated in the Mexico City market prior to 1840 remains obscure, but after acquiring the Marquisate they ranked among the leading suppliers of sheep for the *abasto*. In addition, they enjoyed a share of the market in San Miguel Allende.[18] At times, however, because of Indian depredations and drought, Jacobo had to purchase locally a flock or two of some fifteen hundred head in order to meet the family's commitments to buyers in central Mexico. Judging from the price he paid in Saltillo—fourteen to seventeen reals for prime animals—the Sánchez Navarros made a satisfactory profit selling their sheep in the cities of the central plateau.[19] The main fact that emerges is that by the mid-1840's the Sánchez Navarros were again operating on a national scale in a sheep trade that had largely recovered from the disastrous slump arising from the struggle for independence.

This was not the case with regard to the traffic in wool. As in colonial times, the Sánchez Navarros marketed the bulk of their wool through Saltillo, selling most of their production to middlemen willing to risk transporting it southward in the hope of turning a profit. Yet at the same time a new pattern was emerging, one in which the Sánchez Navarros themselves shipped part of their wool clip directly to San Luis Potosí. This search for a new market reflected the stagnant condition of the wool trade in the early 1820's.

In the spring of 1822, the family's Saltillo warehouse contained twenty-one mule loads of wool rotting for lack of a buyer. José Melchor tried to unload it on his cousin, Román de Letona, the wool merchant. The latter was interested, but not at the *hacendado*'s price, given the condition of both the wool and the market. Letona offered sixteen reals per *arroba*, mentioning that the best wool was selling in Saltillo for twenty-two, and that it retailed in Querétaro for twenty-eight. If José Melchor accepted his offer, Letona planned to take the wool by pack train to San Miguel Allende and attempt to retail it there.[20]

The *hacendado* reluctantly agreed, for he was having trouble marketing the current wool clip, which he had shipped to San Luis Potosí consigned to Rafael Delgado, his future son-in-law. Delgado reported a total lack of interest in the Sánchez Navarro product, adding that the price for top-quality wool in San Luis has dropped to 34 reals per *arroba*. He had decided to send José Melchor's wool on to San Miguel Allende where, if it could not be disposed of on a wholesale basis, it might be retailed over a period of time. He subsequently informed José Melchor that the 12,225 pounds of wool had sold for 2,036 pesos, but that expenses had been heavy, so the net profit was only 1,679 pesos which Delgado had credited to José Melchor's account.[21]

The Saltillo market deteriorated further in 1823, when even at the annual fair José Melchor's agents were unable to make a sale. Since the best offer was a mere nine reals per *arroba*, the wool was left with Román de Letona in hopes that by selling it in small lots to outsiders he might eventually dispose of it at sixteen reals.[22]

Becoming increasingly frustrated as his unsold wool moldered in the Saltillo warehouse, José Melchor tried a novel approach to finding a new market. He offered a substantial quantity of wool to an American merchant, one Stephen Willson, who was in Monclova in 1823 to investigate business opportunities. Willson had become a friend of the Sánchez Navarros, but he had to decline José Melchor's proposition, which involved exporting the wool through the port of Refugio in Texas. The American pointed out that, in addition to the problem of transporting the wool to Refugio, the facilities at that port were primitive, making the whole scheme impractical.[23] This attempt failed, but José Melchor's efforts were not entirely in vain, for in 1824 Willson purchased ten thousand pounds of wool, although neither price nor destination was specified.[24]

By 1824, the wool trade in northern Mexico was beginning to recover from the dislocations of the preceding decade. Prices remained low, but there was a spurt in the volume of wool being handled, perhaps because the textile industry itself was emerging from the doldrums. In any case José Melchor could at least dispose of his production that year. Despite delays caused by a shortage of sacks in which to pack the wool, there developed a brisk trade with Saltillo.[25] One merchant took thirty mule loads, while another bought 6,800 pounds for resale in San Luis Potosí.[26] José Melchor's main customer was his sister, María Guadalupe Sánchez Navarro de Cacho, who was operating her late husband's business in Saltillo. The *hacendado* sold her 17,975 pounds, which she transported using the pack train of their cousin, Román de Letona.[27] These transactions cleared away the backlog at Tapado, which was fortunate since the

August shearing had just produced another 22,675 pounds.[28] Whatever profit José Melchor realized was based on volume of sales, for the price per *arroba* at the 1824 Saltillo fair was only twelve reals.[29]

This evidently continued to be the average price in Saltillo for the remainder of the decade. José Melchor retailed small amounts of wool in the Monclova area, but Saltillo was still the principal outlet.[30] Pack trains regularly plied the road between that city and Tapado; a single shipment in 1825, for example, consisted of sixty-one mule loads.[31] Depressed prices notwithstanding, José Melchor was fortunate to be able to market substantial quantities of wool. In September, 1826, a mule train passed through Saltillo loaded with 12,800 pounds of the *hacendado*'s wool consigned to a buyer in San Luis Potosí. Two years later a shipment to Saltillo totaled 6,750 pounds.[32] By 1829, there was some indication of an increased demand for wool. A foreign merchant from San Luis Potosí, a certain Ricardo Piarte, traveled all the way to Monclova to close a deal for an unspecified but evidently considerable quantity of Sánchez Navarro wool. Besides his dealings with Piarte, the *hacendado*'s shipments for the year included 6,750 pounds sent to Saltillo in April and seventy mule loads dispatched in August in preparation for the September fair.[33]

Prices rose a bit in the early 1830's, as indicated by a contract José Melchor had signed in 1829 to deliver twenty-five mule loads of wool in Saltillo at twelve reals per *arroba*. The *hacendado* fulfilled his part of the bargain, but in a subsequent dispute over the contract he stressed that in 1830 wool inferior to his had sold for a higher price in Saltillo.[34] Most of the 1830 clip went to a buyer in San Luis Potosí who must have paid a satisfactory price, for José Melchor offered another 2,500 pounds to one of the buyer's competitors, and the *hacendado* felt confident enough to demand thirteen reals an *arroba* delivered at Tapado.[35]

Transporting the increased volume of wool caused José Melchor continual problems because sacks were perennially in short supply. At Saltillo the muleteers often had to dump their cargo in the warehouse so they could return the sacks to Hermanas for the next shipment, a procedure that accelerated the deterioration of the wool.[36]

The *hacendado* was especially concerned with preserving the quality of his product because in 1831 large amounts of wool, mostly of inferior quality, were arriving in Saltillo in preparation for the fair. Even so, wool was retailing for sixteen reals in that city, while the following year the retail price rose to eighteen reals.[37] As an indication of the volume in which José Melchor was now dealing, in 1833, besides what he sold at Monclova and at Saltillo, he shipped 15,690 pounds directly to San Luis Potosí and in December was busily planning the next delivery.[38]

The records for the next few years are fragmentary. In 1834, for example, the shipment through Saltillo of only 7,545 pounds of wool can be accounted for, although the total was undoubtedly much greater. Moreover, by then the mild boom of the early 1830's had tapered off, for José Melchor again complained that sales at the fair had been disappointing.[39] The next reference to wool is in 1837, but it is particularly interesting because Apolonia, who had been running the *latifundio* since José Melchor's death the previous year, alluded to having shipped wool directly to Mexico City.[40] Carlos was presumably handling the sales in the capital, as he was doing with the flocks being delivered there. The late 1830's thus marked the reemergence of the Sánchez Navarros in the national economy with respect not only to the sheep trade but also the traffic in wool.

Once they acquired the Marquisate, however, the family changed their pattern of operations. While continuing to participate in the Mexico City sheep trade they discontinued sending wool to the capital, reverting to their earlier practice of dealing with middlemen at the regional level. The likeliest explanation is the difficulty of transportation involved in marketing the wool clip from several hundred thousand animals.

Saltillo remained the center of the Sánchez Navarros' activities, with Jacobo negotiating the sales. One of these, in 1842, was for 12,500 pounds to a cousin, José Luis de Goríbar, who intended to resell the wool in central Mexico.[41] In addition, Jacobo maintained a steady flow into the Saltillo warehouse, both to supply other large buyers and to dispose of wool in small lots, for its retail price that year was eighteen reals.[42] The price trended downward over the next few years and by 1845 reached thirteen to fourteen reals. Yet Jacobo retailed his wool at twelve reals, hoping to undersell his competitors and thereby become the principal supplier for the numerous artisans producing the brightly colored sarapes for which Saltillo was famous.[43]

Regardless of the fluctuations in the Saltillo market, Jacobo had an escape valve because for years he had sent a considerable portion of the annual clip directly to San Luis Potosí, where his brother-in-law, Rafael Delgado, had again established himself as a successful wool broker.[44] As had so often happened, familial connections proved a major factor in advancing the Sánchez Navarros' business interests.

Sheep and wool accounted for most of the family's revenues, but the Sánchez Navarros dealt in a variety of other commodities. They were, for instance, heavily involved in the retail meat business in Santa Rosa, Monclova, and Saltillo. The Santa Rosa trade was a minor enterprise, with small herds of cattle being slaughtered according to demand.[45] Monclova represented the principal market, since it was a sizeable town and the Sánchez Navarros enjoyed a virtual monopoly. Every year, normally in January, large flocks of fattened sheep and goats were brought in for slaughter, a procedure spanning several weeks. Some of the meat was retailed while still fresh, but the bulk was dried for subsequent sale. From a commercial viewpoint the hides and tallow produced were much more valuable than the meat itself. When the tallow was rendered, it was packed in casks for sale throughout the year, being much in demand for making candles and soap.[46] The hides were cured, then packed in bundles for shipment to shoemaking establishments in such cities as Querétaro.[47] The family also participated in the Saltillo meat market, but competition was stiffer in that city. Nevertheless, they maintained an abattoir there. Flocks were pastured outside Saltillo and were slaughtered at the rate of four or five animals a day.[48]

Another aspect of *latifundio* production was the distillation of liquor. José Melchor did not engage directly in this activity but rather collected as rent a share of the *mescal* and *aguardiente* produced by his tenants. Since the customary charge was three twenty-gallon barrels of liquor annually from each tenant operating a *vinatería*, the net profits were small, averaging between 100 and 250 pesos a year.[49] Not until the acquisition of the Marquisate did the Sánchez Navarros become involved in the production of liquor on a major scale. While they owned the Hacienda del Rosario, the family derived a substantial income from the sale of wine and brandy, for Rosario's production was estimated at ten thousand gallons in 1852. The absence of records precludes any further discussion of this aspect of the family's activities.[50]

Agricultural products formed an increasingly important source of income. The sugar cane raised at such haciendas as Soledad and Hermanas was refined into *piloncillo*, for these cones of brown sugar constituted a valuable item of local commerce. *Piloncillo* production was invariably referred to in monetary terms rather than by weight; through the years its price remained remarkably stable, fluctuating between sixteen and eighteen cones for a peso.[51] Except in drought years, such as 1827 when Soledad and San Juan de Sabinas together produced only 153 pesos' worth, José Melchor could count on making several thousand pesos annually from *piloncillo*.[52] In 1830, despite a freeze that killed much of the cane, Hermanas produced nearly 2,000 pesos' worth. Two years later, with refining still in progress, the *mayordomo* reported that over 1,400 pesos of brown sugar had already been processed. By the mid-1840's, the cane crop of Hermanas alone brought in from 5,000 to 6,000 pesos a year.[53]

Cotton surpassed *piloncillo* in terms of the income it produced, but unfortunately documentation is scanty. The acreage devoted to cotton expanded in the 1830's. In 1841–1842, the family's Monclova gin processed some 204,000 pounds of cotton belonging to outsiders, and it seems reasonable that an even greater quantity of Sánchez Navarro cotton passed through the facility.[54] The family's principal market was Saltillo, where an enterprising Irishman, James Hewetson, had built a textile factory, the Hibernia Company.

After 1840 Saltillo also absorbed most of the wheat produced on the *latifundio*. The grist mill in Monclova continued functioning to satisfy local needs, but from 1840 on the family's operations changed markedly; instead of the traditional north-south axis in which wheat from Hermanas and Soledad went to Monclova for milling, the Sánchez Navarros now operated on an east-west axis in which the considerable amounts of wheat grown at San Lorenzo de la Laguna, Rosario, and Patos were shipped eastward. Some of the production was ground into flour at Patos, but most of the wheat went by oxcart to Saltillo, where the Sánchez Navarros' relatives, the Arizpe family, operated large flour mills.

In May, 1846, the Sánchez Navarros suddenly acquired new customers for many of their products. The Mexican War not only disrupted the established pattern of commerce but also produced a serious shortage of staple agricultural commodities, and Jacobo profited accordingly.[55] But the item most critically in demand was horses, for the army was frantically attempting to organize the defense of the Northeast. At one stroke, therefore, the family gained an important market that they had previously failed to exploit. Prior to the war they had concentrated on sheep and goats, the sale of other types of livestock being incidental.

Now the national government ordered 1,000 cavalry horses from Jacobo, for which the *hacendado* received seventeen thousand pesos. He had great difficulty in fulfilling his part of the contract; even the Sánchez Navarros could not produce 1,000 selected horses at the drop of a hat. By September, Jacobo had managed to deliver only 387 animals, and the Americans were driving on Monterrey, the headquarters of Gen. Pedro de Ampudia, commanding the Army Corps of the North. Ampudia angrily ordered Gen. Rafael Vázquez, the commandant general in Coahuila, to secure the remaining 613 horses, emphasizing that if Jacobo did not comply immediately he was to be arrested and taken to Monterrey under guard.[56]

General Vázquez was upset, for he and Jacobo were friends.[57] The *hacendado* had in fact been trying to fulfill the contract, but some of the horses had to be brought from as far away as Durango, being pastured at the Santa Catalina del Alamo and San Lorenzo de la Laguna haciendas. An enemy of Jacobo's in Ampudia's entourage, one Valera, had convinced the general that the delay was evidence of Jacobo's attempting to cheat the government. The matter was resolved satisfactorily, at least from Jacobo's point of view, when a friend of his on Vázquez's staff hurried to Monterrey to explain the situation to Ampudia. The latter reprimanded Valera and detailed a cavalry captain to receive at Saltillo whatever additional horses Jacobo had collected.[58]

Many of these were undoubtedly nags, not only because they were hastily rounded up, but also because the cavalry captain was a friend of Jacobo's cousin, Miguel Sánchez Navarro. The latter wrote to the *hacendado* from Saltillo implying that as long as the animals had four legs the captain would accept them without question.[59]

At the same time as he was providing horses, Jacobo was negotiating to supply Ampudia's army with flour. Early in September the general agreed for him to furnish all the flour the seven-thousand-man garrison at Monterrey required.[60] Unfortunately the city fell on September 24, and by the end of 1846 American columns under Generals Taylor and Wool had occupied Coahuila as well.

Patriotic considerations aside, this development was less than disastrous for the Sánchez Navarros; having lost the Mexican army as customers, the family gained a more free-spending clientele when the American army moved in. Not only did the Americans buy provisions in quantity, but, what was more important, they also paid in cash. Corn for forage ranked among their chief requirements.[61] Deliveries were made on a regular basis from Patos and La Florida, but with increasing reluctance. Even though Jacobo was being paid, the American demand for corn created problems in keeping enough of the grain to ration his own peons.[62]

This was not the case with wheat, one of the main cash crops on the *latifundio*. The American demand for flour seemed insatiable, and Jacobo readily provided all the wheat he could grow. The *hacendado* worked closely with his cousin Arizpe, whose flour mill in Saltillo was the Americans' main source of supply, and with Horace Boultbee, an Irishman long resident in Coahuila, who was one of Jacobo's tenants. Boultbee was in Saltillo making himself generally useful to the American high command, and among other things he functioned as middleman in securing a steady supply of wheat for the occupying forces.

The Americans were paying sixteen pesos a mule load for the flour from Arizpe's mill in March, 1847. Though Arizpe complained that the invaders expected the flour to be processed at an unreasonably rapid rate, nevertheless his mill operated at maximum capacity, and he was being paid in dollars.[63] Boultbee, in his role as middleman, was buying as much of Jacobo's wheat as possible, offering the *hacen-*

dado eight to nine pesos per mule load of 325 pounds. The Irishman's profit as a wheat broker shrank, for by April the volume of wheat pouring into Saltillo enabled the Americans to pay only fourteen pesos a load for flour.[64] By July, Boultbee was offering only seven pesos a load for the current harvest from Patos. For the remainder of the occupation prices stabilized, with Jacobo receiving seven pesos per load from Boultbee, and the Americans paying fourteen pesos for Arizpe's flour.[65] The amount of wheat Jacobo provided the army of occupation is unknown, but, as an indication, a single shipment in May, 1847, totaled 11,700 pounds.[66]

Besides enjoying an assured market for corn and wheat, Jacobo benefited by supplying livestock to the Americans. Their chief requirement was beef cattle, which pleased Jacobo since before the war there had been little demand for the herds raised on the *latifundio*. Very incomplete records show that in 1847 he provided 124 head, as well as 11 mules and 20 horses, but the total number he sold during the occupation was undoubtedly much higher.[67]

Because communications between Coahuila and Mexico City had been disrupted, Carlos was not always aware of just how adroitly Jacobo had adjusted to these new business opportunities. In April, 1847, a worried Carlos urged his brother to hide the family's livestock from the "infamous Yankees."[68] A radically different view of the situation came from Capt. George Hughes, whose job it was to procure supplies for the American army occupying Coahuila. Referring to the Sánchez Navarro clan, Hughes stated that "nearly all our expenditures for supplies have found their way directly or indirectly into the coffers of these princely nabobs."[69]

Jacobo's business dealings were by no means limited to provisioning the Americans. Throughout the occupation he strove to maintain the established markets and even to develop new ones.[70] He managed to keep the Sánchez Navarros in the sheep trade, the very lifeblood of the *latifundio*. His principal accomplishment was that of meeting the family's commitments regarding the *abasto* in Mexico City. The contract that Carlos had signed some years earlier required the annual delivery of 14,480 sheep, which Jacobo dispatched in eight flocks of 1,810 animals each. Although in the spring of 1847 Carlos complained about the miserable condition in which several of the flocks had arrived, Jacobo maintained his schedule, at least up to September, when Mexico City fell to the Americans after a fierce defense.[71] And even before the end of the war in February, 1848, Jacobo had resumed deliveries.[72]

In the period of postwar adjustment the *abasto* contract was especially important, not only for the income it produced but also because the Sánchez Navarros were making strenuous efforts to dispose of as much livestock as possible before the animals were lost either to drought or to Indians. Having an assured market for 14,480 sheep a year was an enormous advantage. Throughout 1848, 1849, and 1850 the flocks were regularly dispatched on the five-hundred-mile, three-month journey to Mexico City.[73]

The contract came up for renewal in January, 1851. Carlos handled the negotiations with Luis del Conde, the family's buyer in the capital. Del Conde agreed to purchase the usual 14,480 sheep, with delivery technically being made at Bonanza. Sánchez Navarro shepherds would drive the animals to the capital in eight flocks beginning in January at intervals of twenty-five to thirty days. Del Conde, however, ran all the risks of delivery, and he agreed to reimburse the Sánchez Navarros for the expenses of the drives as soon as each flock arrived. On the other hand, Del Conde enjoyed the option of having deliveries postponed up to three months. The sheep were sold for the excellent price of 24 reals a head, which totaled a gratifying 43,440 pesos. Del Conde would pay this sum in silver at Mexico City, half in January and the balance within two months after receiving the last flock. And the contract would apply in 1852 as well.[74] The Sánchez Navarros' dealings with Del Conde lasted through 1856 and were presumably on terms that continued to bring in approximately 50,000 pesos a year.[75]

In addition to the lucrative *abasto* contract, the Sánchez Navarros concluded a number of livestock sales in the postwar years. Through 1850 these were on a regional level, involving flocks for the *abasto* in Saltillo and several hundred sheep sold at Bonanza and Mazapil, at twenty reals a head.[76] In 1851, however, sales spurted. When Carlos and Jacobo conferred in Mexico City in January, they decided to dispose of as many sheep as possible. Accordingly, Jacobo wrote to Arizpe, who was managing the *latifundio* in his absence, informing the lawyer that he was negotiating the sale of fifteen to twenty thousand sheep, which he wanted Arizpe to have ready for shipment by April.[77] Complying with Jacobo's instructions, Arizpe prepared to dispatch a flock southward every twenty days.[78]

The Sánchez Navarros sold an impressive number of sheep and goats in 1851. Jacobo closed a deal with one José Luis de Sautto, who wanted several flocks for his Hacienda de la Venta near San Miguel Allende. A shipment of 4,972 sheep and 1,887 goats started for San Miguel, but en route Jacobo diverted the flocks to the Hacienda de Arroyozarco in the state of México, having arranged to sell them there at a better price.[79] He explained to the irate Sautto that their original contract had lapsed, and that it had been imperative to find another buyer. The *hacendado* stressed that additional flocks were on the way from Patos and that these animals could readily be substituted. Accordingly, the two men entered into a verbal contract by which Sautto agreed to pay eleven reals for three-year-old goats, ten reals for two-year-olds, and eight and one-half reals for sheep, in addition to bearing the expenses of delivery.[80] The sheep were obviously culls, as their price was considerably lower than the twenty-four reals the Sánchez Navarros received for those sent to Mexico City.

Once the animals had been delivered, Jacobo's troubles began, for Sautto reneged on the deal. Jacobo demanded that Sautto deposit the money in Mexico City as agreed; and, when the latter refused, Jacobo threatened to sue, claiming he was owed 7,713 pesos for the livestock and 468 for expenses.[81] There followed an acrimonious correspondence lasting for years.[82] Despite the bluster on both sides, neither party really wanted to go to court since this would involve interminable delay and heavy costs. In 1855 they finally resorted to the time-honored practice of arranging an out-of-court settlement, but the available documents do not reveal its terms.[83]

The rest of the Sánchez Navarros' sheep sales for 1851 ended more happily. The flock of 4,972 animals diverted to Arroyozarco that precipitated the clash between Jacobo and Sautto had been sold to Anselmo Zurutuza, a dynamic Spaniard who from Mexico City directed a far-flung network of stagecoach lines.[84] The price he paid is not specified, but it could not have been much more than what Sautto had originally offered, for the Spaniard drove a hard bargain; the Sánchez Navarros found themselves in the unaccustomed position of having to bear the expenses and risks of delivery until the flocks reached Zurutuza's Hacienda de Arroyozarco.[85] Shortly after receiving the initial flock, Zurutuza purchased a second, composed of 4,000 yearling rams.[86] Despite delays caused by the terrific drought in Coahuila, Zurutuza must have been satisfied with the Sánchez Navarros' product, for he purchased still a third flock, of 2,000 ewes.[87] Dealings with the Spaniard, who had taken 10,972 of the family's animals in 1851, were ended by Zurutuza's death the following year.

Nevertheless, Zurutuza had played an indirect role in enabling the Sánchez Navarros to conclude yet another transaction in 1851. For years the Spaniard had been leasing the magnificent sugar hacienda of Atlacomulco in Morelos. His partner in this enterprise was Jesús Goríbar, member of a powerful *hacendado* family—his relative Juan Goríbar, for example, later became the proprietor of the sugar haciendas of Cocoyoc and Casasano in Morelos and of the huge Hacienda de Gallinas in San Luis Potosí, besides being a leading financier in Mexico City.[88] As luck would have it, the Goríbars, several of whom also lived in Saltillo, were distant cousins of the Sánchez Navarros, who used this family connection quite effectively.[89] Jacobo prevailed on the Goríbars to negotiate for him the sale of 5,000 ewes and 250 rams to the brothers Leandro and Miguel Mosso. They were prominent merchants in Veracruz and Mexico City and owned the haciendas of San Sebastián and El Salto. The animals were scheduled for delivery late in the fall, but the lack of pasture along the road delayed the shipment until January, 1852, much to the displeasure of the Mossos.[90]

The difficulties the Sánchez Navarros experienced in meeting their commitments in 1851 because of the drought are best illustrated by the deal Jacobo closed in Mexico City with a certain Mariano Vega, who paid 7,875 pesos for 7,000 two-year-old ewes at nine reals a head, with delivery to be made at Patos. The *administrador* Quirino Benavente confided to Arizpe that it would be hard to supply the necessary animals because of the toll the drought was taking.[91] When Vega's representative arrived to inspect the flock, he accepted only 6,823 head as being fit for the long drive to central Mexico.[92] Vega subsequently requested, and received, a refund for the other 177 head. Despite the condition of the flock he had purchased, Vega was evidently not displeased, for in December he wrote to Jacobo asking whether the *hacendado* could sell him 4,000 sheep and an equal number of goats the next year.[93]

Jacobo was also receiving inquiries from other buyers. The proprietor of a hacienda near Fresnillo, in Zacatecas, was interested in ewes and yearling and two-year-old goats, asking their price, the terms Jacobo would extend, and the route the flocks would take if a sale were consummated.[94] Jacobo also received an inquiry from his old rival Rafael Aguirre, who asked for a loan in order to purchase a hacienda in San Luis Potosí. By way of incentive, Aguirre mentioned that he might need 20,000 to 25,000 ewes, 3,000 to 4,000 goats, and 3,000 to 4,000 rams, presumably to stock the hacienda for which he was negotiating. In his next letter Aguirre also put Jacobo in contact with yet another buyer, who wanted 5,000 goats and 1,200 sheep, offering 10 and 8 reals respectively, with payment to be made at San Luis Potosí, a transaction totaling 7,450 pesos.[95]

Considering the problems they faced, the Sánchez Navarros did extremely well in 1851. Deliveries to Mexico City were made on schedule and with surprisingly light losses en route, enabling the family to fulfill the vital *abasto* contract.[96] The Mexico City market was so lucrative, in fact, that the Sánchez Navarros' business agent in the capital, Juan F. de Puyade, asked to purchase two flocks from Jacobo on credit as a speculation. The *hacendado* refused on the ground that he was hard-pressed to produce enough marketable sheep to meet the family's other sales commitments.[97] During 1851 the Sánchez Navarros sold over 45,000 sheep and 7,000 goats, for which they received close to 100,000 pesos.

Furthermore, Jacobo had received inquiries concerning the possible sale of some 52,000 sheep and more than 8,000 goats. How many of these deals he actually closed is impossible to ascertain since the documentation for the years after 1851 is fragmentary. Besides the usual shipments for the *abasto* in Mexico City, the only transaction recorded for 1852 is Jacobo's sale of 1,200 sheep and 700 goats to a Miguel Ferreira, who took delivery at the Hacienda de Bonanza. The animals all sold for 9 reals a head, making a total of 2,127 pesos.[98] The *abasto* trade continued without interruption, but, although Jacobo was doubtless involved in numerous other livestock transactions, the next reference to his activities is not until 1855. A buyer from San Miguel Allende inquired as to the terms Jacobo was willing to extend; if the latter would grant credit for one year, the buyer would take a "considerable number" of sheep and goats for fattening. Jacobo replied that it was now too late in the year to sell this type of stock, but that the following year he could provide some 8,000 goats and 2,000 sheep, the rest of his marketable animals already having been committed for sale.[99]

By the late 1850's, Bonanza, the southernmost hacienda in the *latifundio*, had replaced Patos as the main delivery point for livestock shipments. In December, 1857, however, there broke out a savage civil war that convulsed Mexico for the next three years, making it impossible for the Sánchez Navarros to get their flocks through to Mexico City, and the *abasto* contract ended. Reduced once again to a regional market, the family found it difficult to sell their livestock even on this basis. The accounts maintained between the two haciendas indicate a drastic curtailment in shipments, with only 2,256 goats being sent to Bonanza in 1857 and 6,278 in 1859.[100]

As the civil war came to a close in 1860, business began to improve. In November, Jacobo dispatched a flock of 1,810 sheep from Bonanza to San Luis Potosí, repeating the operation in May, 1861. This second flock produced 4,298 pesos, the animals having sold for 19 reals each. Anticipating continued improvement in the trade, the *hacendado* had some 12,000 sheep transferred from Hermanas to Bonanza. His assessment of the situation proved much too optimistic, for during the rest of the year only one other flock, consisting of 1,567 sheep, was sold.

The French Intervention completed the ruin of the sheep trade. During 1862, Jacobo shipped a single flock to San Luis Potosí, the 5,508 sheep bringing 14 reals a head, for a total of 9,639 pesos.[101]

Two years later, Carlos was negotiating a sale in Mexico City, for he sent an agent to the *latifundio* to report on the condition of some 8,000 sheep and 10,000 goats.[102] Whether the sale was concluded is, however, unknown. The last recorded transaction involving sheep occurred in 1865, when a buyer from San Luis Potosí took delivery of 600 head at Patos.[103] Thus, for the Sánchez Navarros the sheep trade, the principal source of income from their *latifundio*, came to a dismal end, a far cry from the boom years of the early 1850's.

That era had also been a time of rapid growth in the sale of other kinds of livestock, a development that dated from the Mexican War. As with sheep, the family made strenuous efforts in the postwar years to dispose of cattle and mules, and for the same reasons—a favorable market plus the prospect of losing the livestock to drought and to Indians. Up to 1851, the Sánchez Navarros' outlets were regional ones. Besides a few animals sold at Patos, Jacobo sent herds of cattle to Saltillo for slaughter and to supply that city's bull ring. He also shipped a few yearlings to Mazapil.[104]

The peak year for cattle sales was 1851, many of these transactions being with individuals who also purchased sheep. Jacobo sold one hundred yearlings to José Luis de Sautto at 10 pesos each, but, as with the sheep and goats he had bought from the *hacendado*, Sautto refused to pay the 1,000 pesos for the livestock plus the 135 pesos in trail expenses.[105]

Jacobo had somewhat better luck selling cattle to Anselmo Zurutuza. The Spaniard ordered 500 head, which were driven to Arroyozarco in the late spring in two herds of 250 head each.[106] The drives were disasters. Whereas sheep withstood the rigors of the trail fairly well, the cattle, already weakened by the drought, perished in droves along the way. Exactly 204 head reached Arroyozarco, and they arrived in miserable condition.[107] Since the cattle had been delivered at Jacobo's risk, Zurutuza's only obligation was to pay for 204 animals. And the shrewd Spaniard adamantly refused to pay the agreed-on price, insisting on a reduction because of the herd's condition. The Sánchez Navarros' business agent in Mexico City promptly informed Jacobo of Zurutuza's attitude, adding that Jacobo could not imagine "how annoying and disagreeable this man is in all his dealings."[108]

Disagreeable or not, Zurutuza ultimately had his way: Jacobo grudgingly agreed to a reduction, and Zurutuza paid 2,266 pesos for the
cattle.[109]

Despite the disappointing results of these ventures, Jacobo continued to ship livestock to Mexico City. He was negotiating the sale not
only of cattle but of mules as well, once again using the good offices of
his cousins the Goríbars. The latter arranged the sale of three hundred
yearlings, probably at 10 pesos a head, to the brothers Mosso but politely declined to buy four hundred mules Jacobo was also sending to
the capital. The Goríbars assured the *hacendado* that since his mules
were of high quality he would have no trouble finding a buyer, and
they would certainly do what they could to help.[110] Yet when the
mules reached Mexico City their condition left much to be desired,
and the family's business agent had difficulty finding a purchaser. He
finally managed to sell the four hundred animals for 23 pesos, 4 reals
each; the 9,400 pesos produced was below Jacobo's expectations, but
under the circumstances the *hacendado* had little cause for complaint.[111]

During 1851 Jacobo also developed a new outlet for mules closer
to home. He was one of the principal stockholders in a mining company at Catorce, in San Luis Potosí. The directors of the company
asked Jacobo to sell them forty of his best mules for use in the smelter, a request to which the *hacendado* acceded with alacrity. The directors were delighted with the superior quality of the stock he
provided.[112]

The *hacendado* in all likelihood continued to make shipments to
Catorce, as well as engaging in various other transactions involving
cattle and mules, but here again we have only isolated glimpses of his
activities. In the mid-1850's he was still supplying the Saltillo bull
ring, a venture that lasted through 1862, when he sold twenty-three
bulls for 420 pesos. The only other reference to cattle sales is for
1864–1865, when some three hundred head were sold from one of
the subdivisions of Patos.[113] As had occurred with the sheep trade, the
combination of civil war and foreign invasion beginning in 1857
wrecked the Sánchez Navarros' traffic in livestock.

The same process destroyed the family's wool trade. With the end of the Mexican War, the demand for wool increased, and Jacobo resumed shipments to Saltillo.[114] Over the next two years, however, an enormous backlog developed: in 1850, some 52,000 pounds from Hermanas were dispatched to Saltillo by oxcart, and Patos contributed another 100,000 pounds. Yet by May less than 5,000 pounds had been sold in Saltillo or forwarded on to San Luis Potosí.[115] Jacobo sold an additional quantity at the Saltillo fair, but tons of wool remained in the family's warehouse.

The situation improved somewhat in 1851. Jacobo found a new market when a merchant from the border town of Eagle Pass, Texas, a certain D. T. Rich, asked to buy the entire spring clip from Hermanas. Though the documents fail to establish whether this deal was closed, in all probability it was. By ridding himself—at whatever price—of the 26,000-pound Hermanas wool clip, Jacobo could concentrate on marketing the 50,000 pounds produced that spring at Patos, to say nothing of the existing backlog.[116]

The backlog constituted a formidable problem. Trains of oxcarts periodically journeyed from Patos to Saltillo, adding their loads to the already-bursting warehouse; one train of eight carts, for instance, carried 12,575 pounds in August, 1851.[117] The Saltillo market was saturated, and Jacobo increased his shipments to San Luis Potosí, where Rafael Delgado still acted as the family's broker. The San Luis operation produced a modest profit at best, for Jacobo had to ship the wool there at his own expense, and freight rates increased sharply in the early 1850's because of the drought and the danger of Indian attacks along the road.[118] These conditions, coupled with the inferior quality of the Sánchez Navarros' wool, drastically reduced potential profits, but the alternative was that of losing the wool altogether through spoilage.

Delgado had indifferent success in marketing the wool he received in 1851, partly because the San Luis market was sluggish due to the influx of wool from neighboring haciendas.[119] Nonetheless, Jacobo increased his shipments, sending another 29,850 pounds. Delgado informed him that their only hope was to wholesale the wool at a considerable discount to buyers who demanded extended credit.[120]

It was probably on this disadvantageous basis that the wool shipped to Delgado in succeeding years was sold. In contrast to the livestock trade, a market for wool existed even during the bitter civil war of the late 1850's. In August, 1859, for example, Jacobo sent 29,200 pounds to San Luis Potosí consigned to Delgado. Volume dropped sharply in 1860, when from Bonanza the *hacendado* shipped 6,375 pounds, which at 18 reals per *arroba* produced only 575 pesos. The decrease may well have reflected the fact that by the early 1860's the Sánchez Navarros had developed a new outlet for wool, exporting it in quantity through Brownsville, Texas. In October, 1861, they had 37,500 pounds of wool at Brownsville; at 12 reals per *arroba* this consignment was valued at 2,250 pesos.

Still, San Luis Potosí remained the principal regional market. Jacobo's next shipment to Delgado, in April, 1862, when the French Intervention was already under way, consisted of 4,900 pounds, at 16 reals, for a mere 392 pesos. In August, however, Delgado sold an additional 24,400 pounds, at 16 reals; the sale amounted to a much more satisfactory 2,032 pesos. Moreover, that same month the *hacendado* disposed of another 14,950 pounds at Saltillo, also at 16 reals, for 1,196 pesos.[121] This was evidently the last burst of activity with respect to wool sales. In 1864, with Coahuila caught up in the military campaigns of the French Intervention, the Sánchez Navarros had to evacuate their warehouse in Saltillo. The wool was transported by oxcart to Patos for safekeeping, but there it spoiled for lack of buyers.[122]

The wool trade had been conducted along traditional lines with only a few innovations being discernible. One was the practice, after the Mexican War, of shipping wool by oxcart rather than by mule train. Another, which had been adopted by the early 1860's, was the use at Hermanas of a press for baling wool, a much more efficient method than the traditional one of having peons jump on the wool to compress it.[123] Last, to some extent the Sánchez Navarros shifted away from the colonial trade pattern by developing new markets in the United States at Eagle Pass and Brownsville.

This was not the case with regard to the remaining *latifundio* products, whose marketing more closely conformed to tradition. The meat trade, which declined in relative importance after the Mexican War, was carried on largely at Patos, Saltillo, and later Bonanza. In 1851, the Sánchez Navarros leased their Monclova slaughterhouse to a foreigner for ten years, confining themselves to butchering small flocks for local consumption.[124]

The scattered records for agricultural commodities prevent any detailed analysis of production in the years after the Mexican War. One can only state that *piloncillo*, cotton, and *aguardiente* continued to be important products at Hermanas, while at that hacienda and at Patos there were at times surpluses of beans for sale at Saltillo and Monclova.[125] Wheat, long the principal cash crop, still went to Arizpe's grist mill in Saltillo, 1,357 bushels being sent there in 1851 alone.[126] The most noticeable agricultural change was the vastly increased production of maize, which came to rival wheat as a cash crop. Not only was the *latifundio* self-sufficient but also there were substantial amounts left over to market even in such drought years as 1851, when Jacobo sold at Saltillo 3,681 bushels at about five pesos per fanega.[127] And between 1857 and 1860, an annual average of 7,095 bushels was shipped from Patos to Bonanza. Some of the maize was consumed at Bonanza, but most of it was transshipped to San Luis Potosí for sale.[128] As late as 1865, the Sánchez Navarros were marketing corn not only in Coahuila but also in Monterrey, receiving between five and six pesos a fanega.[129]

The one unique feature of *latifundio* production in the national period was mining, which dated from the acquisition of the Marquisate in 1840. At that time the Albarradón silver mine at Bonanza, which had once been a lucrative property, was in a ruinous condition and its output was negligible.[130] With their accustomed energy, the Sánchez Navarros set out to remedy this situation. They had extensive assays made of the Bonanza deposits, and over the next fifteen years the brothers invested substantial sums in capital improvements. Not only did they rejuvenate the Albarradón, but they also developed two additional mines. They also restored the existing facilities and modernized the entire smelting process by importing the latest furnaces from Germany, together with German experts to install and operate the machinery. To provide a reliable fuel supply for the smelter, the Sánchez Navarros exploited three small coalfields in the vicinity. Linking this growing complex together was a narrow-gauge railway built in 1856.[131]

Conforming to habit, the Sánchez Navarros put a cousin, Marcial Beráin, in charge of Bonanza. Production figures exist only for the late 1850's and early 1860's, but by then most of the capital improvements had been made, and the mines should have been returning their maximal yield. The price for silver remained stable, ranging between 8 pesos and 8 pesos 2 reals per marco (7.4 Troy ounces) delivered at Bonanza. But production fell far short of expectations: 6,432 pesos' worth in 1856, 8,965 pesos in 1860, 20,601 in 1861, and 12,102 in 1862.[132]

Overshadowing this lackluster performance was the dismaying fact that by the 1860's the mines were playing out.[133] The overall picture after 1860 was one of unrelieved gloom. As of 1862, the only profitable part of the operation was the smelter, but this gain was cancelled by the losses at the mines and coalfields.[134] Compounding the losses was the heavy investment in equipment; in December, 1859, the Sánchez Navarros owed ninety thousand pesos for machinery to one French firm alone.[135] It is doubtful whether the brothers were able to amortize their investment, for the French Intervention ruined the mining activities at Bonanza. Yet, unlike other phases of *latifundio* operations, the Bonanza mines were already in marked decline by the time of the Intervention.

Viewing *latifundio* production as a whole, the most notable development in the national period was an enormous increase in virtually all areas, resulting primarily from the acquisition of the Marquisate. At the same time, however, there was a significant shift away from ranching and toward agriculture and mining, a trend that exemplified the historical pattern of *hacendados* becoming mining magnates and vice versa.

11. Commerce

The comfortable pattern of commerce by which the Sánchez Navarros purchased manufactured goods from the mercantile houses to whom they sold sheep was shattered by the insurrection in 1810. Even after independence, the turbulent conditions in Mexico made it impossible for the family to reestablish the orderly system they had enjoyed in the viceregal era. For the Sánchez Navarros, who had retrenched into Coahuila during the decade 1810–1820, the early national period represented a time of rebuilding, as they struggled to reorganize and expand their commercial enterprises.

The first priority was the preservation of existing assets. Although José Melchor spent much of his time in legal battles over land, he did not neglect the family's accounts receivable, making a determined effort to collect outstanding debts. This proved extremely difficult, for with business activity at a low ebb many of the *hacendado*'s debtors could not pay because they themselves were trying to recover money owed to them. In most cases the best José Melchor could do was to secure a fresh acknowledgment of indebtedness, thereby safeguarding his legal rights until conditions improved. With more important affairs requiring his personal attention, José Melchor often availed himself of his numerous relatives to perform the chore of harassing his debtors.[1]

The *hacendado* began relying to an increasing degree on Apolonia to handle the collection of debts.[2] Apolonia took her responsibilities seriously; not only did she press debtors, but she also sharply criticized José Melchor for continuing to make loans, a practice of which she vehemently disapproved. Once in 1828 she informed her husband that in accordance with his instructions she had delivered forty pesos to a borrower. She had done so, however, "with great repugnance, because around here one has to work hard just to see a peso, especially the way things are at present—for one to collect what is rightfully his, he has to spend twice as much."[3]

José Melchor was painfully aware of this truth. Not only was he still engaged in the costly Elizondo litigation, but he was also trying to collect the balance of his account with Gabriel de Yermo, the Spanish merchant prince and *hacendado* who had been the Sánchez Navarros' principal buyer in the late colonial period. Yermo had since returned to Spain with whatever liquid assets he had been able to salvage from the revolution. José Melchor was pressing a claim for nearly ten thousand pesos against Yermo's haciendas in Morelos, but as late as 1833 the claim was still not settled.[4]

Debts played a role in enlarging the Sánchez Navarros' urban holdings, for José Melchor sometimes resorted to the time-honored practice of accepting real estate in lieu of cash. In this manner he acquired three more houses and three lots.[5] But the *hacendado*'s main concern was that of improving his urban properties, not adding to them. The mansion he owned in Monterrey presented no problem. Since it was one of the most desirable dwellings in that city, José Melchor was able to keep it rented at three hundred pesos a year.[6] His Saltillo residence, though, required attention. In 1822 part of the rambling structure was converted into an abattoir and butcher shop, and the following year the edifice was requisitioned by the government for billeting troops. They left the place a shambles, and José Melchor had to spend considerable sums on renovation before the building could serve as the family's townhouse.[7]

The *hacendado* had also been improving his properties in Monclova and Santa Rosa. The most notable phase of this program came in 1831, when he entered into an agreement with an American engineer,

John Blacaller, who had been operating the Sánchez Navarros' grist mill in Monclova in return for half the profits. Under the new arrangement the American supervised the demolition of the mill and the construction of a larger and more modern facility on the same site. In addition, next to the mill he built a cotton gin, equipped with American machinery. José Melchor defrayed all the costs, Blacaller operated the facilities, and they divided the profits equally.[8] This ambitious project showed José Melchor's willingness to take an occasional flier in industrial enterprises. The new grist mill and cotton gin, which continued in operation through the 1850's, proved to be a much better investment than had a previous venture.

In 1822, José Melchor had become half owner of a silver mine, the Pabellón, near Santa Rosa. Though potentially profitable, the mine flooded with distressing frequency.[9] Reluctant to invest the large amounts necessary to bring the Pabellón into full production, José Melchor in 1825 tried to interest foreign capitalists in the enterprise. An American mercantile house in Mexico City dispatched a representative, Stephen Willson, a man who had several years' experience trading in Coahuila and who had already established personal and business ties with José Melchor. Willson's mission was to examine mining prospects not only in the vicinity of Santa Rosa but in Nuevo León as well.[10] The political instability in Mexico, however, ultimately dissuaded the American financiers from investing. The Pabellón operated sporadically through 1828 when it was abandoned.[11]

Except for the cotton gin and the Pabellón mine, José Melchor's commercial activities were of a more traditional nature. As in the past the *hacendado*'s basic aim was twofold: to dominate local commerce and to ensure a steady supply of goods for the *latifundio*. With regard to the local retail trade many items such as candles, tallow, hides, mutton, flour, and a number of agricultural commodities, were supplied from the Sánchez Navarros' own resources. The manufactured articles, mainly clothing and textiles, required both for commerce and for the *latifundio* were another matter. In examining how José Melchor met this demand, one finds that the most noticeable development was a marked trend toward greater local self-sufficiency.

Since the Hacienda de Tapado now boasted a carpenter, he built not only furniture but also oxcarts and wooden mills for grinding cane, items whose components had to be imported from Monterrey in the colonial period.[12] Furthermore, at Tapado and Hermanas about half of the sacks required for transporting wool were produced, another item that had been imported prior to independence.[13] Perhaps the major change was the establishment at Tapado in the early 1820's of an *obraje*. This workshop, manned by one or two weavers, annually turned out several dozen bolts of cloth for dressing the peons.[14] The demand for clothing far outstripped the *obraje*'s capacity, so José Melchor relied heavily on artisans in Monclova and Santa Rosa to supply sombreros, cotton and woolen textiles, sarapes, and shoes for the peons.[15] Nevertheless, local sources could not possibly meet all the needs of an expanding labor force. On various occasions the *mayordomo* of Hermanas reported that the workers were inadequately clothed and urgently requested the restocking of the *tienda de raya*.[16]

It was therefore necessary to procure in Saltillo a variety of merchandise. At each September fair José Melchor bought a stock of goods, which, whenever possible, were transported to the *latifundio* by his own pack train.[17] The bulk of the *hacendado*'s purchases consisted of clothing for the peons, but he also bought cacao, cigarettes, black powder for use at the Pabellón mine and in his various irrigation projects, woolsacks, stationery, iron bars for window grills, molds for making *piloncillo*, and ornaments for the chapel at Soledad.[18] Although most of the merchandise coming from Saltillo went to supply the *latifundio*, that city was also the source of certain amenities to brighten Apolonia's existence; for example, she ordered imported silks, a selection of flowerpots, and several varieties of carnations. On occasion she even had luxuries brought from as far away as San Luis Potosí.[19]

The Sánchez Navarros' trade with San Luis Potosí represented the family's most important new mercantile connection at the regional level. It stemmed logically from two factors: first, José Melchor amassed credits from the sale of livestock and wool to San Luis dealers, and second, these merchants could provide articles that were sometimes unobtainable in Saltillo. Thus, on a lesser scale, the San Luis trade approximated the commercial pattern the Sánchez Navarros had enjoyed with Mexico City in the colonial period.

José Melchor's original contact was Rafael Delgado, who in 1822 and 1823 made several shipments consisting primarily of cheap footwear: 528 pairs of shoes at 8 pesos a dozen.[20] When Delgado married the Sánchez Navarros' daughter in 1824 and moved to Coahuila, this in no way lessened the commerce with San Luis Potosí, for José Melchor simply transferred his business to other mercantile houses. The flow of goods was evidently fairly heavy, but the only items referred to specifically were cacao, bar chocolate, burlap for woolsacks, crates of candies, a shipment of coconuts, and ten dozen *rebozos*.

Though San Luis Potosí figured prominently in the Sánchez Navarros' regional trade, José Melchor also maintained business connections in several other cities. In contrast to the colonial period, he no longer dealt with merchants in San Miguel Allende, but he did have occasional transactions with those in Querétaro, León, and Guadalajara.[21]

The *hacendado* barely participated in commerce at the national level. From time to time he did place orders in Mexico City, but in comparison with the family's activities prior to independence this traffic was insignificant.[22] José Melchor's failure to trade with the capital was not due to a lack of business connections there. Rather, given the frequent political convulsions the country was experiencing, Mexico City could not be relied on as a dependable source of supply.

This situation was the background for a significant shift in the Sánchez Navarros' trade pattern—a partial reorientation toward the United States. The earliest instance, in 1829, was hardly breathtaking: José Melchor ordered from New Orleans two large kettles, which were shipped overland through San Antonio. Two years later, though, when the *hacendado* established the cotton gin in Monclova, he imported the machinery from the United States. The equipment was landed at Matamoros, and José Melchor paid a considerable sum to have it freighted via Monterrey and Saltillo.[23]

This route continued to be used in the 1840's, when Jacobo and Carlos were directing the Sánchez Navarro empire. In 1842, Jacobo decided that the family's enhanced status required the remodeling and redecoration of their Saltillo residence as well as the main house at Patos. The project involved replacing the shabbier pieces with furniture purchased in the United States. The elegant new furnishings, packed in seven large crates, came in by way of Matamoros and Monterrey.[24]

At the same time, Jacobo was negotiating to expand the family's Monclova cotton gin, which his cousin Miguel Blanco managed. The business had been yielding a satisfactory profit, but Jacobo planned to raise working capital by taking in several other partners, among them James Hewetson, an Irishman long resident in Coahuila, and a countryman of Hewetson's, one Nicholas Pendergast.[25] Meetings were held in Monclova, and the partners agreed to purchase additional machinery. A few months later, however, they decided to suspend the purchase, a course of action with which Carlos concurred. From his vantage point in Mexico City, he advised that the present state of the economy made capital investments of this type a risky proposition. Nevertheless, should the situation improve, he would arrange to have funds transferred to the United States to pay for the equipment. Conditions evidently did improve, for in 1843 Jacobo dispatched Blanco on a buying trip, and he returned through Matamoros with an unspecified amount of American ginning machinery and other merchandise.[26]

The Sánchez Navarros' use of Matamoros as a port of entry reflected a major development in northeastern Mexico—the decline of Saltillo as a commercial center and its eventual displacement by the Matamoros-Monterrey axis. Despite being temporarily retarded by the Mexican War, Monterrey rose to mercantile dominance in the second half of the nineteenth century. The temporary loss of Matamoros due to the war was not a crippling blow for the Sánchez Navarros, because the majority of the goods they required had still been coming through Saltillo.

The Saltillo trade had increased notably after 1840, since, with the acquisition of the Marquisate, Jacobo had to provide for a vastly increased labor force, most of it in the general vicinity of Saltillo. He therefore refocused the commercial activities of the family in Coahuila, allowing its participation in retail trade to decline and instead concentrating on supplying the landholding. Jacobo depended on Saltillo to keep the *latifundio* going. The *hacendado*'s agent in that city was hard pressed to procure and ship the necessary merchandise as well as handle the attendant paperwork and financial arrangements. Trains of mules and oxcarts loaded with textiles and clothing continually plied between Saltillo and the main *cascos*. These items were available in greater quantities, for by 1844 the Irishman James Hewetson had established in Saltillo a textile mill, the Hibernia Company.[27] This firm became the principal supplier of cheap cotton cloth for Jacobo, who thereby saved himself not only the middlemen's profits on textiles brought from central Mexico but also the freight charges. This of course was not the case for most of the other manufactured articles Jacobo bought in Saltillo. Following long-established practice, his heaviest purchases were during the September fair. The 1845 fair was memorable in that Jacobo acquired an unusually large stock of goods, in anticipation of the impending conflict with the United States.[28]

As war approached, Jacobo intensified his efforts to stockpile merchandise. He financed buying trips to Tampico by San Luis businessmen, and he also dispatched one of his cousins to Durango for the same purpose.[29] Once war broke out, the *hacendado*'s regional purchases declined drastically, and he was reduced to relying on what could be supplied through Saltillo.[30] He managed to keep the *latifundio* work force reasonably well supplied, as is illustrated by a shipment sent from Patos to San Lorenzo de la Laguna in October, 1847. The cargo included sixteen dozen scarves, fourteen dozen *rebozos*, one hundred sombreros, and four thousand needles; the total value of the merchandise was some ten thousand pesos.[31]

The problems that the Mexican War caused the Sánchez Navarros in their business dealings at the national level were of a different nature. Though little merchandise came from Mexico City, the capital nevertheless figured prominently in the family's affairs. With Carlos living in Mexico City, the Sánchez Navarros' commercial position was greatly strengthened, for besides negotiating various deals he served as a financial clearinghouse. It was Carlos who managed most of the family's funds, writing drafts to pay for the merchandise Jacobo bought and cashing drafts coming in from the sale of *latifundio* products. Since the economy functioned on credit, Carlos's connections within the business community and his consequent ability to transfer money wherever needed were invaluable. Complementing Carlos's role, Jacobo's agent in Saltillo would make disposition of the drafts flowing through that office and would then shift some of the funds to Mexico City by issuing drafts in favor of Carlos.[32] At times there were delays in sending these instruments, causing Carlos to complain bitterly because he had already committed the funds to meet pressing obligations in the capital.[33] Yet on the whole the procedure operated efficiently; Jacobo was the only businessman in Coahuila who could write drafts on funds in Mexico City with the assurance that they would be honored.[34]

During the war the national financial system centered in Mexico City began to collapse, a development reminiscent of the situation during the struggle for independence. The effects on the Sánchez Navarros' cash flow were disastrous. Although Jacobo was profiting by provisioning the Americans in Coahuila, he found it increasingly difficult to transfer funds to Mexico City, where Carlos desperately needed the money. Sending cash to the capital was obviously out of the question, and, as the system of credit broke down, few businessmen were able to handle sizeable drafts, such as one that Jacobo wrote in the spring of 1847 for 46,700 pesos.[35] Consequently, the Sánchez Navarro brothers had to issue drafts for much smaller amounts—10,000 to 20,000 pesos—against merchants in intermediate cities, such as Zacatecas, San Luis Potosí, and San Miguel Allende. After discounting the paper these businessmen then wrote letters of credit of their own, and by this cumbersome and time-consuming expedient the Sánchez Navarros did succeed in shifting some of their funds.[36]

With the reestablishment of peace in 1848, the financial system began to recover, and money flowed more freely.[37] The postwar years constituted a time of intense business activity for the Sánchez Navarros. Not only did Carlos work feverishly to clear up pending deals, but with the capital raised by selling several of their haciendas the family in 1850 also retired the mortgage on the *latifundio*.

The Sánchez Navarros formulated a new policy in 1851, when Jacobo joined Carlos and Apolonia in Mexico City to review their situation. The outcome of these discussions was that in addition to managing the *latifundio* Jacobo would also direct most of the financial affairs; Carlos departed on an extended European sojourn, doubtless motivated in part by a desire to recuperate from the pressure under which he had been working for years.[38] Jacobo's new responsibilities were not as onerous as might have been the case, for Carlos left behind a well-organized office. Juan F. de Puyade, the family's business agent, was both reliable and experienced. Besides handling routine matters, such as provisioning the trail crews and cashing drafts, Puyade maintained four sets of daily accounts: these were for Carlos, Jacobo, general expenses, and the *latifundio*. After familiarizing himself with the situation, Jacobo returned to Coahuila, leaving the Mexico City office in Puyade's capable hands. The latter kept Jacobo informed through frequent correspondence, and each month he sent copies of the daily accounts.[39]

Jacobo performed surprisingly well as an absentee financier, though he got off to a discouraging start: 35,000 pesos invested in the Mexico City commercial house of William de Drusina, a German-born merchant and *hacendado*, were lost when that firm went bankrupt in March, 1851.[40] This setback, however, was really Carlos's fault, for it was he who had placed the funds with Drusina.

The investments that Jacobo handled by himself usually turned out more satisfactorily. Through Carlos he had met many of the capital's leading financiers, among them José Ignacio Baz and Alejandro Bellangé, a Frenchman who had lived in Mexico for some twenty years and was extremely well connected in financial and social circles, eventually becoming the head of a major French commercial house in the capital.[41] Baz and Bellangé were directors of the Compañía Restauradora del Mineral de Catorce, a company formed to revive the silver mines at Catorce, in San Luis Potosí. Although the company had bright prospects, such large amounts of capital had been required so frequently from the shareholders that most of them had withdrawn from the enterprise, while several of those remaining were trying to sell their stock for whatever it would bring.[42]

Baz and Bellangé urged Jacobo to invest, but, being somewhat sceptical of the rosy picture the directors painted, the *hacendado* shrewdly decided to do some checking first. He availed himself of the familial intelligence network, writing to his cousin Arizpe, who in turn contacted some of his own relatives residing in Catorce for a first-hand report on the company's possibilities. The report was favorable, and Jacobo became one of the principal stockholders. Within months the stock's value soared, for the company hit a rich new vein of silver.[43]

One of the difficulties involved in financial transactions was the problem of safely transferring funds between cities because of the threat of Indians and highwaymen. When it was necessary to ship large amounts of coin, businessmen would usually wait for the departure of a convoy called a *conducta*, which had a military escort.[44] Whenever possible merchants preferred to rely on drafts.

Even so, for a time in 1851 the Sánchez Navarros' office in Mexico City became the depository for a disturbingly large amount of cash. As a result of Jacobo's management, the family's coffers were literally overflowing. By November, the office contained 99,045 pesos in cash and 6,720 in drafts payable to the bearer.[45] Puyade was extremely nervous at having so much money on hand, and he implored Jacobo to draw against his account.[46]

The *hacendado* was pondering how to invest the funds, and an opportunity soon appeared. Rafael Aguirre, who had bought the Hacienda del Rosario in 1848, wrote to Jacobo asking for a loan of 50,000 or 60,000 pesos in order to purchase the Hacienda de Gallinas in San Luis Potosí. Jacobo was reluctant to extend the loan merely on Aguirre's signature, for the latter already owed him 16,000 pesos. He blandly informed Aguirre that although the Sánchez Navarros did have some money in Mexico City the funds did not even total 50,000 pesos.[47] But, in response to Aguirre's pleas, Jacobo finally agreed to loan him up to 100,000 pesos at interest if the credit were fully guaranteed by third parties of unquestioned financial standing.[48] The profusely grateful Aguirre managed to find guarantors acceptable to Jacobo, who in the meantime had once again used the family intelligence network to check the guarantors' credit rating. On this occasion he received a report from Rafael Delgado, since the guarantors were prominent businessmen-*hacendados* in San Luis Potosí.[49] Having protected himself, Jacobo made Aguirre a loan of 50,000 pesos. Within a matter of weeks, however, Aguirre returned the money because the deal to purchase the hacienda had fallen through.[50]

Almost immediately Jacobo had the opportunity to make another substantial loan. Manuel de Ibarra, proprietor of the Hacienda de Abajo near Parras, wrote that his brothers had appointed him to represent their interests in San Luis Potosí and Tamaulipas, and he asked to borrow seventy thousand pesos for a year, offering as collateral a mortgage on the extensive Hacienda de Cruces, in Tamaulipas. Ibarra explained that he and his brothers had substantial accounts receivable but were desperately short of cash, adding that Jacobo was "the only person in these parts who is not in debt and has money available."[51]

This was precisely Jacobo's problem—trying to decide what to do with the liquid assets at his disposal. Land remained the safest form of investment, but the Sánchez Navarros were rather well off in that respect. Business opportunities in Mexico City were clouded by a wave of failures among mercantile houses, that of the brothers Del Conde, who were Jacobo's sheep buyers, being a notable exception.[52] On the other hand, even the prestigious English banking firm of Mackintosh was having difficulty in meeting its obligations on schedule.[53] Jacobo was already involved in trying to collect 15,500 pesos owed him by Jorge Luis Hammeken, a well-known Mexico City financier. After allowing Hammeken to refinance at 1 percent interest per month, Jacobo had to sue him in the Mercantile Tribunal, whereupon a settlement was quickly arranged out of court. By the end of 1851 the debt was liquidated.[54] Whatever ruffled feelings the affair produced were evidently smoothed over, for Jacobo continued doing business with Hammeken for years afterward.[55]

The lack of security for investments in Mexico City was a major factor in Jacobo's decision in the early 1850's to channel much of the family's venture capital into mining. His initial speculation, in the Compañía Restauradora at Catorce, was going well, and there seemed to be no reason why the Sánchez Navarros could not develop their own silver mines at Bonanza. Carlos, who was residing in France at the time,[56] not only concurred but also played an important role by contacting European manufacturers of mining equipment, by secur-

ing the services of foreign experts, and by handling the complex arrangements for financing. During the next few years, there arrived at
Bonanza several hundred thousand pesos' worth of equipment and
machinery, besides a contingent of European technicians.[57] The mining operations at Bonanza added an important new dimension to the
Sánchez Navarros' financial activities, since a great part of their investment capital was now being channeled into improving the *latifundio*
itself.

Though the director of this economic empire and one of the leading
businessmen in the country, Jacobo remained provincial in his style
of living, as is shown by the articles he bought in Mexico City. During
his stay in the capital the only items he sent back to Patos were two
bottles of Rhine wine for himself, and a pair of elaborate chandeliers
for his wife. These were transported by the returning trail crews.[58]
Despite careful packing, the second chandelier arrived in damaged
condition. This distressed Puyade, who explained to Jacobo that,
since there were six men in the trail crew, by taking turns carrying
the chandelier they should have been able to transport it without
incident "to the ends of the earth."[59]

Although in later years Jacobo's purchases from Mexico City increased, they still remained surprisingly modest for a man in his position. He seems not to have been overly concerned with fashionable at-
tire, for during half a decade he ordered a mere three cravats, a dozen
white linen shirts and six colored ones, two pairs of trousers, and
two vests. It is to be hoped that his wife was not fashion conscious
either, for in the same period she received a dozen pairs of silk hose.
Jacobo did, however, buy her three books of music. His own taste in
reading matter ran to the conservative Mexico City newspaper *El
Universal*. Occasionally he ordered a few reams of imported English
or French stationery for his personal correspondence, or a saddle, or a
few bottles of Rhine wine. Jacobo's one weakness was a good cigar,
and he had them shipped to Patos by the hundred.[60]

Carlos, by contrast, definitely enjoyed gracious living, as befitted
one who moved easily among the elite of the capital. An urbane and
polished man of the world, he had maintained an account with an
exclusive London firm of men's clothiers even before embarking on

his European sojourn in 1851.[61] During his residence on the Continent, Carlos managed to spend a respectable amount of the liquid assets Jacobo was accumulating.

For one thing, he maintained his Mexico City residence, a monthly expenditure that included 140 pesos in rent for the mansion, as well as 50 to 75 pesos in wages for the staff of servants. Moreover, he was educating his daughter and a niece at Las Vizcaínas, a fashionable school for girls in the capital. Carlos was well read, his interests ranging from the French newspaper *Trait d'Union* to scholarly works, such as the conservative Lucas Alamán's *Historia de Méjico*. The books he accumulated in Europe were shipped back by the crate to enrich his personal library. His wine cellar was also enriched to the point that it must have been one of the finest in Mexico City, for he sent back 331 cases of French wines. Always conscious of his social position, Carlos purchased a coach and a carriage of the latest model.[62] Returning by way of New York and Veracruz in late 1856, an even more cosmopolitan Carlos resumed his place in Mexico City's business and social circles. Heads doubtless turned as he was frequently driven in his elegant new vehicles to his box at the Iturbide Theater, a favorite gathering place of the capital's elite.[63]

Yet the social whirl did not dominate Carlos's life, for he spent most of his time confronting a series of business crises. To Jacobo's relief, in 1856 Carlos resumed management of the Sánchez Navarros' finances. The times, however, were less than favorable for business. Within eighteen months of Carlos's return, civil strife again wracked Mexico when the bitter War of the Reform broke out at the end of 1857. The ensuing three years of warfare between Liberals and Conservatives severely curtailed the Sánchez Navarros' commercial activities precisely when the brothers needed all the money they could raise in order to pay for their investment at Bonanza. Increasingly, the Sánchez Navarros found themselves being limited to regional and local trade.

Since the main objective in this type of commerce remained that of supplying the *latifundio*, Jacobo had been supervising these activities throughout the preceding decade. Saltillo and its annual fair still constituted the pivot of regional trade.[64] But the fair could provide only a part of the goods needed on the *latifundio*. During the rest of the year the *administrador* received from his subordinates a stream of requests, which he tried to fill in Saltillo. Clothing for the peons was in greatest demand, but the requests included such items as cruppers, rope, stationery, iron, tin, and wax.[65]

The Saltillo fair itself was becoming a dismal affair, a far cry from its heyday in the eighteenth century.[66] Jacobo continued to rely on Saltillo as a source of supply despite the problems arising from political instability and the attendant business uncertainties. There are few references to dealings in Saltillo for the late 1850's, but, aside from one instance of Jacobo's buying a case of cognac to send to Patos, they all concern the difficulty of stocking the store at Bonanza, which at times lacked even such basic commodities as soap.[67]

To make matters worse, the rest of the Sánchez Navarros' regional commerce contracted in the 1850's. The long-standing connection with Rafael Delgado in San Luis Potosí declined.[68] And the renewed turmoil adversely affected Jacobo's developing trade with Monterrey. Whereas in 1851 the only purchase from that city consisted of two wooden mills for grinding cane, by 1855 Jacobo had established important business ties with Lorenzo Olivier, a merchant, financier, and industrialist in Monterrey whose holdings included a lead smelter. Olivier not only purchased the silver produced at Bonanza, paying for it in thirty-day notes against firms in New Orleans and New York, but he also supplied some of the cheap calico required for the *latifundio*.[69]

This mutually profitable association suffered as a result of Santiago Vidaurri's rise to power. As has been mentioned, Jacobo had serious personal and political differences with Vidaurri, to the detriment of the Sánchez Navarros' interests. In retaliation for the pressure Vidaurri had been applying, Jacobo in 1858 declined to assist the governor financially. Vidaurri was taking an active part in the War of the Reform on the Liberal side and had arranged for a considerable arms purchase in the United States. Since Vidaurri's administration was chronically short of funds, the governor asked several prominent citizens to guarantee payment. Jacobo refused to accept the ten-thousand-peso obligation assigned to him. The *hacendado* explained that in recent years he and Carlos had suffered such a series of financial reverses that they had signed a formal agreement between themselves not to commit their signatures to any new ventures.[70] Dampening whatever satisfaction Jacobo derived from discomfiting Vidaurri was the stark fact that the Sánchez Navarros were indeed experiencing serious financial difficulties.

By avoiding any new commitments they managed to weather the War of the Reform, though much of their liquid capital was consumed by the disappointing mining venture at Bonanza. In 1861, upon the conclusion of the war, Carlos and Jacobo began taking stock of their situation, with an eye to dividing the family holdings between them.[71]

Whatever prospects there were of a business revival ended abruptly in 1862 with the French Intervention, leaving Carlos and Jacobo more than ever on the defensive financially. For the first time since the curate José Miguel began building the family's empire, the Sánchez Navarros found themselves in the uncomfortable position of being land poor. Their lack of liquid assets became so critical by 1862 that in order to raise a paltry 6,701 pesos owed in taxes, they had to sell some real estate.[72] Carlos disposed of the Monterrey mansion that had belonged to the family since 1794, as well as some miscellaneous property near Saltillo, to Luis Cepeda for 14,000 pesos, which enabled him to surmount this crisis.[73]

The crises became more frequent as the Intervention progressed. Trade routes to central Mexico being interdicted by the fighting, Jacobo imported what merchandise he could through Matamoros and Monterrey, with mixed results. In 1862, he brought in 2,850 pesos' worth of machinery from the United States for Bonanza, while two years later a consignment that included textiles and clothing for Hermanas and a piano for Patos reached its destination safely. The freighters transporting this cargo could count themselves fortunate, for on the road they passed the charred wreckage of a train of oxcarts belonging to Jacobo that Indians had destroyed a few months earlier as it was returning from Matamoros.[74]

With the Sánchez Navarros' commercial network collapsing, Jacobo necessarily concentrated on keeping the hacienda stores stocked. For the first three years of the Intervention he succeeded reasonably well.

To cite one instance, in 1862 the store at Bonanza carried a respectable variety of merchandise, valued at 5,314 pesos.[75] Beginning in 1864 the fighting in Coahuila intensified, and even local commerce stagnated.[76] This soon ceased to matter, for the triumphant Liberals sacked the various *cascos* as they drove the French and their Imperialist allies from the state. The wreckage of the Sánchez Navarros' commercial empire was mute evidence that business could not survive, let alone flourish, without political stability in Mexico.

12. Politics

Politics played the decisive role in the Sánchez Navarros' affairs after independence. Having become politicized during the revolutionary war, the family found it impossible to disengage, since the turbulent situation in Mexico meant that in the final analysis the retention of their privileged position depended on making the right choices politically. Basically conservative and elitist, the Sánchez Navarros were nevertheless pragmatists, striving to work within the system—whatever it might be at the moment. The degree of their involvement conformed to the pattern established in the colonial period, for as a rule they shunned public office, preferring to achieve their ends by influencing those in power. This was usually done through friends and relatives, many of whom were officeholders themselves, who represented a wide range of political viewpoints. What one is dealing with in the case of the Sánchez Navarros, therefore, is kinship politics, in which ideology was oftentimes of secondary importance.

In 1822 the dominant political figure in Mexico was the ambitious Gen. Agustín de Iturbide; under his auspices the nation was in the process of establishing the machinery of government. This involved the election of a constituent congress as well as provincial deputations for the various regions of Mexico. In Coahuila the Sánchez Navarros could justifiably feel satisfied with the family's political prospects. José Melchor had already established his credentials as an ardent supporter of Iturbide by having opportunely espoused the Plan of Iguala in 1821. Disdaining public office, José Melchor used his influence to further the careers of several relatives. An election held in Monclova resulted in his cousin Melchor Múzquiz becoming a deputy to the constituent congress. Another cousin, José Ignacio Sánchez Navarro, the curate of Saltillo, not only served as one of the three electors in this vote but immediately thereafter was chosen as a deputy to the provincial deputation for the Northeast.[1]

Shortly thereafter, in March, 1822, Iturbide cowed the national congress into electing him Emperor Agustín I. The new monarch proved unable to consolidate his rule, and early in 1823 a Federalist rebellion erupted in central Mexico and rapidly gained adherents. Coahuilans joined the movement to overthrow Iturbide with the same enthusiasm they had earlier shown for his accession to power. In the face of mounting opposition, Iturbide bowed to the inevitable and left the country in April, 1823.

With the triumph of Federalism it became necessary once again to organize the machinery of government, and another round of elections occurred. Again the Sánchez Navarros obtained their fair share of representation. José Melchor's cousin the priest José Miguel Ramos Arizpe went to Mexico City as a deputy in the new constituent congress, where he performed brilliantly. Elected as his alternate, moreover, was another of José Melchor's cousins, Domingo de Letona, who had been the family's business agent in the capital for so many years. Even José Melchor reluctantly accepted public office as one of the seven Coahuilan deputies to the provincial deputation. Nor was José Melchor alone, for among the other deputies was his cousin Rafael Ecay Múzquiz, while still another cousin, Víctor Blanco, was one of the three alternates in the delegation.[2]

With his political position apparently secure, José Melchor abruptly declined to serve in the provincial deputation, obtaining instead the comparatively insignificant position of postmaster of Santa Rosa, which he held until 1826.[3] The explanation for his surprising choice of offices was twofold. First, the *hacendado* had never really been enthusiastic about being a deputy; second, his presence was urgently required in Santa Rosa where a serious situation had developed. While concentrating on national politics, José Melchor had neglected to keep his fences mended in Santa Rosa, to the detriment of the lawsuits he had pending in that locality.

Matters had seemed well in hand, for not only were José Melchor's representatives pressing the suits, primarily the one against the Elizondo family, but also the *alcalde* and municipal council of Santa Rosa were partisans of the *hacendado*. The *alcalde* could be relied on to ignore the Elizondos' arguments in the land dispute, causing the latter to complain that most of the citizenry in Santa Rosa were either clients or friends of José Melchor.[4]

This being the case, the *hacendado* was understandably complacent. The Elizondos and their allies, however, worked diligently to mobilize everyone who resented the Sánchez Navarros' domination of the Santa Rosa region, and in a close election in 1823 they managed to install one of their supporters as *alcalde*. From then on, José Melchor experienced mounting frustration as the new *alcalde* consistently ruled against him.[5]

In spite of his economic power and political connections, José Melchor was by no means omnipotent in Coahuila, as is shown by the amount of trouble he received from petty officials. Not only was the *alcalde* of Santa Rosa now openly hostile, but his counterpart in Monclova was also emboldened to defy the Sánchez Navarros.[6] This growing wave of opposition had the covert or at least tacit support of many townspeople in Monclova and Santa Rosa who were enjoying José Melchor's discomfiture, and it took the *hacendado* four years to regain control of the situation.

Santa Rosa remained the focal point of opposition, for here José Melchor faced the enmity of the *alcalde* as well as the parish priest, José Antonio Quirós, with whom the *hacendado* was also engaged in a land dispute. To overcome this alliance José Melchor launched a counterattack by rallying his supporters to recapture control of local government. But an election in 1825 returned another Elizondo partisan as *alcalde*, and that worthy promptly took the offensive.[7]

Enthusiastically executing a ruling by the Audiencia of Guadalajara that the Elizondos had been unjustly deprived of their land, in 1826 the *alcalde* ordered the seizure of property belonging to José Melchor's brother, who owned a ranch near Santa Rosa.[8] José Melchor's fury at learning of this unprecedented treatment of the Sánchez Navarros increased when one of his informants reported early in 1827 that the family was being openly insulted on the streets of Santa Rosa by jubilant Elizondo partisans.[9] This marked the nadir of the *hacendado*'s prestige in Santa Rosa, but these reverses merely caused José Melchor to redouble his efforts to regain control of the community. That summer he finally succeeded when his followers won a majority of seats on the municipal council and elected as *alcalde* Melitón Castellano, brother of the *mayordomo* of Hermanas and one of José Melchor's staunchest supporters.[10]

The *hacendado* now began paying off old scores. First, his brother's property was returned. Next, the municipal council launched a savage campaign to discredit and remove the local priest Quirós. They sent a report to the governor detailing the curate's alleged misconduct, citing his lack of respect for the current local authorities, his brutality toward his peons at the Hacienda de Nacimiento, his neglect of his ecclesiastical duties, and his having for the last seven years kept a mistress, by whom he had a bastard son. The new *alcalde* sent José Melchor a copy of the report, stating, "I believe we have carried out all your instructions in this matter."[11] Not only was the curate Quirós removed, but also his lawsuit over land was now hopeless, for the *alcalde* rejected every argument presented, as he was also doing in the Elizondo case.[12]

José Melchor could now concentrate on his campaign to establish a supreme court for Coahuila. Ever since his attorney suggested this in 1826 as the way to win the lawsuits pending in the Audiencia of Guadalajara, the *hacendado* had been exerting every bit of political pressure he could muster. One tactic was to have the Monclova municipal council petition for the creation of the court because several of the smaller towns would follow Monclova's lead. But José Melchor first had to reassert his dominance over local government in Monclova, no easy matter. In December, 1826, his supporters met total defeat when they tried to have the petition passed by the municipal council.

Their next attempt resulted in the council meeting erupting into a freewheeling brawl between the *hacendado*'s partisans and his enemies.[13] José Melchor persisted, and in 1827 his forces carried the day: not only was the petition sent to the state legislature, but also the *hacendado* was elected *alcalde* of Monclova. Having made his point, José Melchor declined to serve, stepping aside for one of his cronies.[14]

The collapse of opposition in Monclova in turn reflected the *hacendado*'s successful lobbying in Saltillo, where he had influential contacts in the state government. His connections began with the governors, each of whom between August, 1824, and August, 1827, was a cousin of his. In addition, the *hacendado* could count on the enthusiastic support of the Baron de Bastrop, a leading member of the legislature. In fact it was Bastrop, one of José Melchor's co-conspirators in the 1811 plot to capture the insurgent leaders, who urged his fellow legislators to create the supreme court immediately, citing the abuses that various *alcaldes* were committing.[15] José Melchor jubilantly reported to his attorney the legislature's willingness to serve his special interest.[16] Much to the *hacendado*'s disgust, however, that body first took up the matter of writing a state constitution, and, as debate dragged on for months, his impatience increased accordingly. José Melchor remained in Saltillo through the end of 1826, fuming at the delay and spurring his legislative allies to greater activity on his behalf.[17] Finally, in June, 1827, he had the satisfaction of learning that the long-awaited law providing for a supreme court had been passed.[18]

Since it was now only a matter of time until his pending lawsuits came before that tribunal, where he had every confidence of winning favorable judgments, José Melchor repaid his political debts by supporting his friends in the legislature, whose speaker was none other than his cousin the curate José Ignacio Sánchez Navarro.[19] Throughout 1828 he was in the thick of the factional strife in Coahuila, working for the removal of certain local officials who resisted the legislature's efforts to assert itself.[20] Much of the *hacendado*'s activity was of a clandestine nature, in which he communicated secretly with local leaders in order to sway opinion in favor of the legislature. His task was easier because he belonged to the Masonic order, as did several of his correspondents, and the Masonic oath provided protection against the unauthorized disclosure of information. Furthermore, at least one of José Melchor's associates, the commander of the Presidio de Río Grande, took the added precaution of burning all confidential letters he received from the *hacendado*.[21]

José Melchor's discreet involvement in state politics did not go unrewarded, for one of the legislators, Ramón García Rojas, not only took charge of presenting the pending lawsuits before the supreme court but also arranged what proved to be the victorious settlement with the Elizondo family. García Rojas easily persuaded José Melchor to loan sixty pesos to the legislator's friend Santiago del Valle, whom the Elizondos had chosen as their arbiter in the settlement; moreover, García Rojas prevailed on the Elizondos to accept as the third arbiter— from whose ruling there was no appeal—Juan Vicente Campos, the congressman from Coahuila, who was an intimate friend of José Melchor.[22] It came as no surprise, therefore, when in May, 1829, Campos ruled that the Elizondos had lost their tenacious struggle to retain San Juan de Sabinas. Shortly thereafter the supreme court confirmed José Melchor's title to the lands in dispute with the curate Quirós, the Hacienda de Nacimiento.[23] Political involvement, however reluctant, had thus been a vital part of José Melchor's success in expanding the *latifundio* by some 137,000 acres.

Even while engaged in his own particular battles, the *hacendado* had remained abreast of events outside Coahuila. Much of his information came from correspondents in Mexico City and Monterrey, but he also subscribed to several periodicals, among them the Mexico City newspaper *Aguila Mexicana*.[24] Perceiving which way the political winds were blowing, the *hacendado* tacked accordingly.

The Federalist republic established in 1824 was in serious trouble by 1828, as evidenced by the disputed presidential election of that year. Force of arms resolved the controversy, elevating the Liberal candidate, Gen. Vicente Guerrero, to the presidency in 1829. Almost immediately his vice-president, Gen. Anastacio Bustamante, began planning his own bid for power, and in 1830 he deposed Guerrero. Under Bustamante, whose regime lasted from 1830 to 1832, the government became openly reactionary. Behind a façade of Federalism, the new administration sought to allay the rising fears of the upper classes by pacifying the country and preserving as much of Mexico's colonial heritage as possible.

This policy met with the relieved approval of José Melchor, who like many of his countrymen looked back nostalgically on the stability of the viceregal period. Although the *hacendado* had operated quite effectively under the preceding Liberal administrations, Bustamante's style was much more to his liking. It promised not only a climate of security in which to conduct business, but also the preservation of the Sánchez Navarros' hard-won local power.

José Melchor had the local situation well in hand at the time of Bustamante's accession in 1830. In the course of winning the various land disputes, the *hacendado* had crushed his leading rivals and had reemerged as a political power in Coahuila, a position he firmly intended to maintain. José Melchor's political machine functioned smoothly. In troublesome Santa Rosa, for example, his followers controlled the local offices from 1830 to 1832. Moreover, in 1830 his brother-in-law Juan Estevan Beráin became the parish priest. Though in 1831 Beráin was transferred, the loss was offset by the appointment of one of José Melchor's friends as commander of the garrison.[25] Reinforcing this influence, in May, 1831, the *hacendado*'s cousin and business associate José María de Letona became governor, occupying that position until September, 1832, when he died in office.

José Melchor even had access to President Bustamante himself. The intermediary was Juan Vicente Campos, still the congressman from Coahuila and still an intimate friend of the *hacendado*. Campos not only presented to the chief executive José Melchor's recommendations for combatting Indian depredations in Coahuila but also worked diligently to arouse support for the proposal in the chamber of deputies and the senate.[26] José Melchor's ties with the Bustamante regime continued with the election in 1832 of his cousin the priest José Ignacio Sánchez Navarro as congressman from Coahuila.[27]

This advantage proved short-lived, for the long-expected rebellion against Bustamante broke out in 1832. Leading the revolt was Gen. Antonio López de Santa Anna, the unscrupulous opportunist who dominated the political scene for three decades following independence. Santa Anna's pretext for this rebellion was the reestablishment of the Federalist system, whose self-styled champion he professed to be. Though at first the congressman José Ignacio Sánchez Navarro discounted the rebels' chances of success and referred to Santa Anna in disparaging terms, the revolt made rapid headway.[28] To José Melchor the impending collapse of Bustamante's administration and the stability it represented was nothing less than a catastrophe. Writing to his wife, the *hacendado* lamented, "God grant that my foreboding be ill founded, but I foresee much suffering and the total ruin of the Nation itself."[29]

José Melchor's gloomy prognostication proved somewhat exaggerated. His correspondents duly kept him informed of Bustamante's desperate efforts to retain power, when José Melchor's cousin Gen. Melchor Múzquiz served as interim president for four months while Bustamante personally led the army, and of the disorganization following the latter's downfall in December, 1832.[30] Nonetheless, Mexico managed to survive under a Liberal regime nominally headed by the victorious Santa Anna. The latter, exhibiting the political cunning that had become his trademark, spent little time in the presidency, delegating the thankless task of administering the bankrupt nation to his vice-president, Valentín Gómez Farías, a dedicated reformer. Gómez Farías's policies, especially his efforts to break the power of the Church and the army, proved extremely controversial, and opposition mounted against the hapless vice-president. The wily Santa Anna, who had in effect disassociated himself from his own regime, led a successful rebellion in 1834 against Gómez Farías and the Liberals, this time as the self-styled champion of Centralism.

With the country undergoing such bewildering vicissitudes, José Melchor had been concentrating on maintaining his influence in Coahuila by means of the political machine he had organized. Shortly before elections he drew up lists of acceptable candidates for local office and distributed them to his partisans with instructions to get out the vote.[31] The *hacendado* coordinated these maneuvers with his allies in the state legislature. Even while convalescing in Saltillo from his near-fatal attack of cholera in 1833, he repeatedly left his sickbed for informal strategy sessions.[32] José Melchor still adhered to his basic technique of remaining in the background and influencing events through intermediaries. Having on various occasions declined to hold public office himself, he nevertheless felt no compunction about lecturing his supporters on their civic responsibilities. When the cashier of the Monclova store expressed reluctance to serve as an alderman of that city, the *hacendado* pompously rebuked him, pointing out that, if honest men shirked their responsibilities, the nation was doomed.[33]

Yet, as the situation became increasingly menacing, José Melchor made himself increasingly scarce. In 1834 not only was Santa Anna engaged in overthrowing Gómez Farías but also civil war was raging in Coahuila between Monclova, which adhered to Federalism, and Saltillo, which supported Santa Anna. The *hacendado* sought to maintain an even lower political profile than usual until the current round of revolution had ended, in order to keep his options open. His trip that year to visit his sons at school in Mexico City provided a convenient pretext for leaving Coahuila at a critical juncture. After his return in the fall he went into virtual seclusion.[34]

In October he announced his imminent departure for Monterrey to take mineral baths for his rheumatism.[35] A week later, though, he sent a confidential letter by messenger informing the cashier of the Monclova store that he had actually taken refuge at the Estancia de la Mota, the Sánchez Navarro hacienda east of Monclova. José Melchor stated that the discomforts of traveling to La Mota by an unfrequented route would be amply justified if by having done so he achieved "my objective of not becoming involved in the revolution, which is precisely the thing from which I'm fleeing, because I don't want to find myself committed to any of the factions."[36] He planned to seclude himself at one of his haciendas near Santa Rosa, and he emphasized the necessity of being kept informed of the contending factions' troop movements, to avoid any awkward encounters on the road.

José Melchor presumably kept moving from one hacienda to another often enough to avoid having to take sides as Santa Anna moved in the spring of 1835 to crush the Federalist legislature stubbornly holding out in Monclova. In fact, José Melchor decided that another visit to Mexico City was in order, and he departed in May.[37] Once again his reason for going was to visit his sons in school, but one may speculate that while in the capital he prudently established relations with the Centralist regime.

Upon his return to Coahuila in October, the *hacendado* went into retirement.[38] Besides having lost whatever zest he may have had for politics, his health was rapidly failing. When Santa Anna led his army through Monclova in February, 1836, on his way north to conduct the disastrous campaign in Texas, José Melchor was unable to pay his respects to that illustrious personage, because he was confined to his bed at the Hacienda de Soledad. Three of Santa Anna's generals, however, asked to be remembered to the *hacendado*, which strengthens the supposition that José Melchor had made useful contacts while in Mexico City.[39]

In June, 1836, José Melchor died, worn out by the strain of directing the Sánchez Navarros' complex affairs. Yet with politics, as with other matters, the *hacendado* had done an impressive job of protecting the family's interests. By opportunely switching his allegiance during the preceding quarter century from royalist to Iturbidist to Federalist to Centralist, he had guided the family safely through one of the most unstable periods in Mexican history.

At the time of his death José Melchor's political machine was in disarray, but the Sánchez Navarros still had a great deal of residual influence in Coahuila. Apolonia's domineering personality often sufficed to overawe local functionaries.[40] Furthermore, she had been privy to many of her late husband's intrigues and was thus able to advise Jacobo as he began dealing with his father's old associates. In addition, friends of the family could be relied on to alert Jacobo to the machinations of the Sánchez Navarros' rivals.[41] But on balance the four years following José Melchor's death represented a holding action, for not until the purchase of the Marquisate in 1840 did the Sánchez Navarros' political power increase markedly.

This development was largely a function of the family's new position as the largest *hacendados* in Mexico, but it also reflected progressively efficient teamwork between Jacobo in Coahuila and

Carlos in Mexico City. The latter's role was particularly important, for the Centralists had written a new constitution converting the states into departments, which meant that the country was being run from Mexico City. Carlos's contacts in the capital were invaluable in helping to resolve some of the Sánchez Navarros' problems in Coahuila. Although the brothers, sensibly enough, were nominal Centralists, they still sought to retain as much local power as possible; therefore, it is difficult to make a neat categorization of their political affiliations. For example, they were supporters of Santa Anna, who by 1841 had recovered the prestige he had lost in the 1836 debacle and was again the dominant political figure in Mexico. Yet the Sánchez Navarros' support of Santa Anna stemmed not from admiration of the man but from the lack of an alternative. Like their father, Carlos and Jacobo wanted a government that could provide the stability necessary for the profitable operation of the family's enterprises.

The brothers also emulated José Melchor in that they preferred to work behind the scenes to achieve their ends. This technique was especially well suited to the situation obtaining under the Centralist republic, for oftentimes the governors of Coahuila were generals appointed from Mexico City. The task before Carlos and Jacobo was thus not one of building a political machine capable of winning elections but rather one of finding ways to influence specific officials. In doing so the brothers naturally turned to their network of relatives and friends.

This was certainly the case in the first crisis they experienced, that concerning payment of the *alcabala* on the purchase of the Marquisate. It will be remembered that the Coahuilan authorities insisted that the Sánchez Navarros pay the transfer tax, something the brothers refused to do. The national government then ordered the military governor of Coahuila to seize their properties, though a subsequent directive allowed the governor to use his own judgment in the matter. Fortunately for the Sánchez Navarros, they not only knew what actions the governor planned to take almost as soon as he himself had decided, but they also received excellent advice about countering these moves: the governor's military secretary, Col. Rafael González, was a second cousin of the Sánchez Navarros, and from Saltillo he kept Jacobo abreast of the governor's intentions, besides mailing periodic reports to Carlos in Mexico City.[42]

It was González who alerted the brothers to the fact that the governor had sent a writ to the capital requiring Carlos to show cause why the Sánchez Navarros should not pay the *alcabala*. The writ promptly became mislaid somewhere within the Ministry of War, bringing the proceedings to a standstill for months. In a letter to Jacobo, Carlos disclaimed any role in these mysterious happenings, stating that he had not tried to use his influence, because he was confident that the law was on his side.[43] Nevertheless, an unidentified general high in the ministry was definitely intervening on the Sánchez Navarros' behalf. When the governor of Coahuila, Gen. Francisco Mejía, inquired about the writ, he received a remarkable reply from the ministry: the unnamed general returned the document unanswered, along with a covering letter blandly announcing that no one there knew of a Carlos Sánchez Navarro, nor was his address known, nor was it known whether he might be a soldier, and if so to what unit he belonged. Colonel González gleefully reported this development to his cousin Jacobo, adding that the letter "shows that Carlos has not lacked friends, for which I am delighted."[44] The identity of Carlos's benefactor remains obscure, but it may be speculated that Gen. Melchor Múzquiz, the Sánchez Navarros' uncle and sometime interim president of the republic, had taken a hand in the matter. Múzquiz not only had widespread connections within the army but was also a prominent figure in Centralist circles.[45]

Though the Sánchez Navarros had some influence with the national government, the committee of Aguayo's creditors wielded considerably more. In 1843 the government ruled that the committee was not liable for the *alcabala*. As for the Sánchez Navarros, they had to pay only a token tax. The affair thus serves to illustrate how two powerful interests could conclude an enormous real estate transaction and evade paying virtually all of the taxes due on it.

While final settlement was pending, the Sánchez Navarros had been coping with other troubles growing out of the *alcabala* affair. The governor, General Mejía, understandably resented the cavalier treatment he had received from Carlos's ally in the Ministry of War, and Mejía developed a pronounced animus against the Sánchez Navarros. Since he was on the scene, Jacobo bore the brunt of Mejía's anger, which the latter vented by siding with the aggressive Aguirre family, who claimed a tract on the northwestern boundary of the Marquisate. As Jacobo's lawyer and cousin Juan N. de Arizpe ruefully pointed out, the *hacendado* "should expect nothing favorable" while Mejía held office, an opinion the governor's military secretary confirmed.[46]

With Mejía already predisposed against the Sánchez Navarros, there occurred still another incident that aroused the governor's ire. In November, 1842, a leading Mexico City newspaper published an anonymous letter ridiculing Mejía for his incompetence in repelling Indian incursions. Arizpe brought the letter to Jacobo's attention and warned him that in Saltillo it was generally thought that the Sánchez Navarros had written it. Accordingly, Jacobo should be prepared, for, when Mejía returned from an expedition against Indian raiders, he would be furious.[47] In all probability Carlos and Jacobo had nothing to do with the offending letter because the last thing they wanted was to exacerbate their already tense relations with Mejía. A more likely explanation is that their rivals the Aguirres were responsible. The latter sent a copy of the newspaper in question by messenger to Mejía at his field headquarters, along with a covering letter noting that only the Sánchez Navarros had reason to perpetrate such a calumny. When Mejía returned to Saltillo, he was indeed livid with rage, threatening to sue the newspaper and reiterating his intention of crushing the impertinent Sánchez Navarro brothers. Arizpe advised Jacobo to stay out of Mejía's way for a time until the matter blew over, "as it did the last time."[48]

Jacobo took the advice, spending his time at Patos and Bonanza and rarely setting foot in Saltillo. While waiting for the passage of time to soothe Mejía's feelings, Jacobo also mobilized his friends to intercede with the governor. Besides Arizpe and Colonel González, the *hacendado* called on old friends of his father, such as Juan Vicente Campos, the ex-congressman, and Jesús M. Ibarra, the departmental treasurer.[49] Ibarra had already proved himself zealous in protecting

Jacobo's interests; not only was he a relative but he was also a tenant, leasing one of the haciendas composing the Marquisate.[50] Jacobo's trump, however, lay in the fact that Mejía's second-in-command was none other than Col. José Juan Sánchez Navarro, his uncle.

José Juan had always been on terms of warm affection with Apolonia and José Melchor. When in 1828 as a captain he journeyed through Coahuila to command the escort of Gen. Manuel de Mier y Terán on the latter's famous tour of inspection in Texas, the Sánchez Navarros outdid themselves in extending hospitality to their cousin. Not only were José Juan and his wife transported across the *latifundio* in José Melchor's own coach, but they were also entertained at each of the *cascos* along the way.[51] José Juan remained in northeastern Mexico, and the friendship endured over the years. In 1831 he became adjutant inspector for Nuevo León and Tamaulipas, continuing in that post until the Texas revolution. He fought at San Antonio in December, 1835, and took part in the siege of the Alamo the following March; in his diary he recorded a valuable first-hand account of these engagements.[52] He was subsequently promoted to lieutenant colonel and assigned to troop duty on the northern frontier, where he gained a formidable reputation as an Indian fighter. We have seen how in 1842 José Juan responded with alacrity to Apolonia's appeal for help against the Indians. He now responded to his nephew Jacobo's appeal by using his influence to help calm Mejía.

Matters eventually worked out to Jacobo's satisfaction. Mejía refrained from taking any drastic action against the Sánchez Navarros, and in March, 1843, José Juan succeeded him as interim governor. Unfortunately José Juan held office only one month, until a new general could arrive from Mexico City. Still, Jacobo enjoyed cordial relations with José Juan's successor. Even when in May, 1844, Mejía was reassigned to his old position, which he occupied until January, 1845, there was little of the tension that had characterized his previous dealings with Jacobo. One reason was that the *hacendado* and the Aguirres were in the process of reaching an out-of-court settlement to their land dispute, and the Aguirres had less cause to incite Mejía against the Sánchez Navarros.[53] A more compelling reason for Jacobo's improved relations with the military was the impending conflict with the United States. As the army began reinforcing the northern frontier in 1845, Gen. Mariano Arista, commanding the Northeast, found Jacobo's financial connections with Mexico City indispensable in arranging the transfer of funds to finance the army's operations.[54]

When hostilities broke out in 1846, the army's state of readiness left much to be desired: every major battle was lost. Nor was the political situation conducive to a vigorous war effort. In August, 1846, a revolt overturned Centralism and restored the Federalist system, necessitating a monumental changing of governmental gears in the midst of foreign invasion. Moreover, the new Federalist president was none other than the mercurial Santa Anna, who made a triumphant return from exile. His principal collaborator in the administration was Valentín Gómez Farías, the reformer whom Santa Anna had deposed in 1834. Leaving Gómez Farías to cope with insoluble political and economic problems, Santa Anna took personal command of the army, leading it to defeat.

The war was a disaster for the nation but not for the Sánchez Navarros, who engaged in some adroit political maneuvering. When the Americans occupied Coahuila in December, 1846, Jacobo was spared the humiliation of watching them march into Saltillo, for he had taken Apolonia to stay with Carlos in Mexico City. The *hacendado*'s absence proved most unfortunate, for the Aguirre clan seized control of the state government in a bloodless coup. They persuaded the incumbent governor to resign, held an irregular election, and installed José María Aguirre as governor with wide powers to rule by decree. Jacobo was thunderstruck when he learned of these developments in a letter from Arizpe, who grimly emphasized the gravity of the situation. The Sánchez Navarros' interests were now menaced by enemies both domestic and foreign.[55] Jacobo immediately set out for Coahuila, and he must have spent his time on the journey pondering how to retrieve the situation. The only encouraging element in the picture was that the lieutenant governor, Eduardo González, was a cousin of the Sánchez Navarros, but under the circumstances there seemed little that González could do.

At what point in his analysis Jacobo grasped the solution one cannot say, but grasp it he did; real power in Coahuila lay not with Governor Aguirre and his minions but with the American forces of occupation. By reaching an accommodation with the Americans he could effectively neutralize the Aguirres. What was happening in Coahuila reflected one of the major weaknesses of Mexican society during the war— the propensity of factions to try to destroy each other rather than uniting against the common foe.

Jacobo's decision to collaborate with the Americans stemmed both from his determination to checkmate the Aguirres and from some very practical considerations. First was the overriding necessity of safeguarding the family's properties. Second was the prospect of doing a profitable business by supplying the American army. Third, given the defenseless condition of the inhabitants of Coahuila, resistance in the form of guerrilla warfare would be futile.

The *hacendado* discovered to his delight that the American commander in Coahuila, Gen. John Wool, welcomed collaboration. Wool's policy was one of conciliation, and he offered broad guarantees to those Mexicans prepared to cooperate with the army.[56] Taking the American at his word, Jacobo declared his neutrality in the war, supplied whatever provisions the conquerors required, and soon established excellent relations with Wool himself. The general and his entourage received lavish hospitality when they visited Patos.[57]

Wool would have been less than human had he not been flattered by the attentions of the Sánchez Navarros and the other landowning families who were assiduously cultivating his favor. By establishing a *rapprochement* with this element, Wool not only enjoyed their society but also used them to ensure a steady stream of provisions for the army and to control the population. In turn the *hacendados* benefited handsomely by supplying the Americans and by having Wool protect their properties.[58]

Yet beneath the surface cordiality there was growing hostility on the part of the Mexicans. In no small measure it resulted from outrages by the unruly volunteer units in the army of occupation.[59] A particular problem was the Texas Rangers, who perhaps more than any other American troops viewed the war as a splendid opportunity to kill Mexicans, combatant and noncombatant alike; General Taylor finally had to ask the War Department not to send him any more troops from Texas.[60] Jacobo was well aware of the abuses being committed, for twice Patos was the scene of volunteer atrocities. On one occasion Arkansas cavalrymen got out of control and went on a rampage of rape and murder. Wool had to dispatch dragoons to restore order.[61] The other tragedy involved Texas Rangers running amok when one of their comrades, who had gotten drunk and had assaulted the resident priest, was seized and tortured by the enraged inhabitants. According to one of Wool's dragoons, the affair was hushed up to avoid embarrassing the army.[62]

Wool probably interpreted Jacobo's acquiescence in this matter as further evidence of the *hacendado*'s friendship. It apparently never occurred to the general that Jacobo might be playing a double game, biding his time until a telling blow could be struck against the invader. In contrast to Wool's naïveté, some of his own officers were more perceptive. Capt. George Hughes, for one, observed that "this powerful family, together with their relations, the Blancos, the Yvarros [*sic*], and the Zuloagos [*sic*], own nearly the entire state and its population. They have taken no open or active part in the present war, and have preserved friendly and even kindly relations with many of our officers; but the Blancos and Sanchezes are understood to be prepared, under more promising circumstances, to uphold the Mexican government with their wealth and influence."[63] Their opportunity came when Santa Anna moved north from San Luis Potosí to drive the Americans from Saltillo, a campaign that culminated in the decisive battle of Buenavista on February 22–23, 1847.

Jacobo and his relatives assisted the Mexican army in various ways. Juan N. de Arizpe secretly stockpiled flour for use by Santa Anna's forces and subsequently took to the hills at the head of a guerrilla band, as did another cousin, Miguel Blanco. The latter, with the rank of colonel, raised a large force of rancheros and endeavored to cut off any American retreat from Saltillo.[64] A nephew, Manuel Sánchez Navarro, who had been Jacobo's business agent in Saltillo and who was a militia captain, likewise took up arms. He guided Gen. José V. Miñón's cavalry brigade to the Hacienda de Encarnación fifty miles south of Saltillo, where on January 23 they surrounded and captured an eighty-man scouting party of Arkansas and Kentucky cavalry.[65] Jacobo was much more circumspect, adhering to his policy of remaining in the background. Rather than openly committing himself by leading his retainers in partisan warfare as did the Aguirres, he used his position and network of informants to secure military intelligence for transmittal to Santa Anna's headquarters, where his uncle José Juan Sánchez Navarro served as a staff officer.[66]

All these efforts were in vain. During two days of savage fighting at Buenavista, Santa Anna came very close to winning the victory he so desperately needed, but Taylor's battered lines managed to hold: the Mexican army began its disastrous retreat back to San Luis Potosí. In the aftermath of the climactic encounter, Jacobo's last gesture toward aiding his countrymen was to contribute one hundred pesos to a fund administered by his uncle José Ignacio Sánchez Navarro, who was once again the curate of Saltillo, to succour wounded Mexican prisoners of war.[67]

Having backed the losing side, Jacobo withdrew to his Hacienda de Bonanza where he nervously waited to learn what retribution the Americans would exact. The *hacendado* could write off as the fortunes of war the damage to his estates of Aguanueva and Buenavista, but it was the rest of his properties—to say nothing of his person— that now concerned him. It came as no surprise to learn that Wool was furious, not only with Jacobo but also with the other landowners and public officials who had broken their pledge of neutrality by aiding Santa Anna. Jacobo's immediate task was to ascertain how much the Americans knew about his clandestine activities. Since most of his associates, being Mexicans, were also under a cloud, the resourceful *hacendado* availed himself of the Irishman Boultbee to make the necessary inquiries.

In a carefully worded letter Boultbee reassured Jacobo that the Americans had little evidence linking him to espionage. Regarding the *hacendado*'s personal safety, the Americans were not persecuting those who had taken up arms, and even people such as Arizpe had received safe-conducts. Jacobo had nothing to fear. Greatly relieved, he returned to Patos where he pursued a campaign to get back in Wool's good graces.[68] Boultbee's intercession on Jacobo's behalf brought to light the real source of Wool's anger—the general's feelings were hurt. Wool had been bitterly disillusioned to discover that the Mexicans did not love him for himself alone—their good will had been largely a matter of expediency. He was particularly disappointed with Jacobo, whose actions he interpreted as a betrayal of friendship.[69] Jacobo immediately instructed Boultbee to see Wool again at the earliest opportunity and at all costs convince him of the *hacendado*'s innocence and of his warm affection for the general. The Irishman probably used a liberal application of blarney, for a few days later he triumphantly conveyed a message from Wool to the effect that the general was planning a reconciliation.[70]

Having extricated himself from an extremely awkward situation, Jacobo redoubled his efforts to maintain cordial relations with Wool. Life for Jacobo settled into a comfortable routine in which he sold supplies to the Americans and basked under Wool's protection. To avoid jeopardizing his hard-won position, Jacobo now followed a policy of strict neutrality regarding the war. Guerrilla bands occasionally harassed traffic on the highway south of Saltillo, but there is no evidence that Jacobo gave them anything except perhaps moral support.[71] Nor did he allow himself to be drawn into assisting a proposed counteroffensive from San Luis Potosí by Gen. José Urrea, a counteroffensive that in any case never materialized.[72] Jacobo's technique of catering to Wool's desire for friendship saw him safely through the remainder of the war.

As the Americans evacuated Coahuila in the summer of 1848, Jacobo could congratulate himself for having successfully walked a perilous political tightrope. His services to the Mexican cause prior to Buenavista established his credentials as a patriot, while at the same time he had enjoyed profitable commercial relations with the Americans during the occupation. Above all, the *latifundio* had emerged almost unscathed from the conflict.

In the postwar era the Sánchez Navarros not only expanded their economic base but also reached the height of their political power. As shown by Rafael Aguirre's approaching Jacobo for a substantial loan in 1851, the Aguirre clan lacked the financial resources to continue competing for domination of the state. The Sánchez Navarros' resurgence was evident by the fall of 1848, when they helped persuade José María Aguirre to resign as governor. His successor, Eduardo González, was both Jacobo's cousin and his tenant at the Hacienda de Aguanueva. Even when González's term ended, the Sánchez Navarros' interests were protected, for the next two governors were also friends of the family. Thus, through 1850 the Sánchez Navarros had extraordinary influence in the state capitol.

Another source of influence was Jacobo's uncle, José Juan Sánchez Navarro. He had emerged from the war with the rank of general and in 1848 became the commandant general of Coahuila, holding that post until his death in June, 1849.[73] The general's brother, the priest José Ignacio Sánchez Navarro, further reinforced the family's power. Besides being a cultured individual and the owner of the finest private library in Saltillo, José Ignacio enjoyed tremendous popularity in that city, popularity that in 1848 was put to good use when he was elected senator from Coahuila. Having capped his political career, José Ignacio had the satisfaction of fulfilling his ecclesiastical ambitions. Upon the expiration of his senatorial term in 1850, he was elected bishop of Linares, with a diocese encompassing the whole Northeast. Unfortunately, he died in Mexico City in August, 1851, shortly before his consecration.[74] That same year, however, Carlos was elected as the alternate from Coahuila to the senate.[75] Given the family's economic power and their political, military, and ecclesiastical connections, Coahuila at mid-century resembled a fief of the Sánchez Navarros.

Jacobo continued to operate behind the scenes, his direct involvement in politics being limited to serving on the governor's advisory council.[76] The *hacendado* worked principally through his cousin and lawyer Juan N. de Arizpe, who was an influential member of the legislature. A brief examination of the property tax structure of Coahuila indicates just how effectively the Sánchez Navarros ran the state to suit themselves.

The legislature decreed in 1850 that councils of appraisal in the municipalities would prepare valuations of property, which would then be taxed at the annual rate of 30 reals per 1,000 pesos valuation.[77] In practice the councils of appraisal were careful not to offend the Sánchez Navarros, tamely accepting the latter's declaration of what their properties were worth.[78] With their holdings valued at 413,500 pesos for tax purposes, the Sánchez Navarros owed 1,550 pesos. But they in turn passed on 826 pesos of the tax to their tenants. Thus, while owning half the state the Sánchez Navarros themselves in 1851 paid a mere 724 pesos in property taxes.[79]

Jacobo also used his political connections when he decided in 1851 to seek compensation from the United States for losses at the hands of the Indians. His closest associate was, ironically enough, ex-governor José María Aguirre. The latter cooperated, partly because the Aguirre haciendas had also suffered heavy losses and partly because the Aguirres owed Jacobo money and hoped to borrow more.[80] The event setting the depredations claims project in motion was Aguirre's appointment in January, 1851, as minister of justice in Gen. Mariano Arista's cabinet, an event that Jacobo jubilantly reported to Arizpe. Jacobo's jubilation increased, for Aguirre subsequently became the acting minister of the treasury as well.[81] Assured of Aguirre's support, Jacobo lost no time in taking advantage of "the present favorable circumstances." He sent Arizpe detailed instructions on how to gather documentation to support an initial claim of 300,000 to 500,000 pesos. Arizpe made good use of his political contacts to ensure that Coahuilan officials from the governor on down produced the documentation in accordance with Jacobo's instructions.[82] But all this effort was in vain, for, as we have seen, the Sánchez Navarros' claims, which ultimately totaled $865,165, were disallowed.

Though the Sánchez Navarros failed in the matter of claims, it was certainly not due to a lack of influence with the national government. On the contrary, their influence increased, reaching its height during Santa Anna's last administration in 1853–1855. That worthy, who had gone into exile at the end of the Mexican War, was restored to the presidency in 1853 by the Conservatives, who had rebelled against the moderate policies of the postwar regimes. Once in power, Santa Anna established a military dictatorship. This was not precisely what the Conservatives had envisioned, but at least Santa Anna offered

some hope of stability. He therefore enjoyed the support of the privileged elements in society, including of course the Sánchez Navarros
and most of their business associates.

Santa Anna rewarded the family in rather spectacular fashion. For
years one of the Sánchez Navarros' greatest aggravations had been
that of having to deal with two sets of state officials, because the
Hacienda de Bonanza extended southward into Zacatecas. Jacobo
brought this situation to the dictator's attention and requested that
Bonanza become part of Coahuila. Santa Anna, allegedly in return
for a substantial bribe, was more than happy to oblige. Over the protests of the Zacatecan authorities, he issued a decree changing the
boundary of Coahuila to include all of Bonanza.[83]

The Bonanza affair is noteworthy both as the most blatant example
of the Sánchez Navarros' political influence and as the last time they
were able to exert such influence. Their fortunes were closely linked
with those of Santa Anna, and by 1855 he was in serious difficulty.
A resurgent Liberal faction had risen in arms the year before, and the
shabby opportunist found himself unable to repress the rising tide
of opposition. Giving up the struggle, he went into exile and obscurity. Mexico entered a new era, the period of the Reform, in which
Liberals strove with mixed success to eliminate the colonial heritage
that had so tragically retarded the country's development since independence.

For the Sánchez Navarros, too, Santa Anna's downfall marked the
end of an era. From 1855 on, the family was increasingly on the defensive as its members tried to maintain their privileged position.
The immediate threat was in Coahuila itself, where the Sánchez Navarros had lost the political initiative. It will be recalled that Santiago
Vidaurri rose to prominence by heading the revolution against Santa
Anna in the Northeast. During the fighting a portent of what lay in
store for the Sánchez Navarros was seen in the defection of their
cousin Miguel Blanco. He had been closely associated with the
family, first as manager of the Monclova cotton gin and later as
mayordomo of Hermanas. Now, however, Blanco cast his lot with
Vidaurri, becoming in turn his secretary, his agent in Coahuila, one
of his hand-picked representatives in congress, and finally a general

in the Liberal forces.[84] Blanco was able to ride the wave of the future, but the Sánchez Navarros were deeply committed to the past.

Having been one of the pillars of the old regime, Jacobo learned to his sorrow that neither wealth nor connections counted for much in the face of naked force. When Vidaurri's partisans overran Coahuila in the summer of 1855, they did not confine themselves to plundering the *latifundio*; they sacked Jacobo's mansion in Saltillo as well.[85] Other prominent citizens of Saltillo, which had been a stronghold of support for Santa Anna, suffered a similar fate. When they lodged outraged protests with Vidaurri, they were summarily imprisoned and subjected to various indignities. Jacobo, for instance, was forced to ride on a mule under armed guard down to Monterrey to explain his conduct to Vidaurri.[86]

Though he was soon released, the experience had been traumatic for the haughty *hacendado* accustomed to having his way. Jacobo suffered a further humiliation when Vidaurri rejected out of hand his claim for damages, contemptuously suggesting that the *hacendado* had padded the bill. Jacobo thereupon sent a dignified reply requesting that the claim be returned to him, for he preferred a monetary loss to having his integrity questioned.[87]

Jacobo also issued a thinly veiled warning that he would withhold financial support from Vidaurri's administration.[88] The threat of using the Sánchez Navarros' economic power was the only weapon left to Jacobo, because the family's political influence in Coahuila was rapidly evaporating. Not only did Vidaurri possess overwhelming military force, but also he, too, had a widespread familial intelligence network. Especially in northern Coahuila this net proved invaluable in whipping up support for the strongman.[89] Rapidly consolidating his position in February, 1856, Vidaurri boldly annexed Coahuila to Nuevo León and defied the national government to do anything about it.

In light of this stunning *fait accompli*, Jacobo's only recourse was to journey to Mexico City in hopes of finding allies among the anti-Vidaurri faction in the Liberal administration. The *hacendado* met with nothing but frustration. Although many Liberals did oppose Vidaurri's seizure of power, and although the annexation of Coahuila figured prominently in the debates of the constituent congress, the national government was simply too weak to bring the northern chieftain to heel; and it reluctantly accepted the status quo. Compounding Jacobo's bitter disappointment, congress took up the matter of Bonanza at the request of the governor of Zacatecas. In the course of the tumultuous debate, Guillermo Prieto, whose Liberal credentials were unimpeachable, rose to speak in defense of Jacobo, but the weight of sentiment was against the *hacendado*. Various congressmen—among them Miguel Blanco—attacked Jacobo as a reactionary whose family had monopolized landed wealth in Coahuila and had ruthlessly dominated local government there. Accompanied by the influential Mexico City businessman Antonio Escandón, Jacobo lobbied desperately in the halls of congress, but as the debate neared a vote the *hacendado* began to despair. His state of mind can be inferred from his challenging one of his more vocal detractors to a duel. The congressman discreetly declined, on the ground that as a representative of the people he was accountable only to the nation.[90] The outcome of the Bonanza controversy was that in December, 1856, by the surprisingly close vote of forty-eight to forty-two, congress annulled Santa Anna's decree and restored part of the hacienda to Zacatecas.[91] Having tried to repel the Sánchez Navarros' enemies in Coahuila and in Mexico City simultaneously, Jacobo had been defeated on both fronts.

He now received a welcome reinforcement, for Carlos returned from Europe and assumed the task of strengthening the family's connections with the Liberal regime. Jacobo was thus free to concentrate on the situation at home. In some respects it had improved. Though Vidaurri's supporters continued to harass some of the Sánchez Navarros' tenants, relations between Vidaurri himself and Jacobo had warmed slightly. The former still had the *hacendado*'s claim for damages under advisement, but he was doing nothing to satisfy it.[92] Jacobo finally sent for Carlos in hopes that he could get results from Vidaurri. Carlos, who had done a remarkable job of ingratiating himself with the Liberals, arrived at Patos in the spring of 1857 armed with letters of introduction from President Ignacio Comonfort and from Manuel Payno, who had been Comonfort's minister of the treasury. To these letters Vidaurri sent a gracious reply stating that no such introductions were necessary, for he fondly remembered having been Carlos's classmate in grammar school in Monclova.[93]

Carlos's diplomatic approach proved effective. An outwardly cordial correspondence developed between him and Vidaurri, followed by a meeting in Mexico City at which Carlos tactfully broached the subject of his brother's claim.[94] Vidaurri was amenable to honoring a reduced claim, a condition to which Carlos readily agreed. Even so, the Sánchez Navarros could hope to recover only a small fraction of their losses, for the claim would be paid in government bonds, which, as Carlos pointed out, were worth 5 percent of their face value. The main benefit for the brothers lay in eliminating this major source of friction with Vidaurri. True to his word, Vidaurri approved the claim, and Carlos presented it to the national government for payment in September, 1857.[95]

As matters developed, the claim was never paid, for within a few months Mexico plunged into yet another round of civil war: the savage three-year War of the Reform, the showdown between Liberals and Conservatives that had been brewing for decades. Ironically, it was President Comonfort's desire to avoid a civil war at all costs that touched off the conflict, for in December, 1857, he acquiesced to a reactionary coup in Mexico City aimed at abolishing the Liberal constitution adopted only nine months earlier. In January, 1858, Comonfort resigned in favor of the rebel leader, Gen. Félix Zuloaga. The majority of Liberals considered Comonfort a traitor who had delivered the government to their implacable enemies. As far as Liberals were concerned, the legitimate president was now Benito Juárez, who had been next in line under the constitution. Battle lines were quickly drawn. The Conservatives under Zuloaga held Mexico City and had the support of the Church and the regular army. The Liberals rallied around Juárez, who established his capital at Veracruz and began organizing a coalition of regional strongmen whose private armies constituted the bulk of Liberal fighting strength.

Both Carlos and Jacobo sympathized with the Conservatives, but

in Jacobo's case all he could do was to sympathize: Vidaurri dominated
the Northeast, and Vidaurri was a Liberal. Jacobo's attitude therefore
was one of passive resistance. When in 1858 Vidaurri asked him to
underwrite 10,000 pesos of a 100,000-peso loan to purchase arms in
Texas, Jacobo prudently agreed in principle but deliberately at-
tached impossible stipulations: not only must the Liberals triumph
in six months but Vidaurri must still be governor at that time. Jacobo
blandly explained that he had confidence only in Vidaurri's ability
to repay public debts.[96] Vidaurri dryly thanked Jacobo for his pa-
triotism and explained at length why it was humanly impossible to
give such guarantees. Jacobo replied that he well understood all these
arguments but reiterated that Vidaurri alone inspired him with confidence. This time the strongman curtly stated that since it was evident
Jacobo had no intention of cooperating the matter was closed. Vidaurri ended on an ominous note, saying that his exchange with Jacobo
had been instructive, for it showed who supported the state government.[97]

Compared with Jacobo, Carlos was much better off, for he was
rising in Conservative circles. Within days of their coup in December, 1857, the Conservatives reorganized the Mexico City municipal
council, and Carlos figured as one of the new aldermen.[98] Moreover,
when a year later the Conservatives met to select a replacement for
Gen. Félix Zuloaga as their president, Carlos was one of the 147
electors.[99]

The balloting came out in favor of Gen. Miguel Miramón, who
despite his youth was by far the ablest Conservative field commander.
The dashing general-president was able to win brilliant victories but
not to crush the Liberal faction. After being on the defensive for the
first two years of the war, the Liberals began to gain the upper hand
in 1860. A major factor in their ascendancy was their control of the
port of Veracruz, which deprived the Conservative regime in Mexico
City of vital tax revenues. To meet the crisis, Miramón of necessity
resorted to various money-raising expedients, including imposing
forced loans on his own partisans. By the fall of 1860, however, even
dedicated Conservatives were reluctant to contribute, because a Li-

beral victory was only a matter of time. In September a 300,000-peso loan was levied on forty of the leading Mexico City businessmen, and among those who preferred going to jail rather than paying their quota was Carlos, who doubtless saw no point in continuing to finance a losing cause.[100] While it is not known how long he remained in prison or whether he finally contributed his share, whatever money he advanced could soon be written off as a bad investment. By January, 1861, the Conservatives had collapsed and Miramón was on his way to European exile, while Juárez was triumphantly establishing his government in Mexico City.

Although the Sánchez Navarros' fortunes had continued to decline during the War of the Reform, the brothers emerged from that conflict in surprisingly good condition considering the fact that they were on the losing side. The forced loans Vidaurri had imposed on Jacobo were insignificant compared to those some of the strongman's subordinates had extorted from other *hacendados*. A striking instance was the 100,000-peso levy placed on the lordly Hacienda de Ciénega de Mata in Jalisco, owned by the Rincón Gallardo family; the tribute was later reduced to 50,000 pesos, which was still no bargain.[101] The most important result of the war was that the Sánchez Navarro *latifundio* remained intact, because the thrust of Liberal land reform had been toward the nationalization and sale of haciendas belonging to the Church.[102]

Nevertheless, there was no question but that the Sánchez Navarros were slipping. One indication was the strong political comeback that their old rivals the Aguirres had made by opportunely boarding the Vidaurri bandwagon, which again underscored the disagreeable fact that while the Sánchez Navarros might command wealth it was Vidaurri who wielded power.[103] In 1861, Vidaurri began tightening the screw in earnest, ordering the seizure of the haciendas of Nacimiento and Encinas for alleged arrears in taxes. The situation became so serious that Carlos even made one of his infrequent trips to Coahuila in an effort to placate Vidaurri.[104] He evidently failed, for in 1862 the state government also seized the Hacienda de Hermanas.

Their backs to the wall, the Sánchez Navarros viewed the French

Intervention as a godsend, for it provided the opportunity to strike back at Vidaurri in particular and Liberals in general. Like other Conservatives, the Sánchez Navarros viewed the Intervention as a resumption of the War of the Reform—as yet another round in their continuing struggle against the Liberals.

Conservative exiles had been instrumental in arousing Napoleon III's interest in the Mexican venture, and what began as an exercise in gunboat diplomacy by England, France, and Spain to collect debts from Juárez's bankrupt government became by 1862 a unilateral effort by France to establish a protectorate over Mexico. Despite assurances from the Conservatives and the clergy that most Mexicans would welcome the French, Napoleon discovered that the Juárez regime commanded widespread support and was offering a fierce resistance. As the French expeditionary force confidently marched inland toward Mexico City, the invaders suffered a stunning defeat before the walls of Puebla on May 5, 1862. With French national honor now at stake, Napoleon dispatched powerful reinforcements to Mexico, abandoning any hope of a cheap conquest. It took the French until the summer of 1863 to fight their way to Mexico City. What ensued was in many respects a repetition of the War of the Reform: the French and their Conservative allies held the capital, while Juárez fell back into the North, trying to form a coalition of regional strongmen and grimly preparing for protracted guerrilla warfare.

Juárez was relying heavily on Vidaurri, who repeatedly assured the embattled president of his steadfast support. Vidaurri was, in fact, already engaged in raising money to purchase arms abroad. In describing the project to Juárez, he mentioned that forced loans would be an effective device, adding that Jacobo Sánchez Navarro, for one, could easily stand a levy of thirty thousand pesos.[105] While planning this further extortion, Vidaurri maintained outwardly cordial relations with the Sánchez Navarros.[106]

Yet Vidaurri was beginning to waver in his allegiance to the Republican cause, for the French continued to expand the area over which they had nominal control, occupying major cities and forcing Juárez to retreat ever northward. It seemed that Napoleon's venture might succeed after all, and, symbolizing the growing pacification of the country, the Archduke Maximilian of Austria arrived in June, 1864, to begin his reign as the French-sponsored Emperor Maximilian. Neither the handsome, well-meaning, but incompetent Maximilian nor his beautiful and ambitious consort, Carlota, realized the extent to which they were pawns whose throne rested on French bayonets.

Believing it only a matter of time until the remnants of Juárez's followers were crushed, the Imperial pair threw themselves into an agreeable round of social activities. Within days of their arrival in Mexico City they held a series of glittering functions designed to impress distinguished Mexicans whose support they sought. Among the first to dine at the Imperial table were Carlos and Jacobo.[107]

This signal mark of royal esteem was not wasted on the Sánchez Navarros. Taking the most momentous gamble in the family's history, the brothers decided to link their destinies to Maximilian's, for their only hope of retaining their wealth and position lay in the triumph of the Emperor. Their commitment made, the brothers resumed their customary roles in directing the family enterprises. Jacobo returned to Coahuila to manage the *latifundio*, while Carlos remained in Mexico City where he soon became a familiar figure at court.

The urbane Carlos was in his element, unlike those members of Mexico City society whose awkward efforts to adapt to court life produced amused sneers from Maximilian's European retinue. Yet some of the Europeans who infested the court at Chapultepec Castle were only down-at-the-heels adventurers. Curiously enough, the archtype of these unsavory individuals became Carlos's protege, and from this relationship there resulted profound consequences for Maximilian.

Agustín Fischer's chief talent was a remarkable ability to live by his wits. Born a German Lutheran, he emigrated in 1845 to Texas, where he eked out a living as a notary's clerk. He went to California during the gold rush but, failing to strike it rich, drifted to Mexico around 1852. Fischer's life then took a strange turn, for he became, of all unlikely things, a Jesuit. Unfortunately, his weakness for women cost him his position as secretary to the bishop of Durango. We next find him living in ecclesiastical exile as the curate in Parras, where in the early 1860's he met Carlos and his wife during one of their visits to Patos. Fischer was undeniably charming, and he soon ingratiated himself with the Sánchez Navarros. Ever on the alert for the main chance, he went to Mexico City in December, 1863, and carefully cultivated the friendship. He reportedly became the confessor for Carlos's wife, who was instrumental in persuading her husband to present the good father to Maximilian. Carlos did so, and the Emperor was delighted.[108]

Had Carlos not been available, the resourceful Fischer would have found some other means of gaining access to Maximilian, but the very fact that his sponsor was someone of Carlos's prominence heightened the favorable impression Fischer made on the Emperor. The unscrupulous priest rapidly gained Maximilian's complete trust, which he parlayed into a meteoric rise as a courtier, becoming the Emperor's chaplain, his private secretary, his representative to the Vatican, and eventually secretary to the Imperial cabinet. In the person of this poor man's Rasputin, Carlos had a powerful ally at court.

Carlos himself continued to bask in the Imperial favor. In the fall of 1864 he was appointed one of Maximilian's chamberlains, and his wife, the socially prominent Dolores Osio, became one of Carlota's ladies-in-waiting.[109] For Dolores, who consistently ranked among the most fashionably dressed at court, life was a pleasant round of levées, banquets, visits to the theater, and balls at Chapultepec Castle.[110] As for Carlos, his ceremonial duties included that of acting as escort for diplomats presenting their credentials to Maximilian.[111]

Among the new faces appearing at court was one Carlos never imagined seeing in such surroundings: that of Santiago Vidaurri, who defected from the Republicans in 1864. Maximilian welcomed Vidaurri as a symbol of impending Republican collapse and in January, 1865, made him a councilor of state.[112] Thus by a convolution of Mexican politics, Vidaurri, the radical Liberal, and Carlos, the arch-Conservative, were now staunch Imperialists.

By 1865 things were going badly for the Imperialists. The armies of Juárez were regaining the initiative, particularly in the North, and the outcome of the Civil War in the United States ended any possibility of an alliance between the Confederacy and Maximilian. Nevertheless the Imperial government proposed to resettle Confederates as a barrier to help stem the Republican tide.

In casting about for suitable lands, one of the areas the Imperialist authorities considered was the vast Sánchez Navarro domain.[113] Carlos jumped at the chance to sell part of the *latifundio*, for in view of the military situation he was eager to liquidate his holdings. Accordingly, he offered two million acres for a total of one million pesos; a separate price would be negotiated for the livestock and improvements, and the form of payment would be left up to the Imperial treasury.[114] Although one official considered the price excessive and suggested to Maximilian that the lands could simply be expropriated, the government received Carlos's proposal favorably.[115] A professional surveyor was dispatched to Coahuila to examine the property and submit a detailed report.[116]

Carlos's anxiety stemmed from the fact that he stood to lose his lands altogether: in 1863 the Juárez regime had decreed the property of those collaborating with the French subject to confiscation.[117] Now, in 1865, Juárez was beginning to act. He instructed his commanding general in the North to confiscate the Sánchez Navarros' holdings, adding that this was the opportunity to break the family's monopoly in Coahuila.[118] On November 22, 1865, the Republican governor of that state issued a decree confiscating all of Carlos's property.[119] The Republicans could implement the measure only in piecemeal fashion, though, for Imperialist forces still battled them savagely. In the midst of this perilous situation, the surveyor was diligently carrying out his mission, dodging bands of Juarista irregulars as he traveled across the *latifundio*.[120] After several narrow escapes, he managed to reach the Imperialist lines, and in May, 1866, submitted his report on the Sánchez Navarro properties.[121]

By then the report was only of academic interest, for the Republicans had gained the upper hand in Coahuila, and in June they began confiscating the Sánchez Navarros' properties with a vengeance. Neither Juárez nor his subordinates were able to exercise much control as the Republican soldiery sacked each *casco* and helped themselves to anything that caught their fancy.[122] Trying to bring some degree of order out of this chaos, the governor asked Juárez whether Jacobo's property was also subject to confiscation, since the *hacendado* had served as Imperialist prefect of Matamoros for two months in 1865. It was.[123] The authorities proceeded to dispose of the *latifundio* in a haphazard manner, hurriedly carving out parcels and selling them on credit to deserving Republicans.[124]

Back in Mexico City, Carlos raged as he learned the extent of the disaster that had overtaken his family. His honors and decorations— he had received the Swedish Order of the North Star and was a knight commander in the Imperial Order of Guadalupe—were scant compensation for Maximilian's inability to protect the Sánchez Navarro *latifundio*.[125] Even Carlos's elevation to grand chamberlain was largely an empty honor, for the court was disintegrating.[126]

This situation resulted in part from the absence of Carlota, who had left Mexico in July to importune Napoleon III for continued aid to Maximilian's regime, an unsuccessful mission that cost the tragic young Empress her sanity. The fundamental cause of the deepening gloom in Mexico City, however, was precisely Napoleon's decision to liquidate the Mexican venture and withdraw the French expeditionary force. As the French accelerated their preparations for evacuation, the gloom turned into panic.[127]

The Conservatives' panic increased when, after much vacillation, Maximilian announced his intention of abdicating. This was the only sensible course open to him, for without French support the Empire's days were numbered. Up to now the Conservatives had been lukewarm in their support of the Emperor because his policies had been entirely too liberal for their liking. Yet Maximilian represented their last faint hope; as the case of the Sánchez Navarros so painfully illustrated, Conservatives could expect little mercy from a victorious Republican government. Despite frantic entreaties, Maximilian remained adamant, and in October he left Mexico City, planning to sail from Veracruz. Since the Austrian warship coming for him had not yet arrived, the Emperor stopped at Orizaba to rest and to wind up his affairs. Among other things he wrote a gracious letter of farewell to Carlos, the grand chamberlain.[128] He also instructed Carlos to liquidate various accounts and to dispose of his personal property.[129] Far from complying, Carlos was at that moment pounding along the road to Orizaba.[130]

The Conservatives had decided to make a last concerted effort to persuade Maximilian to stay. Their principal instrument was the sinister Father Fischer, who had come to dominate the Emperor.[131] To reinforce the arguments of Fischer and the others on the scene, several of their colleagues hurried out from Mexico City. Among them was Carlos, whom Maximilian's physician described as "one of the most rabid Conservatives," as well he might be, for the doctor went on to mention that once Carlos had been considered "the wealthiest landowner in Mexico."[132] No sooner did Carlos arrive in Orizaba than he closeted himself with Fischer and several other courtiers to work out strategy. Together they bombarded Maximilian with arguments against abdication, appealing to his sense of honor, stressing that he was abandoning his loyal subjects, and making the most extravagant promises of forthcoming Conservative military and financial support. After two days of this the Emperor sent Carlos back to Mexico City, ostensibly because the grand chamberlain needed to supervise the closing up of the palace. Even on the point of departure, though, Carlos made yet another appeal, employing "his customary verbosity."[133] Carlos's trip had not been in vain, for under intense pressure the Emperor finally yielded. The Orizaba meeting proved to be a turning point in Maximilian's life, for he had delivered himself into the hands of the Conservatives.

Promises availed little in the face of reality. The year 1867 opened on a somber note, with the Republican armies growing stronger every day. In January, Maximilian's leading advisors convened at the Hacienda de la Teja near Mexico City to discuss the deteriorating situation. A roll-call vote was taken on the question of whether the Empire was capable of continuing the war. The vote showed the demoralization of the Conservatives by this time: of the thirty-three notables present, seven voted for Maximilian's abdication, nine—including Vidaurri—abstained, and only seventeen were resolutely in favor of fighting to the bitter end. Among the latter were Fischer and Carlos, who was now the minister of the Imperial household. Carlos, in fact, was the most impassioned of the speakers, delivering a rather Church-illian oration in which he declared that the war must be fought at all costs, "even with daggers," if it came to that.[134]

As of February 5, the day he watched the last French contingent march out of Mexico City, Maximilian was on his own. The Imperial army had several competent generals, among them Miguel Miramón, the Conservative ex-president during the War of the Reform, but the Emperor's forces could not begin to match the Republicans in leader-ship, manpower, equipment, or morale. In an effort to raise the flag-ging spirits of his troops, Maximilian decided to go to the front, and on February 13 he left for Querétaro where Imperialist forces were concentrating.

Carlos, in his capacity as minister of the Imperial household, re-mained in Mexico City. His task became increasingly difficult as the weeks passed; Maximilian kept demanding large sums to pay the army at Querétaro, but the treasury was empty. Maximilian became so desperate that he finally ordered Carlos to sell the Imperial coaches, horses, and other property so that at least the household payroll could be met.[135] The heroic efforts Carlos was making to raise money earned the Emperor's approval, for when he reshuffled his cabinet Carlos continued as minister of the household.[136]

In the meantime the situation at Querétaro worsened. The city had become a trap for the Imperialists; their foes dominated the surround-ing heights and were constantly tightening their siege lines. After much consultation and vacillation, Maximilian approved a plan to have a body of cavalry under Gen. Leonardo Márquez break through the Republican lines. Márquez's mission was to fight his way to Mexico City, somehow raise a relief force, and return to lift the siege. The Emperor invested Márquez with sweeping powers to act as his sur-rogate and so informed Carlos. In the event that Márquez could not hold the capital, Maximilian had given him strict orders to protect Car-los, "one of my loyal and devoted friends." The Emperor also sent Carlos detailed instructions regarding the disposition of his property in case Mexico City fell to the Republicans.[137]

General Márquez, accompanied by Vidaurri, effected the breakout from Querétaro and succeeded in reaching the capital. Vidaurri took charge of matters there, presiding over a cabinet meeting at which Carlos and the other ministers dejectedly discussed ways of replenishing the treasury.[138] Meanwhile, Márquez decided on his own initiative to march to the relief of Puebla, for the Imperialist garrison in that strategic city was under fierce attack by Gen. Porfirio Díaz's army. Puebla fell before Márquez could arrive, and immediately thereafter Díaz inflicted a crushing defeat on Márquez's column. As the shattered remnants of this force streamed back into Mexico City, it was evident that, far from being able to rescue Maximilian, the Imperialists in the capital would themselves soon be under siege.

Following Díaz's encirclement of Mexico City, matters moved swiftly to a climax. In beleaguered Querétaro, one of Maximilian's favorite officers treacherously allowed the enemy to penetrate the Imperialist lines on the night of May 14, resulting in the capture of the Emperor and his entire army. From his prison cell in Querétaro, Maximilian continued to issue instructions for Carlos to settle various outstanding accounts, such as liquidating the civil list.[139] In fact, one of the last letters the Emperor wrote was to Carlos, "one of my most faithful friends," giving him further instructions on this matter and ending with a touching passage of farewell.[140] Six days later the Emperor was dead: on the morning of June 19, Maximilian was conducted to a hill on the outskirts of Querétaro and there, together with his generals, Mejía and Miramón, was executed by a firing squad.

Carlos was in no position to carry out his monarch's last wishes, for, with Díaz battering at the gates, pandemonium reigned in Mexico City.[141] Carlos was nearing nervous exhaustion from his futile efforts to protect Maximilian's property. With discipline rapidly breaking down, the Austrian troops guarding the palace had smashed into the Imperial winecellars and had become gloriously drunk on Maximilian's vintage stock, selling what they could not consume. In the same manner, the soldiery did a brisk business selling the linens, tableware, and other palace furnishings to the proprietors of hotels and restaurants.[142] This exercise in private enterprise came to an abrupt halt on June 21, when Mexico City fell to Díaz.

The most prominent Imperialists went into hiding, for it was common knowledge that Díaz intended to shoot a number of them. In the ensuing manhunt Carlos fell into the hands of the Republicans and was imprisoned. He was less fortunate than Fischer or General Márquez, both of whom evaded capture. But Carlos was much luckier than Vidaurri, who was captured and then executed in a particularly degrading manner—shot in the back by a firing squad while reportedly being forced to kneel in a pile of excrement.[143]

Epilogue

The fall of the Empire ruined the Sánchez Navarros. Writing to Arch-duke Charles Louis, Carlos lamented that he had lost his entire personal fortune in the Imperial cause.[1] This was no exaggeration. Not until 1868 did Carlos secure his release from prison, and he had been reduced to selling his silver service to pay the expenses incurred during his incarceration.[2] The ex-minister then went into exile, living in very straitened circumstances in Paris with his wife and five young children.[3] While in the French capital he maintained contact with other Conservative exiles there, including the polished José Manuel Hidalgo, who had played a major role in promoting the disastrous French Intervention.[4]

By 1870, however, the Juárez government felt confident enough to grant amnesty to former Imperialists, and Carlos's dreary existence as an expatriate ended. He took his family back to Mexico City, where they joined Jacobo and Apolonia. In many respects Apolonia's was the most pathetic case: she was nearing eighty, was almost blind, and for years had lived quietly in Coahuila completely aloof from politics, yet because of her sons' activities she too had been ruined.[5] Carlos's unceasing efforts to rebuild the family fortune met with scant success. At the beginning of 1872, for instance, he filed a suit in Berlin against Baron Anton von Magnus, the former Prussian minister to Maximilian's government. Carlos alleged that he had given the baron ten

thousand pesos of his own money to be used for Maximilian's legal
defense at Querétaro. Von Magnus, however, proved to the satisfaction of the Berlin municipal court that the sum came from the sale of
the late Emperor's silver and was in no way Carlos's personal property.[6]

Carlos spent the remainder of his life in genteel poverty, dying on
October 10, 1876, at the age of sixty. Reaction in the Mexico City
press varied. One newspaper merely reported that "Don Carlos Sánchez Navarro, a member of Mexican high society, died."[7] Yet the
leading Liberal paper gave him a surprisingly generous obituary:

> We regret to inform our readers that day before yesterday Don Carlos
> Sánchez Navarro died at 7:15 A.M.
>
> This is a lamentable occurrence. Mr. Sánchez Navarro was always a chari-
> table man and lavished his benevolence whenever the opportunity arose. A
> victim, on the other hand, of the hate and rancor of men, his immense
> holdings in Coahuila were expropriated without his being able to recover
> them. But we sincerely hope that the not too distant future will bring other
> public officials inspired by a feeling of justice who will grant it in full
> measure to his worthy family who today face a miserable future.
>
> May his soul rest in peace, and to all his family we extend our heartfelt
> sympathy.[8]

The passage of time brought about a partial realization of the newspaper's pious hope. The confiscation of the *latifundio* having occurred
in 1866, the Juárez regime enacted a law on August 12, 1867, sub-
stituting fines for outright confiscation in the case of Imperialists. The
Sánchez Navarros availed themselves of this measure, and on July 20,
1868, the national government ordered that whatever property had not
yet been disposed of be returned to the family.[9] The order produced
an immediate and angry reaction from the governor of Coahuila, who
wrote Juárez an open letter chiding the president and implying a betrayal of Liberal ideals. The governor recapitulated the Sánchez Navarros' role as collaborators during the Intervention and denounced the
brothers for having constituted the greatest obstacle to the development of Coahuila.[10] The governor need not have worried. Though at
first glance the order appeared to favor the Sánchez Navarros, in reality it upheld the confiscation: most of the family's property had already

been sold and was thus not returnable, besides which the only right the Sánchez Navarros had gained was that of paying their numerous creditors from the little that was left. Under these circumstances the family did not bother to try.

Not until the late 1870's, with the political passions of the Intervention cooling and with a different regime in power, did Carlos's heirs succeed after prolonged litigation in recovering a portion of the family's properties in Coahuila.[11] Yet they subsequently sold these estates, so that for all practical purposes the Sánchez Navarro *latifundio* had passed into history as of 1866. Not so the family, however; in the century since the Intervention they have made an impressive financial comeback, and today the Sánchez Navarros once again rank among the most distinguished of Mexican families.

Conclusion

In less than a century an obscure provincial family in northern Mexico amassed the largest landholding in Latin America. By virtue of unremitting labor, shrewdness, and luck, the rise of the Sánchez Navarros was spectacular; their fall was even more so. Had the third generation of *hacendados* not committed the catastrophic error of allying themselves inextricably with Maximilian, the family would in all probability have retained their *latifundio* until the Revolution of 1910. Politics, not indolence or mismanagement, caused the Sánchez Navarros' downfall. After 1867 a new landowning elite emerged in Coahuila, composed of men who had supported Juárez during the Intervention. And herein lies the crucial point—individual families like the Sánchez Navarros might rise and fall, but the hacienda system continued to flourish. What occurred was merely a change in the composition of the *hacendado* element, not in the pattern of land tenure itself. In fact, the whole process of concentration of landownership that had been going on since the sixteenth century reached its height between 1867 and 1910, after which the Revolution finally destroyed the *latifundio*.

Viewing the Sánchez Navarros within the context of the hacienda system, two broad questions come to mind. First, is the traditional

colonial-national period division valid? In the case of the Sánchez Navarros there is ample justification for this approach, since the year
1821 was indeed a watershed in the family's history. The colonial period had been dominated by the curate José Miguel, and upon his
death in 1821 all the family's wealth was concentrated in the hands of
José Melchor, who thus had a base from which to expand in the
national period.

Yet for the hacienda as an institution, independence produced little
significant change except for the end of entailment. Therefore, as has
recently been suggested, a more meaningful approach is to treat the
period 1750–1850 as an integral unit.[1] And here again the case of the
Sánchez Navarros bears out the validity of this timeline. One may suggest the need for a series of studies comparing the classical *hacendados*—such as the Sánchez Navarros—whose roots lay in the colonial
period, with the new breed of Liberal *hacendados*—such as Gen. Luis
Terrazas—who dominated the second half of the nineteenth century.

The second question is to what extent did the Sánchez Navarros
conform to the generalizations that have been advanced concerning
hacendados and haciendas? The most striking adherence to stereotype
concerns size. The Sánchez Navarro domain—an area the size of West
Virginia—exemplifies the trend toward concentration of landownership. Yet even here the stereotype applies more to northern Mexico
than to other parts of the country, which strengthens the case for considering the northern hacienda as a distinct type. Instead of thinking
in terms of "the Mexican hacienda," we need to explore much more
fully the regional variations in the institution, for only in this manner
can meaningful syntheses eventually be produced.[2] For example, William B. Taylor's recent study ably demonstrates that the hacienda that
developed in Oaxaca differed in many important respects—including
size—from its northern counterpart.

Another area where the Sánchez Navarros conform to stereotype is
debt peonage, which formed the core of the labor system they employed. Beyond any question, the peons received harsh treatment.
Still, the evidence would seem to support Charles Gibson's idea that
peonage was the best of available worlds for laborers in the late colonial period. The same cannot be said for the national period, however.

Not only did working conditions become more hazardous, but also, as the labor force increased, the element of paternalism which traditionally served to ameliorate abuse declined noticeably. But again, Gibson has suggested that peonage was more widespread in the peripheral areas, such as Coahuila, than in central Mexico where labor was more abundant.

Third, the Sánchez Navarros fit the stereotype concerning inefficient use of land and reliance on traditional methods of production. They owned a great deal more land than they could ever use, and ranching was carried on in accordance with time-honored practices. Yet the family should be viewed within the context of the times; a semiarid region ravaged by periodic droughts and incessant Indian raids was hardly conducive to scientific ranching or farming. Even today, sixty-five years after a fundamental social revolution stressing agrarian reform, much of the land in Coahuila is still used inefficiently.

As for the prevailing picture of the *hacendado* leading a life of luxurious idleness, the stereotype simply does not apply in the Sánchez Navarros' case. Beginning with the curate José Miguel's modest commercial ventures in the 1750's, a business mentality was the family's salient characteristic. The Sánchez Navarros were entrepreneurs, which explains much of their success. They built the *latifundio* primarily to make money, prestige being but a secondary consideration.

The very process by which the family amassed their properties does not substantiate the generalization that *hacendados* tended to usurp land. This charge has validity in some cases, but the most that can be said of the Sánchez Navarros is that they engaged in sharp practice on occasion, for their *latifundio* expanded by a series of legal transactions. Often a landowner's ultimate success or failure depended not on his technical proficiency but on his ability to win the interminable legal battles that were such an ingrained part of the hacienda system.

Hacendados are often characterized as absentee landowners: the Marquises of Aguayo fit this generalization, but the Sánchez Navarros do not. Their basic pattern was not only to live on their estates but also to lavish personal attention on improving their properties. Nevertheless, staying on the land conferred no particular merit in itself; the Vázquez Borregos, the Garza Falcóns, and the Elizondos also lived on their estates, yet each of these families declined. The crucial difference was that the Sánchez Navarros had liquid assets, resulting from commerce, which enabled them to withstand periods of adversity in ranching and ultimately to crush their competitors. It was precisely because the Sánchez Navarros were not entirely dependent on their *latifundio* that they made such a notable success of it.

The development of the *latifundio* was therefore a single aspect—albeit the major one—of their rise to power. The family's extensive commercial activities belie the generalization that the objective of every *hacendado* was to make his estates self-sufficient. The Sánchez Navarros produced for a market, much of the time for a national market, and they purchased most of the manufactured articles needed on the *latifundio*. Thus, the family's fortune rested firmly on the twin pillars of ranching and commerce. Nor were the Sánchez Navarros atypical; their principal business associates in both the colonial and national periods were men who combined being *hacendados*, merchant princes, and mining magnates. It seems reasonable to speculate, therefore, that future research will increasingly show that the leading members of the "*hacendado* element" in Mexican history were also the leaders of the business community.

The importance of the familial aspect in the building of the Sánchez Navarros' empire cannot be overstated. Just as the *latifundio* was profoundly influenced by the Sánchez Navarros' commercial and political activities, in all these areas the Sánchez Navarros derived incalculable assistance from their widespread network of family connections. By working through their relatives and friends, the Sánchez Navarros could exert considerable influence at the state and even at the national levels while they themselves remained discreetly in the background. Without discounting the importance of ideology in the history of Mexico, a great deal more research needs to be done with regard to kinship politics, for, as we have seen, this was a major factor in enabling the Sánchez Navarros to surmount political upheavals. And even when the family began to decline in 1855 as a result of the revolution of Ayutla, what was fundamentally involved was not so much opposition to the Liberal ideology but rather the inability to reach an accommodation with Santiago Vidaurri, who was effectively employing kinship politics himself. If there is one element that runs through the Sánchez Navarros' political activities it is pragmatism, for they were prepared to work with anyone who would work with them. It was only when the family's options narrowed in the late 1850's that they committed themselves irrevocably to the Conservative cause.

The history of the Sánchez Navarros is one of an elite clan striving to protect its vested interests. It is a model that may be useful not only for the study of the hacienda but for other areas of Latin American history as well.

NOTES

ABBREVIATIONS USED

ADAS	Archivo del Ayuntamiento, Saltillo
AGEC	Archivo General del Estado de Coahuila
AGENL	Archivo General del Estado de Nuevo León
AGENL-C	Congreso, 1814
AGENL-VA	Vidaurri Archive
AGN	Archivo General de la Nación
AGN-AP	Abasto y Panaderías
AGN-EE	Expulsión de Españoles
AGN-IC	Industria y Comercio
AGN-JE	Justicia Eclesiástica
AGN-M	Mercedes
AGN-PI	Provincias Internas
AGN-T	Tierras
JJSNP	José Juan Sánchez Navarro Papers
MCSN	Manuscritos de la Casa Sánchez Navarro
NA	National Archives
SN	Sánchez Navarro
SNP	Sánchez Navarro Papers
WMAP	William Marshall Anderson Papers

INTRODUCTION

1. Jacques Lambert, *Latin America*, trans. Helen Katel, p. 59; see also Stanley J. and Barbara H. Stein, *The Colonial Heritage of Latin America*, pp. 137–138.

2. Charles Gibson, *The Aztecs under Spanish Rule*, pp. 406–407.

3. François Chevalier, *La formation des grandes domains au Mexique*, ed. Lesley Byrd Simpson and trans. Alvin Eustis as *Land and Society in Colonial Mexico*.

See also François Chevalier (ed.), *Instrucciones a los Hermanos Jesuitas Administradores de Haciendas (manuscrito mexicano del siglo XVIII)*, and idem, "The North Mexican Hacienda: Eighteenth and Nineteenth Centuries," in *The New World Looks at Its History*, ed. Archibald R. Lewis and Thomas F. McGann, pp. 95–107.

4. General works: Manuel Romero de Terreros, *Antiguas Haciendas de México*; William H. Dusenberry, *The Mexican Mesta*; Isabel González Sánchez (ed.), *Haciendas y ranchos de Tlaxcala en 1712*, and her thesis, "Situación Social de Indios y Castas en las Fincas Rurales, en Vísperas de la Independencia de México"; Enrique Florescano, "El problema agrario en los últimos años del virreinato, 1800–1821," *Historia Mexicana* 20, no. 4 (April–June 1971): 477–510, and his *Precios del maíz y crisis agrícolas en México (1708–1810)*; Luis González y González, "La hacienda queda a salvo," *Historia Mexicana* 6, no. 1 (July–September 1956): 24–38; Jan Bazant, "The Division of Some Mexican *Haciendas* during the Liberal Revolution, 1856–1862," *Journal of Latin American Studies* 3, part 1 (May 1971): 25–37; Hermes Tovar Pinzón, "Las haciendas jesuitas de México, índice de documentos existentes en el Archivo Nacional de Chile," *Historia Mexicana* 20, no. 4 (April–June 1971): 563–617, and 21, no. 1 (July–September 1971): 135–180; Friedrich Katz, "Labor Conditions on Haciendas in Porfirian Mexico: Some Trends and Tendencies," *Hispanic American Historical Review* 54, no. 1 (February 1974): 1–47.

Specific haciendas: José Mancebo Benfield, *Las lomas de Chapultepec*; Edith Boorstein Couturier, "Hacienda of Hueyapan: The History of a Mexican Social and Economic Institution, 1550–1940," Ph.D. dissertation, and her "Modernización y Tradición en una Hacienda (San Juan Hueyapan, 1902–1911)," *Historia Mexicana* 18, no. 1 (July–September 1968): 35–55; Ward J. Barrett, *The Sugar Hacienda of the Marqueses del Valle*; Roland E. Chardon, "Hacienda and Ejido in Yucatán: The Example of Santa Ana Cucá," *Annals of the Association of American Geographers* 53 (1963): 174–193; Paulino del Pozo Rosillo, "La hacienda de Peñasco, S.L.P.," *Archivos de Historia Potosina* 1, no. 2 (October–December 1969): 107–114; Bohumil Badura, "Biografía de la Hacienda de San Nicolás de Ulapa," *Ibero-Americana Pragensia* 4 (1970): 75–111.

Regional studies: Roland E. Chardon, *Geographic Aspects of Plantation Agriculture in Yucatan*; Arnold Strickson, "Hacienda and Plantation in Yucatan," *América Indígena* 25, no. 1 (January 1965): 35–63; Bernardo García Martínez, *El Marquesado del Valle*; G. Micheal Riley, "Land in Spanish Enterprise: Colonial Morelos, 1522–1547," *The Americas* 27, no. 3 (January 1971): 233–251, and his *Fernando Cortes and the Marquesado in Morelos, 1522–1547*; William B. Taylor, *Landlord and Peasant in Colonial Oaxaca*.

Elite families: Jan Bazant, "Los bienes de la familia de Hernán Cortés y su venta por Lucas Alamán," *Historia Mexicana* 19, no. 2 (October–December 1969): 228–247; José Fuentes Mares, *. . . Y México se Refugió en el Desierto*.

5. James Lockhart, "Encomienda and Hacienda: The Evolution of the Great Estate in the Spanish Indies," *Hispanic American Historical Review* 49, no. 3 (August 1969): 429; see also Robert G. Keith, "Encomienda, Hacienda and Corregimiento in Spanish America: A Structural Analysis," *Hispanic American Historical Review* 51, no. 3 (August 1971): 431–446.

6. J. H. Hexter, *Reappraisals in History*, p. 20.

7. Eric R. Wolf and Edward C. Hansen, *The Human Condition in Latin America*, p. 201.

8. "Sánchez Navarro Papers (1658–1895)," *The Library Chronicle of the University of Texas* 1, no. 1 (Summer 1944): 31–32; Lota M. Spell, *Research Materials for the Study of Latin America at the University of Texas*, p. 7.

9. Charles H. Harris III, *The Sánchez Navarros*, and "A Mexican *Latifundio*: The Economic Empire of the Sánchez Navarro Family, 1765–1821," Ph.D. dissertation.

10. Frank Tannenbaum, *The Mexican Agrarian Revolution*, pp. 104–105.

1. THE FAMILY AND THE LAND

1. Nicolás de Lafora, *Relación del viaje que hizo a los Presidios Internos situados en la frontera de la América Septentrional Perteneciente al Rey de España*, ed. Vito Alessio Robles, pp. 178–179; Jacobo de Ugarte to the Marquis of Croix, December 14, 1769, AGN-PI, vol. 24, exp. 1, fols. 10–10v.

2. Lafora, *Relación del viaje*, pp. 195–196.

3. Vito Alessio Robles, *Coahuila y Texas en la época colonial*, pp. 19–21, 35 (hereafter cited as *Coahuila y Texas*).

4. Juan Agustín de Morfi, *Viaje de indios y diario del Nuevo México*, ed. Vito Alessio Robles, p. 213 (hereafter cited as *Viaje*).

5. Lafora, *Relación del viaje*, pp. 197–198.

6. Alfred Barnaby Thomas (ed.), *Teodoro de Croix and the Northern Frontier of New Spain, 1776–1783*, p. 88; Lafora, *Relación del viaje*, p. 196.

7. Cornelius H. Muller, "Vegetation and Climate of Coahuila, Mexico," *Madroño* 9 (1947): 33.

8. Thomas F. Glick, *Irrigation and Society in Medieval Valencia*, pp. 193–195; United States, Senate, *Report of the Special Committee of the United States Senate on the Irrigation and Reclamation of Arid Lands*, IV, 250–251.

9. Donald D. Brand, "The Early History of the Range Cattle Industry in Northern Mexico," *Agricultural History* 35, no. 3 (July 1961): 135.

10. Jacinto de Barrios to the Marquis of Cruillas, April 8, 1766, AGN-PI, vol. 25, exp. 9, fol. 340v.

11. Vito Alessio Robles, *Francisco de Urdiñola y el norte de la Nueva España*, pp. 65–66; Alessio Robles, *Coahuila y Texas*, p. 164.

12. Alessio Robles, *Coahuila y Texas*, pp. 147, 291, map between pp. 292 and 293, 578; Vito Alessio Robles, *Bosquejos históricos*, pp. 16, 66.

13. Alessio Robles, *Coahuila y Texas*, pp. 293–294; Alessio Robles, *Bosquejos históricos*, p. 82; Ricardo Ortega y Pérez Gallardo, *Historia Genealógica de las Familias más antiguas de México*, I, "Marquesado de Aguayo," 1–5.

14. Morfi, *Viaje*, pp. 215, 219.

15. "Testimonio del Real Título de Composición . . . ," cited in Alessio Robles, *Bosquejos históricos*, pp. 15–16.

16. Comisión de Límites de Coahuila, *Documentos relativos a la línea divisoria y mapas que determinan los límites del estado de Coahuila con el de Durango y Zacatecas*, pp. iv–v.

17. Eduardo Guerra, *Historia de la Laguna*, pp. 7, 22.

18. Compañía Agrícola Industrial, Colonizadora, Limitada del Tlahualilo, S.A. versus the Federal Government of the Republic of Mexico, *Allegations Presented by*

Jorge Vera Estañol, Special Attorney for the Federal Government before the III Hall of the Supreme Court of Justice of the Nation, trans. Ernesto Lara de Gogorza, p. 48; *Mapa de los Estados de Parras.*

19. "Referentes á la Joya—2 Cuads—. . . ," SNP (2922) and (2881); SNP (3515); "Título de 198 sitios de ganado mayor . . . ," SNP (2925).

20. Manuel Romero de Terreros, *Antiguas Haciendas de México*, pp. 99–100; Morfi, *Viaje*, pp. 145–147; Pastor Rouaix (comp.), *Diccionario geográfico, histórico, y biográfico del Estado de Durango*, p. 22.

21. "Título de 198 sitios de ganado mayor . . . ," SNP (2925); SNP (1790); SNP (2881).

22. *Legajo*, SNP (2892).

23. Lafora, *Relación del viaje*, p. 172; Pedro Tamarón y Romeral, *Demostración del vastísimo obispado de la Nueva Vizcaya, 1765*, ed. Vito Alessio Robles, p. 110.

24. Alessio Robles, *Coahuila y Texas*, p. 578.

25. Alessio Robles, *Bosquejos históricos*, pp. 85–87.

26. "V. E. en nombre de Su Mag^d . . . ," February 8, 1751, AGN-M, vol. 79, fols. 4–5; Tamarón y Romeral, *Demostración*, p. 111.

27. Tamarón y Romeral, *Demostración*, p. 111; Lafora, *Relación del viaje*, p. 172.

28. Alessio Robles, *Coahuila y Texas*, pp. 405–406, 510–511.

29. Ibid., pp. 551–553; "Linderos de Soledad con Vázquez Borrego," November 12, 1739–October 16, 1762, SNP (455); "S. Exª aprueba y confirma las Dilig^s . . . ," March 24, 1757, AGN-M, vol. 75, fols. 185–186.

30. "Linderos de Soledad con Vázquez Borrego," November 12, 1739–October 16, 1762, SNP (455); Miguel de la Garza Falcón to the Viceroy, November 5, 1743, AGN-PI, vol. 177, exp. 6, fols. 257–257v; petition from José Vázquez Borrego to Col. José de Escandón. The petition is undated but the document following it in the *expediente* is dated February 15, 1753, AGN-PI, vol. 172, exp. 9, fols. 162–162v.

31. "Linderos de Soledad con Vázquez Borrego," November 12, 1739–October 16, 1762, SNP (455); Miguel de la Garza Falcón to the Viceroy, November 5, 1743, AGN-PI, vol. 177, exp. 6, fol. 257.

32. "V. E. confirma la mrzd de 196 sitios . . . ," November 3, 1745, AGN-M, vol. 75, fol. 42v; Esteban L. Portillo, *Anuario Coahuilense para 1886*, p. 447.

33. Robert S. Weddle, *San Juan Bautista*, p. 226.

34. Petition from José Vázquez Borrego to Col. José de Escandón, AGN-PI, vol. 172, exp. 9, fol. 162v.

35. Vito Alessio Robles, *Saltillo en la historia y en la leyenda*, p. 115 (hereafter cited as *Saltillo*); Alessio Robles, *Coahuila y Texas*, p. 83.

36. "Para q la just^a mas cercana . . . ," August 26, 1748, AGN-M, vol. 75, fols. 86–86v; "Reconfirma la adjudica^on . . . ," October 2, 1748, AGN-M, vol. 75, fol. 89; *legajo*, January 13, 1747, SNP (459).

37. "Documentos sacados de los Autos sobre Texas, existentes en el Oficio del Superior Gobierno de esta Corte," *Boletín del Archivo General de la Nación* 29, no. 3 (1958): 408.

38. "Copia simple de títulos . . . ," SNP (463); *legajo*, September 17, 1714–May 29, 1726, SNP (466)–(471); deed, June 15, 1755, SNP (2912).

39. *Legajo*, January 12, 1729–January 2, 1731, SNP (2574); "Documentos primordiales de la Estancia . . . ," SNP (2921).

40. "Certifico en forma haber cumplido . . . ," February 22, 1759, SNP (2352); "Autos del juicio seguido en Guadalajara . . . ," 1753–1763, SNP (2679).

41. Carlos Sánchez Navarro [y Peón] (ed.), *La Guerra de Tejas*, pp. 83–84; Alessio Robles, *Bosquejos históricos*, p. 32.

42. Alessio Robles, *Saltillo*, pp. 14, 48, 59; "Copia de la escritura . . . ," 1594, ADAS, *carpeta* 1, *legajo* 2; "MCXCI As—Treslado de la fundacion . . . ," AGN-T, vol. 191, exp. 7, fols. 39–42.

43. "Quaderno 1º—Contiene la nobleza de don José Melchor Sánchez Navarro . . . ," cited in Alessio Robles, *Francisco de Urdiñola*, pp. 112–119. There was a Sánchez Navarro family in Tlaxcala in the eighteenth century, but I have been unable to establish any connection between them and the Sánchez Navarros in Coahuila. See Isabel González Sánchez (ed.), *Haciendas y ranchos de Tlaxcala en 1712*, p. 37.

44. "No. 7—Sⁿ Esteban Nᵃ Tlascala—Año de 1701 . . . ," AGN-T, vol. 191, exp. 7, fols. 18v–19v, 21v–22v.

45. Alessio Robles, *Coahuila y Texas*, pp. 212, 218, 242; SNP (2907); SNP (2922); SNP (463).

46. Alessio Robles, *Coahuila y Texas*, pp. 373, 537.

47. "Lista de los Militares . . . ," August 31, 1738, AGN-PI, vol. 177, exp. 4, fol. 188; December 9–10, 1766, SNP (2933); Josefa Andrea Jiménez to José Miguel SN (Sánchez Navarro), December 14, 1784, SNP (1922); Portillo, *Anuario Coahuilense*, pp. 458, 460; December 16, 1766, SNP (2933); April 13, 1784, SNP (2377).

48. "Reconocimiento E inventario . . . ," January 2, 1775, MCSN; Alessio Robles, *Francisco de Urdiñola*, p. 116; July 11, 1742, SNP (3067); José Martín SN to José Miguel SN, October 4, 1759, SNP (1717).

49. "Venta de un Molino de pan . . . ," 1705, ADAS, *carpeta* 6, *legajo* 52.

50. Cristóbal José SN to José Miguel SN, November 14, 1756, SNP (1207); November 29, 1758, SNP (3365); Manuel Francisco SN to same, October 19, 1787, SNP (3372); "Quaderno de registros de Minas . . . ," 1759, AGEC, *legajo* 3, *carpeta* 214; Israel Cavazos Garza, "Laguna de Sánchez," *El Porvenir*, November 28, 1971, p. 2-B.

51. José Domingo de Letona to José Miguel SN, December 2, 1817, SNP (3557); María Francisca Javiera de Urquiza to same, November 3, 1809, SNP (1835); "Nombramiento de Cura de Santiago de la Monclova . . . ," cited in Vito Alessio Robles (comp.), *Bibliografía de Coahuila, histórica y geográfica*, p. 384.

52. Decree by the Bishop of Guadalajara, June 2, 1758, SNP (1787).

53. Santiago Regato to José Miguel SN, December 7, 1756, SNP (3368).

54. "Compra de la esquina de la Plaza . . . ," September 19, 1756, SNP (2666); "Debe el Br. Dn. Joseph Miguel Sánchez Navarro . . . ," October 2, 1757, SNP (3363).

55. Deeds, March 27, 1760, SNP (2550), and March 28, 1760, SNP (2893).

56. "D. Gregorio Sánchez Navarro . . . ," unsigned account prepared at Mexico City, June 1, 1759, SNP (2247).

57. "Cuaderno en que consta . . . ," 1761–1767, SNP (2064).

58. Lorenzo Cancio to the Marquis of Cruillas, October 30, 1762, AGN-PI, vol. 22,

exp. 7, fols. 150–151; [draft—Marquis of Cruillas] to Lorenzo Cancio, December 11, 1762, AGN-PI, vol. 22, exp. 7, fol. 166.

59. Beginning in 1764, he was tithe administrator for both Coahuila and Texas. See José Martín SN to José Miguel SN, May 25, 1762, SNP (1716); *legajo*, September 22, 1766, SNP (148).

60. Woodrow Borah, "The Collection of Tithes in the Bishopric of Oaxaca in the Sixteenth Century," *Hispanic American Historical Review* 21, no. 3 (August 1941): 386, 389.

61. Fernando Vázquez Borrego to José Miguel SN, February 29, 1763 [*sic*], SNP (3337); September 12, 1764, SNP (1742); "Razón del ganado menor . . . ," 1766, SNP (1602); "Cuenta y razón del ganado menor . . . ," July 1, 1766, SNP (1681).

62. Francisco de Mata to José Miguel SN, June 14, 1762, SNP (2101); Bartolomé de Rivera to same, January 24, 1763, SNP (1334).

63. Jacobo de Ugarte to the Marquis of Croix, February 7, 1770, AGN-PI, vol. 24, exp. 1, fols. 22–23; *legajo*, August 22, 1769–February 3, 1770, SNP (3048).

64. Morfi, *Viaje*, pp. 281–282.

65. "Razón del herradero . . . ," July 15, 1763, SNP (2105).

66. Bill of sale, October 25, 1763, SNP (267); receipt, November 16, 1763, SNP (2229).

67. Baltazar Colomo and Juan Bautista Farías to José Miguel SN, January 10, 1767, SNP (3313).

68. *Legajo*, September 22, 1766, SNP (148).

69. Certificate, October 8, 1779, AGN-PI, vol. 195, exp. 1, fols. 58v–59.

70. Manuel Francisco SN to José Miguel SN, November 14, 1764, SNP (1330).

71. Francisco de Mata to José Miguel SN, June 14, 1762, SNP (2101).

72. "No. 6—Hermanas y Tapado . . . ," September 15, 1694–December 6, 1768, SNP (2907); deeds, October 19, 1764, and July 6, 1767, SNP (2567); "No. 12—Sánchez Navarro—Títulos de la finquita . . . ," May 19, 1727–November 8, 1769, SNP (2924).

73. "No. 5—'Hermanas' y Tapado . . . ," October 27, 1725–December 22, 1770, SNP (2913).

74. "No. 8—Terrenos de 'Ojo Caliente' . . . ," SNP (2906).

75. "No. 1—'Ojo Caliente' . . . ," SNP (2915); "No. 4—Hermanas y Tapado . . . ," SNP (2912); "No. 7—Hermanas y Tapado . . . ," SNP (2908); "Documentos primordiales de la Estancia . . . ," SNP (2921); "No. 13—San Antonio del Potrero y La Cieneguilla . . . ," SNP (465).

76. "No. 29—Disposición testamentaria . . . ," August 9, 1771, SNP (488).

77. "Documentos de los terrenos . . . ," MCSN.

78. Eric R. Wolf and Edward C. Hansen, *The Human Condition in Latin America*, p. 74.

79. "Reconocimiento E inventario . . . ," January 2, 1775, MCSN.

80. François Chevalier, *Land and Society in Colonial Mexico*, ed. Lesley Byrd Simpson and trans. Alvin Eustis, p. 32.

81. Juan Ignacio de Moya to José Miguel SN, December 2, 1772, SNP (3059); "Cuenta de Dn. Joseph Vicente Arizpe . . . ," December 2, 1772, SNP (792).

82. "Quaderno 2º—Ynformación sobre Limpieza de Sangre . . . ," June 6–12, 1812, MCSN.

83. Lorenzo Cancio to the Marquis of Cruillas, June 16, 1762, AGN-PI, vol. 22, exp. 8, fol. 219; "Linderos de Soledad con Vázquez Borrego," November 12, 1739–October 16, 1762, SNP (455); *legajo*, June 30, 1769, SNP (457); certificate by Antonio Bonilla, November 1, 1776, AGN-PI, vol. 24, exp. 57, fols. 270–271.

84. Morfi, *Viaje*, p. 298.

85. "Linderos de Soledad con Vázquez Borrego," November 12, 1739–October 16, 1762, SNP (455).

86. "Este documento simple . . . ," November 19, 1739–March 8, 1788, SNP (2911-A).

87. "Memorial sobre la pretención . . . ," March 6, 1788, SNP (2911); *legajo*, 1697–1788, SNP (2579); [Fernando Vázquez] Borrego to José Miguel SN, December 27, 1786, SNP (2056).

88. "Testimonio de una transacción . . . ," July 31, 1804, SNP (2910).

89. Juan Ignacio de Arizpe to José Miguel SN, July 8, 1802, SNP (1078); September 10, 1802, SNP (1080).

90. Juan Ignacio de Arizpe to José Miguel SN, January 1, 1803, SNP (3358); January 23, 1803, SNP (78); decree by Governor Antonio Cordero, March 14, 1803, SNP (2532).

91. "Testimonio de una transacción . . . ," July 31, 1804, SNP (2910).

92. Juan Ignacio de Arizpe to José Miguel SN, September 10, 1802, SNP (1080).

93. "Reconocimiento E inventario . . . ," January 2, 1775, MCSN; José Vicente Arizpe to José Miguel SN, August 23, 1784, SNP (1970); August 26, 1784, SNP (1973); "——3—'Hermanas y Tapado' . . . ," July 3, 1691–September 10, 1784, SNP (2932).

94. *Legajo*, 1759, SNP (2680); unsigned copy of Castilla y Terán's will, November 18, 1791, SNP (489); "Documentos de los terrenos . . . ," MCSN; "Copia Simple de Escrita Original . . . ," February 9, 1880, SNP (456); [Manuel Francisco S]N to José Miguel SN, January 18, 1792, SNP (3444); February 29, 1792, SNP (3433).

95. "No. 2—Hermanas y Tapado . . . ," 1704–December 24, 1798, SNP (2916); "No. 7—Hermanas y Tapado . . . ," SNP (2908).

96. *Legajo*, January 13, 1747, SNP (459); certificate, December 13, 1763, SNP (2559); Domingo de Berrio to José Miguel SN, September 4, 1801, SNP (2075); October 16, 1801, SNP (2076).

97. Certificate, October 10, 1801, SNP (2560); Domingo de Berrio to José Miguel SN, December 11, 1801, SNP (2077); "N 61—Títulos de 52 sitios . . . ," MCSN.

98. [Draft—José Melchor SN] to Manuel Salcedo, May 1, 1811, SNP (1700); partial inventory of José Miguel SN's estate, April 18–May 30, 1821, SNP (2919).

99. Deeds: June 4, 1789, SNP (477); February 10, 1798, SNP (2563); September 15, 1800, SNP (2564); October 31, 1800, SNP (487); December 4, 1800, SNP (2566); September 25, 1805, SNP (481); November 19, 1805, SNP (479); August 17, 1808, SNP (480); August 11, 1809, SNP (483); November 3, 1813, SNP (2568); February 7, 1816, SNP (484); December 22, 1816, SNP (2570); receipt, September 14, 1800, SNP (2572); list, May 1, 1818, SNP (2649); "Lista formada por el Sor Prev. D. José Miguel Sánchez Navarro . . . " (hereafter cited as 1819 List), January 23, 1819, SNP (2562).

100. 1819 List, January 23, 1819, SNP (2562); deed, October 31, 1800, SNP (487).

101. Juan Ignacio de Arizpe to José Miguel SN, December 16, 1790, SNP (3320).

102. Juan Ignacio de Arizpe to José Miguel SN, January 30, 1801, SNP (76); mortgage, January 31, 1801, SNP (2561).

103. "Quaderno en que consta la Cuenta . . . ," January 31, 1801–January 27, 1818, SNP (2592); *legajo*, January 27, 1818, SNP (2662); *legajo*, November 4, 1820, SNP (2664).

104. Certified copy of a *legajo*, May 3, 1822, SNP (2675).

105. Alessio Robles, *Coahuila y Texas*, p. 553; "Copia simple de Escritura . . . ," April 10, 1809, SNP (2543).

106. Elizondo's petition to the Bishop of Linares, SNP (2673); decree by Bishop Primo Feliciano Marín de Porras, May 27, 1809, SNP (2667); Elizondo's undated petition to the Commandant General of the Interior Provinces and the latter's approval, December 25, 1809, SNP (2668).

107. Alessio Robles, *Coahuila y Texas*, p. 553.

108. *Legajo*, March 30, 1815, SNP (2928).

109. "Autos de D. Melchor Shes Nabarro . . . ," 1826, AGEC, *legajo* 18, *carpeta* 827; [draft—José Melchor SN] to José Alejandro Treviño, January 1, 1820, SNP (3362); "Autos seguidos por D. Melchor Sanches Nabarro . . . ," 1824, AGEC, *legajo* 15, *carpeta* 767.

110. Certified copy of a *legajo*, May 3, 1822, SNP (2675).

111. "Año de 1819—Quaderno en qᵉ consta . . . ," MCSN.

112. [Draft—José Melchor SN] to Ramón García Rojas, June 29, 1818, SNP (1223); "Sobre cuestión de Aguas . . . ," 1826, AGEC, *legajo* 17, *carpeta* 812.

113. "Año de 1819—Quaderno en qᵉ consta . . . ," MCSN.

114. Summary of the inventories of the Aguayo *latifundio* in 1815 and 1826, SNP (2883); see also the following inventories for 1815: "Ynventario de la Hazienda de Parras . . . ," SNP (2927), and "Ynventario de la Hazᵃ de Bonanza," July 1, 1815, SNP (2885).

115. Mexico, Instituto Nacional de Antropología e Historia, Dirección de Monumentos Coloniales, *Edificios coloniales artísticos e históricos de la República Mexicana que han sido declarados monumentos*, pp. 38, 84.

116. Alessio Robles, *Coahuila y Texas*, p. 507.

2. RANCHING

1. Bernardo José Carrasco to José Miguel SN, March 26, 1777, SNP (3408); [Manuel Francisco S]N to [same], May 5, 1777, SNP (2681); [José Miguel] SN to Manuel Francisco SN, April 17, 1774, SNP (3508).

2. Morfi, *Viaje*, pp. 290–291; Juan Agustín de Morfi, *Diario y Derrotero (1777–1781)*, ed. Eugenio del Hoyo and Malcolm D. McLean, p. 86.

3. [Manuel Francisco S]N to José Miguel SN, April 25, 1780, SNP (542); August 11, 1784, SNP (3004); January 10, 1786, SNP (1986); Tomás Torres to same, July 14, 1784, SNP (2971); Juan Antonio de Olivares to same, August 22, 1784, SNP (1815); *legajo*, May 12, 1784–January 5, 1833, SNP (2661).

4. Commission signed by the King of Spain, July 15, 1790, MCSN.

5. [Manuel Francisco S]N to José Miguel SN, January 18, 1792, SNP (3444).

6. "Cuenta y razón . . . ," August, 1774, SNP (2505).

7. "No. 29—Disposición testamentaria . . . ," August 9, 1771, SNP (488); "Copia de la Cu^ta de D. Fernando Basques Borrego . . . ," 1761, SNP (1615); Fernando Vázquez Borrego to José Miguel SN, June 20, 1765, SNP (1743).

8. Fernando Vázquez Borrego to José Miguel SN, January 14, 1762, SNP (553); September 12, 1764, SNP (1742); January 23, 1765, SNP (1745).

9. "Cuaderno en que consta . . . ," 1761–1767, SNP (2064); Fernando Vázquez Borrego to José Miguel SN, May 7, 1769, SNP (3336).

10. "Cuaderno en que consta . . . ," 1761–1767, SNP (2064); Francisco de Mata to José Miguel SN, May 19, 1766, SNP (566); Manuel Reyes to same, May 19, 1773, SNP (3056); contract, January 15, 1772, SNP (1643).

11. Francisco de Mata to José Miguel SN, July 15, 1771, SNP (1313); "Tanto de la Cuenta . . . ," August 27, 1776, SNP (3610).

12. Francisco de Mata to José Miguel SN, March 6, 1767, SNP (1260); Manuel Francisco SN to same, January 10, 1786, SNP (1986); Andrés Vicente de Urizar to same, April 26, 1786, SNP (2045); José Antonio Rodríguez to same, September 24, 1820, SNP (777); [José Miguel] SN to Manuel Francisco SN, May 9, 1792, SNP (3508).

13. Winifred Kupper, The Golden Hoof, pp. 19–20.

14. William H. Dusenberry, The Mexican Mesta, p. 3.

15. Certificate by José Miguel SN, January 5, 1762, AGN-PI, vol. 25, exp. 5, fol. 169.

16. Robert Maudslay, Texas Sheepman, ed. Winifred Kupper, p. 114; Kupper, Golden Hoof, p. 52.

17. [José Miguel] SN to Manuel Francisco SN, January 30, 1788, SNP (3508).

18. Kupper, Golden Hoof, pp. 152–155; Maudslay, Texas Sheepman, pp. 118–119; "Hacienda de Sn. Ignacio del Paso Tapado . . . ," August 28, 1786, SNP (3421); [José Miguel] SN to Manuel Francisco SN, May 9, 1792, SNP (3508); [Juan Ignacio de] Arizpe to José Miguel SN, September 2, 1802, SNP (1077); Leovigildo Islas Escárcega (comp.), Diccionario rural de México, p. 58.

19. [Manuel Francisco S]N to José Miguel SN, February 8, 1786, SNP (2935).

20. [Manuel Francisco S]N to José Miguel SN, June 15, 1790, SNP (3454); January 18, 1792, SNP (3444); February 29, 1792, SNP (3433).

21. "No. 6—Hermanas y Tapado . . . ," SNP (2907); "Reconocimiento E inventario . . . ," January 2, 1775, MCSN.

22. [Manuel Francisco S]N to José Miguel SN, February 13, 1787, SNP (2059); Ignacio de Castro to same, ———, 1787, SNP (2936); June 7, 1787, SNP (2003); July 7, 1787, SNP (2011); July 20, 1787, SNP (2034); July 28, 1787, SNP (2012).

23. Donald D. Brand, "The Early History of the Range Cattle Industry in Northern Mexico," Agricultural History 35, no. 3 (July 1961), p. 136.

24. See Luis Navarro García, Don José de Gálvez y la Comandancia General de las Provincias Internas del Norte de Nueva España, and Max L. Moorhead, The Apache Frontier.

25. "Estado que manifiesta . . . ," May 3, 1767, AGN-PI, vol. 25, exp. 9, fol. 387.

26. Jacobo Ugarte to the Marquis of Croix, February 7, 1770, AGN-PI, vol. 24, exp. 1, fol. 18.

27. Jacobo Ugarte to the Viceroy, November 27, 1771, AGN-PI, vol. 24, exp. 1,

fols. 71–71v; [draft—Viceroy Antonio de Bucareli] to Jacobo Ugarte, December 21, 1771, AGN-PI, vol. 24, exp. 1, fol. 57.

28. Francisco de Mata to José Miguel SN, March 6, 1767, SNP (1260); Vicente de Alderete to the Marquis of Croix, July 18, 1768, AGN-PI, vol. 22, exp. 10, fols. 324–325, 328; Manuel Rodríguez to same, September 8, 1768, AGN-PI, vol. 22, exp. 9, fol. 315v; Jacobo Ugarte to Viceroy Antonio Bucareli, November 4, 1771, AGN-PI, vol. 24, exp. 1, fol. 74v–75; same to Melchor de Peramás, July 3, 1773, AGN-PI, vol. 24, exp. 36, fol. 162; same to Viceroy Antonio Bucareli, August 10, 1773, AGN-PI, vol. 24, exp. 39, fols. 178–182; January 28, 1774, AGN-PI, vol. 24, exp. 45, fols. 204v, 207.

29. "Estado de los Presidios . . . ," AGN-PI, vol. 24, exp. 24, fols. 129–130. The document is undated but is in the correspondence for 1773.

30. Morfi, *Viaje*, pp. 264–265; [draft—the Viceroy] to Jacobo Ugarte, August 14, 1773, AGN-PI, vol. 24, exp. 40, fol. 183.

31. Manuel Rodríguez to the Marquis of Croix, March 19, 1769, AGN-PI, vol. 22, exp. 1, fols. 23–23v; *legajo*, August 22, 1769–February 3, 1770, SNP (3048).

32. Certificate by José Miguel SN, April 4, 1770, AGN-PI, vol. 24, exp. 1, fol. 38.

33. Bernardo Manuel de Umarán to José Miguel SN, ——— 8, 1771, SNP (1322).

34. [Manuel Francisco S]N to José Miguel SN, December 24, 1775, SNP (760); December 6, 1776, SNP (2493); Jacobo Ugarte to Viceroy Antonio Bucareli, July 9, 1776, AGN-PI, vol. 24, fols. 258v, 259v.

35. José Díez Tamayo to José Miguel SN, July 8, 1777, SNP (1307).

36. Alfred Barnaby Thomas (ed.), *Teodoro de Croix and the Northern Frontier of New Spain, 1776–1783*, pp. 60–62; [Manuel Francisco S]N to José Miguel SN, May 3, 1784, SNP (2973).

37. Ignacio de Castro to José Miguel SN, December 11, 1785, SNP (2944); [Manuel Francisco S]N to same, February 8, 1786, SNP (2935); February 14, 1786, SNP (1980).

38. Pedro Tueros to José Miguel SN, February 21, 1786, SNP (1880).

39. [Manuel Francisco S]N to José Miguel SN, February 21, 1786, SNP (3029).

40. Francisco Castellano to José Miguel SN, February 21, 1786, SNP (1890); Marcos Laureano Suárez to same, August 2, 1786, SNP (3051); [Manuel Francisco S]N to same, September 7, 1786, SNP (2954).

41. Miguel José de Emparán to Viceroy Revillagigedo, March 24, 1790, AGN-PI, vol. 160, exp. 2, fol. 185; April 8, 1790, AGN-PI, vol. 160, exp. 2, fol. 191; "Extracto que manifiesta . . . ," June 3, 1790, AGN-PI, vol. 160, exp. 2, fol. 208; Miguel José de Emparán to Viceroy Revillagigedo, July 29, 1790, AGN-PI, vol. 160, exp. 2, fol. 219.

42. "Estado que manifiesta . . . ," April 8, 1790, AGN-PI, vol. 160, exp. 2, fol. 191.

43. Miguel José de Emparán to Viceroy Revillagigedo, March 23, 1790, AGN-PI, vol. 24, exp. 85, fols. 353v, 356; [draft—Viceroy Revillagigedo] to Miguel de Emparán, April 14, 1790, AGN-PI, vol. 24, exp. 85, fol. 355; [Miguel José de] Emparán to Viceroy Revillagigedo, August 11, 1790, AGN-PI, vol. 160, exp. 2, fol. 226.

44. Miguel José de Emparán to Viceroy Revillagigedo, April 22, 1790, AGN-PI,

vol. 24, exp. 86, fols. 357–365; "Villa de Santiago . . . ," August 26, 1791, AGN-PI, vol. 56, exp. 1, fols. 464–471.

45. Joseph F. Park, "Spanish Indian Policy in Northern Mexico, 1765–1810," *Arizona and the West* 4, no. 4 (Winter 1962): 343–344.

46. [Manuel Francisco S]N to José Miguel SN, June 13, 1791, SNP (3438); July 10, 1791, SNP (3429); January 14, 1792, SNP (3341); January 18, 1792, SNP (3444); José Antonio SN to same, June 26, 1791, SNP (1682).

47. Juan Ignacio de Arizpe to José Miguel SN, September 25, 1801, SNP (1075); October 10, 1801, SNP (1071); Domingo de Berrio to same, December 11, 1801, SNP (2077).

48. Morfi, *Viaje*, p. 289.

49. C. W. Towne and E. N. Wentworth, *Shepherd's Empire*, pp. 251–252; Maudslay, *Texas Sheepman*, pp. 39–40, 117; Kupper, *Golden Hoof*, p. 86.

50. [José Miguel] SN to Manuel Francisco SN, April 17, 1774, SNP (3508); Felipe Padilla to José Miguel SN, September 21, 1775, SNP (3011); [Manuel Francisco S]N to same, July 5, 1776, SNP (3591); Pedro Simón de la Cruz to same, November 23, 1776, SNP (1332).

51. [Manuel Francisco S]N to [José Miguel SN], February 7, 1802, SNP (845); [José Miguel S]N to Francisco Castellano, April 13, 1802, SNP (29).

52. Antonio Cordero to José Miguel SN, May 28, 1802, SNP (1050); Francisco Castellano to same, June 2, 1802, SNP (808); [Juan Ignacio de] Arizpe to same, July 8, 1802, SNP (1078); a similar disaster had occurred in Monclova in October, 1767. See Jacinto de Barrios to the Marquis of Croix, October 12, 1767, AGN-PI, vol. 25, exp. 9, fol. 405.

53. Francisco Castellano to José Miguel SN, June 2, 1802, SNP (808); Mariano José Monzón to same, July 11, 1802, SNP (1030).

54. [José Miguel S]N to Francisco Castellano, July 17, 1802, SNP (36); José Gerónimo Cacho to José Miguel SN, July 22, 1802, SNP (2066).

55. José Miguel SN (the nephew) to José Miguel SN (the curate), September 17, 1802, SNP (969).

56. [José Melchor S]N to Francisco Castellano, December 31, 1801, SNP (3300); [José Miguel S]N to same, August 25, 1802, SNP (14).

57. Juan Ignacio de Arizpe to José Miguel SN, August 17, 1802, SNP (1029); August 28, 1802, SNP (1082); [Manuel Francisco S]N to same, September 1, 1802, SNP (83); [José Miguel S]N to Francisco Castellano, August 25, 1802, SNP (14).

58. [Manuel Francisco S]N to José Miguel SN, February 13, 1805, SNP (840); José Melchor SN to same, March 4, 1805, SNP (716).

59. José Melchor SN to José Miguel SN, April 4, 1805, SNP (718).

60. George T. M. Davis, *Autobiography of the Late Col. Geo. T. M. Davis*, pp. 107–108; Josiah Gregg, *Diary and Letters of Josiah Gregg*, ed. Maurice Garland Fulton, I, 270; William Marshall Anderson, *An American in Maximilian's Mexico, 1865–1866*, ed. Ramón Eduardo Ruiz, pp. 92–93.

61. Certificate, November 6, 1781, SNP (2585); *merced*, March 9, 1786, SNP (2380); deed, March 9, 1786, SNP (2380); deed, March 18, 1786, SNP (2376); José Melchor SN to María Francisca Apolonia de Beráin, May 30, 1807, SNP (3311).

62. José Antonio Ecay Múzquiz to José Miguel SN, February 13, 1813, SNP

(1893); February 19, 1813, SNP (1902); José Melchor SN to same, May 7, 1813, SNP (1854); November 18, 1813, SNP (1855); August 27, 1817, SNP (2864); José Luis Gorostiza to same, October 18, 1813, SNP (1911); same to [José] Melchor SN, October 29, 1813.

63. Ward J. Barrett, *The Sugar Hacienda of the Marqueses del Valle*, p. 7.

64. [Manuel Francisco S]N to José Miguel SN, July 5, 1771, SNP (1309).

65. [Manuel Francisco S]N to José Miguel SN, January 8, 1780, SNP (713); the Sánchez Navarros planted 11.5 *cargas*, or mule loads, of wheat. A *carga* equaled 5.15 bushels, and a *fanega*, or half a *carga*, equaled 2.58 bushels. Manuel Carrera Stampa, "The Evolution of Weights and Measures in New Spain," *Hispanic American Historical Review* 29, no. 1 (February 1949): 15; the amount of wheat planted was therefore 23 *fanegas*. It took 69 *fanegas* of seed to plant a *caballería* (103 acres) of wheat and 12 *fanegas* to plant a *caballería* of maize. Mariano Galván (comp.), *Ordenanzas de Tierras y Aguas ó sea Formulario Geométrico-Judicial para la designación, establecimiento, mensura, amojonamiento y deslinde de las poblaciones y todas sus suertes de tierras, sitios, caballerías y criaderos de ganados mayores y menores, y mercedes de agua*, p. 164.

66. [Manuel Francisco S]N to José Miguel SN, August 11, 1784, SNP (3004); Román de Letona to same, September 15, 1784, SNP (1956).

67. Father José Badiola to José Miguel SN, July 2, 1785, SNP (1992); Ignacio de Castro to same, January 3, 1786, SNP (2953); June 30, 1787, SNP (2026); [Manuel Francisco S]N to same, March 20, 1786, SNP (1811); September 7, 1786, SNP (2954); José Román de Letona to same, September 13, 1786, SNP (3391).

68. [Draft—Viceroy Manuel Antonio Flores] to Pedro de Tueros, June 1, 1788, AGN-PI, vol. 24, exp. 66, fol. 308.

69. Miguel José de Emparán to Viceroy Revillagigedo, June 28, 1790, AGN-PI, vol. 24, exp. 77, fol. 340; [draft—Viceroy Revillagigedo] to Miguel de Emparán, July 20, 1790, AGN-PI, vol. 24, exp. 77, fol. 341; Miguel José de Emparán to Viceroy Revillagigedo, January 24, 1791, AGN-PI, vol. 24, exp. 101, fol. 405.

70. [Manuel Francisco S]N to José Miguel SN, June 13, 1791, SNP (3438); "No. 7—Hermanas y Tapado . . . ," SNP (2908).

71. [Manuel Francisco S]N to José Miguel SN, February 29, 1792, SNP (3433).

72. José Antonio de Treviño to José Miguel SN, August 12, 1795, SNP (3458); [Manuel Francisco S]N to same, December ——, 1795, SNP (868); same to Francisco Castellano, June 22, 1798, SNP (3295).

73. [Manuel Francisco S]N to [José Miguel SN], February 7, 1802, SNP (845).

74. Mariano José Monzón to José Miguel SN, November 16, 1801, SNP (1036); Domingo de Berrio to same, December 11, 1801, SNP (2077); [José Miguel S]N to Francisco Castellano, May 12, 1802, SNP (31).

75. José Gerónimo Cacho to José Miguel SN, May 28, 1802, SNP (2068); Islas Escárcega (comp.), *Diccionario rural de México*, p. 84.

76. Since October, 1801, corn had sold for 3 reals per *almud*. In January, 1802, it had dropped to 2½ reals in Monterrey but at nearby Cadereyta it commanded 3 pesos a *fanega*. Mariano José Monzón to José Miguel SN, January 7, 1802, SNP (1043).

77. Juan Francisco Montemayor to José Miguel SN, June 22, 1802, SNP (853). The corn shortage in Monterrey had been approaching famine conditions. The price had reached 4 reals per *almud*, although in July, 1802, it was down to 2½ reals.

The forecast was that the price would reach 3 reals because of the current poor harvest. At Saltillo corn was selling for 4 reals an *almud*. Mariano José Monzón to José Miguel SN, July 11, 1802, SNP (1030).

78. [José Miguel S]N to Francisco Castellano, June 11, 1802, SNP (30); the price of grain increased steadily in Saltillo. By mid-July, 1802, corn sold for 4 pesos, 4 reals a *fanega*, while wheat and flour brought 15 pesos a *carga*. The prospects were for prices to continue rising. José Camacho to José Miguel SN, July 14, 1802, SNP (1022).

79. José Gerónimo Cacho to José Miguel SN, July 22, 1802, SNP (2066).

80. [José Melchor S]N to Francisco Castellano, May 27, 1803, SNP (11); same to José Miguel SN, April 7, 1804, SNP (638); June 1, 1804, SNP (824); [Manuel Francisco S]N to same, August 7, 1804, SNP (3297).

81. José Melchor SN to José Miguel SN, May 12, 1805, SNP (1730); May 16, 1805, SNP (703); December 18, 1805, SNP (820); José María Arcaute to same, June 1, 1806, SNP (1971).

82. [José Antonio] Chacón to José Miguel SN, July 9, 1806, SNP (1805).

83. José Melchor SN to José Miguel SN, October 29, 1816, SNP (1861); Juan Bernardino Quinteros to same, January 22, 1817, SNP (2198); Anderson, *An American in Maximilian's Mexico*, p. 93.

84. José Ignacio González to José Miguel SN, February 16, 1816, SNP (3038).

85. Pedro Rodríguez to [José Melchor SN], February 19, 1815, SNP (100).

86. José Antonio Chacón to José Miguel SN, May 22, 1807, SNP (2463); José Melchor SN to Faustino Castellano, May 24, 1809, SNP (1096); same to María Francisca Apolonia de Beráin, May 30, 1807, SNP (3311).

87. José Melchor SN to José Miguel SN, June 8, 1811, SNP (2469); November 28, 1811, SNP (1907); ——— to José Melchor SN, October 11, 1811, SNP (2626).

88. José Estevan del Castillo to José Miguel SN, May 8, 1812, SNP (1877); July 9, 1812, SNP (2432); José Luis Gorostiza to same, June 4, 1814, SNP (1937); June 12, 1814, SNP (2431); July 18, 1814, SNP (3400); October 6, 1814, SNP (1350); November 20, 1814, SNP (1800).

89. José María de Letona to José Miguel SN, March 18, 1816, SNP (2878); March 29, 1816, SNP (2202); June 24, 1816, SNP (1932); José Melchor SN to same, July 9, 1816, SNP (1974); José Santiago Villarreal to same, October 10, 1816, SNP (1910). Corn was selling in Saltillo for four pesos, four reals a *fanega*, the same as in Monclova. See José María de Letona to José Melchor SN, November 11, 1816, SNP (3468).

90. José Melchor SN to José Miguel SN, October 29, 1816, SNP (1861).

91. José Melchor SN to José Miguel SN, November 7, 1816, SNP (2879); January 20, 1817, SNP (1456).

92. José Melchor SN to José Miguel SN, December 23, 1817, SNP (1909); February 13, 1818, SNP (1924); José Santiago Villarreal to same, April 26, 1818, SNP (1926); ——— to José Melchor SN, March 8, 1818, SNP (2977).

93. Manuel Castellano to José Miguel SN, May 17, 1818, SNP (1860); June 7, 1818, SNP (1441); May 22, 1819, SNP (1417); September 12, 1819, SNP (1395); November 30, 1819, SNP (1402); José Melchor SN to same, May 19, 1818, SNP (1440); May 21, 1818, SNP (1404); August 24, 1818, SNP (1436); Mariano José

Monzón to same, May 26, 1818, SNP (1388); Juan Nepomuceno de la Peña to same, May 26, 1818, SNP (1426); Manuel Castellano to José Melchor SN, October 16, 1819, SNP (2631); May 31, 1820, SNP (599).

94. José Melchor SN to José Miguel SN, November 3, 1818, SNP (1403); José Gerónimo Cacho to same, September 27, 1818, SNP (1385); Manuel Castellano to same, January 2, 1819, SNP (1394); January 13, 1819, SNP (1412); same to José Melchor SN, May 31, 1820, SNP (599); May 7, 1819, SNP (2607); Martín Rodríguez to same, August 21, 1820, SNP (570).

95. [Manuel Francisco S]N to José Miguel SN, February 13, 1805, SNP (840); José Luis Gorostiza to same, November 20, 1814, SNP (1800).

96. José Luis Gorostiza to José Miguel SN, June 12, 1814, SNP (2431).

97. José Melchor SN to José Miguel SN, June 16, 1814, SNP (1870); June 28, 1814, SNP (1961).

98. José Melchor SN to José Miguel SN, July 9, 1816, SNP (1974).

99. José Melchor SN to José Miguel SN, December 14, 1816, SNP (1858); José Gerónimo Cacho to José Melchor SN, January 16, 1817, SNP (3463).

100. José Melchor SN to José Miguel SN, December 23, 1817, SNP (1909); December 24, 1817, SNP (1450).

101. José Luis Gorostiza to José Miguel SN, July 18, 1814, SNP (3400); October 6, 1814, SNP (1350); October 7, 1814, SNP (1875).

102. Receipt by Pedro Valdés, January 24, 1815, SNP (987); "Noticia de las contribuciones . . . ," June 30, 1814, AGENL-C; Francisco Vidaurri to the Secretary of the Provincial Deputation, June 27, 1814, AGENL-C; receipt by José María de Uranga, November 6, 1815, SNP (1340).

103. Francisco Adam to [José Melchor SN], April 23, 1817, SNP (1314); José Melchor SN to José Miguel SN, April 27, 1817, SNP (1975).

104. Governor Antonio García de Texada to José Melchor SN, and draft of the latter's reply, April 29, 1817, SNP (3024); José Melchor SN to José Miguel SN, April 30, 1817, SNP (2196); Antonio Muñiz to [José] Melchor SN, May 1, 1817, SNP (3348).

105. José Melchor SN to José Miguel SN, April 4, 1805, SNP (718); May 7, 1806, SNP (831); Manuel Royüela to same, March 5, 1806, SNP (836).

106. José Gerónimo Cacho to José Miguel SN, February 22, 1814, SNP (2433); José Melchor SN to same, April 7, 1814, SNP (1897); José Luis Gorostiza to same, July 5, 1814, SNP (1865).

107. José Melchor SN to José Miguel SN, July 9, 1816, SNP (1974); August 16, 1816, SNP (2876); August 23, 1816, SNP (2868).

108. José Gerónimo Cacho to José Melchor SN, December 9, 1816, SNP (3462).

109. José Melchor SN to José Miguel SN, January 13, 1817, SNP (2204); January 20, 1817, SNP (1456).

110. José Melchor SN to José Miguel SN, January 26, 1817, SNP (2195); March 28, 1817, SNP (2200).

111. José Melchor SN to José Miguel SN, January 21, 1817, SNP (2877); January 26, 1817, SNP (2195); Juan B. Quinteros to same, January 22, 1817, SNP (2198).

112. José Melchor SN to José Miguel SN, June 12, 1817, SNP (1925).

113. Juan Nepomuceno de la Peña to José Miguel SN, August 10, 1817, SNP (1445); José Melchor SN to same, August 11, 1817, SNP (1844); August 17, 1817, SNP (1901); August 21, 1817, SNP (1449); August 23, 1817, SNP (2862); August 24, 1817, SNP (1903); August 27, 1817, SNP (2864).

114. José Melchor SN to José Miguel SN, September 4, 1817, SNP (1443).

115. José Melchor SN to José Miguel SN, November 23, 1817, SNP (2199); November 12, 1817, SNP (1452); Antonio García de Texada to the Commandant General, November 18, 1817, AGN-PI, vol. 244, exp. 20, fol. 273.

116. Antonio García de Texada to the Commandant General, November 26, 1817, AGN-PI, vol. 244, exp. 20, fol. 275; José Melchor SN to José Miguel SN, December 6, 1817, SNP (1446).

117. Antonio García de Texada to the Commandant General, December 29, 1817, AGN-PI, vol. 244, exp. 20, fols. 295-296v, 305v.

118. José Melchor SN to José Miguel SN, November 3, 1818, SNP (1403); December 13, 1818, SNP (1438).

119. [José] Melchor [SN] to [María Francisca Apolonia Beráin de SN], September 5, 1819, SNP (3145).

120. Manuel Castellano to José Miguel SN, September 12, 1819, SNP (1395).

121. Manuel Castellano to José Miguel SN, October 16, 1819, SNP (2631); November 30, 1819, SNP (1402).

122. Carlos Sánchez Navarro y Peón, *Memorias de un Viejo Palacio (La Casa del Banco Nacional de México), 1523-1950*, pp. 213-214.

3. LABOR

1. Jacinto de Barrios to the Marquis of Cruillas, April 19, 1766, AGN-PI, vol. 25, exp. 9, fols. 332-334.

2. "Cuaderno en que consta . . . ," 1761-1767, SNP (2064); account, December 11, 1772, SNP (3611); Francisco de Mata to José Miguel SN, June 14, 1762, SNP (2101); June 1, 1763, SNP (554); January 13, 176—, SNP (147); José de Herrera to same, March 21, 1763, SNP (1326); Fernando Vázquez Borrego to same, January 14, 1762, SNP (553).

3. Juan Antonio Villavisencio to José Miguel SN, February 17, 1769, SNP (90); account, May 1-July 19, 1766, SNP (1982).

4. [Fernando Vázquez] Borrego to José Miguel SN, December 27, 1786, SNP (2056); Martín Valdez to same, June 21, 1775, SNP (754); José Cayetano Maldonado to same, June 20, 1784, SNP (2050); September 12, 1784, SNP (2999); May 3, 1785, SNP (2061).

5. [José Miguel] SN to Manuel Francisco SN, July 19, 1793, SNP (3508).

6. José Camacho to [José Miguel SN], September 12, 1804, SNP (2599); March 13, 1806, SNP (837).

7. Vicente García to José Miguel SN, September 12, 1810, SNP (1864); José Ignacio Sánchez Castellano to same, November 13, 1811, SNP (1840); José Luis Gorostiza to José Melchor SN, October 29, 1813, SNP (1059); José Melchor SN to José Miguel SN, August 23, 1816, SNP (2868); Manuel Castellano to same, September 1, 1817, SNP (1458); same to José Melchor SN, July 15, 1820, SNP (101); inventories, January 27 and February 6, 1818, SNP (2662).

8. Accounts for 1775, included in SNP (3611); Juan Ignacio de Arizpe to José Miguel SN, March 15, 1802, SNP (1070); [Manuel Francisco S]N to Francisco Castellano, March 21, 1802, SNP (52).

9. Juan Antonio Caviedes to José Miguel SN, July 27, 1765, SNP (1941).

10. "Cuenta y razón . . . ," August, 1774, SNP (2505); Marcos Laureano Suárez to José Miguel SN, August 12, 1784, SNP (3019); Francisco Castellano to same, March 1, 1786, SNP (1834); Marcos Laureano Suárez to same, August 2, 1786, SNP (3051); [José Miguel] SN to Manuel Francisco SN, January 30, 1788, SNP (3508); same to Francisco Castellano, February 12, 1803, SNP (3299).

11. "Cuenta y razón . . . ," August, 1774, SNP (2505); Marcos Laureano Suárez to José Miguel SN, August 12, 1784, SNP (3019); "Hacienda de Sn. Ignacio del Paso Tapado . . . ," August 28, 1786, SNP (3421); José Melchor SN to Faustino [Castellano], August 20, 1809, SNP (1152); same to José Miguel SN, March 11, 1813, SNP (1908); August 16, 1816, SNP (2876); August 11, 1817, SNP (1844); August 24, 1818, SNP (1436).

12. José Melchor SN to José Miguel SN, March 4, 1805, SNP (716).

13. [Manuel Francisco S]N to José Miguel SN, January 8, 1780, SNP (713); January 27, 1784, SNP (2982); October 3, 1784, SNP (1951); June 15, 1790, SNP (3454); January 18, 1792, SNP (3444); Ignacio de Castro to same, January 6, 1786, SNP (2687); José Román de Letona to same, January 6, 1787, SNP (2017); [José Miguel] SN to Manuel Francisco SN, November 21, 1787, SNP (3508).

14. José Melchor SN to José Miguel SN, June 8, 1811, SNP (2469); November 1, 1815, SNP (586); April 7, 1818, SNP (1929); José Estevan del Castillo to same, October 9, 1812, SNP (1863); José Ignacio González to same, October 12, 1813, SNP (1905); Manuel Castellano to same, January 13, 1819, SNP (1412); José Luis Gorostiza to José Melchor SN, October 6, 1814, SNP (1350); Manuel Castellano to same, October 16, 1819, SNP (2631).

15. Felipe Padilla to José Miguel SN, May 20, 1785, SNP (3022); Ignacio de Castro to same, May 30, 1787, SNP (2937); July 7, 1787, SNP (2011); June 30, 1787, SNP (2026); José Melchor SN to same, June 1, 1804, SNP (824); May 16, 1805, SNP (703); José María Arcaute to same, June 1, 1806, SNP (1971); José Antonio Chacón to same, May 22, 1807, SNP (2463); José Luis Gorostiza to same, June 12, 1814, SNP (2431); [José Melchor SN] to Francisco Castellano, May 27, 1803, SNP (11); June 14, 1803, SNP (13); same to Faustino Castellano, May 24, 1809, SNP (1096).

16. Alessio Robles, *Coahuila y Texas*, p. 590, note 2; "Cuaderno en que consta . . . ," 1761–1767, SNP (2064); Fernando Vázquez Borrego to José Miguel SN, January 14, 1762, SNP (553); "Año de 1800. Testimonio . . . ," SNP (490).

17. Bill of sale, October 25, 1763, SNP (2670); receipt, November 16, 1763, SNP (2229); "Escritura de la Mulata Bernabela," December 10, 1779, SNP (2934); [Manuel Francisco S]N to José Miguel SN, January 8, 1780, SNP (713); March 20, 1786, SNP (1811); José Luis Gorostiza to same, October 7, 1814, SNP (1875); [José Miguel] SN to Manuel Francisco SN, March 19, 1793, SNP (3508); [Manuel Francisco S]N to Francisco Castellano, November 4, 1802, SNP (53); partial inventory of José Miguel SN's estate, April 18–May 30, 1821, SNP (2919).

18. "No. 38. Escritura de la Casa . . . ," December 2, 1813, SNP (2347); José

Melchor SN to José Miguel SN, November 11, 1815, SNP (10); José Domingo de Letona to same, May 31, 1816, SNP (3555).

19. Ignacio Gregorio to José Miguel SN, June 20, 1787, SNP (2018); Francisco Castellano to same, June 16, 1797, SNP (2460); José Estevan del Castillo to José Faustino Castellano, June 6, 1808, SNP (1117); Isidro de Aguilar to same, July 3, 1808, SNP (1121); *legajo*, September 17, 1800–November 17, 1805, SNP (3075).

20. C. W. Towne and E. N. Wentworth, *Shepherd's Empire*, pp. 59, 61; Robert Maudslay, *Texas Sheepman*, ed. Winifred Kupper, p. 129, note 2.

21. José Luis Gorostiza to José Miguel SN, June 12, 1814, SNP (2431); [Manuel Francisco S]N to same, July 5, 1771, SNP (1309).

22. Fernando Vázquez Borrego to José Miguel SN, August 20, 1781, SNP (1806); José Gerónimo Cacho to same, July 22, 1802, SNP (2066); September 7, 1804, SNP (682).

23. [Manuel Francisco S]N to José Miguel SN, July 5, 1776, SNP (3591); May 3, 1784, SNP (2973); Ignacio de Castro to same, December 11, 1785, SNP (2944); José Melchor SN to same, May 7, 1813, SNP (1854).

24. Manuel Castellano to José Melchor SN, October 16, 1819, SNP (2631); same to José Miguel SN, November 30, 1819, SNP (1402).

25. [Manuel Francisco S]N to José Miguel SN, January 9, 1785, SNP (2620); March 2, 1786, SNP (3045); January 18, 1792, SNP (3444); Ignacio de Castro to same, May 30, 1787, SNP (2937); José Luis Gorostiza to same, October 18, 1813, SNP (1911); Martín Rodríguez to José Melchor SN, August 21, 1820, SNP (570); Manuel Castellano to same, October 16, 1819, SNP (2631).

26. "Cuaderno en que consta . . . ," 1761–1767, SNP (2064); Pedro Flores y Valdés to José Miguel SN, July 7, 1764, SNP (1331); Juan Antonio Villavisencio to same, February 17, 1769, SNP (90).

27. "Cuenta y razón . . . ," August, 1774, SNP (2505); accounts in SNP (3611).

28. Charles Gibson, *The Aztecs under Spanish Rule*, pp. 251–252; William B. Taylor, *Landlord and Peasant in Colonial Oaxaca*, p. 149; Isabel González Sánchez, "Situación Social de Indios y Castas en las Fincas Rurales, en Vísperas de la Independencia de México," thesis, p. 79.

29. "Razón de los Gastos . . . ," September 17, 1800–November 17, 1805, SNP (3075); José Estevan del Castillo to José Faustino Castellano, June 6, 1808, SNP (1117); July 3, 1808, SNP (1085); Isidro de Aguilar to same, July 3, 1808, SNP (1121); José Antonio Armendáriz to José Miguel SN, February 17, 1813, SNP (1874).

30. Román de Letona to José Melchor SN, May 26, 1815, SNP (3354).

31. "Año de 1819—Quaderno en q^e consta . . . ," MCSN.

32. See O. P. Eklund and Sydney P. Noe, *Hacienda Tokens of Mexico*.

33. The amount was 2 *almudes*. An *almud* equalled 6.88 dry quarts. Juan Antonio Villavisencio to José Miguel SN, February 17, 1769, SNP (90); account, May 1–July 19, 1766, SNP (1982); Fernando Vázquez Borrego to José Miguel SN, July 3, 1776, SNP (3585); Zebulon M. Pike, *The Expeditions of Zebulon Montgomery Pike*, ed. Elliott Coues, II, 679.

34. The amount was 1 *fanega*, 2 *almudes*. Francisco de Mata to José Miguel SN, September 16, 1764, SNP (582). The standard ration was 2½ *almudes* of corn.

"Cuaderno en que consta . . . ," 1761–1767, SNP (2064); [José] Estevan [del Castillo] to José Miguel SN, July 9, 1812, SNP (2432); José Melchor SN to same, October 29, 1816, SNP (1861); August 23, 1816, SNP (2868); Manuel Castellano to same, September 19, 1817, SNP (1447); January 13, 1819, SNP (1412); Ignacio de Castro to same, January 26, 1786, SNP (2687); [Manuel Francisco S]N to same, June 15, 1790, SNP (3454); "Hacienda de Sn. Ignacio del Paso Tapado . . . ," August 28, 1786, SNP (3421).

35. Francisco Castellano to José Miguel SN, September 18, 1786, SNP (1881).

36. For an example of a peon's purchasing power in the 1770's and 1780's see Charles H. Harris III, "A Mexican *Latifundio*: The Economic Empire of the Sánchez Navarro Family, 1765–1821," Ph.D. dissertation, pp. 299–303.

37. Friedrich Katz, "Labor Conditions on Haciendas in Porfirian Mexico: Some Trends and Tendencies," *Hispanic American Historical Review* 54, no. 1 (February 1974): 6–7.

38. Francisco Castellano to José Miguel SN, March 5, 1786, SNP (3028); José Román de Letona to same, December 23, 1786, SNP (3379); Ignacio de Castro to same, May 30, 1787, SNP (2937); [José] Estevan [del Castillo] to same, October 9, 1812, SNP (1863); José Luis Gorostiza to same, July 18, 1814, SNP (3400); "Razón de los efectos . . . ," January 12, 1789, SNP (3508); "Noticia de los Efectos Comprados . . . ," October 1, 1801, SNP (1027).

39. [Manuel Francisco S]N to José Miguel SN, January 8, 1780, SNP (713); "Cuaderno en que consta . . . ," 1761–1767, SNP (2064).

40. Accounts in a letter from Francisco Antonio Gómez de la Casa to José Miguel SN, October 19, 1781, SNP (1623).

41. "Cuaderno en que consta . . . ," 1761–1767, SNP (2064); account, December 11, 1772, SNP (3611).

42. "Quadrante de la Hazienda . . . ," February 23, 1791–November 1, 1794, SNP (88).

43. "Cuaderno en que consta . . . ," 1761–1767, SNP (2064).

44. [José Miguel] SN to Manuel Francisco SN, January 13, 1789, SNP (3508); José Gerónimo Cacho to José Miguel SN, May 28, 1802, SNP (2068); memorandum, May 29, 1805, SNP (2992).

45. Father Iñigo de San José to José Miguel SN, April 18, 1802, SNP (613); June 15, 1802, SNP (681).

46. For an example of a father-son debt see Harris, "A Mexican *Latifundio*," p. 300.

47. Ignacio de Castro to José Miguel SN, January 3, 1786, SNP (2953); José Antonio Chacón to same, May 22, 1807, SNP (2463); [Manuel Francisco S]N to [same], May 5, 1777, SNP (2681); José Luis Gorostiza to same, July 18, 1814, SNP (3400); José Román de Letona to same, January 6, 1787, SNP (2017).

48. José Román de Letona to José Miguel SN, December 23, 1786, SNP (3379); José Melchor SN to same, August 23, 1816, SNP (2868); Manuel Castellano to same, September 1, 1817, SNP (1458); November 30, 1819, SNP (1402).

49. [Manuel Francisco S]N to José Miguel SN, February 29, 1792, SNP (3433).

50. [Manuel Francisco S]N to José Miguel SN, July 5, 1776, SNP (3591); Tomás Torres to same, July 14, 1784, SNP (2971); [José Miguel S]N to [Francisco] Castellano, May 4, 1802, SNP (34).

51. [José Miguel S]N to [Francisco] Castellano, September 4, 1802, SNP (70); [José Melchor SN] to same, May 27, 1803, SNP (11); Manuel Castellano to José Melchor SN, May 7, 1819, SNP (2607); Juan José de Cárdenas to same, June 21, 1819, SNP (1752); Martín Rodríguez to same, August 21, 1820, SNP (570).

52. Fernando Vázquez Borrego to José Miguel SN, September 8, 1774, SNP (1358); July 3, 1776, SNP (3585); July 31, 1776, SNP (2495).

53. José Gerónimo Cacho to José Miguel SN, January 26, 1802, SNP (1692); May 28, 1802, SNP (2068); July 22, 1802, SNP (2066); September 7, 1804, SNP (682).

54. José Gerónimo Cacho to José Miguel SN, September 7, 1804, SNP (682); José Joaquín del Fierro to same, January 1, 1785, SNP (2996); José Nepomuceno Gil to same, May 28, 1785, SNP (2989); José Máximo Elizondo to same, September 30, 1801, SNP (116).

55. María Ignacia Palau to José Miguel SN, February 25, 1788, SNP (3342); Francisco Antonio Sánchez de Zamora to same, February 26, 1788, SNP (3343); [Manuel Francisco S]N to same, March 2, 1786, SNP (3045); January 23, 1787, SNP (1885).

56. Juan Bautista de Elguézabal to [José] Miguel SN, April 1, 1802, SNP (1046); April 14, 1802, SNP (1045); May 12, 1802, SNP (1047).

57. [José Miguel] SN to Manuel Francisco SN, July 19, 1793, SNP (3508); August 16, 1793, SNP (3508); Mariano José Monzón to José Miguel SN, March 15, 1802, SNP (1042); April 26, 1802, SNP (1033); May 16, 1802, SNP (1038); July 5, 1802, SNP (1031); June 11, 1804, SNP (681-B); Domingo de Berrio to same, June 1, 1802, SNP (2079).

58. Francisco de Mata to José Miguel SN, July 10, 1771, SNP (1311); Ignacio de Castro to [same], October 2, 1785, SNP (2939); May 30, 1787, SNP (2937); Román de Letona to same, April 16, 1786, SNP (2686); January 6, 1787, SNP (2017); Francisco Castellano to same, May 7, 1802, SNP (905); José Melchor SN to same, May 7, 1813, SNP (1854); same to Faustino Castellano, April 20, 1809, SNP (1095).

59. [José Miguel] SN to Manuel Francisco SN, March 19, 1793, SNP (3508).

60. Juan Ignacio de Arizpe to José Miguel SN, August 17, 1802, SNP (1029); August 28, 1802, SNP (1082); Manuel Francisco SN to same, September 1, 1802, SNP (83); [José Miguel S]N to Francisco Castellano, August 25, 1802, SNP (14).

61. Francisco Castellano to José Miguel SN, December 17, 1802, SNP (1028); [Manuel Francisco S]N to same, September 16, 1804, SNP (1345).

62. José Melchor SN to María Francisca Apolonia de Beráin [de SN], May 30, 1807, SNP (3311).

63. José Melchor SN to Faustino [Castellano], August 20, 1809, SNP (1152).

64. José Melchor SN to José Miguel SN, April 7, 1818, SNP (1929).

65. José Melchor SN to José Miguel SN, June 16, 1814, SNP (1870).

66. Pablo Martínez del Río, El suplicio del hacendado y otros temas agrarios, p. 12.

4. LATIFUNDIO PRODUCTION

1. Robert C. West, The Mining Community in Northern New Spain, pp. 61–63.

2. José Antonio Fernández de Jáuregui Urrutia, Descripción del Nuevo Reino de León (1735–1740) por Don Josseph Antonio Fernández de Jáuregui Urrutia su

Gobernador y Capitán General, ed. Malcolm D. McLean and Eugenio del Hoyo, p. 99; Francisco de Mata to José Miguel SN, July 8, 1783, SNP (2956).

3. Andrés Vicente de Urizar to José Miguel SN, July 20, 1785, SNP (3603).

4. "Reconocimiento E inventario . . . ," January 2, 1775, MCSN.

5. Domingo Narciso de Allende to José Miguel SN, February 20, 1781, SNP (2023); Hubert H. Bancroft, *History of Mexico,* IV, 104.

6. "El Sr. D. Manuel Fran^co Sanchez Navarro . . . ," October 12, 1787, SNP (3506).

7. José Miguel SN to Andrés Vicente de Urizar, January 12, 1785, SNP (81).

8. Andrés Vicente de Urizar to José Miguel SN, May 11, 1785, SNP (3604).

9. Andrés Vicente de Urizar to José Miguel SN, May 25, 1785, SNP (3605); July 20, 1785, SNP (3603).

10. "El Sr. D. Manuel Fran^co Sanchez Navarro . . . ," October 12, 1787, SNP (3506).

11. Ibid.; Andrés Vicente de Urizar to José Miguel SN, July 11, 1787, SNP (2039); May 31, 1786, SNP (2042); September 27, 1786, SNP (2044); August 22, 1787, SNP (2040).

12. Donald B. Cooper, *Epidemic Disease in Mexico City, 1761–1813,* pp. 70–74.

13. Fernando Manuel de Umarán to José Miguel SN, February 21, 1787, SNP (2058).

14. "R1. Prov^n Receptoria . . . ," January 14, 1788, AGN-T, vol. 2966, exp. 48, fols. 1–2; "R1. Prov^n Receptoria . . . ," March 6, 1788, AGN-T, vol. 2966, exp. 71, fols. 1–2.

15. See two articles by J. Ignacio Rubio Mañé in the *Boletín del Archivo General de la Nación* 2, no. 4 (October–December 1961): "Los Allendes de San Miguel el Grande," pp. 517–556, and "Los Unzagas de San Miguel el Grande," pp. 557–568.

16. José Domingo de Letona to José Miguel SN, May 12, 1790, SNP (3526).

17. José María de Unzaga to José Miguel SN, March 2, 1787, SNP (2055); Domingo de Berrio to same, December 11, 1801, SNP (2077); Bancroft, *History of Mexico,* IV, 104–105.

18. Ricardo Ortega y Pérez Gallardo, *Historia Genealógica de las Familias más antiguas de México,* II, "Condado de Bassoco," 7–8; D. A. Brading, *Miners & Merchants in Bourbon Mexico, 1763–1810,* pp. 124–128.

19. José Domingo de Letona to José Miguel SN, September 3, 1789, SNP (3530).

20. José Domingo de Letona to José Miguel SN, May 12, 1790, SNP (3526).

21. [Manuel Francisco S]N to José Miguel SN, February 29, 1792, SNP (3433).

22. [José Miguel] SN to Manuel Francisco SN, May 31, 1792, SNP (3508).

23. [José Miguel] SN to Manuel Francisco SN, July 8, 1792, SNP (3508).

24. [José Miguel] SN to Manuel Francisco SN, May 31, 1792, SNP (3508); ——— 15, 1792, SNP (3508).

25. José Antonio de Treviño to José Miguel SN, August 12, 1795, SNP (3458); José Domingo de Letona to same, September 31 [*sic*], 1795, SNP (3529).

26. Receipt, September 2, 1797, SNP (771).

27. Domingo de Berrio to José Miguel SN, September 4, 1801, SNP (2075); June 1, 1802, SNP (2079); July 9, 1802, SNP (2080); February 4, 1803, SNP (3356); April 5, 1805, SNP (720); February 28, 1806, SNP (973).

28. Lucas Alamán, *Historia de Méjico desde los primeros movimientos que pre-*

pararon su independencia en el año de 1808 hasta la época presente, I, 238, note 1.

29. "Cotejo de las cavezas . . . ," April 12, 1804–August 7, 1805, AGN-AP, vol. 5, exp. 10, fol. 5; "Cotejo de los Carneros . . . ," April 12, 1804–August 7, 1805, AGN-AP, vol. 5, exp. 10, fol. 5v; "Razón de los carneros . . . ," August 9, 1805, AGN-AP, vol. 5, exp. 11, fol. 19; "D^n Gab^l de Yermo mejorando la apelacion . . . ," October 24, 1805, AGN-AP, vol. 5, exp. 10, fol. 1; petition by Gabriel de Yermo, May 12, 1806, AGN-AP, vol. 5, exp. 10, fols. 6–7; the *síndico procurador*'s legal opinion, August 8, 1806, AGN-AP, vol. 5, exp. 10, fol. 11.

30. Alessio Robles, *Coahuila y Texas*, pp. 392–393.

31. Manuel Carrillo to José Miguel SN, March 19, 1806, SNP (838).

32. Domingo de Berrio to José Miguel SN, December 11, 1801, SNP (2077).

33. José Antonio SN to José Miguel SN, November 10, 1786, SNP (3381); December 18, 1786, SNP (3374); February 19, 1787, SNP (1976).

34. [Manuel Francisco S]N to José Miguel SN, October 19, 1787, SNP (3372); José Antonio SN to same, February 11, 1788, SNP (3063).

35. Francisco de la Maza, *San Miguel de Allende*, p. 44.

36. Domingo de Berrio to José Miguel SN, February 28, 1806, SNP (973); José Camacho to same, March 13, 1806, SNP (837); March 19, 1806, SNP (972); March 21, 1806, SNP (2100).

37. Manuel Carrillo to José Miguel SN, March 19, 1806, SNP (838); José Camacho to same, March 19, 1806, SNP (972); April 20, 1806, SNP (739).

38. Román de Letona to José Miguel SN, September 9, 1809, SNP (1156).

39. [Manuel Francisco S]N to [José Miguel SN], February 7, 1802, SNP (845); same to Francisco Castellano, April 4, 1804, SNP (60); November 4, 1802, SNP (53); Mauricio de Alcocer to same, December 1, 1802, SNP (62); Francisco Castellano to José Miguel SN, December 17, 1802, SNP (1028); [José Melchor S]N to same, April 7, 1804, SNP (638); Román de Letona to Faustino Castellano, January 31, 1810, SNP (1184); February 28, 1810, SNP (1194).

40. [Manuel Francisco S]N to José Miguel SN, January 8, 1780, SNP (713); January 23, 1787, SNP (1885); August 7, 1804, SNP (3297); Ignacio de Castro to same, December 11, 1785, SNP (2944); ——— Carranza to same, February 27, 1786, SNP (3027); Francisco Castellano to same, March 9, 1786, SNP (2945); José Antonio SN to same, February 19, 1787, SNP (1976); José Miguel SN to Francisco Castellano, February 7, 1801, SNP (3301); May 12, 1802, SNP (31); [José Melchor S]N to same, December 31, 1801, SNP (3300); May 7, 1806, SNP (831); same to Faustino Castellano, January 26, 1809, SNP (1103); February 23, 1809, SNP (1093).

41. [Manuel Francisco S]N to José Miguel SN, January 9, 1785, SNP (2620).

42. "Cuenta y razón . . . ," August, 1774, SNP (2505); "Hacienda de Sn. Ignacio del Paso Tapado . . . ," August 28, 1786, SNP (3421); José Melchor SN to Faustino [Castellano], August 20, 1809, SNP (1152); same to José Miguel SN, August 24, 1817, SNP (1903); August 24, 1818, SNP (1436).

43. Robert S. Smith, "Sales Taxes in New Spain, 1575–1770," *Hispanic American Historical Review* 28, no. 1 (February 1948): 14; "Alcabala de Entrega de Carneros . . . ," 1779–1801, SNP (1079); see also the Marquis of Aguayo to José Miguel SN, September 16, 1801, SNP (3576); Juan Ignacio de Arizpe to same, October 17, 1801, SNP (1081); October 24, 1801, SNP (1072).

44. "Quadrante de la Hazienda . . . ," February 23, 1791–November 1, 1794, SNP (88); [José Miguel S]N to [Francisco] Castellano, September 4, 1802, SNP (70).

45. [José Miguel S]N to Francisco Castellano, April 13, 1802, SNP (29); July 17, 1802, SNP (36); September 4, 1802, SNP (70); February 12, 1803, SNP (3299); Juan Ignacio de Arizpe to José Miguel SN, April 13, 1800, SNP (1066); Mariano José Monzón to same, June 11, 1804, SNP (681-B); [Manuel Francisco S]N to same, August 7, 1804, SNP (3297); José Melchor SN to same, June 1, 1804, SNP (824); May 12, 1805, SNP (1730); May 16, 1805, SNP (701); same to Faustino [Castellano], August 20, 1809, SNP (1152).

46. Román de Letona to José Miguel SN, July 21, 1811, SNP (1343).

47. José Melchor SN to José Miguel SN, November 28, 1812, SNP (1898); June 28, 1814, SNP (1961); José Antonio Múzquiz to same, February 19, 1813, SNP (1902); José Luis Gorostiza to same, July 18, 1814, SNP (3400).

48. José María de Letona to [José] Melchor SN, May 26, 1815, SNP (3553); same to José Miguel SN, March 18, 1816, SNP (2878); June 24, 1816, SNP (1932).

49. [José Bernardino] Quinteros to José Miguel SN, February 22, 1816, SNP (2874); José Melchor SN to same, July 9, 1816, SNP (1974); May 12, 1817, SNP (2867); August 24, 1817, SNP (1903); October 29, 1816, SNP (1861); Manuel Castellano to same, June 7, 1818, SNP (1441); José María de Letona to José Melchor SN, November 11, 1816, SNP (3468); Manuel Castellano to same, October 16, 1819, SNP (2631).

50. José Antonio Medina to José Miguel SN, October 10, 1812, SNP (749); José Melchor SN to same, June 28, 1814, SNP (1961); July 9, 1816, SNP (1974); May 12, 1817, SNP (2867); Manuel Castellano to same, January 13, 1819, SNP (1412); José Luis Gorostiza to same, October 7, 1814, SNP (1875); same to José Melchor SN, October 6, 1814, SNP (1350); José María de Letona to same, May 26, 1815, SNP (3353); Román de Letona to same, May 26, 1815, SNP (3354).

5. COMMERCE

1. José Gregorio SN to José Miguel SN, May 18, 1762, SNP (3432).

2. Francisco de Mata to José Miguel SN, July 18, 1763, SNP (555).

3. "Cuaderno en que consta . . . ," 1761–1767, SNP (2064); Francisco de Mata to José Miguel SN, September 28, 1761, SNP (583); May 7, 1762, SNP (584); July 1, 1762, SNP (552); January 6, 1763, SNP (2097); July 18, 1763, SNP (555); April 4, 1764, SNP (1708); September 16, 1764, SNP (582); May 19, 1766, SNP (566); ———— to same, August 12, 1764, SNP (950); José Felipe Galván to same, August 13, 1764, SNP (1329); Fernando Vázquez Borrego to same, February 29 [sic], 1763, SNP (3337); December 28, 1765, SNP (556).

4. Pedro Flores y Valdés to José Miguel SN, July 7, 1764, SNP (1331).

5. Francisco de Mata to José Miguel SN, September 28, 1761, SNP (583); May 7, 1762, SNP (584); January 6, 1763, SNP (2097); February 17, 1772, SNP (91).

6. Jacobo de Ugarte to the Marquis of Croix, February 7, 1770, AGN-PI, vol. 24, exp. 1, fols. 22–23.

7. Max L. Moorhead, "The Private Contract System of Presidio Supply in Northern New Spain," *Hispanic American Historical Review* 41, no. 1 (February 1961): 33, 53.

8. Manuel Rodríguez to the Marquis of Croix, April 11, 1769, AGN-PI, vol. 22, exp. 1, fols. 28–28v; certificate by Father Diego Ximénez, February 13, 1772, AGN-PI, vol. 24, exp. 3, fol. 84; Vicente Rodríguez to José Miguel SN, March 12, 1776, SNP (3595).

9. [Draft—the Viceroy] to Manuel Rodríguez, May 27, 1769, AGN-PI, vol. 22, exp. 1, fol. 30; Marquis of Croix to Jacobo Ugarte, January 19, 1770, AGN-PI, vol. 24, exp. 1, fols. 31–31v.

10. Manuel Rodríguez to the Marquis of Croix, March 16, 1770, AGN-PI, vol. 22, exp. 1, fol. 59; "Contaduría Gral. de Rl. Hacienda . . . ," October 27, 1772, SNP (3606).

11. "Reconocimiento E inventario . . . ," January 2, 1775, MCSN.

12. For the complete inventory of the store see Charles H. Harris III, "A Mexican *Latifundio*: The Economic Empire of the Sánchez Navarro Family, 1765–1821," Ph.D. dissertation, pp. 304–312.

13. José Miguel González to [José] Melchor SN, October 26, 1819, SNP (3205); "Recibo que otorgó . . . ," May 18, 1811, SNP (2251).

14. "Razón de los efectos . . . ," October 4, 1776, SNP (1983).

15. Moorhead, "Private Contract System," pp. 33–34.

16. Juan Antonio Serrano to José Miguel SN and Manuel [Francisco SN], June 16, 1776, SNP (3594); Vicente Rodríguez to José Miguel SN, March 12, 1776, SNP (3595).

17. Morfi, *Viaje*, pp. 282–283. For an example of the practices Morfi referred to see Santiago Guadalupe de Pruneda to José Miguel SN, November 29, 1775, SNP (759).

18. "En dhº día se saco tanto . . . ," October 21, 1777–September 15, 1787, SNP (3507).

19. Moorhead, "Private Contract System," pp. 35–36; Lorenzo Cancio to the Marquis of Cruillas, June 16, 1762, AGN-PI, vol. 22, exp. 8, fol. 219; [José Miguel] SN to Manuel Francisco SN, August 9, 1788, SNP (3508); Juan de Ugalde to the Commandant General of the Interior Provinces, March 12, 1782, AGN-PI, vol. 13, exp. 13, fols. 411–413; same to Viceroy Alonzo Núñez de Haro, September 7, 1787, AGN-PI, vol. 13, exp. 13, fols. 408v–409.

20. José Domingo de Letona to José Miguel SN, October 20, 1784, SNP (2054); January 11, 1785, SNP (1966); April 20, 1785, SNP (3520); April 27, 1785, SNP (2046).

21. Francisco Castellano to José Miguel SN, August 26, 1784, SNP (1814).

22. José Miguel SN to Andrés Vicente de Urizar, January 12, 1785, SNP (81); Andrés Vicente de Urizar to José Miguel SN, May 11, 1785, SNP (3604).

23. Andrés Vicente de Urizar to José Miguel SN, May 25, 1785, SNP (3605); July 20, 1785, SNP (3603); April 26, 1786, SNP (2045).

24. Andrés Vicente de Urizar to José Miguel SN, April 26, 1786, SNP (2045); José Domingo de Letona to same, January 25, 1786, SNP (1892); Domingo de Berrio to same, February 1, 1786, SNP (1891).

25. Andrés Vicente de Urizar to José Miguel SN, April 26, 1786, SNP (2045); May 31, 1786, SNP (2042); José Antonio SN to same, August 4, 1786, SNP (1882); Donald B. Cooper, *Epidemic Disease in Mexico City, 1761–1813*, pp. 70–85.

26. Andrés Vicente de Urizar to José Miguel SN, September 27, 1786, SNP (2044); December 13, 1786, SNP (2043); José Antonio SN to same, December 18, 1786, SNP (3374); January 17, 1787, SNP (1812); February 19, 1787, SNP (1976).

27. Urizar explained that the muleteers refused to travel north because there was no forage along the trail and because they would have to pay twelve pesos a mule load for corn and thirty-five for flour. On the route to Acapulco, not only was there abundant forage but also corn cost only four pesos and flour seven.

28. "Memoria de los efectos . . . ," May 19, 1787, SNP (2014); Andrés Vicente de Urizar to José Miguel SN, July 11, 1787, SNP (2039). Illustrating the wide fluctuation in the price of staples was Urizar's comment in August that heavy rains around Mexico City were ensuring an excellent maize crop, and corn was now selling for five pesos per mule load, while the price of wheat was in excess of nine pesos. On the other hand in Durango, which was in the grip of a drought, corn was said to be extremely expensive, and flour commanded thirty pesos a mule load. Andrés Vicente de Urizar to José Miguel SN, August 22, 1787, SNP (2040).

29. "El Sr. D. Manuel Franco Sanchez Navarro . . . ," December 11, 1782–October 12, 1787, SNP (3506); Andrés Vicente de Urizar to José Miguel SN, May 11, 1785, SNP (3604).

30. [José Miguel] SN to Manuel Francisco SN, January 1, 1788, SNP (3508); January 30, 1788, SNP (3508).

31. Mariano José Monzón to José Miguel SN, February 5, 1788, SNP (3422); María Ignacia Palau [de SN] to same, February 25, 1788, SNP (3342).

32. "El Sr. D. Manuel Franco Sanchez Navarro . . . ," December 11, 1782–October 12, 1787, SNP (3506); José María de Unzaga to Manuel Francisco SN, March 16, 1787, SNP (3507); April 12, 1787, SNP (3507); June 22, 1787, SNP (3508); Domingo de Berrio to same, June 16, 1787, SNP (3507); April 25, 1788, SNP (3505); May 8, 1788, SNP (3504); June 20, 1788, SNP (3507).

33. Commission signed by the King of Spain, July 15, 1790, MCSN; "Cuenta de gastos hechos . . . ," July 21, 1790, SNP (1712); Andrés, Obispo del No Ro de León to José Miguel SN, December 2, 1790, SNP (1339).

34. José Antonio de Treviño to José Miguel SN, December 23, 1790, SNP (3405); Juan de la Brena to same, April 9, 1791, SNP (3439); [José Miguel] SN to Manuel Francisco SN, March 19, 1793, SNP (3508).

35. "Escritura de la Casa de Monterrey," August 6, 1774–January 30, 1794, SNP (3616).

36. Pedro Valdés to José Miguel SN, March 1, 1794, SNP (3402); Lucas de Foronda to same, April 25, 1795, SNP (3481); José Domingo de Letona to same, October 14, 1795, SNP (3527).

37. Domingo de Berrio to Manuel Francisco SN, January 29, 1790, SNP (3508); "Cuenta Factura . . . ," August 29, 1794, SNP (2616); "Memoria de los efectos . . . ," October 13, 1794, SNP (902); Juan Antonio de Zavala to Domingo de Berrio y Zavala, December 11, 1794, SNP (773); "Cuenta de lo que tengo remitido . . . ," December 13, 1794, SNP (2619); "El Sor D. Manl Franco Sanchez Nabarro . . . ," August 31, 1795, SNP (2615); "El Sr. Lizdo Dn José Migl Sánchez Navarro . . . ," September 3, 1796, SNP (951).

38. José Domingo de Letona to José Miguel SN, March 17, 1790, SNP (3525);

September 31 [*sic*], 1795, SNP (3529); José Antonio SN to same, June 5, 1791, SNP (1683); Antonio de Bassoco to same, November 14, 1798, SNP (98).

39. José Miguel SN's account with Bassoco, December 4, 1793–September 7, 1810, MCSN.

40. See William L. Schurz, "The Royal Philippine Company," *Hispanic American Historical Review* 3, no. 4 (November 1920): 491–508.

41. Manuel Francisco SN's account with Rábago, October 21, 1777–September 15, 1787, SNP (3507); José Miguel SN's account with Bassoco, December 4, 1793–September 7, 1810, MCSN; José Antonio SN to José Miguel SN, February 18, 1790, SNP (3323); José Domingo de Letona to same, September 21, 1799, SNP (3550); María Gertrudis Lobo Guerrero to same, August 13, 1799, SNP (3321).

42. Accounts, September 17, 1800–January 2, 1810, SNP (3075); account, September 12, 1801, SNP (2083); Francisco Castellano to José Miguel SN, June 2, 1802, SNP (808); February 26, 1803, SNP (2090); [Juan Ignacio de] Arizpe to same, July 8, 1802, SNP (1078).

43. Francisco Gerónimo Cacho to Manuel Francisco SN, September 14, 1801, SNP (785); José Gerónimo Cacho to José Miguel SN, October 19, 1802, SNP (2604); September 7, 1804, SNP (682); AGN-IC, vol. 27, fols. 4, 149–192v.

44. "Cuenta de Cargo y data . . . ," April 30–October 1, 1801, SNP (2084); [José Miguel S]N to [Francisco] Castellano, May 2, 1802, SNP (66); José Camacho to José Miguel SN, February 24, 1802, SNP (1023); May 5, 1802, SNP (1025); June 11, 1802, SNP (1024); June 16, 1802, SNP (1021); July 14, 1802, SNP (1022); January 19, 1805, SNP (3298); José Melchor SN to same, May 16, 1805, SNP (703); "Cuenta que manifiesto de la Lana . . . ," October 4, 1802–1803, SNP (1637); account, February 1, 1802–April 12, 1803, SNP (3075); account, February 1, 1803, SNP (1753).

45. José Domingo de Letona to José Miguel SN, July 24, 1799, SNP (3541); [Manuel Francisco S]N to same, October 3, 1800, SNP (2089).

46. [Manuel Francisco S]N to José Miguel SN, October 6, 1801, SNP (1026); "Noticia de los Efectos Comprados . . . ," October 1, 1801, SNP (1027).

47. [Manuel Francisco S]N to José Miguel SN, September 9, 1803, SNP (835); Manuel Royüela to same, October 19, 1803, SNP (2070); José Camacho to [same], September 12, 1804, SNP (2599).

48. Domingo de Barasorda to Francisco Castellano, December 9, 1800, SNP (73); Domingo de Berrio to José Miguel SN, September 4, 1801, SNP (2075); December 11, 1801, SNP (2077); April 1, 1802, SNP (2078); June 1, 1802, SNP (2079); July 9, 1802, SNP (2080); February 4, 1803, SNP (3356); José María de Allende to same, April 2, 1802, SNP (71); José Camacho to same, June 11, 1802, SNP (1024); "El Sr. D. Domingo de Berrio . . . ," February 4, 1803, SNP (560).

49. José Domingo de Letona to José Miguel SN, July 24, 1799, SNP (3541); José Miguel SN's account with Yermo, March 3, 1801–January 15, 1806, SNP (2249).

50. Letona's account, November 25, 1800–October 23, 1802, SNP (3455).

51. José Domingo de Letona to José Miguel SN, January 9, 1802, SNP (3542); March 30, 1802, SNP (3544); July 2, 1802, SNP (3543); José Miguel SN's account, April 6–May 17, 1802, SNP (2085).

52. José Domingo de Letona to José Miguel SN, October 10, 1804, SNP (3537); November 21, 1804, SNP (3538); November 28, 1804, SNP (3533); José Riveiro de Aguilar to José Domingo López de Letona, December 4, 1804, SNP (3423).

53. Letona's account, November 25, 1800–October 23, 1802, SNP (3455); José Miguel SN's account, March 3, 1801–January 15, 1806, SNP (2249); José Román de Letona to José Miguel SN, June 29, 1802, SNP (2082); José Camacho to same, February 24, 1802, SNP (1023); June 11, 1802, SNP (1024); July 28, 1802, SNP (1020); José Domingo de Letona to same, March 16, 1803, SNP (2523); December 14, 1803, SNP (3540); June 20, 1804, SNP (3549); September 12, 1804, SNP (3534).

54. Juan Ignacio de Arizpe to José Miguel SN, ——— 17, 1802, SNP (1029); José Domingo de Letona to same, September 21, 1799, SNP (3550); María Gertrudis Lobo to same, October 21, 1801, SNP (114); Mariano José Monzón to same, June 7, 1801, SNP (1041); April 26, 1802, SNP (1033); June 11, 1804, SNP (681-B); Letona's account, November 24, 1800–October 23, 1802, SNP (3455); "Cargo y producido de la Lana . . . ," October 5, 1801, SNP (1027); "Quaderno en que consta la Cuenta . . . ," January 31, 1801–January 27, 1818, SNP (2592).

55. Rafael Trinidad Ramos y Arizpe to José Miguel SN, September 22, 1801, SNP (115).

56. Simón de Herrera to José Miguel SN, January 2, 1802, SNP (1706); Juan Manuel Mexía to same, January 2, 1802, SNP (1707); Antonio de Bassoco to same, March 20, 1802, SNP (2074); Rafael Trinidad Ramos y Arizpe to same, September 22, 1801, SNP (115); promissory note by Simón de Herrera, January 2, 1802, SNP (1795); "Cuenta que manifiesto de la Lana . . . ," October 4, 1802–1803, SNP (1637).

57. José Domingo de Letona to José Miguel SN, September 21, 1799, SNP (3550); September 12, 1804, SNP (3534); November 28, 1804, SNP (3533); Antonio de Bassoco to same, October 12, 1803, SNP (95); Gabriel de Yermo to same, October 5, 1803, SNP (96); November 21, 1804, MCSN; February 27, 1805, MCSN; [Manuel Francisco S]N to Francisco Castellano, January 22, 1805, SNP (17).

58. José Melchor SN to José Miguel SN, February 27, 1805, SNP (715); March 4, 1805, SNP (716); Domingo de Berrio to same, April 5, 1805, SNP (720); Miguel de Vargas Machuca to same, April 11, 1805, SNP (712). Manuel Francisco's other heirs included his second wife, his daughter María Josefa, and his sons José Miguel and Manuel Salvador.

59. Juan Manuel Mexía to José Miguel SN, March 18, 1805, SNP (842).

60. José Domingo de Letona to José Miguel SN, July 17, 1805, SNP (3535); July 24, 1805, SNP (3569).

61. Antonio de Bassoco to José Miguel SN, April 10, 1805, SNP (75); Gabriel de Yermo to same, April 20, 1805, SNP (3470).

62. José Melchor SN to José Miguel SN, December 18, 1805, SNP (820); José Domingo de Letona to same, December 25, 1805, SNP (3532); José Agustín Martínez to same, June 17, 1806, SNP (978); José Melchor SN to Faustino Castellano, June 3, 1806, SNP (56); José Miguel SN's account, March 3, 1801–January 15, 1806, SNP (2249); José Miguel SN's account with Bassoco, December 4, 1793–September 7, 1810, MCSN.

63. José Francisco González de Velasco to Juan Ignacio de Arizpe, July 28, 1809, SNP (1155).

64. José Domingo de Letona to José Miguel SN, July 17, 1805, SNP (3535); December 25, 1805, SNP (3532).

65. José Domingo de Letona to José Miguel SN, July 17, 1805, SNP (3535); July 24, 1805, SNP (3569).

66. Asunción Lavrin, "The Role of the Nunneries in the Economy of New Spain in the Eighteenth Century," *Hispanic American Historical Review* 46, no. 4 (November 1966): 388–390.

67. José Domingo de Letona to José Miguel SN, December 25, 1805, SNP (3532); March 19, 1806, SNP (3539); April 23, 1806, SNP (3551).

68. José Patricio Villarreal to José Miguel SN, December 30, 1805, MCSN; Mariano José Monzón to same, January 20, 1806, SNP (819).

69. Anna Rosalía SN to José Miguel SN, May 1, 1806, SNP (3407); José Gregorio SN to same, March 21, 1805, SNP (702); Mariano José Monzón to same, January 20, 1806, SNP (819); Bishop Primo [Feliciano Marín de Porras] to same, February 2, 1806, SNP (2657); "Quaderno en que consta la Cuenta . . . ," January 31, 1801–January 27, 1818, SNP (2592).

70. Pedro Valdés to José Miguel SN, January 31, 1805, SNP (3338); José Melchor SN to same, May 16, 1805, SNP (703); Francisco Molina to Francisco Castellano, September 14, 1806, SNP (176); Román de Letona to same, September 18, 1806, SNP (6); [José] Ignacio de Arizpe to Faustino Castellano, April 30, 1809, SNP (1090); José Francisco de Castillo to same, May 10, 1809, SNP (1086).

71. Antonio Muñiz to Francisco Castellano, February 6, 1805, SNP (59); Francisco Molina to same, September 14, 1806, SNP (176); Antonio Muñiz to same, October 17, 1806, SNP (57); Julián de Goríbar to Faustino Castellano, February 5, 1809, SNP (1092); [Antonio] Muñiz to same, March 26, 1809, SNP (1101); Julián de Goríbar to same, August 19, 1809, SNP (1149); José María Valdés to same, February 21, 1809, SNP (1087); José Camacho to José Miguel SN, April 20, 1806, SNP (739).

72. José Miguel SN's account with Yermo, June 9, 1806–May 7, 1810, SNP (2250); José Miguel SN's account with Bassoco, December 4, 1793–September 7, 1810, MCSN.

73. José Miguel SN's account with Yermo, June 9, 1806–May 7, 1810, SNP (2250); Andrés Florentino Ramos to Faustino Castellano, November 7, 1809, SNP (1144); José Rafael Alarid to same, June 28, 1809, SNP (1163); July 12, 1809, SNP (1161); July 19, 1809, SNP (1160); August 2, 1809, SNP (1145); August 9, 1809, SNP (1157); José Francisco de Castillo to same, July 18, 1809, SNP (1162); [José] Ignacio de Arizpe to same, August 30, 1809, SNP (1158).

74. Gabriel de Yermo to José Miguel SN, October 22, 1808, SNP (2248); José Miguel SN's account with Yermo, June 9, 1806–May 7, 1810, SNP (2250).

75. José María Valdés to Faustino Castellano, February 21, 1809, SNP (1087); [Antonio] Muñiz to same, March 26, 1809, SNP (1101); "Ymbentario en que Constan los Libros . . . ," May 18, 1811, SNP (3294); "Inventario de los Documentos . . . ," May 18, 1811, SNP (2251).

76. José Melchor SN to José Miguel SN, November 28, 1811, SNP (1907);

[José] Ignacio de Arizpe to José Melchor SN, June 4, 1812, and draft of the latter's reply, June 28, 1812, SNP (3054).

77. Mariano José Monzón to José Melchor SN, May 21, 1812, SNP (109).

78. Invoices, June 3–July 10, 1812, SNP (1055); forms prepared by the masters of the *Dulce Nombre de Jesús* and the *Merced*, June 18, 1812, SNP (1056) and (1057).

79. Bill of lading, June ——, 1812, SNP (1054); José Vicente Díaz to José Melchor SN, June 24, 1812, SNP (2984); invoices, June 3–July 10, 1812, SNP (1055); "Factura de los Efectos . . . ," July 8, 1812, SNP (1377).

80. José Alejandro Sánchez to [José] Melchor SN, March 9, 1814, SNP (1335); José María de Letona to same, May 26, 1815, SNP (3353); Román de Letona to same, May 26, 1815, SNP (3354).

81. José Melchor SN to José Miguel SN, June 28, 1814, SNP (1961).

82. Between October, 1811, and September, 1812, the Sánchez Navarros had incurred 1,199 pesos in taxes on merchandise moving through Monclova. "Cuenta p^r menor de las Partidas de Alc^a . . . ," October 11, 1811–September 1, 1812, SNP (1603).

83. Román de Letona to José Melchor SN, May 26, 1815, SNP (3354).

84. José Luis de Cárdenas to José Miguel SN, July 13, 1814, SNP (1921); José Melchor SN to same, June 16, 1814, SNP (1870).

85. "Quaderno 4°—Contiene los Certificados del Caudal . . . ," January 19–February 22, 1813, MCSN.

86. Sebastián Rodríguez and Faustino Castellano to José Miguel SN, February 22, 1813, SNP (3046); José Melchor SN to same, June 16, 1814, SNP (1870).

87. Román de Letona to José Melchor SN, May 26, 1815, SNP (3354); José Melchor SN to José Miguel SN, November 11, 1815, SNP (10).

88. The Ecclesiastical Cabildo of Monterrey to General Joaquín de Arredondo, February 7, 1816, AGN-PI, vol. 172, exp. 2, fol. 128; [José Miguel S]N to José Melchor SN, August 23, 1816, SNP (1749); José Melchor SN to José Miguel SN, August 23, 1816, SNP (2868).

89. José Domingo de Letona to José Miguel SN, November 27, 1816, SNP (3556); Mariano José Monzón to same, February 4, 1818, SNP (1386); José Miguel SN to Bishop José Ignacio de Aranzivia, February 19, 1819, and the latter's reply, February 28, 1819, SNP (2655).

90. José Domingo de Letona to José Miguel SN, November 27, 1816, SNP (3556).

91. Ibid.; August 19, 1817, SNP (3567); December 2, 1817, SNP (3557); February 24, 1819, SNP (3558); Ricardo Ortega y Pérez Gallardo, *Historia Genealógica de las Familias más antiguas de México*, II, "Condado de Bassoco," 1, 8; see also Pedro Cantón to José Miguel SN, April 28, 1818, SNP (1873).

92. José Domingo de Letona to José Miguel SN, August 12, 1818, SNP (3554); December 2, 1817, SNP (3557); September 16, 1818, SNP (979); February 24, 1819, SNP (3558); April 28, 1819, SNP (981).

93. José Melchor SN to José Miguel SN, July 9, 1816, SNP (1974).

94. José María de Letona to José Melchor SN, March 12, 1816, SNP (587); José Melchor SN to José Miguel SN, September 23, 1816, SNP (2197); account, September 30, 1816, SNP (592).

95. José María de Letona to José Melchor SN, November 11, 1816, SNP (3468); Juan Crouset to same, November 13, 1816, SNP (3467); Miguel Múzquiz to same, November 19, 1816, SNP (3459); José Gerónimo Cacho to same, January 16, 1817, SNP (3463); José María de Letona to same, January 20, 1817, SNP (3461); José Gerónimo Cacho to José Miguel SN, September 27, 1818, SNP (1385); same to [José] Melchor SN, April 12, 1819, SNP (3137); Francisco Vidaurri to [same], July 31, 1820, SNP (2640).

96. Receipt, November 6, 1816, SNP (990); [José] Melchor [SN] to María Francisca Apolonia Beráin de SN, September 2, 1819, SNP (3139); Antonio Rivas to José Miguel SN, February 25, 1819, SNP (1429); José Miguel Ecay Múzquiz to same, October 31, 1812, SNP (110); June 7, 1814, SNP (107); June 30, 1814, SNP (108); March 3, 1819, SNP (1409); "Quaderno en que consta la Cuenta . . . ," January 31, 1801–January 27, 1818, SNP (2592).

97. José Miguel Lobo Guerrero to José Miguel SN, October 10, 1813, SNP (74); Antonio Pacheco Alarcón and Martín Gutiérrez y Fernández to same, December 25, 1818, SNP (1796).

98. Román de Letona to José Melchor SN, May 26, 1815, SNP (3354); José Miguel González to same, October 26, 1819, SNP (3205); Rafael Trinidad Ramos Arizpe to José Miguel SN, July 8, 1816, SNP (2974); June 9, 1817, SNP (1444); September 2, 1817, SNP (1721); October 12, 1817, SNP (3009); José María de Letona to same, June 9, 1817, SNP (1931).

99. José Luis de Cárdenas to José Miguel SN, July 13, 1814, SNP (1921); Ana Petra de la Peña to same, October 20, 1815, SNP (1317); November 1, 1817, SNP (1846); José Ignacio SN to same, March 12, 1817, SNP (1318); José Melchor SN to Nicolás Elizondo, January 22, 1815, SNP (541); José Miguel González to [José] Melchor SN, October 26, 1819, SNP (3205); Fermín de Goyzueta to same, February 7, 1817, SNP (3460); June 9, 1820, SNP (1747); Manuel María de Oca to same, December 20, 1820, SNP (3181); Pedro de la Fuente Fernández to same, December 31, 1820, SNP (910); Pedro Varela y Herrera to Fermín de Goyzueta, June 8, 1820, SNP (1748).

100. "No. 38. Escritura de la Casa . . . ," December 2, 1813, SNP (2347).

101. "Obligación de D. Migl. Musquiz Longoria . . . ," September 1, 1816, SNP (2590); "N. 36—Escriptura de la Casa . . . ," October 4, 1819, SNP (3072).

102. "Fincas de los Molinos," January 27, 1818, SNP (2662).

103. "33 Escritᵃ de la casa de Dᵃ Teresa Galindo . . . ," August 12, 1820, SNP (2348).

104. Contract, April 10, 1820, SNP (2593).

6. POLITICS

1. Miguel José de Emparán to Viceroy Revillagigedo, March 24, 1790, AGN-PI, vol. 160, exp. 2, fol. 185.

2. Vito Alessio Robles, *Coahuila y Texas, desde la consumación de la independencia hasta el tratado de paz de Guadalupe Hidalgo*, II, 437 (hereafter cited as *Coahuila y Texas, desde la consumación*).

3. Certified copies of Royüela's baptismal certificate and those of his parents: June 3, 1784, SNP (1830); September 16, 1784, SNP (1826); October 5, 1792, SNP (1832).

4. Vito Alessio Robles, *Bosquejos históricos*, p. 236; Royüela's commission as treasurer at Saltillo, September 23, 1792, SNP (2903); Documents concerning Royüela's admission to the Order of Charles III: April 5, 1794, SNP (1825); August 28, 1794, SNP (1831); August 28, 1794, SNP (1821); September 4, 1794, SNP (1828); September 5, 1794, SNP (1823); October 24, 1795, SNP (1822).

5. Manuel Royüela to Manuel Francisco SN, February 12, 1800, SNP (738).

6. Zebulon M. Pike, *The Expeditions of Zebulon Montgomery Pike*, ed. Elliott Coues, II, 686–687.

7. Juan Ignacio de Arizpe to José Melchor SN, January 6, 1810, SNP (3127); José Joaquín Ugarte to Faustino Castellano, February 14, 1810, SNP (1185).

8. "Quaderno 3º—Testimonio de los documentos . . . ," MCSN (hereafter cited as "1812 Testimonio").

9. Alessio Robles, *Coahuila y Texas*, pp. 630–634; for Jiménez's account of the engagement see J. E. Hernández y Dávalos (ed.), *Colección de Documentos para la Historia de la Guerra de Independencia de México de 1808 á 1821*, II, 332–334.

10. "Relación—De las ocurrencias desde el año de 1810 . . . ," October 5, 1824, AGN-JE, vol. 40, exp. 2, fol. 31 (hereafter cited as "1810 Relación").

11. Carlos Pérez Maldonado, *El Excmo. y Rvmo. Sr. Dr. Don Primo Feliciano Marín de Porras y la emboscada de Baján*, p. 35.

12. See, for example, Hugh M. Hamill, Jr., *The Hidalgo Revolt*, pp. 208–209.

13. Alessio Robles, *Coahuila y Texas*, pp. 632–633, note 9; see also José M. de la Fuente, "Notas Históricas: El Coronel Elizondo," *Boletín de la Sociedad Mexicana de Geografía y Estadística* 1 (1902): 726–727.

14. Mexico, Secretaría de Relaciones Exteriores, *Fr. Gregorio de la Concepción y su proceso de infidencia*, p. 20.

15. Petition from Manuel Royüela to the King, December 1, 1815, SNP (2905); Alessio Robles, *Coahuila y Texas*, pp. 634–635, 640.

16. "1810 Relación"; Alessio Robles, *Coahuila y Texas*, pp. 635, 640; "1812 Testimonio."

17. "1812 Testimonio."

18. Alessio Robles, *Coahuila y Texas*, pp. 636, 639.

19. "1812 Testimonio"; see also Charles A. Bacarisse, "The Baron de Bastrop: Life and Times of Philip Hendrik Nering Bögel, 1759–1827," Ph.D. dissertation.

20. "1812 Testimonio"; Alessio Robles, *Saltillo*, p. 194; "Nota individual y circunstanciada de los Españoles . . . ," February 18, 1828, AGN-EE, vol. 4, exp. 12, fol. 145; Sebastián Rodríguez to Francisco Castellano, February 1, 1804, SNP (2); Alessio Robles, *Coahuila y Texas*, pp. 639–640.

21. "1812 Testimonio"; Alessio Robles, *Saltillo*, p. 199.

22. "1812 Testimonio."

23. "1810 Relación"; [José Estevan del] Castillo to José Melchor SN, March 18, 1811, SNP (1693).

24. "1810 Relación"; for the royalist dispatches relating the events at Baján see Hernández y Dávalos (ed.), *Colección de Documentos*, II, 416–424.

25. "1810 Relación"; Pedro García, *Con el cura Hidalgo en la Guerra de Independencia*, p. 184.

26. Esteban L. Portillo, *Anuario Coahuilense para 1886*, under the date Novem-

ber 1, 1878; "Relación de los individuos aprehendidos . . . ," March 28, 1811, AGN-PI, vol. 239, exp. 4, fol. 174v.

27. José Eleuterio González, *Obras completas*, II, 501, 503; for José Juan Sánchez Navarro's account of his imprisonment see José M. de la Fuente, *Hidalgo íntimo*, pp. 367–368.

28. Melchor Múzquiz to Faustino Castellano, December 27, 1809, SNP (1138); José Domingo de Letona to José Miguel SN, December 25, 1816, SNP (3345); August 19, 1817, SNP (3567); Angel María Garibay K. et al. (comps.), *Diccionario Porrúa de historia, biografía y geografía de México*, p. 1082.

29. José Domingo de Letona to José Miguel SN, December 25, 1816, SNP (3345).

30. Hernández y Dávalos (ed.), *Colección de Documentos*, VI, 317, 539–553; for a summary of José Domingo de Letona's career see Genaro García and Carlos Pereyra (eds.), *Documentos inéditos ó muy raros para la historia de México*, XXI, 40–41; though in the mid-1820's Letona was occupying a clerical post in Morelia, his participation in family affairs had virtually ceased. See Román de Letona to José Melchor SN, July 12, 1825, SNP (230); April 18, 1826, SNP (239).

31. Hernández y Dávalos (ed.), *Colección de Documentos*, II, 214.

32. General Nemesio Salcedo to José Miguel SN, April 8, 1811, MCSN; April 9, 1811, MCSN.

33. [Draft—José Melchor SN] to Manuel Salcedo, May 1, 1811, SNP (1700).

34. Simón de Herrera to [José] Melchor SN, May 13, 1812, MCSN; undated notes from Herrera and Salcedo accompanying this letter, MCSN.

35. Miguel de Vargas Machuca to José Melchor SN, June 15, 1812, MCSN; undated draft of José Melchor SN's petition prepared by Vargas Machuca, MCSN.

36. "Quaderno 1º—Contiene la nobleza de don José Melchor Sánchez Navarro . . . ," cited in Vito Alessio Robles, *Francisco de Urdiñola y el norte de la Nueva España*, pp. 112–119; "Quaderno 2º—Ynformación sobre Limpieza de Sangre . . . ," June 6–12, 1812, MCSN; "1812 Testimonio"; "Quaderno 4º—Contiene los Certificados del Caudal . . . ," January 19–February 22, 1813, MCSN.

37. Antonio Cordero to Manuel Royüela, September 11, 1812, SNP (2276).

38. Alessio Robles, *Coahuila y Texas*, p. 660; [Manuel Royüela] to the Viceroy, January 15, 1818, SNP (2904); Julián Fernández de Navarrete to same, April 25, 1814, SNP (1820).

39. Alessio Robles, *Coahuila y Texas*, p. 660.

40. Manuel Royüela to Commandant General Joaquín de Arredondo, March 11, 1816, SNP (2898); "Juicio de la cuenta . . . ," December 5, 1817, SNP (2899); [draft—Manuel Royüela to Viceroy Apodaca], March 6, 1818, SNP (2264); unsigned statement, May ——, 1818, SNP (2896); see also the following undated documents: SNP (2275); SNP (2902); SNP (2273).

41. José Gerónimo Cacho to [José] Melchor SN, January 6, 1817, SNP (3464); same to José Miguel SN, February 3, 1817, SNP (1845); Manuel Royüela to same, March 17, 1817, SNP (1463); José Domingo de Letona to same, July 2, 1817, SNP (3547); March 5, 1817, SNP (3560); [draft—Manuel Royüela] to the Royal Treasurer in Mexico City, undated, SNP (2902); Viceroy Apodaca to Manuel Royüela, April 10, 1818, SNP (1829); certified copy of Royüela's burial certificate, May 14, 1819, SNP (1827).

42. Alessio Robles, *Coahuila y Texas*, p. 660.

43. Nettie Lee Benson, *La diputación provincial y el federalismo mexicano*, p. 13, note 7; [José] Miguel Ramos Arizpe to José Miguel SN, March 4, 1805, SNP (699); October 12, 1805, SNP (843); October 7, 1809, SNP (1940).

44. Miguel Ramos Arizpe, *Report That Dr. Miguel Ramos de Arizpe, Priest of Borbon and Deputy in the Present General and Special Cortes of Spain for the Province of Coahuila, One of the Four Eastern Interior Provinces of the Kingdom of Mexico, Presents to the August Congress on the Natural, Political, and Civil Conditions of the Provinces of Coahuila, Nuevo León, Nuevo Santander, and Texas of the Four Eastern Interior Provinces of the Kingdom of Mexico*, ed. Nettie Lee Benson.

45. Benson, *Diputación provincial*, pp. 17–19, 21.

46. Portillo, *Anuario Coahuilense*, pp. 71–75; José Ignacio SN to José Miguel SN, July 24, 1805, SNP (3578); November 14, 1816, SNP (325); January 14, 1817, SNP (2203); April 21, 1818, SNP (1904); July 20, 1819, SNP (1416).

47. José Melchor's brother had been the *alcalde* of Monclova in 1811. Certificate, December 19, 1811, SNP (2580); Víctor Blanco was to hold several public posts in Monclova and was eventually elected senator from Coahuila. Zapopan Ramón, "Hombres Notables de Monclova," *Monclova: Quincenal de actualidades y anuncios*, September 20, 1937, p. 5.

48. "1810 Relación"; certified copy of the Monclova district election results, March 6, 1814, AGENL-C; Benson, *Diputación provincial*, p. 30; notice of the provincial deputation's election, March 21, 1814, AGENL-C.

49. Melchor Núñez de Esquivel to José Miguel SN, May 16, 1814, SNP (1871).

50. José Melchor SN to the Provincial Deputation, May 28 and June 4, 1814, AGENL-C.

51. José Melchor SN to José Miguel SN, June 16, 1814, SNP (1870); June 28, 1814, SNP (1961).

52. José Melchor SN to the Provincial Deputation, June 30, 1814, AGENL-C; Viceroy Calleja to General Joaquín de Arredondo, August 18, 1814, AGENL-C.

53. Receipt, November 6, 1815, SNP (1340); "1810 Relación."

54. Benson, *Diputación provincial*, p. 64, note 59.

55. "1810 Relación."

56. Petition by Juan Marcelino González and Nicolás del Moral to the Ayuntamiento of Saltillo, September 27, 1821, SNP (3066); Portillo, *Anuario Coahuilense*, pp. 71–72; Mexico, Secretaría de la Defensa Nacional, *La Correspondencia de Agustín de Iturbide después de la Proclamación del Plan de Iguala*, ed. Vito Alessio Robles, II, 99.

57. "1810 Relación."

58. Legend at the bottom of a portrait of José Miguel Sánchez Navarro in possession of Doña Blanca Villar Villamil de Sánchez Navarro, Marquesa de Monte Hermoso, Mexico City; Zapopan Ramón, "Hombres Notables de Monclova," September 20, 1937, p. 5; "Derechos del Funeral . . . ," May 19, 1821, MCSN; "Apunte de lo que toca . . . ," undated, MCSN.

59. Alessio Robles, *Coahuila y Texas*, p. 509.

60. Partial inventory of José Miguel SN's estate, April 18–May 30, 1821, SNP

(2919); [José] Melchor SN to [María Francisca Apolonia Beráin de SN], February 28, 1821, SNP (3143).

7. THE FAMILY AND THE LAND

1. Charles C. Cumberland, *Mexico*, p. 141.

2. Rafael Delgado to [José] Melchor SN, May 14, 1822, SNP (849); August 5, 1822, SNP (3129); August 18, 1823, SNP (3118); September 15, 1823, SNP (3211); certificate, November 7, 1825, SNP (461).

3. José Melchor SN to Rafael Delgado, July 20, 1824, SNP (993); August 1, 1824, SNP (994); Rafael Delgado to José Melchor SN, July 27, 1824, SNP (3089); November 16, 1824, SNP (3239); December 12, 1824, SNP (3236); December 18, 1824, SNP (3270).

4. Rafael Delgado to José Melchor SN, July 8, 1824, SNP (3219).

5. "1810 Relación"; Rafael Delgado to José Melchor SN, July 21, 1824, SNP (3082); same to Apolonia Beráin de SN and Vicenta Delgado, December 18, 1825, SNP (3184); [draft—José Melchor SN] to the *alcalde* of San Luis Potosí, October 12, 1825, MCSN.

6. Rafael Delgado to José Melchor SN, July 21, 1824, SNP (3082); August 23, 1824, SNP (3100); Vicenta Delgado to same, July 27, 1824, SNP (809); August 19, 1824, SNP (3200).

7. Rafael Delgado to José Melchor SN, January 17, 1825, SNP (3235); January 19, 1825, SNP (3233).

8. Rafael Delgado to José Melchor SN, September 26, 1825, SNP (211); September 1, 1826, SNP (2474); same to Apolonia Beráin de SN and Vicenta Delgado, December 18, 1825, SNP (3184); December 29, 1825, SNP (3147).

9. Rafael Delgado to José Melchor SN, May 24, 1826, SNP (1781); May 27, 1826, SNP (236).

10. Rafael Delgado to José Melchor SN, September 1, 1826, SNP (2474); same to Apolonia Beráin de SN, November 3, 1826, SNP (1302).

11. Apolonia [Beráin de SN] to [José] Melchor [SN], December 27, 1826, SNP (1655); June 19, 1827, SNP (2099); Juan José de Cárdenas to same, January 3, 1827, SNP (1352).

12. José Toribio del Castillo to [José] Melchor SN, September 27, 1826, SNP (2482); Carlos and Jacobo [SN] to [Apolonia Beráin de SN], October 17, 1826, SNP (263); November 28, 1826, SNP (169); December 5, 1826, SNP (166).

13. Apolonia Beráin [de SN] to [José] Melchor [SN], June 19, 1827, SNP (3412); Rafael Delgado to Apolonia Beráin [de SN], November 3, 1826, SNP (1302).

14. Apolonia Beráin de S[N] to [José] Melchor [SN], July 17, 1827, SNP (1017).

15. Passport issued at Monclova, August 16, 1827, SNP (3581); passport issued at Saltillo, September 24, 1827, SNP (1064).

16. Apolonia Beráin de SN to [José] Melchor [SN], January 2, 1828, SNP (2771); April 30, 1828, SNP (2772).

17. Román de la Garza to José Melchor SN, March 5, 1828, SNP (2762).

18. Antonio Vázquez to José Melchor SN, January 28, 1828, SNP (2747); Fran-

cisco Ignacio Castañeda to same, February 18, 1828, SNP (2756); Apolonia Beráin de SN to same, January 30, 1828, SNP (2714); Carlos and Jacobo [SN] to [Apolonia Beráin de SN], May 6, 1828, SNP (2837).

19. [José Melchor S]N to [Juan José de] Cárdenas, September 20, 1828, SNP (2839); October 7, 1828, SNP (2857); November 1, 1828, SNP (2848); Apolonia Beráin [de SN] to same, October 9, 1829, SNP (1292); Manuel Castellano to José Melchor SN, August 19, 1829, SNP (1271).

20. [José] Melchor [SN] to Apolonia Beráin de SN, May 25, 1830, SNP (3570).

21. Apolonia Beráin de S[N] to José Melchor SN, May 26, 1830, SNP (3571).

22. Apolonia Beráin de S[N] to Jacobo and Carlos SN, September 1, 1830, SNP (2440).

23. Apolonia Beráin de S[N] to José Melchor SN, March 9, 1831, SNP (733).

24. José Ignacio SN to José Melchor SN, February 15, 1832, SNP (84).

25. [José] Melchor [SN] to Apolonia [Beráin de SN], July 22, 1832, SNP (1019); Carlos and Jacobo SN to same, August ——, 1832, SNP (793).

26. Jacobo and Carlos SN to [Apolonia Beráin de SN], August 28, 1833, SNP (930); Juan Vicente Campos to [José] Melchor SN, September 21, 1833, SNP (1759).

27. [Draft—José Melchor SN] to Simona de Jesús Mendoza de Rojas, October 30, 1833, SNP (1652).

28. Apolonia Beráin de SN to [Juan José de] Cárdenas, November 13, 1833, SNP (1233); Máximo Valdés to José Melchor SN, December 11, 1833, SNP (2424); Manuel Castellano to same, December 28, 1833, SNP (724).

29. Francisco Adam to [José] Melchor SN, August 2, 1834, SNP (693); José Melchor SN to Matías ——, October 13, 1834, SNP (2901).

30. Passport issued at Saltillo, May 15, 1835, SNP (3316).

31. Passport issued at Saltillo, October 29, 1835, SNP (591).

32. Jacobo SN to [Juan José de Cárdenas?], June 23, 1836, SNP (2606); [José Melchor S]N to same, April 30, 1833, SNP (3485).

33. José Antonio Rodríguez to José Melchor SN, July 17, 1822, SNP (3417); José Alejandro de Treviño Gutiérrez to same, February 27, 1823, SNP (82); note, September 19, 1824, SNP (3248).

34. Memorandum, September 19, 1824, SNP (3248); transcript of the proceedings before the *alcalde* of Monclova, December 3, 1824, SNP (2358); Rafael Delgado to José Melchor SN, December 12, 1824, SNP (3236); December 18, 1824, SNP (3270); certified copy of testimony taken at San Buenaventura, December 16–17, 1824, MCSN; "Prontuario de los papeles . . . ," undated, SNP (3609).

35. Emilio Langberg to Francisco Beráin, September 24, 1855, MCSN; October 3, 1855, MCSN; Rafael de la Fuente to same, January 3, 1856, MCSN.

36. José Melchor SN to José Miguel SN, February 1, 1821, SNP (1431); February 13, 1821, SNP (1425); February 28, 1821, SNP (1434); March 15, 1821, SNP (1421); March 29, 1821, SNP (1420).

37. Francisco Vidaurri to José Melchor SN, April 25, 1822, SNP (3332).

38. Copy of the judgment, May 2, 1822, SNP (1698); *legajo*, November 10, 1819–May 3, 1822, SNP (2675).

39. Francisco Vidaurri to José Melchor SN, May 3, 1822, SNP (3335).

40. Francisco Vidaurri to José Melchor SN, May 26, 1822, SNP (3424).

41. Unsigned copy of José María Echais's petition to the *alcalde* of Santa Rosa, September 11, 1822, SNP (1249); José Francisco del Castillo to José Melchor SN, September 12, 1822, SNP (3331).

42. Unsigned copy of a petition to the Audiencia of Guadalajara and that tribunal's ruling, November 28, 1822, MCSN.

43. Juan Bautista Fresquet to Fermín de Goyzueta, July 31, 1823, SNP (3116); Fermín de Goyzueta to José Melchor SN, August 1, 1823, SNP (3117); Rafael Delgado to same, August 18, 1823, SNP (3118).

44. Unsigned copy of the Audiencia of Guadalajara's ruling, October 3, 1823, SNP (2235).

45. "Autos seguidos por D. Melchor Sanches Nabarro . . . ," 1824, AGEC, *legajo* 15, *carpeta* 767.

46. José Melchor SN to Román de Letona, April 27, 1824, SNP (225).

47. Expense account, August 18, 1825, SNP (2239); petition from Pedro Agustín Ballesteros to the *alcalde* of Santa Rosa, July 28, 1825, MCSN; drafts of petitions from Rafael Delgado to same, August 20, 25, 27, September 9 and 19, 1825, MCSN; Rafael Delgado to [José] Melchor SN, August 21, 1825, SNP (205); José Alejandro de Treviño Gutiérrez to Rafael Delgado, September 14, 1825, MCSN.

48. "Autos de D. Melchor Shes Nabarro . . . ," 1826, AGEC, *legajo* 18, *carpeta* 827; "Sobre cuestión de aguas . . . ," 1826, AGEC, *legajo* 17, *carpeta* 812; unsigned copies of petitions from José Melchor SN to the *alcalde* of Santa Rosa, February 6–25, 1826, SNP (2206); expense account, May, 1826, SNP (2236); Rafael Delgado to [José Melchor SN], May 21, 1826, SNP (1783).

49. Rafael Delgado to José Melchor SN, July 28, 1826, SNP (137); August 4, 1826, SNP (2458); August 25, 1826, SNP (1065); Rafael Villalobos to same, August 1, 1826, SNP (2446); José Mauricio de Alcocer to same, August 10, 1826, SNP (2459).

50. Copy of a petition from Juan Bautista Fresquet to the Audiencia of Guadalajara, August 21, 1826, SNP (2245).

51. [Rafael Delgado] to José Melchor SN, August 25, 1826, SNP (1065); José Alejandro de Treviño [Gutiérrez] to same, September 22, 1826, SNP (1062).

52. José Alejandro de Treviño [Gutiérrez] to José Melchor SN, October 23, 1826, SNP (1063); [José Melchor SN] to [José Miguel SN], November 22, 1826, SNP (1300).

53. [Draft—José Melchor SN] to José Alejandro de Treviño [Gutiérrez], December 13, 1826, SNP (941); [draft—same] to Agustín Martínez, December 16, 1826, SNP (941).

54. Rafael del Valle to [José] Melchor SN, December 18, 1826, SNP (948); January 4, 1827, SNP (1353).

55. Juan Vicente Campos to [José] Melchor SN, June 23, 1827, SNP (1018).

56. [José] Miguel [SN] to [José Melchor SN], July 8, 1827, SNP (2448).

57. "Testimonio del espediente . . . ," September 27, 1827–June 3, 1829, SNP (2914) (hereafter cited as "1829 Testimonio").

58. The third arbiter was Juan Vicente Campos. See Juan Vicente Campos to [José] Melchor SN, November 18, 1826, SNP (3015); June 23, 1827, SNP (1018).

59. "1829 Testimonio"; "Noticia de los frutos cozechados . . . ," May 2, 1822–
August 24, 1828, MCSN; José Francisco del Castillo to José Melchor SN, March 6,
1828, SNP (2744); March 23, 1828, SNP (2746); Agustín Martínez to same,
March 23, 1828, SNP (1220).

60. "1829 Testimonio."

61. José Francisco del Castillo to José Melchor SN, January 27, 1828, SNP
(2751); January 27, 1828, SNP (1219); unsigned copy of a petition from José
María de Aguirre to the *alcalde* of Santa Rosa, February 22, 1828, SNP (1210);
Melitón Castellano to José Francisco del Castillo, February 24, 1828, SNP (2739);
draft of a petition from the Ayuntamiento of Santa Rosa to the Chief of Department, February 27, 1828, SNP (2759).

62. José Melchor SN to Apolonia Beráin de SN, April 2, 1829, MCSN; unsigned
copy of the Supreme Court's decision, August 25, 1829, SNP (2602).

63. License from Dr. José León Lobo, acting bishop at Monterrey, for Echais and
Quirós to build a chapel and cemetery at their Hacienda de la Purísima, June 18,
1826, SNP (2654); "N. 21—Escritura de la Haz^a de la Purisima . . . ," February 11,
1832, MCSN.

64. José Melchor SN to Apolonia Beráin de SN, April 2, 1829, MCSN.

65. Deed, October 17, 1823, SNP (2350); Francisco Vidaurri to José Melchor SN,
October 22, 1823, SNP (3244); ———, 1824, SNP (3238); Juan Antonio de Urtea-
ga and Catarina de la Garza to same, March 7, 1828, SNP (3511); deed, December 3, 1827, SNP (2553); deed, March 28, 1828, SNP (1792); deed, August 18,
1829, SNP (2555); deed, March 24, 1832, SNP (458); "No. 20—Contiene 28
horas . . . ," August 16, 1832, SNP (1793); deed, July 21, 1835, SNP (2227);
deed, March 6, 1837, SNP (2226).

66. Certified copy of the deed, July 13, 1829, SNP (2546).

67. Certificate, June 23, 1827, SNP (2365); certificate, December 22, 1829, SNP
(3663); "N. 24—Escritura de transacion . . . ," December 23, 1829, MCSN.

68. "N. 27—Escritura de 2 dias y 8 oras de agua . . . ," May 2, 1831, SNP
(1794); "N. 28—Escritura de seis horas de Agua . . . ," January 10, 1825–June 15,
1834, SNP (1791).

69. Deed, July 20, 1829, SNP (2551).

70. Carlos [SN] to Apolonia Beráin de SN, May 24, 1837, SNP (694); May 31,
1837, SNP (692).

71. Jesús de la Garza to Jacobo SN, June 11, 1838, SNP (732); Manuel Mestre
Ghigliazza (comp.), *Efemérides biográficas (defunciones-nacimientos)*, p. 126.

72. This account of the vicissitudes of the Marquisate of Aguayo generally fol-
lows that in Alessio Robles, *Coahuila y Texas, desde la consumación*, II, 245–265.

73. Angel María Garibay K. et al. (comps.), *Diccionario Porrúa de historia, biografía y geografía de México*, pp. 1428–1429; Frances Erskine Calderón de la
Barca, *Life in Mexico*, ed. Howard T. and Marion Hall Fisher, p. 423.

74. Manuel Dublán and José María Lozano (eds.), *Legislación Mexicana*, I, 528–
531.

75. Alessio Robles, *Coahuila y Texas, desde la consumación*, I, 142–144; Dublán
and Lozano (eds.), *Legislación*, I, 662–664.

76. Dublán and Lozano (eds.), *Legislación*, I, 545.

77. J. Fred Rippy, *British Investments in Latin America, 1822–1949*, p. 25.

78. Ralph Willard Hidy, *The House of Baring in American Trade and Finance*, p. 67.

79. Alessio Robles, *Coahuila y Texas, desde la consumación*, II, 250.

80. *Mapa de los Estados de Parras.*

81. Inventories of Parras, Patos, Bonanza, and Cuatrociénegas, 1826, SNP (2894); "No. 20—Valores a que quedan reducidos . . . ," 1815 and 1826, SNP (2883); Vito Alessio Robles, *Francisco de Urdiñola y el norte de la Nueva España*, p. 66.

82. Lorenzo de Zavala, *Ensayo Histórico de las Revoluciones de México*, ed. Alfonso Toro, II, 138–139; Dublán and Lozano (eds.), *Legislación*, II, 64–65; see also Albert M. Gilliam, *Travels over the Table Lands and Cordilleras of Mexico*, pp. 215–216.

83. Alessio Robles, *Coahuila y Texas, desde la consumación*, II, 252–256.

84. Minutes of a meeting of the committee of creditors, May 13, 1830, SNP (1798); Frank W. Johnson, *A History of Texas and Texans*, ed. Eugene C. Barker, with the assistance of Ernest W. Winkler, I, 350.

85. H. P. N. Gammel (ed.), *The Laws of Texas, 1822–1897*, I, 268; certified copy of a summons issued to James Grant, July 21, 1830, SNP (2920); "Testimonio de las Escrituras . . . ," July 13, 1833–December 16, 1840, SNP (2884).

86. Alessio Robles, *Coahuila y Texas, desde la consumación*, II, 256–264; Dublán and Lozano (eds.), *Legislación*, III, 33–35.

87. Gammel (ed.), *Laws of Texas*, I, 272, 357; Dublán and Lozano (eds.), *Legislación*, III, 42–43; José Vasconcelos, *Don Evaristo Madero (Biografía de un patricio)*, pp. 108–109; Alessio Robles, *Coahuila y Texas, desde la consumación*, I, 510, 521, 530, II, 24, 84; Johnson, *A History of Texas*, I, 421, 423, 426.

88. The companies' interest was valued at 160,000 pesos. Alessio Robles, *Coahuila y Texas, desde la consumación*, II, 265; Alessio Robles, *Coahuila y Texas*, pp. 508–509.

89. Tom Lea, *The King Ranch*, II, 533–534; Jim Berry Pearson, *The Maxwell Land Grant*, p. 76; J. Evetts Haley, *The XIT Ranch of Texas, and the Early Days of the Llano Estacado*, p. 3.

90. José Fuentes Mares, *. . . Y México se Refugió en el Desierto*, pp. 169–170.

91. "Testimonio del Real Título de Composición . . . ," cited in Vito Alessio Robles, *Bosquejos históricos*, pp. 15–16; Compañía Agrícola Industrial, Colonizadora, Limitada del Tlahualilo, S.A. versus the Federal Government of the Republic of Mexico, *Allegations Presented by Jorge Vera Estañol, Special Attorney for the Federal Government before the III Hall of the Supreme Court of Justice of the Nation*, trans. Ernesto Lara de Gogorza, p. 48.

92. "Escritura de venta del día y medio de agua . . . ," May 4, 1840, SNP (2351).

93. Alessio Robles, *Coahuila y Texas, desde la consumación*, II, 245; Valeriano Sánchez to Carlos SN, September 6, 1841, SNP (1686).

94. Rafael González to Jacobo SN, April 9, 1842, SNP (867); April 23, 1842, SNP (884); May 7, 1842, SNP (872).

95. Carlos SN to Jacobo SN, May 25, 1842, SNP (1614); Rafael González to same, June 15, 1842, SNP (1632); September 4, 1842, SNP (889); J. M. Ibarra to same, November 7, 1842, SNP (1013); unsigned copy of a dispatch from the Ministry of the Treasury to the treasurer of the Department of Coahuila, October 17, 1843, SNP (1634).

96. J. M. Ibarra to Jacobo SN, July 25, 1842, SNP (895).

97. Carlos [SN] to Jacobo SN, May 25, 1842, SNP (1614); June 22, 1842, SNP (992); Rafael González to same, June 11, 1842, SNP (874).

98. Juan N. de Arizpe to Jacobo SN, August 26, 1842, SNP (986); December 3, 1842, SNP (1636); December 8, 1842, SNP (1628); Rafael González to same, September 4, 1842, SNP (889).

99. Carlos [SN] to Jacobo SN, July 9, 1843, SNP (540).

100. José María Pompa to Jacobo SN, June 21, 1843, MCSN; J. M. Ibarra to same, June 29, 1843, MCSN.

101. Josiah Gregg, Diary and Letters of Josiah Gregg, ed. Maurice Garland Fulton, I, 292, 295; Juan N. de Arizpe to Jacobo SN, July 21, 1845, MCSN; August 6, 1845, MCSN; Crisóstomo Charles to same, ——— 21, 1845, MCSN; for Arizpe's career up to this point see Esteban L. Portillo, Anuario Coahuilense para 1886, p. 41.

102. George W. Hughes, Memoir Descriptive of the March of a Division of the United States Army under the Command of Brigadier General John E. Wool, from San Antonio de Bexar, in Texas, to Saltillo, in Mexico, p. 40 (hereafter cited as Memoir).

103. Carlos [SN] to Jacobo [SN], March 24, 1847, MCSN; April 14, 1847, MCSN.

104. José Rafael Jove to Jacobo SN, November 6, 1847, SNP (2635).

105. José María de la Fuente to Quirino Benavente, June 8, 1847, SNP (1635).

106. Eduardo Guerra, Historia de la Laguna, pp. 296–297.

107. Adolphus Wislinzenus, Memoir of a Tour to Northern Mexico Connected with Col. Doniphan's Expedition in 1846 and 1847, p. 70.

108. Guerra, Historia de la Laguna, pp. 33–35.

109. J. Jiménez and Leonardo Zuloaga to Juan N. de Arizpe, January 1, 1851, SNP (316); January 16, 1851, SNP (317); Jacobo SN to same, January 15 and 16, 1851, SNP (289) and (290); Guerra, Historia de la Laguna, pp. 42–43, 299.

110. During the colonial period the hacienda was named Santa María de las Parras. It had since become known as the Hacienda del Rosario, or sometimes as the Hacienda de Arriba, to distinguish it from the Ibarra family's Hacienda de San Lorenzo de Parras, or Hacienda de Abajo, some four miles away.

111. John Russell Bartlett, Personal Narrative of Explorations and Incidents in Texas, New Mexico, California, Sonora, and Chihuahua, connected with the United States and Mexican Boundary Commission, during the years 1850, '51, '52, and '53, II, 486–488 (hereafter cited as Personal Narrative); Alessio Robles, Coahuila y Texas, p. 266.

112. Alessio Robles, Coahuila y Texas, desde la consumación, II, 265.

113. J. Jiménez and Leonardo Zuloaga to Juan N. de Arizpe, January 1, 1851, SNP (316); January 16, 1851, SNP (317).

114. Samuel E. Chamberlain, My Confession, ed. Roger Butterfield, pp. 79, 111–112; estimate of materials and labor, November 19, 1847, SNP (964); see also unsigned note of same date, SNP (963).

115. This transaction may also have included the Hacienda de Buenavista. Alessio Robles, Coahuila y Texas, desde la consumación, II, 266.

116. Unsigned copy of a petition from Guadalupe Echais to "Exmo Sor," December 1, 1858, SNP (2586); A. M. Gibson, *The Kickapoos*, p. 201; United States, Senate, *Affairs of the Mexican Kickapoo Indians*, III, 2201–2202.

117. For Vidaurri's rise to power see Edward H. Moseley, "The Public Career of Santiago Vidaurri, 1855–1858," Ph.D. dissertation.

118. Carlos SN to Santiago Vidaurri, September 23, 1857, AGENL-VA (8181); Jacobo SN to same, April 21, 1860, AGENL-VA (8188); [draft—Santiago Vidaurri] to Jacobo SN, April 18, 1860, AGENL-VA (8187); August 29, 1860, AGENL-VA (8190); [draft—same] to Carlos SN, April 27, 1860, AGENL-VA (8189).

119. "Ynventario de los intereses pertenecientes á la Compañia . . . ," September 13, 1857–December 12, 1862, SNP (2889).

8. RANCHING

1. Manuel Castellano to José Melchor SN, May 19, 1822, SNP (864); September 30, 1822, SNP (2611); October 6, 1823, SNP (3103); August 22, 1824, SNP (3197).

2. Manuel Castellano to José Melchor SN, September 22, 1824, SNP (3214); Apolonia Beráin de SN to same, January 2, 1828, SNP (2771).

3. Manuel Flores to [José] Melchor SN, October 11, 1823, SNP (3225).

4. Francisco Vidaurri to José Melchor SN, May 26, 1822, SNP (3424); May 27, 1822, SNP (3333); report by Francisco Vidaurri, April 29, 1822, SNP (3334).

5. Francisco Quintana to [José] Melchor SN, January 23, 1824, SNP (3221); June 22, 1824, SNP (3216).

6. José Melchor SN to Rafael Delgado, July 10, 1824, SNP (997); Apolonia Beráin de SN to [José] Melchor [SN], July 13, 1824, SNP (3191); Rafael Delgado to same, July 13, 1824, SNP (3192).

7. Felipe de los Santos to [José] Melchor SN, October 3, 1824, SNP (3109); Atanacio Muñoz to same, January 1, 1828, SNP (2748); Pedro de Herrera to same, July 6, 1828, SNP (2798); [Atanacio] Rodríguez to same, August 13, 1829, SNP (1295).

8. Atanacio Muñoz to José Melchor SN, May 28, 1828, SNP (2854).

9. Rafael Delgado to José Melchor SN, August 16, 1825, SNP (206); August 21, 1825, SNP (205); same to Apolonia Beráin de SN, November 28, 1825, SNP (3183); Manuel Castellano to Rafael Delgado, November 3, 1825, SNP (259); November 18, 1825, SNP (260).

10. [José] Melchor [SN] to Apolonia Beráin de SN, August 22, 1825, SNP (227); Apolonia [Beráin de SN] to [José] Melchor [SN], December 20, 1826, SNP (87); January 2, 1828, SNP (2771); January 9, 1828, SNP (2710); January 16, 1828, SNP (2697); January 25, 1828, SNP (2712).

11. Apolonia Beráin de SN to [José] Melchor [SN], February 20, 1828, SNP (2782); February 27, 1828, SNP (2719); March 26, 1828, SNP (2774); March 28, 1828, SNP (2738); April 9, 1828, SNP (2701); April 30, 1828, SNP (2772); June 3, 1828, SNP (2796); April 22, 1829, SNP (1269); Manuel Castellano to same, March 27, 1828, SNP (2814).

12. Manuel Castellano to Apolonia Beráin de SN, May 26, 1829, SNP (1272); June 26, 1829, SNP (1291); July 31, 1829, SNP (710).

13. José Melchor SN to [Juan José de] Cárdenas, October 7, 1828, SNP (2857); December 7, 1833, SNP (1239); December 14, 1833, SNP (1234); December 19, 1833, SNP (1237); December 28, 1833, SNP (1225); Manuel Castellano to same, October 16, 1828, SNP (2838); October 30, 1829, SNP (708); November 20, 1833, SNP (1240); December 22, 1833, SNP (1230); December 31, 1833, SNP (1227); March 11, 1834, SNP (1229); Apolonia Beráin de SN to same, November 16, 1833, SNP (1232); December 19, 1833, SNP (1236).

14. [José] Melchor [SN] to Apolonia Beráin de SN, March 9, 1830, SNP (1289).

15. [José] Melchor [SN] to [Apolonia Beráin de SN], February 1, 1830, SNP (1288).

16. [José] Melchor [SN] to Apolonia [Beráin de SN], May 1, 1830, SNP (1298).

17. Manuel Castellano to Juan José de Cárdenas, August 8, 1836, SNP (3607); J. Antonio Tijerina to same, December 18, 1837, SNP (1262) and draft of the latter's reply, December 19, 1837, SNP (1263); Gertrudis, Miguel, and Teresa Flores to Jacobo SN, April 8, 1837, SNP (696); Juan José de Cárdenas to the Ayuntamiento of Monclova, June 12, 1837, SNP (2233).

18. They were San Lorenzo de la Laguna, Aguanueva, Anhelo, Buenavista, Castañuela, La Florida, La Joya, San Juan de Cuatrociénegas, and San Juan de la Vaquería.

19. Manuel Castellano to José Melchor SN, September 30, 1822, SNP (2611); October 6, 1823, SNP (3103); February 28, 1824, SNP (3125); October 21, 1824, SNP (266); May 3, 1826, SNP (215); May 15, 1828, SNP (2844); January 9, 1830, SNP (1273); October 30, 1833, SNP (576); July 18, 1834, SNP (1757); receipt, April 1, 1825, SNP (1777); Atanacio Muñoz to José Melchor SN, January 21, 1828, SNP (2749); March 2, 1828, SNP (2725); March 27, 1828, SNP (2736); [Atanacio] Rodríguez to same, September 9, 1830, SNP (577); [José] Melchor [SN] to Apolonia [Beráin de SN], August 1, 1829, SNP (1283); March 7, 1830, SNP (1290).

20. See "Cuenta General de la Hda de Parras . . . ," January 25, 1841, SNP (2923).

21. George T. M. Davis, *Autobiography of the Late Col. Geo. T. M. Davis*, pp. 107–108; Josiah Gregg, *Diary and Letters of Josiah Gregg*, ed. Maurice Garland Fulton, I, 270.

22. "Inventario de la Hacienda de Hermanas . . . ," March 18, 1863, SNP (2887).

23. Charles H. Harris III, *The Sánchez Navarros*, pp. 9–12.

24. William Marshall Anderson, *An American in Maximilian's Mexico, 1865–1866*, ed. Ramón Eduardo Ruiz, p. 77.

25. Report dealing with lessees at San Antonio del Potrero, April 30, 1823–April 30, 1824, SNP (1280); list of lessees, April 30, 1827, SNP (1279); Gabriel Maldonado to [José] Melchor SN, March 30, 1826, SNP (171); María Antonia de Abrego to same, September 6, 1826, SNP (2450); Apolonia Beráin de SN to same, April 9, 1828, SNP (2701); José Estevan del Castillo to same, January 10, 1830,

SNP (1270); [José Melchor S]N to [Juan José de] Cárdenas, December 19, 1833, SNP (1237); Gertrudis, Miguel, and Teresa Flores to Jacobo SN, April 8, 1837, SNP (696).

26. Francisco Vidaurri to José Melchor SN, May 27, 1822, SNP (3333); "Autos seguidos por D. Melchor Sanches Nabarro . . . ," 1824, AGEC, *legajo* 15, *carpeta* 767.

27. Manuel Castro and Bartolomé de Cárdenas to José Melchor SN, July 17, 1822, SNP (3328); Juan José de Cárdenas to same, October 22, 1830, SNP (1644); Manuel Castellano to same, May 22, 1826, SNP (2479); [José Melchor S]N to [Juan José de] Cárdenas, November 15, 1830, SNP (3413); December 7, 1833, SNP (1239); December 14, 1833, SNP (1234); contract, October 26, 1822, SNP (1610); contract, December 22, 1829, SNP (2663).

28. Manuel Castellano to José Melchor SN, February 28, 1824, SNP (3125); Manuel Salvador SN to same, April 26, 1826, SNP (214); [José Melchor S]N to [Juan José de] Cárdenas, November 6, 1830, SNP (3312); "Quaderno 2º en el que constan los arrendatarios . . . ," November 15, 1825–January 31, 1827, SNP (2422).

29. *Legajo*, October 17, 1830–May 6, 1831, SNP (1208); Ramón Fraire to [José] Melchor SN, May 23, 1828, SNP (2815); petition from José Melchor SN to the Ayuntamiento of Candela, December 5, 1829, MCSN.

30. José Benito Noguera to Jacobo SN, June 5, 1841, MCSN.

31. J. M. Ibarra to Jacobo SN, June 8, 1842, SNP (1481); November 14, 1842, SNP (2636); Juan N. de Arizpe to Juan Vicente Campos, March 16, 1843, SNP (1501).

32. Vicente Carrillo to Valeriano Sánchez, June 16, 1841, SNP (1713); same to Jacobo SN, January 19, 1842, SNP (1484); Juan de Zepeda Almaguer to same, February 1, 1842, SNP (1485); August 16, 1842, SNP (877); August 24, 1842, SNP (876); Jesús María and Joaquín Zepeda to same, April 23, 1847, SNP (965); Eduardo González to same, June 23, 1847, MCSN; July 19, 1847, MCSN; October 27, 1847, SNP (961); February 6, 1848, MCSN; May 5, 1848, MCSN.

33. H. Boultbee to Jacobo SN, January 21, 1847, MCSN; Perfecto de los Santos to same, May 9, 1848, MCSN; Juan N. de Arizpe to same, May 19, 1848, MCSN; Manuel Fernández to Juan N. de Arizpe, January 24, 1851, SNP (347); March 2, 1851, SNP (348).

34. Buenavista and Hedionda Grande: Juan N. de Arizpe to Jacobo SN, April 11, 1847, MCSN; May 10, 1848, MCSN; May 19, 1848, MCSN; Perfecto de los Santos to same, May 9, 1848, MCSN. Aguadulce and San Juan del Retiro: Vicente Carrillo to Valeriano Sánchez, June 16, 1841, SNP (1713); Valeriano Sánchez to Carlos SN, September 6, 1841, SNP (1686); same to Estevan del Castillo, March 15, 1842, SNP (1009); same to Jacobo SN, April 5, 1842, SNP (878); September 6, 1847, MCSN. La Ventura: J. M. Ibarra to Jacobo SN, November 7, 1842, SNP (1013); November 14, 1842, SNP (2636); Juan N. de Arizpe to Quirino Benavente, June 22, 1851, SNP (323). Anhelo and La Joya: J. Ignacio González Paredes to Juan N. de Arizpe, January 27, 1851, SNP (426); February 14, 1851, SNP (429); February 15, 1851, SNP (428). San Juan de Sabinas: Inventory, January 12, 1847, MCSN; H. Boultbee to Jacobo SN, January 21, 1847, MCSN; March 24, 1847, MCSN; January 10, 1848, MCSN; Emilio Bohme to same, June 4, 1856, SNP

(1613); "Ynventario de los intereses pertenecientes á la Compañia . . . ," September 13, 1857–December 12, 1862, SNP (2889). Encinas: Jacobo SN to Juan N. de Arizpe, February 1, 1851, SNP (293); Emilio Langberg to Francisco Beráin, September 24, 1855, MCSN; October 3, 1855, MCSN; Rafael de la Fuente to same, January 3, 1856, MCSN.

35. Resolution by the Ayuntamiento of Parras, December 1, 1841, SNP (810); list of lessees at Patos, December 31, 1849, SNP (3624).

36. In 1828, for example, virtually the entire January lamb crop perished as a result of freezing weather. Manuel Castellano to José Melchor SN, March 27, 1828, SNP (2814). For other records dealing with lambing see: Manuel Castellano to José Melchor SN, October 6, 1823, SNP (3103); February 28, 1824, SNP (3125); October 3, 1824, SNP (221); October 21, 1824, SNP (266); October 23, 1824, SNP (3108); May 15, 1828, SNP (2844); January 9, 1830, SNP (1273); October 30, 1833, SNP (576); July 18, 1834, SNP (1757).

37. There is no evidence that the Sánchez Navarros ever owned Santa Catalina del Alamo. See Pastor Rouaix (comp.), Diccionario geográfico, histórico, y biográfico del Estado de Durango, p. 411; J. Ignacio Gallegos, Compendio de Historia de Durango, 1821–1910, p. 153.

38. Carlos SN to Jacobo SN, February 8, 1849, SNP (1600).

39. Monthly report, March 31, 1862, SNP (2614).

40. "1810 Relación."

41. Frederick Webb Hodge (ed.), Handbook of American Indians North of Mexico, I, 769.

42. Francisco Vidaurri to José Melchor SN, April 25, 1822, SNP (3332); Manuel Castellano to same, September 30, 1822, SNP (2611); July 31, 1825, SNP (255); Bartolomé de Arechabala to same, January 6, 1824, SNP (3126).

43. [José Melchor S]N to Rafael Delgado, September 1, 1825, SNP (782); Manuel Castellano to same, November 18, 1825, SNP (260); [José] Melchor [SN] to Apolonia [Beráin de SN], November 20, 1825, SNP (3148).

44. Víctor Blanco to José Melchor SN, June 25, 1826, SNP (1060).

45. Melitón Castellano and José Francisco del Castillo to José Melchor SN, February 10, 1828, SNP (2849); March 9, 1828, SNP (2781); Manuel Castellano to same, March 27, 1828, SNP (2814); Domingo de Ugartechea to same, March 15, 1828, SNP (2705).

46. Juan Vicente Campos to [José] Melchor SN, April 7, 1830, SNP (783).

47. [José] Melchor [SN] to Apolonia [Beráin de SN], August 2, 1832, SNP (3498); J. Antonio Tijerina to Juan José de Cárdenas, December 18, 1837, SNP (1262), and draft of the latter's reply, December 19, 1837, SNP (1263).

48. Isidro Vizcaya Canales (ed.), La invasión de los indios bárbaros al nordeste de México en los años de 1840 y 1841, p. 50; Ernest Wallace and E. Adamson Hoebel, The Comanches, pp. 45, 298.

49. Paul Horgan, Great River, II, 849, 851.

50. Mexico, Comisión Pesquisidora de la Frontera del Norte, Informe final que en cumplimiento del decreto de 2 de octubre de 1872 rinde al ejecutivo de la unión la comisión pesquisidora de la frontera del norte sobre el desempeño de sus trabajos, pp. 64–66 (hereafter cited as Informe final).

51. Alessio Robles, *Coahuila y Texas, desde la consumación*, II, 234; Vizcaya Canales (ed.), *La invasión*, p. 52.

52. Alessio Robles, *Coahuila y Texas, desde la consumación*, II, 234–236, 242, note 9; Vizcaya Canales (ed.), *La invasión*, p. 181.

53. Alessio Robles, *Coahuila y Texas, desde la consumación*, II, 237–243.

54. Carlos [SN] to Jacobo SN, June 22, 1842, SNP (992).

55. Helen Hunnicut, "A Mexican View of the Texas War," *The Library Chronicle of the University of Texas* 4, no. 2 (Summer 1951): 66, 68.

56. José Juan SN to [José] Estevan del Castillo, November 20, 1842, SNP (1470).

57. José Estevan del Castillo to Jacobo SN, November 20, 1842, SNP (1468).

58. Melchor Lobo to Jacobo SN, November 26, 1842, SNP (1471); Juan N. de Arizpe to same, December 3, 1842, SNP (1636).

59. Hughes, *Memoir*, p. 38; H. Boultbee to Jacobo SN, April 11, 1847, MCSN; Francisco Beráin to the Junta Calificadora de la Villa de Múzquiz, April 3, 1851, SNP (342).

60. Gallegos, *Compendio*, p. 95.

61. United States, House of Representatives, *Correspondence between the Secretary of War and Generals Scott and Taylor, and between General Scott and Mr. Trist*, pp. 334–335.

62. Eduardo González to Jacobo SN, September 16, 1847, MCSN; November 21, 1847, SNP (896).

63. For contemporary—and bitingly contemptuous—foreign travelers' accounts of Mexican inability to cope with depredations see: George Ruxton, *Adventures in Mexico and the Rocky Mountains*, pp. 86–87, 92–93, 96, 110–112, 146, 171–172, and George W. B. Evans, *Mexican Gold Trail*, ed. Glenn S. Dumke, pp. 56, 107, 113–114.

64. Mexico, *Informe final*, pp. 64–66; Bartlett, *Personal Narrative*, II, 447–448.

65. Jacobo SN to Juan N. de Arizpe, February 8, 1851, SNP (292); Harris, *The Sánchez Navarros*, p. 58.

66. Quirino Benavente to Juan N. de Arizpe, February 12, 1851, SNP (1551); February 16, 1851, SNP (411); February 19, 1851, SNP (424); February 23, 1851, SNP (425); March 19, 1851, SNP (418); March 20, 1851, SNP (336); March 23, 1851, SNP (334); April 15, 1851, SNP (1543); April 20, 1851, SNP (3613); Manuel Delgado to same, May 7, 1851, SNP (1533); monthly report, February 28, 1851, SNP (2506); Juan N. de Arizpe to Quirino Benavente, February 22, 1851, SNP (494); March 21, 1851, SNP (2301); May 6, 1851, SNP (674).

67. Francisco Beráin to Juan N. de Arizpe, January 22, 1851, SNP (1520); February 12, 1851, SNP (1517); March 25, 1851, SNP (1525); April 2, 1851, SNP (1514); April 16, 1851, SNP (2160); April 30, 1851, SNP (311); May 7, 1851, SNP (310); monthly report, March 1, 1851, SNP (527).

68. Harris, *The Sánchez Navarros*, p. 78; Francisco Beráin to Juan N. de Arizpe, March 12, 1851, SNP (1518); for Beráin's opinion of the Kickapoos see his letters to Arizpe of June 4 and 11, 1851, SNP (307) and (306).

69. Harris, *The Sánchez Navarros*, p. 79.

70. Francisco Beráin to Jacobo SN, July 2, 1851, SNP (328); same to Juan N. de Arizpe, July 9, 1851, SNP (1542).

71. Quirino Benavente to Juan N. de Arizpe, June 20, 1851, SNP (2156); June 26, 1851, SNP (2157); Pascual Velarde to Quirino Benavente, June 23, 1851, SNP (635).

72. Claudio Aguirre to Quirino Benavente, July 17, 1851, SNP (2339); July 23, 1851, SNP (2321); August 6, 1851, SNP (2519); José María Ortiz to same, July 17, 1851, SNP (2345); Juan N. de Arizpe to same, July 22, 1851, SNP (2329); Miguel Sánchez to same, July 23, 1851, SNP (2342); Demetrio Lucio to Jacobo SN, August 13, 1851, SNP (2515); August 25, 1851, SNP (2516); Claudio Aguirre to Jacobo Elizondo, August 22, 1851, SNP (2529).

73. Mexico, *Informe final*, p. 71; see also Bartlett, *Personal Narrative*, II, 455.

74. Mexico, *Informe final*, p. 81.

75. Manuel [Sánchez] to Jacobo SN, June 25, 1853, SNP (1499); Manuel Beráin to same, July 26, 1856, SNP (922); Jacobo Elizondo to Miguel S. Máynez, September 18, 1864, SNP (1530); November 29, 1864, SNP (2144); Gregorio del Castillo to same, September 24, 1864, SNP (1495); Longino Valero to same, November 8, 1864, SNP (1555); November 8, 1864, SNP (401).

76. Bartlett, *Personal Narrative*, II, 492.

77. Inventory of Patos, April 25, 1857, found in "Cuenta General de la Hda. de Parras . . . ," January 25, 1841, SNP (2923); "Ynventario de los intereses pertenecientes á la Compañia . . . ," September 13, 1857–December 12, 1862, SNP (2889); see also "Inventario de la Hacienda de Hermanas . . . ," March 18, 1863, SNP (2887).

78. J. Fred Rippy, "The Indians of the Southwest in the Diplomacy of the United States and Mexico, 1848–1853," *Hispanic American Historical Review* 2, no. 3 (August 1919): 395–396; Ralph A. Smith, "The Scalp Hunter in the Borderlands, 1835–1850," *Arizona and the West* 6, no. 1 (Spring 1964): 5–22.

79. Paul Neff Garber, *The Gadsden Treaty*, p. 32; Gregg, *Diary*, II, 92.

80. Harris, *The Sánchez Navarros*, pp. 83–84.

81. Ralph P. Bieber (ed.), *Southern Trails to California in 1849*, p. 178.

82. Cosme Garza García (comp.), *Prontuario de leyes y decretos del estado de Coahuila de Zaragoza*, p. 107.

83. Harris, *The Sánchez Navarros*, pp. 82–86; Joseph Warren Revere, *Keel and Saddle*, pp. 205–206.

84. United States, Senate, *Treaty of peace, friendship, limits, and settlement between the United States of America and the Mexican republic, concluded at Guadalupe Hidalgo, on the 2d day of February, in the year 1848*, p. 50.

85. Harris, *The Sánchez Navarros*, pp. 87–88.

86. United States, House of Representatives, *Treaty between the United States of America and the Mexican republic, concluded at the city of Mexico, December 30, 1853*, p. 3.

87. NA, Mexican Docket, Memorials accompanying Claims 129c, 726, 727, 728, and 729; United States, Senate, *Claims on the Part of Citizens of the United States and Mexico under the Convention of July 4, 1868, between the United States and Mexico*, p. 88; cf. Bartlett, *Personal Narrative*, II, 492.

88. John Bassett Moore, *History and Digest of the International Arbitrations to which the United States has been a Party*, II, 1287, 1292, 1305.

89. NA, Mexican Docket, No. 131.

90. Moore, *History and Digest*, II, 1307–1309; see also Rippy, "Indians of the Southwest," p. 396; Francisco Gómez Palacio, *Reclamaciones de indemnización por depredaciones de los indios*, p. 104.

91. NA, Mexican Docket, Memorial accompanying Claim 729.

92. "Testimonio del espediente . . . ," September 27, 1827–June 3, 1829, SNP (2914); Ayuntamiento of Santa Rosa to José Melchor SN, January 26, 1828, SNP (2740); José Francisco del Castillo to same, March 6, 1828, SNP (2744); Ayuntamiento of Abasolo to same, March 26, 1828, SNP (2843); Atanacio Muñoz to same, May 28, 1828, SNP (2854); Valeriano Sánchez to Jacobo SN, September 6, 1847, MCSN; [draft—Santiago Vidaurri] to Carlos SN, July 25, 1863, AGENL-VA (8192).

93. Quirino Benavente to Juan N. de Arizpe, February 9, 1851, SNP (1550); February 19, 1851, SNP (424); Francisco Beráin to same, February 12, 1851, SNP (1517); Claudio Aguirre to Quirino Benavente, February 26, 1851, SNP (516).

94. Claudio Aguirre to Quirino Benavente, March 9, 1851, SNP (2306); March 15, 1851, SNP (2299); April 17, 1851, SNP (1540); Francisco Beráin to the Junta Calificadora de la Villa de Múzquiz, April 3, 1851, SNP (342); Quirino Benavente to Juan N. de Arizpe, April 20, 1851, SNP (3613); April 23, 1851, SNP (1546).

95. Harris, *The Sánchez Navarros*, p. 78.

96. Juan N. de Arizpe to Jacobo SN, June 15, 1851, SNP (430).

97. Francisco Beráin to Jacobo SN, June 18, 1851, SNP (324); same to Juan N. de Arizpe, June 18, 1851, SNP (305).

98. Harris, *The Sánchez Navarros*, p. 62.

99. Rafael Delgado to Jacobo SN, August 14, 1851, SNP (373).

100. [Draft—Jacobo SN] to Luis del Conde, October 5, 1851, SNP (2130).

101. Juan N. de Arizpe to Quirino Benavente, March 1, 1851, SNP (2309); March 29, 1851, SNP (2304); Quirino Benavente to Juan N. de Arizpe, April 13, 1851, SNP (1545).

102. Hughes, *Memoir*, p. 25.

103. Anderson, *An American in Maximilian's Mexico*, pp. 83–86, 89, 93, 95, 98; Gregg, *Diary*, I, 269, 280, II, 91; Hughes, *Memoir*, p. 33; Bartlett, *Personal Narrative*, II, 486–488; John W. Audubon, *Audubon's Western Journal*, ed. Frank H. Hodder, p. 93.

104. Receipt, February 24, 1836, SNP (697).

105. Emilio Langberg to Francisco Beráin, September 24, 1855, MCSN; October 3, 1855, MCSN; Rafael de la Fuente to same, January 3, 1856, MCSN; Saturnino Casas to Juan Farda, August 13, 1855, SNP (861); Comisario de Policía de la Hacienda de Patos to the Ayuntamiento of Saltillo, January 19, 1856, AGENL-VA (8168).

106. Jacobo SN to Santiago Vidaurri, January 29, 1856, AGENL-VA (8166); February 5, 1856, AGENL-VA (8169); February 13, 1856, AGENL-VA (8170);

Jacobo SN's statement of livestock stolen from Patos, January 29, 1856, AGENL-VA (8167).

107. Jacobo SN to Santiago Vidaurri, July 5, 1856, AGENL-VA (8171); Carlos SN to same, August 4, 1857, AGENL-VA (8177); September 23, 1857, AGENL-VA (8181).

108. Emilio Bohme to Jacobo SN, June 4, 1856, SNP (1613); Jesús G. de León to the Juez Auxiliar de Patos, January 24, 1859, SNP (1583); [draft—Santiago Vidaurri] to Jacobo SN, April 18, 1860, AGENL-VA (8187); Jacobo SN to Santiago Vidaurri, April 21, 1860, AGENL-VA (8188).

109. "Ynventario de los intereses pertenecientes á la Compañia . . . ," September 13, 1857–December 12, 1862, SNP (2889); Treasury documents, February 19, 1862, SNP (2213), February 27, 1862, SNP (2211), and February 28, 1862, SNP (2212); petition from Jesús María Aguilar, October 4, 1862, SNP (2222).

110. Manuel Rivera Cambas, *Historia de la Intervención europea y norte-Americana en México y del Imperio de Maximiliano de Hapsburgo*, II, 682; Anderson, *An American in Maximilian's Mexico*, pp. 122–123.

111. Rivera Cambas, *Historia de la Intervención*, III, 194.

112. Ibid., II, caption accompanying plate between pp. 540 and 541, III, 14; Jacobo Elizondo to Miguel S. Máynez, September 21, 1864, SNP (1508); for accounts of the fighting in Coahuila see Vicente Riva Palacio (ed.), *México á través de los siglos*, V, 654–655, 707–708, 746–747, 766; Juan de Dios Arias, *Reseña histórica de la formación y operaciones del cuerpo de ejército del norte durante la intervención francesa, sitio de Querétaro y noticias oficiales sobre la captura de Maximiliano, su proceso íntegro y su muerte*, pp. 9–23; Wilhelm von Montlong, *Authentische Enthüllungen über die letzten Ereignisse in Mexiko*, pp. 150–151, 154–156; Genaro García and Carlos Pereyra (eds.), *Documentos inéditos ó muy raros para la historia de México*, XXVII, 52–54, 73–77, 160–163.

9. LABOR

1. Manuel Castellano to José Melchor SN, July 28, 1824, SNP (3097); August 10, 1824, SNP (3189); same to Juan José de Cárdenas, September 3, 1828, SNP (2828); Miguel Cortines to [José] Melchor SN, January 19, 1830, SNP (2444); [José] Melchor [SN] to Apolonia [Beráin de SN], May 1, 1830, SNP (1298); note by Miguel Morales, November 21, 1833, SNP (1231); J. M. Carrillo y Seguín to Jacobo SN, January 19, 1842, SNP (1484); note by Victorio Morales, October 27, 1850, SNP (3076).

2. See, for example, Manuel Zamora to [José] Melchor SN, April 7, 1823, SNP (3493); Manuel Castellano to same, October 21, 1824, SNP (266).

3. Tomás Valdez to [José] Melchor SN, undated but probably 1823, SNP (3241); Manuel Castellano to same, July 28, 1824, SNP (3097); Andrés de Azcona to same, July 26, 1824, SNP (3194); Atanacio Muñoz to same, January 1, 1828, SNP (2748); Guillermo del Valle to Jacobo SN, February 22, 1852, SNP (1500).

4. [José] Melchor [SN] to Apolonia [Beráin de SN], November 20, 1825, SNP (3148); Apolonia [Beráin de SN] to [José] Melchor [SN], January 25, 1828, SNP (2712); Manuel Beráin to Jacobo SN, July 26, 1856, SNP (922); August 16, 1856, SNP (1622).

5. Francisco Vidaurri to José Melchor SN, May 26, 1822, SNP (3424); May 27,

1822, SNP (3333); "Autos seguidos por D. Melchor Sanches Nabarro . . . ," 1824, AGEC, *legajo* 15, *carpeta* 767.

6. Francisco Vidaurri to José Melchor SN, May 27, 1822, SNP (3333); Manuel Castellano to same, September 30, 1822, SNP (2611).

7. Manuel Castellano to José Melchor SN, May 25, 1824, SNP (3226); same to Rafael Delgado, November 18, 1825, SNP (260).

8. Manuel Castellano to José Melchor SN, September 4, 1826, SNP (2454); November 17, 1827, SNP (3132).

9. Apolonia Beráin de SN to [José] Melchor [SN], January 25, 1828, SNP (2712); Atanacio Muñoz to same, May 28, 1828, SNP (2854); Manuel Castellano to Apolonia Beráin de SN, May 26, 1829, SNP (1272); same to Juan José de Cárdenas, October 30, 1829, SNP (708).

10. Manuel Castellano to Apolonia Beráin de SN, January 2, 1831, SNP (1296); Apolonia Beráin de SN to [Juan José de] Cárdenas, November 16, 1833, SNP (1232).

11. Hughes, *Memoir*, p. 41.

12. Manuel Castellano to José Melchor SN, October 3, 1824, SNP (221); October 10, 1824, SNP (35); May 3, 1826, SNP (215); Atanacio Muñoz to same, May 28, 1828, SNP (2854); Manuel Castellano to Juan José de Cárdenas, October 30, 1829, SNP (708); receipt, August 18, 1834, SNP (1756).

13. Adolphus Wislinzenus, *Memoir of a Tour to Northern Mexico Connected with Col. Doniphan's Expedition in 1846 and 1847*, p. 70; Josiah Gregg, *Diary and Letters of Josiah Gregg*, ed. Maurice Garland Fulton, II, 95.

14. "1855. Raya diaria de los Sirvientes acomodados . . . ," and "Distribución de Sirvientes acomodados . . . ," August 1–December 30, 1855, SNP (3208).

15. Benito Riddell to Jacobo SN, September 4, 1847, MCSN.

16. See, for example, Linacio Luna to Miguel S. Máynez, February 24, 1864, SNP (1497).

17. Account by José María Escobedo at Bonanza, October 1, 1860, SNP (2219).

18. Hughes, *Memoir*, p. 40.

19. Manuel Castellano to José Melchor SN, October 6, 1823, SNP (3103); August 22, 1824, SNP (3197); Juan José de Cárdenas to same, August 9, 1824, SNP (3090).

20. Manuel Flores to [José] Melchor SN, October 11, 1823, SNP (3225); Nicolás Beráin to [same], October 16, 1823, SNP (3245).

21. Francisco Quintana to [José] Melchor SN, January 23, 1824, SNP (3221); Rafael Delgado to same, July 8, 1824, SNP (3219); July 13, 1824, SNP (3192); José Melchor SN to Rafael Delgado, July 10, 1824, SNP (997).

22. Manuel Castellano to José Melchor SN, October 6, 1823, SNP (3103); October 3, 1824, SNP (221); July 3, 1825, SNP (271); September 4, 1826, SNP (2454); May 15, 1828, SNP (2844); same to Apolonia Beráin de SN, January 2, 1831, SNP (1296).

23. Monthly reports, April 30, 1850, SNP (2174) and May 31, 1851, SNP (654); Román Méndez to Carlos Viesca, March 10, 1865, SNP (567).

24. Luis Valdés to Jacobo SN, August 24, 1842, SNP (851).

25. Miguel SN to Jacobo SN, August 31, 1845, MCSN.

26. Francisco Vidaurri to José Melchor SN, May 26, 1822, SNP (3424); Fran-

cisco Quintana to [same], June 22, 1824, SNP (3216); inventory of crops at Patos, July 4, 1851, SNP (3216); Jacobo Elizondo to Miguel S. Máynez, May 12, 1864, SNP (2153).

27. List of harvesters at Hedionda Grande, August 26, 1848, SNP (3618).

28. [Draft—José Melchor SN] to the *alcalde* of San Luis Potosí, October 12, 1825, MCSN.

29. María Beráin y SN to [Apolonia Beráin de SN], January 16, 1823, SNP (172); Apolonia Beráin de SN to [José] Melchor [SN], April 9, 1828, SNP (2701); April 16, 1828, SNP (2727); June 12, 1828, SNP (2805); same to Juan José de Cárdenas, October 9, 1829, SNP (1292).

30. Apolonia Beráin [de SN] to [José] Melchor [SN], August 9, 1824, SNP (3091); [José] Melchor [SN] to Apolonia [Beráin de SN], November 20, 1825, SNP (3148); December 1, 1825, SNP (3151).

31. Apolonia Beráin de SN to [José] Melchor [SN], January 23, 1828, SNP (2717).

32. [José Melchor SN] to Juan José de Cárdenas, October 11, 1829, SNP (1293); Manuel Castellano to same, October 17, 1836, SNP (1587); [José] Melchor [SN] to Apolonia [Beráin de SN], May 1, 1830, SNP (1298).

33. "Cuentas de los gastos . . . ," December 17, 1841–March 4, 1842, MCSN.

34. Luis Valdés to Jacobo SN, November 27, 1842, SNP (1469); Juan F. de Puyade to Quirino Benavente, November 26, 1850, SNP (508).

35. Juan F. de Puyade's monthly accounts, June 30, 1856, SNP (2220) and July 31, 1856, SNP (2209).

36. María Beráin y SN to [Apolonia Beráin de SN], January 16, 1823, SNP (172).

37. [José Melchor SN] to [Juan José de] Cárdenas, April 26, 1833, SNP (3487).

38. "Cuentas de los gastos . . . ," December 17, 1841–March 4, 1842, MCSN.

39. Juan F. de Puyade's monthly accounts, December 30, 1852, SNP (2210), November 30, 1853, SNP (2218), June 30, 1856, SNP (2220), and July 31, 1856, SNP (2209).

40. Francisco Quintana to [José Melchor SN], June 22, 1824, SNP (3216); Atanacio Muñoz to same, May 28, 1828, SNP (2854); vouchers by Francisco Quintana, June 24, 1824, SNP (3215).

41. Manuel Castellano to José Melchor SN, August 22, 1824, SNP (3197); [José] Melchor [SN] to Apolonia [Beráin de SN], March 7, 1830, SNP (1290); March 17, 1830, SNP (1294); Apolonia Beráin de SN to [Juan José de] Cárdenas, December 19, 1833, SNP (1236); Manuel Castellano to same, March 11, 1834, SNP (1229).

42. Miguel SN to Jacobo SN, August 31, 1845, MCSN.

43. Manuel Castellano to José Melchor SN, July 3, 1825, SNP (271).

44. Rafael Delgado to José Melchor SN, December 18, 1824, SNP (3270); Quirino Benavente to Juan N. de Arizpe, January 19, 1851, SNP (2108); list of wages, March 24, 1851, SNP (662).

45. Hughes, *Memoir*, pp. 38–39.

46. William Marshall Anderson, *An American in Maximilian's Mexico, 1865–1866*, ed. Ramón Eduardo Ruiz, p. 97.

47. Note by [José María] Ortiz, September 7, 1843, SNP (1674); Monthly

reports, April 30, 1847, SNP (3078), October 31, 1847, SNP (3617), and March 31, 1851, SNP (2279).

48. José María Ortiz to Quirino Benavente, September 5, 1843, SNP (1673); monthly reports, April 30, 1847, SNP (3078), June 30, 1851, SNP (618), and July 31, 1851, SNP (2323); memorandum by José María Ortiz, June 30, 1851, SNP (618).

49. Monthly reports, October 31, 1847, SNP (3617), May ——, 1848, SNP (3622), May 31, 1850, SNP (3077), July 30, 1850, SNP (2411), February 28, 1851, SNP (2510), March 1, 1851, SNP (2284), and May 1, 1851, SNP (651).

50. [Draft note—José Melchor SN], April 1, 1825, SNP (1777); monthly reports, April 30, 1847, SNP (3078), May 28, 1848, SNP (3622), August 31, 1848, SNP (3618), October 31, 1847, SNP (3617), May 31, 1848, SNP (3622); account for Bonanza, October, 1860–July, 1862, SNP (2223).

51. Monthly reports, April 30, 1847, SNP (3078), October 31, 1847, SNP (3617), May 31, 1848, SNP (3622), August 31, 1848, SNP (3618), November 30, 1849, SNP (796), December 31, 1849, SNP (3624), March 1, 1851, SNP (2284), June 30, 1851, SNP (618), and August 31, 1851, SNP (3172).

52. José María Ortiz to Quirino Benavente, June 19, 1851, SNP (630).

53. Carlos [SN] to Jacobo SN, April 11, 1847, MCSN; memoranda by José María Ortiz, October 31, 1847, SNP (3617), August 1, 1848, SNP (3618), April 1, 1850, SNP (2395), April 30, 1850, SNP (2394), February 1, 1851, SNP (2512) and (2509), March 1, 1851, SNP (2287), March 31, 1851, SNP (2285), April 10, 1851, SNP (2177), and June 1, 1851, SNP (616); memorandum by Quirino Benavente, May 16, 1851, SNP (668); account for Bonanza, October, 1860–July, 1862, SNP (2223).

54. Juan F. de Puyade to Quirino Benavente, November 26, 1850, SNP (508); February 9, 1851, SNP (510); March 1, 1851, SNP (2305); April 5, 1851, SNP (530); May 10, 1851, SNP (671); May 24, 1851, SNP (669); June 13, 1851, SNP (622); July 20, 1851, SNP (2326); August 13, 1851, SNP (3167).

55. "Racionero—1847," [for the Punta de Santa Elena], SNP (3626); "Racionero—1848," [for Hedionda Grande], SNP (3634); "Racionero—1848," [for the Punta de Santa Elena], SNP (3620); "Racionero—1850," [for same], SNP (3160); memoranda by Claudio Aguirre, May 9, 1851, SNP (672) and July 6, 1851, SNP (2337).

56. Quirino Benavente to Demetrio Lucio, December 9, 1850, SNP (3165); Claudio Aguirre to Quirino Benavente, February 26, 1851, SNP (516).

57. Quirino Benavente to Juan N. de Arizpe, April 2, 1851, SNP (337); April 15, 1851, SNP (1543).

58. Juan F. de Puyade to Jacobo SN, December 31, 1851, SNP (304).

59. Memorandum by Rafael Azuela, October 29, 1847, SNP (3617); account book for Patos, 1848, SNP (3635); "1855—Raya diaria de los Sirvientes acomodados . . . ," August 1–December 30, 1855, SNP (3208).

60. José Antonio Rodríguez to José Melchor SN, September 16, 1824, SNP (3228); [José Melchor S]N to [Juan José de] Cárdenas, April 30, 1833, SNP (3485).

61. Vicente Avilez to José Melchor SN, August 9, 1834, SNP (3492).

62. Demetrio Lucio to Quirino Benavente, May 20, 1847, SNP (1324); memoran-

dum by Francisco Frausto, October 22, 1847, SNP (3617); memoranda, February 29, 1848, SNP (3637) and December 20, 1849, SNP (3624).

63. Memorandum by Francisco Frausto, August 3, 1851, SNP (2525).

64. Accounts by Guadalupe Pérez, 1826–January 31, 1827, SNP (2422) and October 17, 1830–May 6, 1831, SNP (1208).

65. Demetrio Lucio to Quirino Benavente, June 28, 1851, SNP (629).

66. Pedro de Herrera to José Melchor SN, July 6, 1828, SNP (2798); Manuel Castellano to same, September 22, 1824, SNP (3214).

67. List by José María Ortiz, September 1, 1843, SNP (1675); monthly reports, April 30, 1847, SNP (3078), October 31, 1847, SNP (3617), April 1, 1848, SNP (3632), May 31, 1848, SNP (3622); account books, 1848, SNP (3635), 1848, SNP (3619), 1849, SNP (3624); monthly reports, May 31, 1851, SNP (654), June 30, 1851, SNP (619); "1855—Raya diaria de los Sirvientes acomodados . . . ," August 1–December 30, 1855, SNP (3208).

68. See, for example, Manuel Castellano to José Melchor SN, June 11, 1828, SNP (2800); monthly reports, May 31, 1848, SNP (3622), April 30, 1850, SNP (2393), May 31, 1851, SNP (649).

69. Monthly report, June 30, 1850, SNP (2415).

70. Cosme Garza García (comp.), *Prontuario de leyes y decretos del estado de Coahuila de Zaragoza*, p. 81; Alessio Robles, *Coahuila y Texas, desde la consumación*, I, 265–267.

71. Manuel Castellano to José Melchor SN, August 22, 1824, SNP (3197); May 26, 1829, SNP (1272); Pedro de Herrera to same, July 6, 1828, SNP (2798); memoranda by Jacinto Barrientos, June 18, 1850, SNP (2421), by Manuel Reyes, August 16, 1848, SNP (3618), and by Felipe Gómez, February 18, 1861, SNP (1581).

72. Nelson Reed, *The Caste War of Yucatan*, p. 11; Manuel Castellano to Rafael Delgado, November 3, 1825, SNP (259); same to José Melchor SN, July 11, 1826, SNP (2455); September 4, 1826, SNP (2454); Apolinar Flores to Saturnino Casas, January 17, 1864, SNP (1492).

73. Miguel Cortines to [José] Melchor SN, January 19, 1830, SNP (2444); Apolonia Beráin de SN to Juan José de Cárdenas, January 28, 1837, SNP (747); memoranda by Rafael Azuela, May 22, 1848, SNP (3622) and ——— 31, 1849, SNP (3624), and by Felipe Gómez, February 18, 1861, SNP (1581).

74. Jacobo SN to Juan Farda, June 12, 1856, SNP (800).

75. Accounts by José María Escobedo, October 1, 1860, SNP (2219); "Ynventario de los intereses pertenecientes á la Compañia . . . ," September 13, 1857–December 12, 1862, SNP (2889).

76. Manuel Castellano to José Melchor SN, October 3, 1824, SNP (221); September 4, 1826, SNP (2454); [José] Melchor [SN] to Apolonia [Beráin de SN], May 1, 1830, SNP (1298).

77. Vouchers for religious ceremonies, October 14–December 15, 1849, SNP (3624), April 14–June 15, 1850, SNP (2416); memoranda, June 30, 1850, SNP (2417) and January 31, 1851, SNP (1575); Juan N. de Arizpe to Quirino Benavente, July 22, 1851, SNP (2329).

78. J. B. de Santisteban, *Indicador particular del administrador de hacienda*, pp. 87–88, 98–99.

79. Father Juan B. Bobadilla to Quirino Benavente, February 17, 1851, SNP (423).

80. Juan José de Cárdenas to José Melchor SN, August 9, 1824, SNP (3090); Manuel Castellano to same, July 3, 1825, SNP (271); [José] Melchor [SN] to Apolonia Beráin de SN, August 22, 1825, SNP (227).

81. José Melchor SN to the Bishop of Monterrey, January 29, 1833, and Bishop José María de Jesús Belaunzarán's reply, February 11, 1833, SNP (2659).

82. Miguel SN to Jacobo SN, January 29, 1844, MCSN.

83. Memorandum by Father Juan E. Beráin, October 31, 1849, SNP (3624); Father Juan B. Bobadilla to Quirino Benavente, February 17, 1851, SNP (423).

84. Jacobo SN to Quirino Benavente, August ——, 1848, SNP (3618); Quirino Benavente to Juan N. de Arizpe, April 20, 1851, SNP (3613).

85. Circular by the Ayuntamiento of San Luis Potosí, May 18, 1825, SNP (1768); Francisco de Paula Treviño to Rafael Delgado, September 14, 1825, MCSN; Francisco Vidaurri to José Melchor SN, July 28, 1825, SNP (231).

86. Manuel Castellano to José Melchor SN, July 3, 1825, SNP (271); July 31, 1825, SNP (255); same to Rafael Delgado, November 18, 1825, SNP (260).

87. Manuel Castellano to Juan José de Cárdenas, October 30, 1829, SNP (708).

88. Agustín Martínez to José Melchor SN, October 13, 1833, SNP (129).

89. Quirino Benavente to Juan N. de Arizpe, February 9, 1851, SNP (1550).

90. Petition from Rafael Delgado to the Governor of Coahuila and Texas, August 9, 1825, SNP (2366); unsigned draft, July ——, 1825, SNP (229); Rafael Delgado to Bartolomé de Cárdenas, July 29, 1825, SNP (2364).

91. Manuel Castellano to José Melchor SN, September 4, 1826, SNP (2454).

92. Apolonia Beráin de SN to [José] Melchor [SN], January 2, 1828, SNP (2771).

93. José Estevan del Castillo to José Melchor SN, May 1, 1826, SNP (200); Eduardo González to Jacobo SN, July 19, 1847, MCSN.

94. Charles H. Harris III, *The Sánchez Navarros*, p. 39. Since it was the *hacendados* who left the written records, one is obviously on shaky ground in attempting to describe the feelings of peons. Therefore, even though dealing with a different area of Mexico at a later period, an invaluable first-hand account of peonage and hacienda life from the peon's point of view is found in Oscar Lewis, *Pedro Martínez*, pp. 6–9, 17–18, 25–26.

95. Manuel Castellano to José Melchor SN, May 25, 1824, SNP (3226); September 22, 1824, SNP (3214); October 3, 1824, SNP (221).

96. Monthly reports, June 30, 1851, SNP (618) and (619).

97. "1855—Raya diaria de los Sirvientes acomodados . . . ," August 1–December 30, 1855, SNP (3208).

98. Manuel Castellano to José Melchor SN, September 30, 1822, SNP (2611); May 25, 1824, SNP (3226); July 28, 1824, SNP (3097); September 22, 1824, SNP (3214); October 3, 1824, SNP (221); Quirino Benavente to Juan N. de Arizpe, April 28, 1851, SNP (420); May 4, 1851, SNP (2159); Jacobo Elizondo to Miguel S. Máynez, November 29, 1864, SNP (2144).

99. Alessio Robles, *Coahuila y Texas, desde la consumación*, I, 266.

100. Melitón Castellano to José Melchor SN, January 13, 1828, SNP (1216).

101. José Francisco del Castillo to José Melchor SN, March 6, 1828, SNP (2744).

102. Melitón Castellano to José Melchor SN, April 20, 1828, SNP (2757).

103. José Francisco del Castillo to José Melchor SN, March 6, 1828, SNP (2744); Melitón Castellano to same, April 20, 1828, SNP (2757).

104. Monthly reports, April 30, 1847, SNP (3078), October 31, 1847, SNP (3617), May 31, 1848, SNP (3622), April 30, 1850, SNP (2393), January 31, 1851, SNP (3325), February 28, 1851, SNP (2506) and (2507), June 30, 1851, SNP (614), (618), and (619), July 31, 1851, SNP (2322); Quirino Benavente to Juan N. de Arizpe, April 28, 1851, SNP (420).

105. Manuel Castellano to José Melchor SN, September 30, 1822, SNP (2611); May 25, 1824, SNP (3226); April 9, 1826, SNP (186).

106. José María Ortiz to Quirino Benavente, June 19, 1851, SNP (630); Carlos [SN] to Jacobo SN, April 11, 1847, MCSN.

107. Manuel Castellano to José Melchor SN, September 30, 1822, SNP (2611); February 28, 1824, SNP (3125); May 25, 1824, SNP (3226); July 28, 1824, SNP (3097); September 22, 1824, SNP (3214); July 17, 1825, SNP (254); August 31, 1833, SNP (3293); Apolonia Beráin de SN to [same], July 27, 1824, SNP (3193); Juan José de Cárdenas to same, August 9, 1824, SNP (3090); Atanacio Muñoz to same, May 28, 1828, SNP (2854); [José] Melchor [SN] to Apolonia [Beráin de SN], May 1, 1830, SNP (1298); [Atanacio] Rodríguez to Manuel Castellano, August 3, 1830, SNP (1277); Memoranda by José María Ortiz, September 1, 1843, SNP (1675) and September 7, 1843, SNP (1674); memorandum, February 7, 1848, SNP (3637).

108. Manuel Castellano to José Melchor SN, February 28, 1824, SNP (3125).

109. [Atanacio] Rodríguez to Manuel Castellano, August 3, 1830, SNP (1277).

110. Manuel Castellano to José Melchor SN, May 25, 1824, SNP (3226); September 22, 1824, SNP (3214).

111. Manuel Castellano to [José Melchor SN], August 31, 1833, SNP (3293).

112. Manuel Castellano to José Melchor SN, July 17, 1825, SNP (254).

113. Manuel Castellano to José Melchor SN, September 30, 1822, SNP (2611).

114. Apolonia Beráin de SN to [José] Melchor [SN], April 9, 1828, SNP (2701).

115. Alessio Robles, *Coahuila y Texas, desde la consumación*, I, 267.

116. José Isidro Hernández to José Melchor SN, April 28, 1822, SNP (847); Manuel Castellano to same, September 22, 1824, SNP (3214).

117. Apolonia Beráin de SN to [José] Melchor [SN], April 16, 1828, SNP (2727).

118. SNP (2816).

119. Apolonia Beráin de SN to [José] Melchor [SN], April 9, 1828, SNP (2701); April 16, 1828, SNP (2727).

120. Manuel Castellano to José Melchor SN, July 28, 1824, SNP (3097).

121. José Estevan del Castillo to [José] Melchor SN, May 27, 1828, SNP (2855); Atanacio Muñoz to same, May 28, 1828, SNP (2854); José Luis de Goríbar to Jacobo SN, May 28, 1847, MCSN; Jacobo Elizondo to same, November 26, 1851, SNP (1589).

122. Manuel Castellano to José Melchor SN, September 22, 1824, SNP (3214); March 9, 1826, SNP (2489); April 9, 1826, SNP (186); September 19, 1826,

SNP (2477); September 24, 1826, SNP (2478); José Estevan del Castillo to same, May 1, 1826, SNP (200).

123. Manuel Zamora to [José] Melchor SN, April 7, 1823, SNP (3493).

124. Juan José de Cárdenas to José Melchor SN, August 9, 1824, SNP (3090); Apolonia Beráin de SN to same, May 4, 1830, SNP (728).

125. Manuel Castellano to José Melchor SN, August 10, 1824, SNP (3189).

126. Manuel Castellano to José Melchor SN, September 30, 1822, SNP (2611); October 3, 1824, SNP (221); July 28, 1824, SNP (3097).

127. Harris, *The Sánchez Navarros*, pp. 40–44.

128. Jacobo Elizondo to Miguel S. Máynez, November 29, 1864, SNP (2144).

129. Daniel Cosío Villegas (ed.), *Historia Moderna de México*, III, 348–349.

10. *LATIFUNDIO* PRODUCTION

1. See Josiah Gregg, *Commerce of the Prairies*, ed. Max L. Moorhead, pp. 265–266.

2. Juan José de Cárdenas to José Melchor SN, September 29, 1823, SNP (3291).

3. Bartolomé de Arechabala to [José] Melchor SN, January 6, 1824, SNP (3126).

4. Román de Letona to José Melchor SN, July 12, 1825, SNP (230); August 9, 1825, SNP (249).

5. Rafael Delgado to José Melchor SN, February 2, 1826, SNP (182); José María de Letona to same, February 30 [*sic*], 1826, SNP (165); April 8, 1826, SNP (238); April 27, 1826, SNP (1779); Román de Letona to same, April 18, 1826, SNP (239); June 3, 1826, SNP (188); Manuel María García to same, August 5, 1826, SNP (2447).

6. Rafael Villalobos to José Melchor SN, August 1, 1826, SNP (2446); August 26, 1826, SNP (2481).

7. Pedro Pablo de Cortines to José Melchor SN, September 26, 1826, SNP (2453).

8. [Draft—José Melchor SN] to Juan Flores, December 11, 1826, SNP (941).

9. José Francisco del Valle to [José] Melchor SN, February 23, 1828, SNP (2779); May 10, 1828, SNP (2823); July 5, 1828, SNP (2822); Apolonia Beráin de SN to same, March 12, 1828, SNP (2775); certificate by José Francisco del Valle, April 29, 1828, SNP (2847).

10. Francisco Bernardino de la Peña to José Melchor SN, June 28, 1828, SNP (2821).

11. Domingo de Ugartechea to [José] Melchor SN, April 3, 1828, SNP (2704).

12. Domingo de Ugartechea to [José] Melchor SN, May 1, 1828, SNP (2834); May 16, 1828, SNP (2790); June 13, 1828, SNP (2786).

13. Juan Martínez to José Melchor SN, January 21, 1830, SNP (2441).

14. Pedro Rodríguez to [José] Melchor SN, May 29, 1830, SNP (3317).

15. Diego Grant to José Melchor SN, October 18, 1830, SNP (898); March 29, 1831, SNP (942); certificate by José de la Luz Méndez, November 1, 1830, SNP (949); [draft—José Melchor SN] to Diego Grant, April 8, 1831, SNP (943).

16. [José] Melchor [SN] to Apolonia Beráin de SN, January 29, 1830, SNP (1286); Joaquín Reynoso to [José] Melchor SN, March 9, 1830, SNP (815); Joaquín de Aguirre to same, April 10, 1830, SNP (781); May 8, 1830, SNP (3573).

17. José María Araujo to Carlos SN, December 16, 1836, SNP (2612).

18. Carlos [SN] to Jacobo SN, May 25, 1842, SNP (1614); June 22, 1842, SNP (992); Luis Valdés to same, August 12, 1842, SNP (886).

19. Worksheet for an account of Jacobo SN, October 8, 1842, SNP (1006); Martín Alcalá to Jacobo SN, November 27, 1842, SNP (1467); December 18, 1842, SNP (1625); Luis Valdés to same, December 20, 1842, SNP (1626).

20. Juan José de Cárdenas to José Melchor SN, April 20, 1822, SNP (865); Román de Letona to same, June 7, 1822, SNP (850).

21. Rafael Delgado to [José] Melchor SN, August 5, 1822, SNP (3129); September 15, 1823, SNP (3211).

22. Román de Letona to José Melchor SN, September 18, 1823, SNP (3256); Juan José de Cárdenas to same, September 29, 1823, SNP (3291).

23. Stephen Willson to [José Melchor SN], October 19, 1823, SNP (3234).

24. Manuel Castellano to José Melchor SN, October 23, 1824, SNP (3108).

25. Manuel Castellano to José Melchor SN, February 28, 1824, SNP (3125); July 3, 1825, SNP (271).

26. Manuel Castellano to José Melchor SN, February 28, 1824, SNP (3125); August 10, 1824, SNP (3189); Apolonia Beráin de SN to [same], July 27, 1824, SNP (3193).

27. María Guadalupe SN de Cacho to [José] Melchor SN, June 29, 1824, SNP (3217); July 28, 1824, SNP (3093); Román de Letona to same, July 30, 1824, SNP (3202); Juan José de Cárdenas to same, August 9, 1824, SNP (3090); Apolonia Beráin [de SN] to [same], August 9, 1824, SNP (3091); Manuel Castellano to same, July 28, 1824, SNP (3097); August 10, 1824, SNP (3189); October 3, 1824, SNP (221).

28. Manuel Castellano to José Melchor SN, August 22, 1824, SNP (3197).

29. Román de Letona to José Melchor SN, October 5, 1824, SNP (3110).

30. Rafael Delgado to José Melchor SN, January 19, 1825, SNP (3233); Apolonia Beráin de SN to same, February 6, 1828, SNP (2752); Manuel Castellano to same, August 3, 1826, SNP (1357); June 11, 1828, SNP (2800); October 16, 1828, SNP (2838).

31. Antonio Margil Cano to José Melchor SN, September 19, 1825, SNP (204); Rafael Delgado to same, September 26, 1825, SNP (211).

32. Manuel Castellano to José Melchor SN, September 19, 1826, SNP (2477); Apolonia Beráin de SN to same, February 27, 1828, SNP (2719).

33. Apolonia Beráin de SN to [José] Melchor [SN], April 22, 1829, SNP (1269); Manuel Castellano to Apolonia Beráin de SN, July 31, 1829, SNP (710); [José] Melchor [SN] to same, August 1, 1829, SNP (1283).

34. Eugenio de Olaez to José Melchor SN, January 12, 1830, and draft of latter's reply, February 21, 1830, SNP (2608).

35. Rafael Villalobos to José Melchor SN, October 12, 1830, SNP (1250).

36. [José Melchor S]N to [Juan José de] Cárdenas, November 6, 1830, SNP (3312); Juan José de Cárdenas to José Melchor SN, November 8, 1830, SNP (1737); Pedro Santa Cruz to same, August 13, 1831, SNP (1648).

37. Pedro Santa Cruz to José Melchor SN, August 27, 1831, SNP (769); Francisco Careaga to same, December 29, 1832, SNP (123).

38. Manuel Castellano to Juan José de Cárdenas, April 30, 1833, SNP (3486); [José Melchor S]N to same, May 26, 1833, SNP (3489); December 28, 1833, SNP

(1225); Francisco Careaga to [José] Melchor SN, June 10, 1833, SNP (2451); same to Juan José de Cárdenas, June 10, 1833, SNP (3490); bill of lading, August 3, 1833, SNP (3491).

39. Manuel Castellano to Juan José de Cárdenas, January 13, 1834, SNP (1226); Vicente Avilez to José Melchor SN, August 9, 1834, SNP (3492); José Melchor SN to Matías ———, October 13, 1834, SNP (2901).

40. Apolonia Beráin de SN to [Juan José de] Cárdenas, November 2, 1837, SNP (2461).

41. J. Luis de Goríbar to Jacobo SN, April 20, 1842, SNP (883).

42. Luis Valdés to Jacobo SN, August 15, 1842, SNP (873); September 1, 1842, SNP (892); November 7, 1842, SNP (1465); December 18, 1842, SNP (1630).

43. Simón Elizondo to Jacobo SN, July 15, 1845, MCSN; August 6, 1845, MCSN.

44. Luis Valdés to Jacobo SN, December 20, 1842, SNP (1626); December 23, 1842, SNP (893).

45. List by [Francisco] Vidaurri, April 29, 1822, SNP (3334); Francisco Vidaurri to José Melchor SN, May 26, 1822, SNP (3424).

46. Rafael Delgado to José Melchor SN, January 19, 1825, SNP (3233); February 2, 1826, SNP (182); Juan José de Cárdenas to same, November 21, 1830, SNP (3339); Apolonia Beráin de SN to same, January 2, 1828, SNP (2771); January 16, 1828, SNP (2697); February 6, 1828, SNP (2752); January 19, 1830, SNP (2428); March 9, 1831, SNP (733); same to [Juan José de] Cárdenas, December 19, 1833, SNP (1236); [José Melchor S]N to same, December 19, 1833, SNP (1237).

47. José Estevan del Castillo to José Melchor SN, June 12, 1826, SNP (1301); Apolonia Beráin de SN to same, January 9, 1828, SNP (2710); January 23, 1828, SNP (2717); January 25, 1828, SNP (2712); January 30, 1828, SNP (2714); February 6, 1828, SNP (2752); Eugenio de Olaez to same, January 12, 1830, SNP (2608); Eugenio Páez to Jacobo SN, February 15, 1844, SNP (1506).

48. Juan José de Cárdenas to José Melchor SN, April 20, 1822, SNP (865); June 9, 1822, SNP (848); Miguel SN to Jacobo SN, January 29, 1844, MCSN; August 31, 1845, MCSN.

49. Manuel Castellano to José Melchor SN, September 8, 1824, SNP (3250); legajo, 1826–January 31, 1827, SNP (2422); legajo, October 17, 1830–May 6, 1831, SNP (1208).

50. See "Cuenta general de la Hda de Parras . . . ," January 25, 1841, SNP (2923).

51. Rafael Delgado to José Melchor SN, January 19, 1825, SNP (3233); Manuel Castellano to same, December 28, 1833, SNP (724); [José Melchor S]N to Juan José de Cárdenas, August 11, 1833, SNP (1244).

52. Atanacio Muñoz to José Melchor SN, January 1, 1828, SNP (2748).

53. Manuel Castellano to José Melchor SN, January 9, 1830, SNP (1273); December 28, 1833, SNP (724); same to Apolonia Beráin de SN, January 2, 1831, SNP (1296); George T. M. Davis, *Autobiography of the Late Col. Geo. T. M. Davis*, p. 108.

54. "No. 2—Noticia de las partidas de algodón . . . ," March 4, 1842, MCSN.

55. Juan N. de Arizpe to Jacobo SN, July 14, 1846, SNP (958).

56. General Pedro de Ampudia to the Commandant General of the Department of Coahuila, September 4, 1846, SNP (957).

57. General Rafael Vázquez to Jacobo SN, September 5, 1846, SNP (956).

58. Juan N. de Arizpe to Jacobo SN, September 9, 1846, SNP (1003); Ignacio Lozano to same, September 9, 1846, SNP (1002).

59. Miguel SN to Jacobo SN, September 10, 1846, MCSN.

60. Juan N. de Arizpe to Jacobo SN, July 14, 1846, SNP (958); Ignacio Lozano to same, September 9, 1846, SNP (1002).

61. Davis, *Autobiography*, p. 108; Josiah Gregg, *Diary and Letters of Josiah Gregg*, ed. Maurice Garland Fulton, I, 276.

62. Juan N. de Arizpe to Jacobo SN, March 30, 1847, MCSN; Eduardo González to same, October 15, 1847, SNP (897); H. Boultbee to same, March 19, 1847, MCSN; Juan Pérez to Quirino Benavente, May 13, 1847, SNP (2624); May 17, 1847, SNP (767).

63. Juan N. de Arizpe to Jacobo SN, March 18, 1847, MCSN; March 30, 1847, MCSN.

64. H. Boultbee to Jacobo SN, March 19, 1847, MCSN; March 28, 1847, SNP (1005); April 6, 1847, MCSN; April 11, 1847, MCSN; April 18, 1847, MCSN.

65. H. Boultbee to Jacobo SN, July 10, 1847, MCSN; July 11, 1847, MCSN; January 6, 1848, MCSN; January 10, 1848, MCSN.

66. José E. del Castillo to Quirino Benavente, May 12, 1847, SNP (120).

67. Jacobo Elizondo to Jacobo SN, March 22, 1847, MCSN; account book for the Punta de Santa Elena, 1847, SNP (3626); E. Domínguez to Demetrio Lucio, May 25, 1848, SNP (3619); Demetrio Lucio to Quirino Benavente, May 31, 1848, SNP (3619).

68. Carlos [SN] to Jacobo [SN], April 14, 1847, MCSN.

69. Hughes, *Memoir*, p. 40.

70. See H. Boultbee to Jacobo SN, March 8, 1847, MCSN; March 13, 1847, MCSN; J. Atenógenes Rodríguez to same, March 27, 1847, MCSN; Simón Elizondo to same, March 13, 1847, MCSN; Jacobo Elizondo to same, March 22, 1847, MCSN; Ignacio Lozano to same, December 19, 1847, MCSN; bills of lading, April 27, 1847, SNP (3078), and May 18, 1847, SNP (1598); Francisco Beráin to Quirino Benavente, October 19, 1847, SNP (2231).

71. Carlos [SN] to Jacobo SN, April 11, 1847, MCSN; April 14, 1847, MCSN; monthly report, October 31, 1847, SNP (3617).

72. Memorandum by José María Ortiz, February 1, 1848, SNP (3637); monthly report, February 29, 1848, SNP (3637).

73. Monthly reports, May 31, 1848, SNP (3622), August 31, 1848, SNP (3618), and December 31, 1849, SNP (3624); memoranda by José María Ortiz, April 1, 1850, SNP (2395), April 30, 1850, SNP (2394), May 31, 1850, SNP (3077), and October 16, 1850, SNP (3076); Juan F. de Puyade to Quirino Benavente, November 26, 1850, SNP (508).

74. Contract, January 2, 1851, SNP (2232).

75. Juan F. de Puyade's monthly accounts, November 30, 1853, SNP (2218) and June 30, 1856, SNP (2220); Juan F. de Puyade to Jacobo SN, July 26, 1856, SNP (860); August 6, 1856, SNP (1511).

76. Eduardo González to Jacobo SN, May 5, 1848, MCSN; monthly reports, May 31, 1848, SNP (3622) and May 31, 1850, SNP (3077); memorandum, April 30, 1850, SNP (2394).

77. Jacobo SN to Juan N. de Arizpe, January 15, 1851, SNP (289); January 16, 1851, SNP (290); February 8, 1851, SNP (292); Francisco Beráin to same, February 19, 1851, SNP (1524); February 26, 1851, SNP (1519); Juan N. de Arizpe to Quirino Benavente, February 22, 1851, SNP (494); March 4, 1851, SNP (2295); memorandum by Francisco Beráin, March 1, 1851, SNP (526).

78. Jacobo SN to Juan N. de Arizpe, February 21, 1851, SNP (295); Juan N. de Arizpe to Quirino Benavente, March 4, 1851, SNP (2295).

79. Monthly reports, February 28, 1851, SNP (2506) and (2507); Jacobo SN to Juan N. de Arizpe, March 5, 1851, SNP (357).

80. [Draft—Jacobo SN] to José Luis de Sautto, March 8, 1851, SNP (3546); April 1, 1851, SNP (2632); same to Juan N. de Arizpe, April 2, 1851, SNP (365).

81. Receipt by Camilo Vázquez, April 24, 1851, SNP (645); memorandum by Quirino Benavente, May 16, 1851, SNP (668); itemized statement by Quirino Benavente, June 6, 1851, SNP (784).

82. José Vicente Díez de Sollano to Jacobo SN, May 19, 1851, SNP (352); [draft—Juan N. de Arizpe] to José Luis de Sautto, June 8, 1851, SNP (581); July 16, 1851, SNP (146); September ——, 1851, SNP (748); same to Quirino Benavente, July 18, 1851, SNP (2332).

83. Antonio Aguado to Jacobo SN, June 18, 1855, SNP (798); June 25, 1855, SNP (797).

84. Angel María Garibay K. et al. (comps.), *Diccionario Porrúa de historia, biografía y geografía de México*, p. 1764.

85. Jacobo SN to Juan N. de Arizpe, March 5, 1851, SNP (357); [draft—same] to José Luis de Sautto, March 8, 1851, SNP (3546); Juan N. de Arizpe to Quirino Benavente, March 22, 1851, SNP (2303).

86. Jacobo SN to Juan N. de Arizpe, March 12, 1851, SNP (299); Juan N. de Arizpe to Quirino Benavente, March 16, 1851, SNP (2298); March 25, 1851, SNP (2302); Quirino Benavente to Juan N. de Arizpe, March 23, 1851, SNP (334).

87. Juan N. de Arizpe to Quirino Benavente, April 1, 1851, SNP (2262); April 6, 1851, SNP (2185); April 8, 1851, SNP (2186); Quirino Benavente to Juan N. de Arizpe, April 2, 1851, SNP (337); April 5, 1851, SNP (1527); April 6, 1851, SNP (1528); Jacobo SN to same, April 16, 1851, SNP (362); A. Zurutuza to Jacobo SN, September 7, 1851, SNP (2127).

88. Garibay et al. (comps.), *Diccionario Porrúa*, p. 1764; Jan Bazant, "The Division of Some Mexican *Haciendas* during the Liberal Revolution, 1856–1862," *Journal of Latin American Studies* 3, part 1 (May 1971): 31, 34.

89. Esteban L. Portillo, *Anuario Coahuilense para 1886*, p. 56; José Manuel Royüela to [José] Melchor SN, May 22, 1830, SNP (1699); José Antonio Goríbar to Jacobo SN, May 1, 1842, SNP (1488).

90. F. de Goríbar to Jacobo SN, October 15, 1851, SNP (368); José de Goríbar to same, November 8, 1851, SNP (1532); Mosso Hermanos to Juan de Goríbar, December 29, 1851, SNP (1599).

91. Pomposo Garces to Juan N. de Arizpe, April 8, 1851, SNP (2191); Juan N. de Arizpe to Quirino Benavente, April 10, 1851, SNP (2189); [draft—Quirino Benavente] to Pomposo Garces, April 11, 1851, SNP (1490); same to Juan N. de Arizpe, April 15, 1851, SNP (1543); April 20, 1851, SNP (3613).

92. Quirino Benavente to Juan N. de Arizpe, April 26, 1851, SNP (422);

April 30, 1851, SNP (419); Juan N. de Arizpe to Quirino Benavente, April 26, 1851, SNP (2180).

93. Mariano Vega to Jacobo SN, May 28, 1851, SNP (433); June 28, 1851, SNP (2112); December 29, 1851, SNP (2167).

94. Francisco de Borja Belaunzarán to Jacobo SN, August 16, 1851, SNP (350).

95. Rafael Aguirre to Jacobo SN, October 30, 1851, SNP (392); November 17, 1851, SNP (398).

96. Juan F. de Puyade to Quirino Benavente, May 24, 1851, SNP (669); June 13, 1851, SNP (622); same to Jacobo SN, June 4, 1851, SNP (436); August 16, 1851, SNP (2135).

97. Juan F. de Puyade to Quirino Benavente, May 24, 1851, SNP (669); same to Jacobo SN, June 25, 1851, SNP (327).

98. Memorandum by Jacobo SN, March 4, 1852, SNP (1640).

99. Manuel González Torres to Jacobo SN, June 13, 1855, SNP (1596); [draft— Jacobo SN] to Manuel González Torres, July 11, 1855, SNP (1595).

100. "Cuenta general de la Hacienda de Bonanza con la de Patos . . . ," 1857– December 31, 1860, SNP (2224).

101. Jacobo SN's account with Bonanza, October, 1860–July, 1862, SNP (2223).

102. Linacio Luna to Miguel S. Máynez, February 24, 1864, SNP (1497); José María Cavazos to same, February 25, 1864, SNP (1498).

103. Vicente Q. Huerta to Miguel S. Máynez, November 25, 1865, SNP (3302).

104. Eduardo González to Jacobo SN, May 5, 1848, MCSN; receipts, ———, 1848, SNP (3619) and September 26, 1850, SNP (3179); memorandum, December 31, 1849, SNP (3624).

105. Jacobo SN to Juan N. de Arizpe, March 5, 1851, SNP (357); itemized statement by Quirino Benavente, June 6, 1851, SNP (784).

106. Jacobo SN to Juan N. de Arizpe, March 12, 1851, SNP (299); Quirino Benavente to same, March 23, 1851, SNP (334); March 30, 1851, SNP (338); April 2, 1851, SNP (337); April 15, 1851, SNP (1543); Francisco Beráin to same, May 14, 1851, SNP (309).

107. Certificate by Ciriaco Lara, June 20, 1851, SNP (2126); "Cuenta que rinde Bacilio Henríquez . . . ," June 25, 1851, SNP (624); "Cuenta que rinde el que suscribe . . . ," June 25, 1851, SNP (625); Juan N. de Arizpe to Jacobo SN, June 22, 1851, SNP (323).

108. Juan F. de Puyade to Jacobo SN, September 6, 1851, SNP (301).

109. A. Zurutuza to Jacobo SN, September 7, 1851, SNP (2127); Juan F. de Puyade to same, October 11, 1851, SNP (2115); November 19, 1851, SNP (2125).

110. Francisco Beráin to Jacobo SN, June 25, 1851, SNP (329); Juan F. de Puyade to same, August 6, 1851, SNP (2136); October 11, 1851, SNP (2115); December 31, 1851, SNP (304); F. de Goríbar to same, October 15, 1851, SNP (368); José de Goríbar to same, November 8, 1851, SNP (1532).

111. Juan F. de Puyade to Jacobo SN, December 3, 1851, SNP (2142); December 24, 1851, SNP (2139); December 31, 1851, SNP (2138).

112. Alejandro Bellangé to Jacobo SN, May 24, 1851, SNP (569); Gonzalo de Pavia to same, June 2, 1851, SNP (431); Juan N. de Arizpe to same, June 15, 1851, SNP (430); June 22, 1851, SNP (323); Gonzalo de Pavia to Juan N. de Arizpe, June 19, 1851, SNP (441).

113. Emilio Bohme to Jacobo SN, June 4, 1856, SNP (1613); Jacobo SN's account with Bonanza, October, 1860–July, 1862, SNP (2223); "Altas y bajas del Ganado Mayor . . . ," January 9, 1864–November 9, 1865, SNP (711).

114. Memoranda, May 5, 16, and 17, 1848, SNP (3622).

115. Memoranda, April 23, 1850, SNP (2392); May 29, 1850, SNP (3077); June 20, 1850, SNP (2413); June 26, 1850, SNP (2412); July 27, 1850, SNP (2414); October 15, 1850, SNP (3076).

116. Francisco Beráin to Juan N. de Arizpe, March 5, 1851, SNP (1515); March 25, 1851, SNP (1525); Juan N. de Arizpe to Quirino Benavente, April 1, 1851, SNP (2262); memorandum, April 9, 1851, SNP (2179).

117. Memorandum, August 23, 1851, SNP (2526).

118. Jacobo SN to Quirino Benavente, August 8, 1851, SNP (2524); Rafael Delgado to Jacobo SN, August 25, 1851, SNP (374).

119. Rafael Delgado to Juan N. de Arizpe, May 22, 1851, SNP (282); same to Jacobo SN, July 10, 1851, SNP (353).

120. Jacobo SN to Quirino Benavente, August 8, 1851, SNP (2524); Rafael Delgado to Jacobo SN, August 25, 1851, SNP (374); September 4, 1851, SNP (375); September 18, 1851, SNP (378).

121. Bill of lading, August 9, 1859, SNP (2520); "Ynventario de los intereses pertenecientes á la Compañia . . . ," September 13, 1857–December 12, 1862, SNP (2889); Jacobo SN's account with Bonanza, October, 1860–July, 1862, SNP (2223) and July 30–August 19, 1862, SNP (2214).

122. Bills of lading, August 9, 1864, SNP (1564), August 10, 1864, SNP (1559), (1563), (1565), and (1566).

123. "Inventario de la Hacienda de Hermanas . . . ," March 18, 1863, SNP (2887).

124. Juan Blackaller to Juan N. de Arizpe, March 13, 1851, SNP (321); memorandum, February 27, 1850, SNP (3077); monthly reports, April 30, 1851, SNP (2169) and (2399), and July 31, 1851, SNP (2312); "Cuenta liquidación de 484 Ovejas . . . ," May 17, 1850, SNP (3077); account, October, 1860–July, 1862, SNP (2223).

125. Piloncillo: memorandum, October 15, 1850, SNP (3076); Francisco Beráin to Quirino Benavente, January 27, 1851, SNP (513); receipt, January 27, 1851, SNP (514); Quirino Benavente to Juan N. de Arizpe, February 23, 1851, SNP (425); cotton: Juan Blackaller to Juan N. de Arizpe, March 13, 1851, SNP (321); *aguardiente*: William Marshall Anderson, *An American in Maximilian's Mexico, 1865–1866*, ed. Ramón Eduardo Ruiz, pp. 99–100; Jacobo Küchler, *Valles de Sabinas y Salinas*, p. 14; beans: Francisco Beráin to Juan N. de Arizpe, January 8, 1851, SNP (1522); Jacobo Elizondo to Miguel S. Máynez, June 6, 1864, SNP (2154).

126. Memorandum, ——, 1848, SNP (3637); Quirino Benavente to Juan N. de Arizpe, January 12, 1851, SNP (2107); February 16, 1851, SNP (411); memorandum, February 21, 1851, SNP (491); Juan N. de Arizpe to Quirino Benavente, April 26, 1851, SNP (2180); inventory of grain at Patos, July 4, 1851, SNP (2316); Marcial Beráin to Juan Farda, June 14, 1856, SNP (1580).

127. Quirino Benavente to Juan N. de Arizpe, January 30, 1851, SNP (413); Juan N. de Arizpe to Quirino Benavente, March 21, 1851, SNP (2301); May 10,

1851, SNP (673); Ignacio Lozano to same, July 27, 1851, SNP (2325); inventory of grain at Patos, July 4, 1851, SNP (2316).

128. "Cuenta general de la Hacienda de Bonanza con la de Patos . . . ," 1857–December 31, 1860, SNP (2224).

129. Receipt by Pedro Zárate, February 27, 1861, SNP (1576); [draft—Santiago Vidaurri] to Carlos SN, June 17, 1863, AGENL-VA (8191); Juan Ramos to Miguel S. Máynez, January 27, 1865, SNP (727).

130. "Ynformacion *ad perpetuam* . . . ," May 20, 1860, SNP (2355).

131. Carlos [SN] to Jacobo SN, May 25, 1842, SNP (1614); Lorenzo Olivier to same, February 17, 1856, SNP (1611); Marcial Beráin to same, July 26, 1856, SNP (922); August 16, 1856, SNP (1622).

132. Lorenzo Olivier to Jacobo SN, February 17, 1856, SNP (1611); Marcial Beráin to same, July 10, 1856, SNP (1639); August 16, 1856, SNP (1622); Jacobo SN's account with Bonanza, October, 1860–July, 1862, SNP (2223) and July 30–August 19, 1862, SNP (2214).

133. Marcial Beráin to Juan Farda, June 14, 1856, SNP (1580); "Ynformacion *ad perpetuam* . . . ," May 20, 1860, SNP (2355).

134. Inventory of Bonanza, October 1, 1860, SNP (2219); "Balance hecho á la Hacienda de Bonanza . . . ," October 1, 1860–June 30, 1862, SNP (2241) and (2242).

135. "Balance hecho á la Hacienda de Bonanza . . . ," October 1, 1860– June 30, 1862, SNP (2241).

11. COMMERCE

1. Román de Letona to José Melchor SN, June 7, 1822, SNP (850); José Gerónimo Cacho to same, October 29, 1822, SNP (3113); December 29, 1822, SNP (3112); Joaquín María Camacho to same, May 14, 1822, SNP (863); May 18, 1823, SNP (168); February 20, 1824, SNP (3123); Apolonia Beráin de SN to same, September 29, 1823, SNP (3257); J. J. Madero to same, October 25, 1823, SNP (3122); Rafael Delgado to same, July 8, 1824, SNP (3219); July 21, 1824, SNP (3082); July 27, 1824, SNP (3089); José Melchor SN to Rafael Delgado, July 10, 1824, SNP (997); July 20, 1824, SNP (993); Manuel de la Garza to same, May 6, 1826, SNP (3319).

2. Rafael Delgado to José Melchor SN, January 19, 1825, SNP (3233); Apolonia Beráin [de SN] to Rafael del Valle, November 16, 1826, SNP (1776); receipt by Juan José de Cárdenas, December 21, 1831, SNP (1799).

3. Apolonia Beráin de SN to [José] Melchor [SN], March 5, 1828, SNP (2726).

4. Apolonia Beráin de SN to [José] Melchor [SN], April 16, 1828, SNP (2727); Francisco de Paula Cabrera to same, April 28, 1828, SNP (2833); [José Melchor S]N to [Juan José de]Cárdenas, November 16, 1833, SNP (1235).

5. "No. 7—escritura de la casa . . . ," April 2, 1822, SNP (2361); "N. 6—Escritura del jiron de tierra . . . ," November 5, 1822, SNP (2918); deeds, November 16, 1822, SNP (2577) and March 24, 1832, SNP (458); "No. 41—Escritura de veinte y siete varas . . . ," October 23, 1824, SNP (2363); [José Melchor S]N to [Juan José de] Cárdenas, May 15, 1833, SNP (3500).

6. Luis de Ugartechea to [José] Melchor SN, November 4, 1830, SNP (1570); Pedro de Ballesteros to same, November 5, 1830, SNP (1304); J. M. Ibarra to

same, November 6, 1830, SNP (3516); [draft—José Melchor SN] to Luis de Ugartechea, November 10, 1830, SNP (1248).

7. Juan José de Cárdenas to José Melchor SN, April 20, 1822, SNP (865); September 29, 1823, SNP (3291); note by Juan José de Cárdenas, undated, SNP (20); Román de Letona to José Melchor SN, June 3, 1826, SNP (188); Víctor Blanco to same, July 8, 1826, SNP (1058); Apolonia Beráin de SN to same, March 26, 1828, SNP (2774).

8. "Compromiso celebrado por D. Juan Blacaller y D. José Melchor Sanchez Navarro . . . ," May 7, 1831, SNP (2547) and (2548).

9. Francisco Vidaurri to José Melchor SN, April 25, 1822, SNP (3332); May 26, 1822, SNP (3424); May 27, 1822, SNP (3333); Manuel de Pinunury to same, July 16, 1824, SNP (3203).

10. Rafael González to José Melchor SN, July 1, 1825, SNP (202); Estevan Julian Willson to same, July 28, 1825, SNP (256); Antonio Margil Cano to same, September 19, 1825, SNP (204).

11. Estevan Julian Willson to José Melchor SN, January 1, 1828, SNP (2696); [draft—Ayuntamiento of Santa Rosa] to the Chief of Department, February 27, 1828, SNP (2759).

12. [Atanacio] Rodríguez to [José Melchor SN], May 15, 1830, SNP (825); September 9, 1830, SNP (577); Agustín Martínez to same, January 4, 1833, SNP (121).

13. Manuel Castellano to Apolonia Beráin de SN, July 31, 1829, SNP (710); [José] Melchor [SN] to same, August 1, 1829, SNP (1283); Manuel Castellano to José Melchor SN, January 9, 1830, SNP (1273).

14. Manuel Castellano to José Melchor SN, September 22, 1824, SNP (3214); October 3, 1824, SNP (221); April 9, 1826, SNP (186); May 3, 1826, SNP (215); receipt by Marcos Vázquez, June 16, 1831, SNP (746).

15. Francisco Vidaurri to José Melchor SN, May 27, 1822, SNP (3333); Juan José de Cárdenas to Apolonia Beráin de SN, August 4, 1823, SNP (3141); Manuel Castellano to José Melchor SN, October 10, 1824, SNP (35); Apolonia [Beráin de SN] to same, December 20, 1826, SNP (87); January 30, 1828, SNP (2714); [José] Melchor [SN] to Apolonia Beráin de SN, January 29, 1830, SNP (1286); same to [Juan José de] Cárdenas, November 6, 1830, SNP (3312); November 15, 1830, SNP (3413); Manuel Castellano to Apolonia Beráin de SN, February 1, 1833, SNP (3415); same to Juan José de Cárdenas, December 31, 1833, SNP (1227).

16. Manuel Castellano to José Melchor SN, September 30, 1822, SNP (2611); May 3, 1826, SNP (215); Atanacio Muñoz to same, January 1, 1828, SNP (2748); Manuel Castellano to Juan José de Cárdenas, August 16, 1828, SNP (2841); December 22, 1833, SNP (1230); January 13, 1834, SNP (1226); same to Apolonia Beráin de SN, January 2, 1831, SNP (1296).

17. Apolonia Beráin de SN to [José] Melchor [SN], February 20, 1828, SNP (2782); Francisco Careaga to same, June 10, 1833, SNP (2451).

18. Apolonia Beráin de SN to [José] Melchor [SN], February 13, 1828, SNP (2730); February 27, 1828, SNP (2719); Manuel Castellano to same, March 5, 1826, SNP (3155); September 24, 1826, SNP (2478); Francisco Quintana to same, January 23, 1824, SNP (3221); Francisco Vidaurri to same, undated, SNP (3238); Rafael Delgado to same, February 2, 1826, SNP (182); Felipe de los Santos to same,

September 8, 1826, SNP (197); José María de la Vega to same, March 13, 1828, SNP (2780); Pedro Santa Cruz to same, August 27, 1831, SNP (769).

19. Juan José de Cárdenas to José Melchor SN, April 20, 1822, SNP (865); Apolonia Beráin de SN to same, February 6, 1828, SNP (2752).

20. Rafael Delgado to [José] Melchor SN, May 14, 1822, SNP (849); August 5, 1822, SNP (3129); Manuel José de Cárdenas to same, June 9, 1822, SNP (848); invoice, May 27, 1823, SNP (3153).

21. Manuel de Pirunury to [José] Melchor SN, July 16, 1824, SNP (3203); Eugenio de Olaez to same, January 12, 1830, SNP (2608); Fermín de Goyzueta to same, July 19, 1822, SNP (3426); January 16, 1823, SNP (3115); Rafael Delgado to [same], August 10, 1826, SNP (2472); José María de Letona to same, December 5, 1826, SNP (167).

22. Antonio de la Vega to [José] Melchor SN, May 14, 1824, SNP (3231); guía, August 30, 1835, SNP (590); invoice, August 30, 1835, SNP (593).

23. Ramón Múzquiz to [José] Melchor SN, January 18, 1830, SNP (2587); "Compromiso celebrado por D. Juan Blacaller y D. José Melchor Sanchez Navarro . . . .," May 7, 1831, SNP (2547) and (2548).

24. Guía, March 23, 1842, SNP (871); receipt by Francisco Pellegrín, June 4, 1842, SNP (870); Luis Valdés to Jacobo SN, May 30, 1842, SNP (869); August 12, 1842, SNP (886).

25. "Reconocimiento de las Cuentas . . . ," March 4, 1842, MCSN; Santiago Hewetson to Jacobo SN, March 4, 1842, SNP (1007).

26. Carlos [SN] to Jacobo SN, May 25, 1842, SNP (1614); July 9, 1843, SNP (540).

27. Invoice, June 28, 1844, SNP (1505); invoice, January 29, 1845, SNP (538); Susan Shelby Magoffin, Down the Santa Fe Trail and into Mexico, ed. Stella M. Drumm, pp. 239–240; Josiah Gregg, Diary and Letters of Josiah Gregg, ed. Maurice Garland Fulton, II, 86.

28. "Facturas de la Feria del Saltillo en 1845," 1845, SNP (1604).

29. Jesús Salas to Jacobo SN, July 29, 1845, MCSN; Rafael Jove to same, May 15, 1846, SNP (1593); Miguel SN to same, September 2, 1846, MCSN.

30. Segundo de Agüero to Jacobo SN, September 13, 1847, MCSN.

31. Invoice, October 6, 1847, SNP (3617).

32. Accounts by Román Flores, February 16, 1842, SNP (1004) and October 8, 1842, SNP (1006); Luis Valdés to Jacobo SN, September 1, 1842, SNP (892); November 12, 1842, SNP (2638); November 14, 1842, SNP (2637); Juan N. de Arizpe to same, December 8, 1842, SNP (1628); Melchor Lobo Pereyra to same, December 24, 1842, SNP (1473); Eduardo González to same, December 25, 1842, SNP (1472); December 29, 1842, SNP (2633); Miguel SN to same, January 29, 1844, MCSN.

33. Carlos [SN] to Jacobo SN, July 9, 1843, SNP (540).

34. Santiago Rodríguez to Jacobo SN, July 24, 1845, MCSN.

35. Carlos [SN] to Jacobo [SN], March 24, 1847, MCSN.

36. Carlos [SN] to Jacobo [SN], April 14, 1847, MCSN; April 28, 1847, MCSN; Miguel SN to same, November [?] 14, 1847, MCSN; Ignacio Lozano to same, December 19, 1847, MCSN.

37. Juan Vicente Campos to Jacobo SN, February 5, 1848, MCSN; May 9, 1848, MCSN; Gregg, *Diary*, II, 226–228.

38. Jacobo SN to Juan N. de Arizpe, January 15, 1851, SNP (289); January 16, 1851, SNP (290); February 21, 1851, SNP (295).

39. Juan F. de Puyade to Jacobo SN, June 4, 1851, SNP (436); Puyade's monthly accounts, December 30, 1852, SNP (2210) and November 30, 1853, SNP (2218).

40. Juan N. de Arizpe to Quirino Benavente, April 1, 1851, SNP (2262); for Drusina see Daniel W. Coit, *Digging for Gold—without a Shovel*, ed. George P. Hammond, pp. 31–35 ff.

41. Lilia Díaz (ed.), *Versión francesa de México*, I, 56, 324, 374, II, 7; Manuel Payno, *Carta que sobre los asuntos de México dirige al señor General Forey comandante en gefe de las tropas francesas el ciudadano Manuel Payno*, p. 72.

42. Jacobo SN to Juan N. de Arizpe, February 26, 1851, SNP (367).

43. Alejandro Bellangé to Jacobo SN, May 24, 1851, SNP (569); José Ignacio Baz to same, May 24, 1851, SNP (434); October 11, 1851, SNP (2121); Gustavo de Pavia to same, June 2, 1851, SNP (431).

44. Charles H. Harris III, *The Sánchez Navarros*, p. 68; Rafael Aguirre to Jacobo SN, September 29, 1851, SNP (390).

45. Juan F. de Puyade to Jacobo SN, September 13, 1851, SNP (2128); October 11, 1851, SNP (2115); November 1, 1851, SNP (355); November 19, 1851, SNP (2125).

46. Juan F. de Puyade to Jacobo SN, November 1, 1851, SNP (355).

47. Jacobo SN to Rafael Aguirre, September 29, 1851, SNP (383); October 18, 1851, SNP (386); Rafael Aguirre to Jacobo SN, October 6, 1851, SNP (388); October 9, 1851, SNP (387); October 27, 1851, SNP (391); Rafael Aguirre's account, November 14, 1851, SNP (384); see also Harris, *The Sánchez Navarros*, pp. 70–71.

48. Rafael Aguirre to Jacobo SN, October 30, 1851, SNP (392); November 3, 1851, SNP (394).

49. Rafael Aguirre to Jacobo SN, November 6, 1851, SNP (397); Rafael Delgado to same, November 3, 1851, SNP (376).

50. Jacobo SN to Rafael Aguirre, November 9, 1851, SNP (393); Rafael Aguirre to Jacobo SN, November 17, 1851, SNP (398); December 18, 1851, SNP (395); December 25, 1851, SNP (396); Juan F. de Puyade to same, December 3, 1851, SNP (2142); December 6, 1851, SNP (2141); December 10, 1851, SNP (2140); December 24, 1851, SNP (2139).

51. Harris, *The Sánchez Navarros*, p. 71.

52. [Draft—Jacobo SN] to Luis del Conde, October 6, 1851, SNP (2130); Luis del Conde to Jacobo SN, October 29, 1851, SNP (2129); Juan F. de Puyade to same, October 1, 1851, SNP (2113).

53. José Ignacio Baz to Jacobo SN, November 26, 1851, SNP (2117).

54. Juan F. de Puyade to Jacobo SN, September 13, 1851, SNP (2128); October 1, 1851, SNP (2113); October 11, 1851, SNP (2115); November 19, 1851, SNP (2125); December 3, 1851, SNP (2142); December 10, 1851, SNP (2140); Puyade's monthly account, December 30, 1852, SNP (2210).

55. Puyade's monthly accounts, November 30, 1853, SNP (2218) and July 31, 1856, SNP (2209); Juan F. de Puyade to Jacobo SN, July 26, 1856, SNP (860).

56. Juan F. de Puyade to Jacobo SN, October 11, 1851, SNP (2115); November 1, 1851, SNP (355).

57. "Balance hecho á la Hacienda de Bonanza . . . ," October 1, 1860–June 30, 1862, SNP (2241); Lorenzo Olivier to Jacobo SN, February 17, 1856, SNP (1611).

58. Jacobo SN to Juan N. de Arizpe, February 15, 1851, SNP (296); Juan F. de Puyade to Quirino Benavente, June 13, 1851, SNP (622); July 20, 1851, SNP (2326) and (2327).

59. Juan F. de Puyade to Jacobo SN, August 15, 1851, SNP (2135).

60. Puyade's monthly accounts, December 30, 1851, SNP (2210), November 30, 1853, SNP (2218), and July 31, 1856, SNP (2209); Juan F. de Puyade to Jacobo SN, July 26, 1856, SNP (860).

61. Statement of account, March 1, 1851, SNP (2123).

62. Puyade's monthly accounts, December 30, 1852, SNP (2210), November 30, 1853, SNP (2218); June 30, 1856, SNP (2220), July 31, 1856, SNP (2209), and February 28, 1857, SNP (2207).

63. Juan F. de Puyade to Jacobo SN, August 6, 1856, SNP (1511).

64. Invoices, October 18 and 31, 1850, SNP (3076).

65. Francisco Beráin to Juan N. de Arizpe, February 19, 1851, SNP (1524); same to Quirino Benavente, February 19, 1851, SNP (521); Claudio Aguirre to same, February 26, 1851, SNP (516); March 1, 1851, SNP (2307); Demetrio Lucio to same, May 3, 1851, SNP (1544); Quirino Benavente to Juan N. de Arizpe, February 12, 1851, SNP (1551); memorandum, April 30, 1851, SNP (2175); Miguel SN to Jacobo Elizondo, August 20, 1851, SNP (2530).

66. Jacobo SN to Rafael Aguirre, September 29, 1851, SNP (383).

67. Jacobo SN to Juan Farda, June 12, 1856, SNP (800); Marcial Beráin to Jacobo SN, July 10, 1856, SNP (1639); July 26, 1856, SNP (922); August 16, 1856, SNP (1622).

68. Rafael Delgado to Jacobo SN, August 14, 1851, SNP (373); August 25, 1851, SNP (374); September 4, 1851, SNP (375); October 27, 1851, SNP (371); same to Juan N. de Arizpe, September 15, 1851, SNP (377); same to Jacobo SN, September 18, 1851, SNP (378); November 3, 1851, SNP (376).

69. Francisco Beráin to Jacobo SN, June 25, 1851, SNP (329); Lorenzo Olivier to same, February 17, 1856, SNP (1611).

70. Jacobo SN to Santiago Vidaurri, June 5, 1858, AGENL-VA (8182); June 8, 1858, AGENL-VA (8184).

71. "Ynventario de los intereses pertenecientes á la Compañia . . . ," September 13, 1857–December 12, 1862, SNP (2889).

72. Treasury statements, February 19 and 27, 1862, SNP (2213) and (2211).

73. Deed, July 30, 1862, SNP (2886).

74. Jacobo SN's account with Bonanza, July 30–August 19, 1862, SNP (2214); Rivero y Cia. to Miguel S. Máynez, December 7, 1864, SNP (1597); Hilario Avila to same, August 3, 1864, SNP (2145).

75. "Balance de la Tienda de Bonanza . . . ," July 30, 1862, SNP (2225); see also "Inventario de la Hacienda de Hermanas . . . ," March 18, 1863, SNP (2887); account book for an unidentified store, 1863–1864, SNP (2423); José María Cavazos

to Miguel S. Máynez, February 25, 1864, SNP (1498); Jacobo Elizondo to same, May 12, 1864, SNP (2153).

76. See Román Méndez to Carlos Viesca, March 10, 1865; Luis Arteaga to Miguel S. Máynez, July 14, 1865, SNP (991).

12. POLITICS

1. "1810 Relación."

2. Ibid.

3. Pedro Valdés to José Melchor SN, October 29, 1823, SNP (3223).

4. Francisco Vidaurri to José Melchor SN, May 26, 1822, SNP (3424); José Francisco del Castillo to same, September 12, 1822, SNP (3331); Nicolás Beráin to same, October 16, 1823, SNP (3245); "Autos seguidos por D. Melchor Sanchez Nabarro . . . ," 1824, AGEC, legajo 15, carpeta 767.

5. Francisco Vidaurri to José Melchor SN, January 17, 1824, SNP (3120); Antonio Crespo to same, October 19, 1824, SNP (224).

6. Petition from Rafael Delgado to the Governor of Coahuila and Texas, August 9, 1825, SNP (2366); certificate by Francisco Ignacio Taboada, May 2, 1826, SNP (1786); same to Jose Melchor SN, April 8, 1826, SNP (173).

7. Rafael Delgado to José Melchor SN, December 9, 1825, SNP (210); December 19, 1825, SNP (180); May 21, 1826, SNP (1783); August 25, 1826, SNP (1065).

8. [José] Miguel SN to [José Melchor SN], October 19, 1826, and draft of latter's reply, November 22, 1826, SNP (1300); January 1, 1827, SNP (1355); Luciano Flores to [José] Miguel SN, December 9, 1826, SNP (1727); December 16, 1826, SNP (3396); [José Miguel SN] to Luciano Flores, December 30, 1826, SNP (1354).

9. José Francisco del Castillo to José Melchor SN, January 23, 1827, SNP (217).

10. "Lista municipal de los Ciudadanos . . . ," May 13, 1827, SNP (2832); Melitón Castellano to José Melchor SN, January 13, 1828, SNP (1216).

11. Agustín Martínez to José Melchor SN, January 21, 1828, SNP (1217); José Francisco del Castillo to same, January 27, 1828, SNP (2751); Melitón Castellano and José Francisco del Castillo to same, February 10, 1828, SNP (2849); February 24, 1828, SNP (2739); draft of the Ayuntamiento of Santa Rosa's report, February 27, 1828, SNP (2759).

12. Melitón Castellano to José Melchor SN, January 27, 1828, SNP (1219); José María de Aguirre to [Melitón Castellano], February 22, 1828, SNP (1210); Melitón Castellano and José Francisco del Castillo to [José Melchor SN], March 9, 1828, SNP (2781); March 23, 1828, SNP (2746); Agustín Martínez to same, March 23, 1828, SNP (1220).

13. Rafael del Valle to [José] Melchor SN, December 18, 1826, SNP (948); January 4, 1827, SNP (1353).

14. Domingo de Ugartechea to [José] Melchor SN, January 16, 1828, SNP (2709); José María Uranga to same, January 16, 1828, SNP (2731); February 20, 1828, SNP (2760).

15. Rafael Delgado to [José Melchor SN], May 21, 1826, SNP (1783); Víctor Blanco to same, July 8, 1826, SNP (1058) and (3608); petition by Felipe Enrique Neri, the Baron de Bastrop, October 20, 1826, SNP (272).

16. José Alejandro de Treviño to José Melchor SN, October 23, 1826, SNP (1063).

17. Felipe Enrique Neri, the Baron de Bastrop, to [José] Melchor SN, November 4, 1826, SNP (2383); Juan Vicente Campos to same, November 18, 1826, SNP (3015); [draft—José Melchor SN] to José Alejandro de Treviño, December 13, 1826, SNP (941); [draft—same] to Agustín Martínez, December 16, 1826, SNP (941).

18. Juan Vicente Campos to [José] Melchor SN, June 23, 1827, SNP (1018).

19. Alessio Robles, Coahuila y Texas, desde la consumación, I, 250.

20. Apolonia Beráin de SN to [José] Melchor [SN], April 23, 1828, SNP (2703); April 30, 1828, SNP (2772); J. Antonio González to same, May 3, 1828, SNP (2842); May 9, 1828, SNP (2817); May 17, 1828, SNP (2820); Francisco Sánchez to same, May 17, 1828, SNP (2785); Ramón García Rojas to same, May 24, 1828, SNP (2792); July 26, 1828, SNP (2831); Domingo de Ugartechea to same, May 29, 1828, SNP (2788); June 13, 1828, SNP (2786); June 27, 1828, SNP (2809); July 11, 1828, SNP (2824); [José] Melchor [SN] to [Juan José de] Cárdenas, August 8, 1828, SNP (2836); August 23, 1828, SNP (2835); October 7, 1828, SNP (2857); the point at issue was Decree No. 50, for which see H. P. N. Gammel (ed.), The Laws of Texas, 1822–1897, I, 211, 317.

21. Domingo de Ugartechea to [José] Melchor SN, May 16, 1828, SNP (2790); June 13, 1828, SNP (2786).

22. Ramón García Rojas to José Melchor SN, May 17, 1828, SNP (2819); May 20, 1828, SNP (2803); May 24, 1828, SNP (2792); José Melchor SN to [Juan José de] Cárdenas, October 7, 1828, SNP (2857).

23. "Testimonio del espediente . . . ," September 27, 1827–June 3, 1829, SNP (2914); copy of the supreme court's ruling, August 29, 1829, SNP (2602).

24. Antonio de la Vega to [José] Melchor SN, May 14, 1824, SNP (3231); José Alejandro de Treviño to same, July 12, 1824, SNP (3102); Mariano Varela to same, July 13, 1824, SNP (3096); José Antonio Rodríguez to same, July 26, 1824, SNP (3086); Antonio Crespo to same, July 29, 1824, SNP (3098); July 30, 1824, SNP (3083); Estevan J. Willson to same, January 1, 1828, SNP (2696); Apolonia Beráin de SN to same, July 27, 1824, SNP (3193); Aguila Mexicana, April 1–4, 1827, SNP (157–160).

25. Pedro Vidaurri to José Melchor SN, January 9, 1830, SNP (806); Juan Martínez to same, January 10, 1830, SNP (3330); Ayuntamiento of Candela to same, January 26, 1830, SNP (2439); Juan Estevan Beráin to same, June 18, 1830, SNP (1715); José Francisco del Castillo to same, July 6, 1831, SNP (3292); [José] Melchor [SN] to [Apolonia Beráin de SN], February 1, 1830, SNP (1288); deed, March 24, 1832, SNP (458).

26. Joaquín Reynoso to [José] Melchor SN, March 9, 1830, SNP (815); Juan Vicente Campos to same, April 7, 1830, SNP (783).

27. Esteban L. Portillo, Anuario Coahuilense para 1886, p. 72.

28. José Ignacio SN to José Melchor SN, February 15, 1832, SNP (84).

29. [José] Melchor [SN] to Apolonia [Beráin de SN], July 22, 1832, SNP (1019).

30. Carlos and Jacobo SN to [Apolonia Beráin de SN], August ——, 1832, SNP (793); December 5, 1832, SNP (3513); Juan Vicente Campos to [José]

Melchor SN, December 21, 1832, SNP (795); December 22, 1832, SNP (122); January 5, 1833, SNP (125); Francisco Careaga to same, December 29, 1832, SNP (123); Angel María Garibay K. et al. (comps.), *Diccionario Porrúa de historia, biografía y geografía de México*, p. 1082.

31. [José] Melchor [SN] to Apolonia [Beráin de SN], July 22, 1832, SNP (1019); August 2, 1832, SNP (3498).

32. Juan Vicente Campos to José Melchor SN, December 22, 1832, SNP (122); January 5, 1833, SNP (125); June 8, 1833, SNP (1351); September 9, 1833, SNP (3457); [José] Melchor [SN] to Apolonia Beráin de SN, March 9, 1833, SNP (3483); same to [Juan José de] Cárdenas, April 26, 1833, SNP (3487); November 16, 1833, SNP (1235).

33. Juan José de Cárdenas to José Melchor SN, December 11, 1833, SNP (1750); December 18, 1833, SNP (2425); [José Melchor S]N to [Juan José de] Cárdenas, December 14, 1833, SNP (1234); December 19, 1833, SNP (1237).

34. José Melchor SN to Matías ———, October 13, 1834, SNP (2901).

35. [José Melchor S]N to Juan José de Cárdenas, October 18, 1834, SNP (1243).

36. [José Melchor S]N to Juan José de Cárdenas, October 24, 1834, SNP (1242); October 27, 1834, SNP (1241).

37. Passport, May 15, 1835, SNP (3316).

38. Passport, October 29, 1835, SNP (591).

39. Juan José de Cárdenas to José Melchor SN, February 6, 1836, SNP (596).

40. J. Antonio Tijerina to [Juan José de Cárdenas], December 18, 1837, SNP (1262); [draft—Juan José de Cárdenas] to J. Antonio Tijerina, December 19, 1837, SNP (1263).

41. Jesús de la Garza to Jacobo SN, June 11, 1838, SNP (732).

42. Rafael González to Jacobo SN, April 9, 1842, SNP (867); April 23, 1842, SNP (884); May 7, 1842, SNP (872); June 11, 1842, SNP (874).

43. Carlos [SN] to Jacobo SN, May 25, 1842, SNP (1614).

44. Rafael González to Jacobo SN, June 15, 1842, SNP (1632).

45. Garibay et al. (comps.), *Diccionario Porrúa*, p. 1082.

46. Juan N. de Arizpe to Jacobo SN, August 26, 1842, SNP (986); Rafael González to same, September 4, 1842, SNP (889).

47. Juan N. de Arizpe to Jacobo SN, December 3, 1842, SNP (1636).

48. Juan N. de Arizpe to Jacobo SN, December 8, 1842, SNP (1628).

49. Juan Vicente Campos to Jacobo SN, December 27, 1842, SNP (1476).

50. J. M. Ibarra to Jacobo SN, June 8, 1842, SNP (1481); November 7, 1842, SNP (1013); November 14, 1842, SNP (2636); June 29, 1843, MCSN; Juan N. de Arizpe to same, December 23, 1842, SNP (1734).

51. Apolonia Beráin de SN to [José] Melchor [SN], January 16, 1828, SNP (2697); January 23, 1828, SNP (2717); Atanacio Muñoz to same, January 21, 1828, SNP (2749); José Juan SN to same, January 26, 1828, SNP (2721); José Juan SN and Ana Petra de la Peña [de SN] to Apolonia Beráin de SN, January 18, 1828, SNP (2720).

52. The diary is in the two-volume index to his records as inspector: JJSNP, Boxes (A 14/71) and (A 14/72). See also Carlos Sánchez Navarro [y Peón] (ed.), *La Guerra de Tejas*, and Helen Hunnicut, "A Mexican View of the Texas War," *The Library Chronicle of the University of Texas* 4, no. 2 (Summer 1951).

53. Juan N. de Arizpe to Jacobo SN, July 21, 1845, MCSN; August 6, 1845, MCSN.

54. Santiago Rodríguez to Jacobo SN, July 24, 1845, MCSN.

55. Juan N. de Arizpe to Jacobo SN, November 16, 1846, MCSN.

56. Harwood Perry Hinton, "The Military Career of John Ellis Wool, 1812–1863," Ph.D. dissertation, p. 195.

57. Francis Baylies, *A Narrative of Major General Wool's Campaign in Mexico in the Years 1846, 1847 & 1848*, p. 21. See also Hughes, *Memoir*, p. 42.

58. Hinton, "Military Career of John Ellis Wool," p. 202.

59. H. Boultbee to Jacobo SN, January 21, 1847, MCSN. See also Josiah Gregg, *Diary and Letters of Josiah Gregg*, ed. Maurice Garland Fulton, I, 315–316, 318, 326–329.

60. United States, House of Representatives, *Correspondence between the Secretary of War and Generals Scott and Taylor, and between General Scott and Mr. Trist*, p. 368.

61. Hinton, "Military Career of John Ellis Wool," p. 208; cf. Gregg, *Diary*, II, 37.

62. Samuel E. Chamberlain, *My Confession*, ed. Roger Butterfield, pp. 173–174.

63. Hughes, *Memoir*, p. 40; see also Gregg, *Diary*, I, 275–276, 282.

64. Juan N. de Arizpe to Jacobo SN, March 18, 1847, MCSN; Portillo, *Anuario Coahuilense*, p. 42; Hughes, *Memoir*, p. 40.

65. Baylies, *Narrative*, p. 21; H. Boultbee to Jacobo SN, March 8, 1847, MCSN; Hughes, *Memoir*, p. 40; United States, *Correspondence between the Secretary of War*, pp. 296–298.

66. Hunnicut, "A Mexican View," p. 68.

67. Eduardo González to Jacobo SN, March 16, 1847, MCSN; receipt by José Ignacio SN, March 28, 1847, MCSN.

68. H. Boultbee to Jacobo SN, March 8, 1847, MCSN; Simón Elizondo to same, March 13, 1847, MCSN; Jacobo Elizondo to same, March 22, 1847, MCSN.

69. H. Boultbee to Jacobo SN, March 16, 1847, SNP (1592); Juan N. de Arizpe to same, March 18, 1847, MCSN.

70. H. Boultbee to Jacobo SN, March 19, 1847, MCSN; March 28, 1847, SNP (1005).

71. Valeriano Sánchez to Jacobo SN, September 6, 1847, MCSN.

72. Susan Shelby Magoffin, *Down the Santa Fe Trail and into Mexico*, ed. Stella M. Drumm, p. 235.

73. Gregg, *Diary*, II, 231–232; Hunnicut, "A Mexican View," p. 68.

74. Gregg, *Diary*, II, 237–238; Portillo, *Anuario Coahuilense*, p. 74; José Ignacio Baz to Jacobo SN, September 13, 1851, SNP (2120).

75. Juan Nepomuceno Almonte, *Guía de forasteros, y repertorio de conocimientos útiles*, p. 38.

76. Cosme Garza García (comp.), *Prontuario de leyes y decretos del estado de Coahuila de Zaragoza*, p. 28.

77. Ibid., p. 256.

78. Francisco Beráin to the Junta Calificadora de la Villa de Múzquiz, April 3, 1851, SNP (342); Rafael Adalpe to Juan N. de Arizpe, April 6, 1851, SNP (343); Francisco Beráin to same, May 14, 1851, SNP (309).

79. "Como Apoderado del Sor. D. Jacobo Sánchez Navarro . . . ," April 26,

1851, SNP (2110); "Valores que las Juntas Calificadoras . . . ," April 26, 1851, SNP (2110); Juan N. de Arizpe to Jacobo SN, June 15, 1851, SNP (430); June 22, 1851, SNP (323).

80. NA, Mexican Docket, Claim 131.

81. Jacobo SN to Juan N. de Arizpe, January 2, 1851, SNP (2168); Angel María Garibay K. et al. (comps.), *Diccionario Porrúa de historia, biografía y geografía de México: Suplemento*, p. 155.

82. Jacobo SN to Juan N. de Arizpe, February 1, 1851, SNP (293); March 12, 1851, SNP (299); undated instructions [February, 1851], SNP (294).

83. Francisco Zarco, *Crónica del Congreso Extraordinario Constituyente, 1856–1857*, ed. Catalina Sierra Casasús, pp. 597, 850–852.

84. Ibid., pp. 593–597; Edward H. Moseley, "The Public Career of Santiago Vidaurri, 1855–1858," Ph.D. dissertation, pp. 110, 245; Garibay et al. (comps.), *Diccionario Porrúa*, p. 209.

85. Jacobo SN to Santiago Vidaurri, February 5, 1856, AGENL-VA (8169).

86. Ibid.; Zarco, *Crónica del Congreso Extraordinario Constituyente*, pp. 113, 151, 854.

87. Jacobo SN to Santiago Vidaurri, February 5 and 13, 1856, AGENL-VA (8169) and (8170).

88. Jacobo SN to Santiago Vidaurri, February 5, 1856, AGENL-VA (8169).

89. Moseley, "Public Career of Santiago Vidaurri," pp. 50, 183–186.

90. Zarco, *Crónica del Congreso Extraordinario Constituyente*, pp. 853–855.

91. Ibid., p. 856.

92. Emilio Bohme to Jacobo SN, June 4, 1856, SNP (1613); Jacobo SN to Santiago Vidaurri, July 5, 1856, AGENL-VA (8171).

93. Carlos SN to Santiago Vidaurri, April 12, 1857, AGENL-VA (8172); [draft—Santiago Vidaurri] to Carlos SN, April 15, 1857, AGENL-VA (8173).

94. Carlos SN to Santiago Vidaurri, May 25, 1857, AGENL-VA (8174); July 4, 1857, AGENL-VA (8175); [draft—Santiago Vidaurri] to Carlos SN, July 8, 1857, AGENL-VA (8176).

95. Carlos SN to Santiago Vidaurri, August 4, 1857, AGENL-VA (8177); September 23, 1857, AGENL-VA (8181); [draft—Santiago Vidaurri] to Carlos SN, August 16, 1857, AGENL-VA (8178); [same] to Jacobo SN, August 16, 1857, AGENL-VA (8179); Jacobo SN to Santiago Vidaurri, August 22, 1857, AGENL-VA (8180).

96. Jacobo SN to Santiago Vidaurri, June 5, 1858, AGENL-VA (8182).

97. [Drafts—Santiago Vidaurri] to Jacobo SN, June 6 and 9, 1858, AGENL-VA (8183) and (8185); Jacobo SN to Santiago Vidaurri, June 8, 1858, AGENL-VA (8184).

98. Vicente Riva Palacio (ed.), *México á través de los siglos*, V, 272.

99. Ibid., p. 346.

100. José Ramón Malo, *Diario de sucesos notables*, ed. Mariano Cuevas, S.J., II, 577; United States, Senate, *Message from the President of the United States, Communicating, In Answer to a Resolution of the Senate of the 25th Ultimo, Papers Relative to Mexican Affairs*, p. 224.

101. Israel Cavazos Garza (ed.), *Epistolario Zaragoza-Vidaurri, 1855–1859*, pp. 56, 71, 74, 77.

102. See Jan Bazant, "The Division of Some Mexican *Haciendas* during the Liberal Revolution, 1856–1862," *Journal of Latin American Studies* 3, part 1 (May 1971).

103. Santiago Roel (ed.), *Correspondencia Particular de D. Santiago Vidaurri, Gobernador de Nuevo León (1855–1864)*, pp. 48, 52.

104. Demetrio Lucio to Carlos SN, October 21, 1861, SNP (2215).

105. Roel (ed.), *Correspondencia Particular*, pp. 173–174; Jorge L. Tamayo (ed.), *Benito Juárez*, VII, 361–362.

106. [Draft—Santiago Vidaurri] to Carlos SN, June 17, 1863, AGENL-VA (8191); July 25, 1863, AGENL-VA (8192); Carlos SN to Santiago Vidaurri, July 30, 1863, AGENL-VA (8193).

107. Manuel Payno, *Cuentas, Gastos, Acreedores y otros asuntos del tiempo de la Intervención francesa y del Imperio*, pp. 697–698.

108. Marianne Oeste de Bopp, *Maximiliano y los alemanes*, pp. 198–201; Egon Caesar Corti, *Maximilian and Charlotte of Mexico*, trans. Catherine Alison Phillips, II, 535; Bertita Harding, *Phantom Crown*, pp. 231–232; José Luis Blasio, *Maximilian Emperor of Mexico*, trans. and ed. Robert H. Murray, pp. 114–115; Paul Gaulot, *L'Expédition du Mexique (1861–1867)*, II, 398; Samuel Basch, *Recuerdos de México*, trans. Manuel Peredo, p. 63.

109. José I. Palomo to Manuel Romero de Terreros, November 10, 1864, in Manuel Romero de Terreros, *Maximiliano y el imperio*, p. 42.

110. Carlota to the Empress Eugénie, February 3, 1865, in Corti, *Maximilian and Charlotte*, II, 880; Ignacio Algara y Gómez de la Casa, *La corte de Maximiliano*, ed. Manuel Romero de Terreros, pp. 26, 53–54, 65.

111. Arnold Blumberg, "A Swedish Diplomat in Mexico, 1864," *Hispanic American Historical Review* 45, no. 2 (May 1965): 279–280, 282.

112. Riva Palacio (ed.), *México á través de los siglos*, V, 691.

113. Ibid., V, 714; Marshal Bazaine to Maximilian, May 29, 1865, in Emile de Kératry, *Elevación y caída del emperador Maximiliano*, trans. Hilarión Frías y Soto, p. 72.

114. Carlos SN to Matthew F. Maury, October 28, 1865, WMAP (AD327); William Marshall Anderson, *An American in Maximilian's Mexico, 1865–1866*, ed. Ramón Eduardo Ruiz, p. xxv (though on p. 118, note 2, the amount is given as ten million acres).

115. Major Loysel to Maximilian, June 5, 1865, in Eugene Lefevre, *Documentos oficiales recogidos en la secretaría privada de Maximiliano*, II, 226.

116. Anderson, *An American in Maximilian's Mexico*, p. xxx; Carlos SN to Miguel S. Máynez, October 14, 1865, WMAP (AD326); M. F. Maury to W. M. Anderson, November 24, 1865, WMAP (AD261); same to Jacobo Küchler, November 24, 1865, WMAP (AD262); J. Küchler to W. M. Anderson, December 29, 1865, WMAP (AD238).

117. José de Jesús Cuevas, *Las confiscaciones en México*, p. 7.

118. Benito Juárez to General Mariano Escobedo, March 27, 1865, in Tamayo (ed.), *Benito Juárez*, IX, 730.

119. Quoted in Cuevas, *Las confiscaciones*, pp. 7–8.

120. W. M. Anderson to Ellen Columba Ryan Anderson, April 6, 1866, WMAP (AD85).

121. Anderson, *An American in Maximilian's Mexico*, pp. 118–125.

122. Cuevas, *Las confiscaciones*, pp. 8–9.

123. Andrés Viesca to Benito Juárez, August 26, 1866, in Tamayo (ed.), *Benito Juárez*, XI, 247–248; Cuevas, *Las confiscaciones*, p. 11; José María Luján (ed.), *El libro secreto de Maximiliano*, p. 102.

124. Cuevas, *Las confiscaciones*, pp. 9–10.

125. *Almanaque Imperial para el año de 1866*, pp. 13, 238.

126. Sara Yorke Stevenson, *Maximilian in Mexico*, p. 223.

127. Ibid., p. 202.

128. Maximilian to Carlos SN, November 8, 1866, in Carlos Sánchez Navarro y Peón (ed.), *Tres Cartas inéditas Del Emperador Maximiliano*, pp. 15–16.

129. Maximilian to Marshal Bazaine, November 12, 1866, in Lilia Díaz (ed.), *Versión francesa de México*, IV, 422–423. See also Kératry, *Elevación y caída del emperador Maximiliano*, pp. 244–245; Charles Blanchot, *Mémoires*, III, 296–297.

130. General Miguel Miramón to Prefect Bureau, November 12, 1866, in E. Masseras, *Un Essai d'Empire au Mexique*, p. 105.

131. Corti, *Maximilian and Charlotte*, II, 731.

132. Basch, *Recuerdos*, p. 63.

133. Ibid., pp. 63, 65.

134. Ibid., p. 221; Lefevre, *Documentos oficiales*, II, 362–367; Tamayo (ed.), *Benito Juárez*, XI, 700–703; Riva Palacio (ed.), *México á través de los siglos*, V, 803–807; Emmanuel Domenech, *Histoire du Mexique*, III, 411–412.

135. Corti, *Maximilian and Charlotte*, II, 784–785, 787.

136. Maximilian to Carlos SN, March 19, 1867, in Sánchez Navarro (ed.), *Tres Cartas*, pp. 17–18.

137. Maximilian to Carlos SN, March 21, 1867, in ibid., pp. 19–24. See also Corti, *Maximilian and Charlotte*, II, 789–790.

138. Leonardo Márquez, *Manifiestos (El Imperio y los Imperiales)*, ed. Angel Pola, p. 46.

139. Maximilian to Agustín Fischer, May 29, 1867, in Felix Salm-Salm, *My Diary in Mexico in 1867, Including the Last Days of the Emperor Maximilian*, II, 48–49.

140. Maximilian to Carlos SN, June 13, 1867, in Díaz (ed.), *Versión francesa*, IV, 494–495.

141. Márquez, *Manifiestos*, pp. 188, 229.

142. Payno, *Cuentas*, p. 724.

143. Hartford Montgomery Hyde, *Mexican Empire*, p. 311.

EPILOGUE

1. José Luis Blasio, *Maximilian Emperor of Mexico*, trans. and ed. Robert H. Murray, p. 184.

2. *Colección de las efemérides publicadas en el Calendario del más antiguo Galván*, p. 176.

3. José de Jesús Cuevas, *Las confiscaciones en México*, p. 13.

4. José Manuel Hidalgo, *Un hombre de mundo escribe sus impresiones*, ed. Sofía Verea de Bernal, pp. 5, 242.

5. In the Memorials they filed with the United States and Mexican Claims Com-

mission in 1870, Carlos and Jacobo listed their place of residence as Mexico City; Cuevas, *Las confiscaciones*, p. 12.

6. Carlos Sánchez Navarro y Peón, *Miramón*, p. 184; Joachim Kühn, *Das Ende des maximilianischen Kaiserreichs in Mexico*, p. 299.

7. *El Correo Germánico*, October 12, 1876, p. 2.

8. *El Siglo Diez y Nueve*, October 12, 1876, p. 3.

9. Cuevas, *Las confiscaciones*, pp. 14–15.

10. Victoriano Cepeda to Benito Juárez, *El Siglo Diez y Nueve*, September 24, 1868, p. 4.

11. Francisco Aguirre Camporedondo, *Juicio de Amparo—cuestión de la finca "El Río," perteneciente a los bienes confiscados a Don Carlos Sánchez Navarro en la época de la Intervención Francesa*; "Copia Simple de la Escritura . . . ," February 9, 1880, SNP (456).

CONCLUSION

1. See William P. McGreevey, "Tierra y trabajo en Nueva Granada, 1760–1845," *Desarrollo Económico* 8, no. 30–31 (July–December 1968): 263–291.

2. See the provocative article by Friedrich Katz, "Labor Conditions on Haciendas in Porfirian Mexico: Some Trends and Tendencies," *Hispanic American Historical Review* 54, no. 1 (February 1974): 1–47.

BIBLIOGRAPHY

ARCHIVAL MATERIAL

Archivo del Ayuntamiento, Saltillo, Coahuila (ADAS).

Archivo General del Estado de Coahuila, Saltillo, Coahuila (AGEC).

Archivo General del Estado de Nuevo León, Monterrey, Nuevo León (AGENL).

———. Congreso, 1814 (AGENL-C).

———. Vidaurri Archive (AGENL-VA).

Archivo General de la Nación, Mexico City (AGN).

———. Abasto y Panaderías, vol. 5 (AGN-AP).

———. Expulsión de Españoles, vol. 4 (AGN-EE).

———. Industria y Comercio, vol. 27 (AGN-IC).

———. Justicia Eclesiástica, vol. 40 (AGN-JE).

———. Mercedes, vols. 75, 79 (AGN-M).

———. Provincias Internas, vols. 13, 22, 24, 25, 56, 160, 172, 177, 195, 239, 244 (AGN-PI).

———. Tierras, vols. 191, 2966 (AGN-T).

José Juan Sánchez Navarro Papers, Archives, University of Texas at Austin (JJSNP).

Manuscritos de la Casa Sánchez Navarro, in possession of Lic. Carlos Sánchez Navarro, Mexico City (MCSN).

National Archives, Washington, D.C., Record Group no. 76. United States and Mexican Claims Commission of 1868 (NA).

Sánchez Navarro Papers, Latin American Collection, University of Texas at Austin (SNP).

William Marshall Anderson Papers, Huntington Library, San Marino, California (WMAP).

THESIS AND DISSERTATIONS

Bacarisse, Charles A. "The Baron de Bastrop: Life and Times of Philip Hendrik Nering Bögel, 1759–1827." Ph.D. Dissertation. University of Texas, 1955.

Couturier, Edith Boorstein. "Hacienda of Hueyapan: The History of a Mexican Social and Economic Institution, 1550–1940." Ph.D. Dissertation. Columbia University, 1965.

González Sánchez, Isabel. "Situación Social de Indios y Castas en las Fincas Rurales, en Vísperas de la Independencia de México." Thesis. Universidad Nacional Autónoma de México, 1963.

Harris, Charles H., III. "A Mexican *Latifundio*: The Economic Empire of the Sánchez Navarro Family, 1765–1821." Ph.D. Dissertation. University of Texas at Austin, 1968.

Hinton, Harwood Perry. "The Military Career of John Ellis Wool, 1812–1863." Ph.D. Dissertation. University of Wisconsin, 1960.

Moseley, Edward H. "The Public Career of Santiago Vidaurri, 1855–1858." Ph.D. Dissertation. University of Alabama, 1963.

PUBLISHED WORKS

Aguirre Camporedondo, Francisco. *Juicio de Amparo—cuestión de la finca "El Río," perteneciente a los bienes confiscados a Don Carlos Sánchez Navarro en la época de la Intervención Francesa.* Saltillo: Tipografía El Golfo de México, 1887.

Alamán, Lucas. *Historia de Méjico desde los primeros movimientos que prepararon su independencia en el año de 1808 hasta la época presente.* 5 vols. Mexico City: J. M. Lara, 1849–1852.

Alessio Robles, Vito, comp. *Bibliografía de Coahuila, histórica y geográfica.* Mexico City: Imprenta de la Secretaría de Relaciones Exteriores, 1927.

———. *Bosquejos históricos.* Mexico City: Editorial Polis, 1938.

———. *Coahuila y Texas, desde la consumación de la independencia hasta el tratado de paz de Guadalupe Hidalgo.* 2 vols. Mexico City: 1945–1946.

————. *Coahuila y Texas en la época colonial.* Mexico City: Editorial Cultura, 1938.

————. *Francisco de Urdiñola y el norte de la Nueva España.* Mexico City: Imprenta Mundial, 1931.

————. *Saltillo en la historia y en la leyenda.* Mexico City: A. del Bosque, 1934.

Algara y Gómez de la Casa, Ignacio. *La corte de Maximiliano: Cartas de don Ignacio Algara.* Edited by Manuel Romero de Terreros. Mexico City: Editorial Polis, 1938.

Almanaque Imperial para el año de 1866. Mexico City: J. M. Lara, 1866.

Almonte, Juan Nepomuceno. *Guía de forasteros, y repertorio de conocimientos útiles.* Mexico City, 1852.

Anderson, William Marshall. *An American in Maximilian's Mexico, 1865–1866: The Diaries of William Marshall Anderson.* Edited by Ramón Eduardo Ruiz. San Marino, Calif.: Huntington Library, 1959.

Arias, Juan de Dios. *Reseña histórica de la formación y operaciones del cuerpo de ejército del norte durante la intervención francesa, sitio de Querétaro y noticias oficiales sobre la captura de Maximiliano, su proceso íntegro y su muerte.* Mexico City: N. Chávez, 1867.

Audubon, John W. *Audubon's Western Journal: 1849–1850. Being the MS. record of a trip from New York to Texas, and an overland journey through Mexico and Arizona to the gold-fields of California.* Edited by Frank H. Hodder. Cleveland: A. H. Clark Co., 1906.

Badura, Bohumil. "Biografía de la Hacienda de San Nicolás de Ulapa." *Ibero-Americana Pragensia* 4 (1970) : 75–111.

Bancroft, Hubert H. *History of Mexico.* 6 vols. San Francisco: A. L. Bancroft & Co., 1883–1888.

Barrett, Ward J. *The Sugar Hacienda of the Marqueses del Valle.* Minneapolis: University of Minnesota Press, 1970.

Bartlett, John Russell. *Personal Narrative of Explorations and Incidents in Texas, New Mexico, California, Sonora, and Chihuahua, connected with the United States and Mexican Boundary Commission, during the years 1850, '51, '52, and '53.* 2 vols. New York and London: D. Appleton & Co., 1856.

Basch, Samuel. *Recuerdos de México: Memorias del médico ordinario del emperador Maximiliano (1866 á 1867).* Translated by Manuel Peredo. Mexico City: N. Chávez, 1870.

Baylies, Francis. *A Narrative of Major General Wool's Campaign in Mexico in the Years 1846, 1847 & 1848.* Albany: Little & Co., 1851.

Bazant, Jan. "Los bienes de la familia de Hernán Cortés y su venta por Lucas Alamán." *Historia Mexicana* 19, no. 2 (October–December 1969): 228–247.

———. "The Division of Some Mexican *Haciendas* during the Liberal Revolution, 1856–1862." *Journal of Latin American Studies* 3, part 1 (May 1971): 25–37.

Benson, Nettie Lee. *La diputación provincial y el federalismo mexicano.* Mexico City: El Colegio de México, 1955.

Bieber, Ralph P., ed. *Southern Trails to California in 1849.* Glendale, Calif.: Arthur H. Clark Co., 1937.

Blanchot, Charles. *Mémoires: L'Intervention Française au Mexique.* 3 vols. Paris: E. Nourry, 1911.

Blasio, José Luis. *Maximilian Emperor of Mexico: Memoirs of His Private Secretary.* Translated and edited by Robert H. Murray. New Haven: Yale University Press, 1941.

Blumberg, Arnold. "A Swedish Diplomat in Mexico, 1864." *Hispanic American Historical Review* 45, no. 2 (May 1965): 275–286.

Borah, Woodrow. "The Collection of Tithes in the Bishopric of Oaxaca in the Sixteenth Century." *Hispanic American Historical Review* 21, no. 3 (August 1941): 386–409.

Brading, D. A. *Miners & Merchants in Bourbon Mexico, 1763–1810.* Cambridge: Cambridge University Press, 1971.

Brand, Donald D. "The Early History of the Range Cattle Industry in Northern Mexico." *Agricultural History* 35, no. 3 (July 1961): 132–139.

Calderón de la Barca, Frances Erskine. *Life in Mexico: The Letters of Fanny Calderón de la Barca.* Edited by Howard T. and Marion Hall Fisher. Garden City: Doubleday, 1966.

Carrera Stampa, Manuel. "The Evolution of Weights and Measures in New Spain." *Hispanic American Historical Review* 29, no. 1 (February 1949): 2–24.

Cavazos Garza, Israel. "Laguna de Sánchez." *El Porvenir* (Monterrey, N.L.), November 28, 1971, p. 2-B.

———, ed. *Epistolario Zaragoza-Vidaurri, 1855–1859.* Mexico City: Primer Congreso Nacional de Historia para el Estudio de la Guerra de Intervención, 1962.

Chamberlain, Samuel E. *My Confession.* Edited by Roger Butterfield. New York: Harper & Bros., 1956.

Chardon, Roland E. *Geographic Aspects of Plantation Agriculture in*

Yucatan. Washington, D.C.: National Academy of Sciences–National Research Council, 1961.

————. "Hacienda and Ejido in Yucatán: The Example of Santa Ana Cucá." *Annals of the Association of American Geographers* 53 (1963): 174–193.

Chevalier, François. *La formation des grandes domains au Mexique: Terre et société aux XVIᵉ–XVIIᵉ siècles*. Paris: Institut d'Ethnologie, 1952.

————. "The North Mexican Hacienda: Eighteenth and Nineteenth Centuries." In *The New World Looks at Its History: Proceedings of the Second International Congress of Historians of the United States and Mexico*, edited by Archibald R. Lewis and Thomas F. McGann, pp. 95–107. Austin: University of Texas Press, 1963.

————, ed. *Instrucciones a los Hermanos Jesuitas Administradores de Haciendas (manuscrito mexicano del siglo XVIII)*. Mexico City: Editorial Jus, 1950.

————. *Land and Society in Colonial Mexico: The Great Hacienda*. Edited by Lesley Byrd Simpson, translated by Alvin Eustis. Berkeley and Los Angeles: University of California Press, 1963.

Coit, Daniel W. *Digging for Gold—without a Shovel: The Letters of Daniel Wadsworth Coit, from Mexico City to San Francisco, 1848–1851*. Edited by George P. Hammond. Denver: Old West Publishing Co., 1967.

Colección de las efemérides publicadas en el Calendario del más antiguo Galván: Desde su Fundación hasta el 30 de Junio de 1950. Mexico City: Antigua Librería de Murguía, 1950.

Comisión de Límites de Coahuila. *Documentos relativos a la línea divisoria y mapas que determinan los límites del estado de Coahuila con el de Durango y Zacatecas*. Saltillo: Imprenta del Gobierno, 1881.

Compañía Agrícola Industrial, Colonizadora, Limitada del Tlahualilo, S.A. versus the Federal Government of the Republic of Mexico. *Allegations Presented by Jorge Vera Estañol, Special Attorney for the Federal Government before the III Hall of the Supreme Court of Justice of the Nation*. Translated by Ernesto Lara de Gogorza. Mexico City: Imprenta de la Secretaría de Fomento, 1911.

Cooper, Donald B. *Epidemic Disease in Mexico City, 1761–1813: An Administrative, Social, and Medical Study*. Austin: University of Texas Press, 1965.

El Correo Germánico (Mexico City), October 12, 1876.

Corti, Egon Caesar. *Maximilian and Charlotte of Mexico*. Translated by

Catherine Alison Phillips. 2 vols. New York and London: Alfred A. Knopf, 1928.

Cosío Villegas, Daniel, ed. *Historia Moderna de México.* 9 vols. Mexico City and Buenos Aires: Editorial Hermes, 1955–1972.

Couturier, Edith Boorstein. "Modernización y Tradición en una Hacienda (San Juan Hueyapan, 1902–1911)." *Historia Mexicana* 18, no. 1 (July–September 1968) : 35–55.

Cuevas, José de Jesús. *Las confiscaciones en México: Expropiación de la familia Sánchez Navarro.* Mexico City: Imprenta de la Constitución Social, 1868.

Cumberland, Charles C. *Mexico: The Struggle for Modernity.* New York: Oxford University Press, 1968.

Davis, George T. M. *Autobiography of the Late Col. Geo. T. M. Davis: Captain and Aid-de-Camp Scott's Army of Invasion (Mexico). From Posthumous Papers.* New York: Jenkins & McCowan, 1891.

Díaz, Lilia, ed. *Versión francesa de México: Informes diplomáticos (1853–1867).* 4 vols. Mexico City: El Colegio de México, 1963–1967.

"Documentos sacados de los Autos sobre Texas, existentes en el Oficio del Superior Gobierno de esta Corte." *Boletín del Archivo General de la Nación* 29, no. 3 (1958) : 371–480.

Domenech, Emmanuel. *Histoire du Mexique: Juarez et Maximilien. Correspondances Inédites des Présidents, Ministres et Généraux Almonte, Santa-Anna, Gutierrez, Miramon, Marquez, Mejia, Woll, Etc., Etc. de Juarez de L'Empereur Maximilien et de L'Empératrice Charlotte.* 3 vols. Paris: Librairie Internationale, 1868.

Dublán, Manuel, and José María Lozano, eds. *Legislación Mexicana.* 34 vols. Mexico City: Imprenta del Comercio, 1876–1904.

Dusenberry, William H. *The Mexican Mesta: The Administration of Ranching in Colonial Mexico.* Urbana: University of Illinois Press, 1963.

Eklund, O. P., and Sydney P. Noe. *Hacienda Tokens of Mexico.* New York: American Numismatic Society, 1949.

Evans, George W. B. *Mexican Gold Trail: The Journal of a Forty-Niner.* Edited by Glenn S. Dumke. San Marino, Calif.: Huntington Library, 1945.

Fernández de Jáuregui Urrutia, José Antonio. *Descripción del Nuevo Reino de León (1735–1740) por Don Josseph Antonio Fernández de Jáuregui Urrutia su Gobernador y Capitán General.* Edited by Malcolm D. McLean and Eugenio del Hoyo. Monterrey: Instituto Tecnológico y de Estudios Superiores de Monterrey, 1963.

Florescano, Enrique. *Precios del maíz y crisis agrícolas en México (1708–1810)*. Mexico City: El Colegio de México, 1969.

————. "El problema agrario en los últimos años del virreinato, 1800–1821." *Historia Mexicana* 20, no. 4 (April–June 1971): 477–510.

Fuente, José M. de la. *Hidalgo íntimo: Apuntes y documentos para una biografía del benemérito cura de Dolores D. Miguel Hidalgo y Costilla*. Mexico City: Tipografía Económica, 1910.

————. "Notas Históricas: El Coronel Elizondo." *Boletín de la Sociedad Mexicana de Geografía y Estadística* 1 (1902): 725–732.

Fuentes Mares, José. *. . . Y México se Refugió en el Desierto: Luis Terrazas, Historia y Destino*. Mexico City: Editorial Jus, 1954.

Gallegos, J. Ignacio. *Compendio de Historia de Durango, 1821–1910*. Mexico City: Editorial Jus, 1955.

Galván, Mariano, comp. *Ordenanzas de Tierras y Aguas ó sea Formulario Geométrico-Judicial para la designación, establecimiento, mensura, amojonamiento y deslinde de las poblaciones y todas sus suertes de tierras, sitios, caballerías y criaderos de ganados mayores y menores, y mercedes de agua*. 5th ed. rev. Paris: Librería de Rosa y Bouret, 1868.

Gammel, H. P. N., ed. *The Laws of Texas, 1822–1897*. 10 vols. Austin: Gammel Book Co., 1898.

Garber, Paul Neff. *The Gadsden Treaty*. Philadelphia: University of Pennsylvania Press, 1923.

García, Genaro, and Carlos Pereyra, eds. *Documentos inéditos ó muy raros para la historia de México*. 36 vols. Mexico City: Viuda de C. Bouret, 1905–1911.

García, Pedro. *Con el cura Hidalgo en la Guerra de Independencia*. Mexico City: Empresas Editoriales, 1948.

García Martínez, Bernardo. *El Marquesado del Valle: Tres siglos de régimen señorial en Nueva España*. Mexico City: El Colegio de México, 1969.

Garibay K., Angel María, et al., comps. *Diccionario Porrúa de historia, biografía y geografía de México*. 2d ed. Mexico City: Editorial Porrúa, 1965.

————. *Diccionario Porrúa de historia, biografía y geografía de México: Suplemento*. Mexico City: Editorial Porrúa, 1966.

Garza García, Cosme, comp. *Prontuario de leyes y decretos del estado de Coahuila de Zaragoza*. Saltillo: Oficina Tipográfica del Gobierno en Palacio, 1902.

Gaulot, Paul. *L'Expédition du Mexique (1861–1867): D'après les docu-

ments et souvenirs de Ernest Louet, Payeur en chef du Corps Expédition-naire. 2d ed. 2 vols. Paris: Société d'éditions littéraires et artistiques, 1906.

Gibson, A. M. *The Kickapoos: Lords of the Middle Border.* Norman: University of Oklahoma Press, 1963.

Gibson, Charles. *The Aztecs under Spanish Rule: A History of the Indians of the Valley of Mexico, 1519–1810.* Stanford: Stanford University Press, 1964.

Gilliam, Albert M. *Travels over the Table Lands and Cordilleras of Mexico. During the Years 1843 and 44; Including a description of California, the principal cities and mining districts of that republic, and the biographies of Iturbide and Santa Anna.* Philadelphia: J. W. Moore; London: Wiley & Putnam, 1846.

Glick, Thomas F. *Irrigation and Society in Medieval Valencia.* Cambridge: Harvard University Press, 1970.

Gómez Palacio, Francisco. *Reclamaciones de indemnización por depredaciones de los indios.* Mexico City: Imprenta del Gobierno, 1872.

González, José Eleuterio. *Obras completas.* 4 vols. Monterrey: Imprenta del Gobierno del Estado, 1885–1887.

González Sánchez, Isabel, ed. *Haciendas y ranchos de Tlaxcala en 1712.* Mexico City: Instituto Nacional de Antropología e Historia, 1969.

González y González, Luis. "La hacienda queda a salvo." *Historia Mexicana* 6, no. 1 (July–September 1956) : 24–38.

Gregg, Josiah. *Commerce of the Prairies.* Edited by Max L. Moorhead. Norman: University of Oklahoma Press, 1954.

———. *Diary and Letters of Josiah Gregg.* Edited by Maurice Garland Fulton. 2 vols. Norman: University of Oklahoma Press, 1941–1944.

Guerra, Eduardo. *Historia de la Laguna: Torreón, su origen y sus fundadores.* Saltillo: Impresora de Coahuila, 1932.

Haley, J. Evetts. *The XIT Ranch of Texas, and the Early Days of the Llano Estacado.* Norman: University of Oklahoma Press, 1953.

Hamill, Hugh M., Jr. *The Hidalgo Revolt: Prelude to Mexican Independence.* Gainesville: University of Florida Press, 1966.

Harding, Bertita. *Phantom Crown: The Story of Maximilian & Carlota of Mexico.* Mexico City: Ediciones Tolteca, 1953.

Harris, Charles H., III. *The Sánchez Navarros: A Socioeconomic Study of a Coahuilan Latifundio, 1846–1853.* Chicago: Loyola University Press, 1964.

Hernández y Dávalos, J. E., ed. *Colección de Documentos para la Historia de la Guerra de Independencia de México de 1808 á 1821.* 6 vols. Mexico City: José María Sandoval, 1877–1882.

Hexter, J. H. *Reappraisals in History: New Views on History and Society in Early Modern Europe.* New York and Evanston: Harper & Row, 1963.

Hidalgo, José Manuel. *Un hombre de mundo escribe sus impresiones: Cartas.* Edited by Sofía Verea de Bernal. Mexico City: Editorial Porrúa, 1960.

Hidy, Ralph Willard. *The House of Baring in American Trade and Finance: English Merchant Bankers at Work, 1763–1861.* Cambridge: Harvard University Press, 1949.

Hodge, Frederick Webb, ed. *Handbook of American Indians North of Mexico.* 2 vols. Washington, D.C.: Government Printing Office, 1959.

Horgan, Paul. *Great River: The Rio Grande in North American History.* 2 vols. New York and Toronto: Rinehart & Co., 1954.

Hughes, George W. *Memoir Descriptive of the March of a Division of the United States Army under the Command of Brigadier General John E. Wool, from San Antonio de Bexar, in Texas, to Saltillo, in Mexico.* Senate Executive Document No. 32, 31st Cong., 1st Sess. Washington, D.C.: Government Printing Office, 1850.

Hunnicut, Helen. "A Mexican View of the Texas War." *The Library Chronicle of the University of Texas* 4, no. 2 (Summer 1951): 59–74.

Hyde, Hartford Montgomery. *Mexican Empire: The History of Maximilian and Carlota of Mexico.* London: Macmillan & Co., 1946.

Islas Escárcega, Leovigildo, comp. *Diccionario rural de México.* Mexico City: Editorial Comaval, 1961.

Johnson, Frank W. *A History of Texas and Texans.* Edited by Eugene C. Barker, with the assistance of Ernest W. Winkler. 2 vols. Chicago and New York: American Historical Society, 1914.

Katz, Friedrich. "Labor Conditions on Haciendas in Porfirian Mexico: Some Trends and Tendencies." *Hispanic American Historical Review* 54, no. 1 (February 1974): 1–47.

Keith, Robert G. "Encomienda, Hacienda and Corregimiento in Spanish America: A Structural Analysis." *Hispanic American Historical Review* 51, no. 3 (August 1971): 431–446.

Kératry, Emile de. *Elevación y caída del emperador Maximiliano: Intervención francesa en México. 1861–1867.* Translated by Hilarión Frías y Soto. Mexico City: Imprenta del Comercio, 1870.

Küchler, Jacobo. *Valles de Sabinas y Salinas: Reconocimiento y descripción de los valles de Sabinas y Salinas en el Departamento de Coahuila, con las haciendas del Nacimiento, San Juan, Soledad, Alamo, Encinas, Hermanas y rancho de la Mota.* Mexico City: Imprenta Imperial, 1866.

Kühn, Joachim. *Das Ende des maximilianischen Kaiserreichs in Mexico: Berichte des königlich preussischen Ministerresidenten Anton von Magnus an Bismarck, 1866–1867.* Göttingen: Musterschmidt-Verlag, 1965.

Kupper, Winifred. *The Golden Hoof: The Story of the Sheep of the Southwest.* New York: Alfred A. Knopf, 1945.

Lafora, Nicolás de. *Relación del viaje que hizo a los Presidios Internos situados en la frontera de la América Septentrional Perteneciente al Rey de España.* Edited by Vito Alessio Robles. Mexico City: Pedro Robredo, 1939.

Lambert, Jacques. *Latin America: Social Structure and Political Institutions.* Translated by Helen Katel. Berkeley and Los Angeles: University of California Press, 1967.

Lavrin, Asunción. "The Role of the Nunneries in the Economy of New Spain in the Eighteenth Century." *Hispanic American Historical Review* 46, no. 4 (November 1966) : 371–393.

Lea, Tom. *The King Ranch.* 2 vols. Boston and Toronto: Little, Brown & Co., 1957.

Lefevre, Eugene. *Documentos oficiales recogidos en la secretaría privada de Maximiliano: Historia de la intervención francesa en Méjico.* 2 vols. Brussels and London, 1869.

Lewis, Oscar. *Pedro Martínez: A Mexican Peasant and His Family.* New York: Random House, 1964.

Lockhart, James. "Encomienda and Hacienda: The Evolution of the Great Estate in the Spanish Indies." *Hispanic American Historical Review* 49, no. 3 (August 1969) : 411–429.

Luján, José María, ed. *El libro secreto de Maximiliano.* 2d ed. Mexico City: Universidad Nacional Autónoma de México, 1963.

McGreevey, William P. "Tierra y trabajo en Nueva Granada, 1760–1845." *Desarrollo Económico* 8, no. 30–31 (July–December 1968) : 263–291.

Magoffin, Susan Shelby. *Down the Santa Fe Trail and into Mexico: The Diary of Susan Shelby Magoffin, 1846–1847.* Edited by Stella M. Drumm. New Haven: Yale University Press, 1926.

Malo, José Ramón. *Diario de sucesos notables.* Edited by Mariano Cuevas, S.J. 2 vols. Mexico City: Editorial Patria, 1948.

Mancebo Benfield, José. *Las lomas de Chapultepec: El Rancho de Coscoa-*

coaco y el Molino del Rey (Estudio histórico, topográfico y jurídico). Mexico City: Editorial Porrúa, 1960.

Mapa de los Estados de Parras: Producido del Original de S.M.L. Staples. Por P. Miguel Alvarez. 1828. N.p., n.d.

Márquez, Leonardo. *Manifiestos (El Imperio y los Imperiales)*. Edited by Angel Pola. Mexico City: F. Vázquez, 1904.

Martínez del Río, Pablo. *El suplicio del hacendado y otros temas agrarios*. Mexico City: Editorial Polis, 1938.

Masseras, E. *Un Essai d'Empire au Mexique*. Paris: G. Charpentier, 1879.

Maudslay, Robert. *Texas Sheepman: The Reminiscences of Robert Maudslay*. Edited by Winifred Kupper. Austin: University of Texas Press, 1951.

Maza, Francisco de la. *San Miguel de Allende: Su historia. Sus monumentos*. Mexico City: Universidad Nacional Autónoma de México, 1939.

Mestre Ghigliazza, Manuel, comp. *Efemérides biográficas (defunciones-nacimientos)*. Mexico City: Antigua Librería Robredo, J. Porrúa, 1945.

Mexico. Comisión Pesquisidora de la Frontera del Norte. *Informe final que en cumplimiento del decreto de 2 de octubre de 1872 rinde al ejecutivo de la unión la comisión pesquisidora de la frontera del norte sobre el desempeño de sus trabajos*. Mexico City: Imprenta del Gobierno, 1874.

———. Instituto Nacional de Antropología e Historia. Dirección de Monumentos Coloniales. *Edificios coloniales artísticos e históricos de la República Mexicana que han sido declarados monumentos*. Mexico City: Editorial Cultura, 1939.

———. Secretaría de la Defensa Nacional. *La Correspondencia de Agustín de Iturbide después de la Proclamación del Plan de Iguala*. Edited by Vito Alessio Robles. 2 vols. Mexico City: Taller Autográfico, 1945.

———. Secretaría de Relaciones Exteriores. *Fr. Gregorio de la Concepción y su proceso de infidencia*. Mexico City: Tipografía Guerrero Hnos., 1911.

Montlong, Wilhelm von. *Authentische Enthüllungen über die letzten Ereignisse in Mexiko*. Stuttgart: Hoffmann, 1868.

Moore, John Bassett. *History and Digest of the International Arbitrations to which the United States has been a Party*. House Miscellaneous Document No. 212, 53d Cong., 2d Sess. 6 vols. Washington, D.C.: Government Printing Office, 1898.

Moorhead, Max L. *The Apache Frontier: Jacobo Ugarte and Spanish-*

Indian Relations in Northern New Spain, 1769–1791. Norman: University of Oklahoma Press, 1968.

————. "The Private Contract System of Presidio Supply in Northern New Spain." *Hispanic American Historical Review* 41, no. 1 (February 1961): 31–54.

Morfi, Juan Agustín de. *Diario y Derrotero (1777–1781).* Edited by Eugenio del Hoyo and Malcolm D. McLean. Monterrey: Instituto Tecnológico y de Estudios Superiores de Monterrey, 1967.

————. *Viaje de indios y diario del Nuevo México.* Edited by Vito Alessio Robles. Mexico City: Bibliófilos Mexicanos, 1935.

Muller, Cornelius H. "Vegetation and Climate of Coahuila, Mexico." *Madroño* 9 (1947): 33–57.

Navarro García, Luis. *Don José de Gálvez y la Comandancia General de las Provincias Internas del Norte de Nueva España.* Seville: Escuela de Estudios Hispano-Americanos de Sevilla, 1964.

Oeste de Bopp, Marianne. *Maximiliano y los alemanes.* Mexico City: Sociedad Mexicana de Geografía y Estadística, 1965.

Ortega y Pérez Gallardo, Ricardo. *Historia Genealógica de las Familias más antiguas de México.* 3d ed. 3 vols. Mexico City: Imprenta de B. Carranza y Compañía, 1908–1910.

Park, Joseph F. "Spanish Indian Policy in Northern Mexico, 1765–1810." *Arizona and the West* 4, no. 4 (Winter 1962): 325–344.

Payno, Manuel. *Carta que sobre los asuntos de México dirige al señor General Forey comandante en gefe de las tropas francesas el ciudadano Manuel Payno.* Mexico City: Imprenta de Vicente G. Torres, 1862.

————. *Cuentas, Gastos, Acreedores y otros asuntos del tiempo de la Intervención francesa y del Imperio. Obra escrita y publicada de orden del gobierno constitucional de la república, por M. Payno. De 1861 á 1867.* Mexico City: Imprenta de Ignacio Cumplido, 1868.

Pearson, Jim Berry. *The Maxwell Land Grant.* Norman: University of Oklahoma Press, 1961.

Pérez Maldonado, Carlos. *El Excmo. y Rvmo. Sr. Dr. Don Primo Feliciano Marín de Porras y la emboscada de Baján.* Monterrey, 1950.

Pike, Zebulon M. *The Expeditions of Zebulon Montgomery Pike.* Edited by Elliott Coues. 3 vols. London and New York: F. P. Harper, 1895.

Portillo, Esteban L. *Anuario Coahuilense para 1886.* Saltillo: A. Prado, 1886.

Pozo Rosillo, Paulino del. "La hacienda de Peñasco, S.L.P." *Archivos de Historia Potosina* 1, no. 2 (October–December 1969): 107–114.

Ramón, Zapopan. "Hombres Notables de Monclova." *Monclova: Quincenal de actualidades y anuncios*, September 20, 1937, p. 5.

Ramos Arizpe, Miguel. *Report That Dr. Miguel Ramos de Arizpe, Priest of Borbon and Deputy in the Present General and Special Cortes of Spain for the Province of Coahuila, One of the Four Eastern Interior Provinces of the Kingdom of Mexico, Presents to the August Congress on the Natural, Political, and Civil Conditions of the Provinces of Coahuila, Nuevo León, Nuevo Santander, and Texas of the Four Eastern Interior Provinces of the Kingdom of Mexico.* Edited by Nettie Lee Benson. Austin: University of Texas Press, 1950.

Reed, Nelson. *The Caste War of Yucatan.* Stanford: Stanford University Press, 1964.

Revere, Joseph Warren. *Keel and Saddle: A Retrospect of Forty Years of Military and Naval Service.* Boston: J. R. Osgood & Co., 1872.

Riley, G. Micheal. *Fernando Cortes and the Marquesado in Morelos, 1522–1547: A Case Study in the Socioeconomic Development of Sixteenth-Century Mexico.* Albuquerque: University of New Mexico Press, 1973.

———. "Land in Spanish Enterprise: Colonial Morelos, 1522–1547." *The Americas* 27, no. 3 (January 1971): 233–251.

Rippy, J. Fred. *British Investments in Latin America, 1822–1949: A Case Study in the Operations of Private Enterprise in Retarded Regions.* Minneapolis: University of Minnesota Press, 1959.

———. "The Indians of the Southwest in the Diplomacy of the United States and Mexico, 1848–1853." *Hispanic American Historical Review* 2, no. 3 (August 1919): 363–396.

Riva Palacio, Vicente, ed. *México á través de los siglos.* 5 vols. Barcelona: Espasa y Cía., 1888–1889.

Rivera Cambas, Manuel. *Historia de la Intervención europea y norte-Americana en México y del Imperio de Maximiliano de Hapsburgo.* 3 vols. Mexico City: Tipografía de Aguilar é Hijos, 1888–1895.

Roel, Santiago, ed. *Correspondencia Particular de D. Santiago Vidaurri, Gobernador de Nuevo León (1855–1864).* Monterrey: Universidad de Nuevo León, 1946.

Romero de Terreros, Manuel. *Antiguas Haciendas de México.* Mexico City: Editorial Patria, 1956.

———. *Maximiliano y el imperio.* Mexico City: Editorial Cultura, 1926.

Rouaix, Pastor, comp. *Diccionario geográfico, histórico, y biográfico del Estado de Durango.* Mexico City: Instituto Panamericano de Geografía e Historia, 1946.

Rubio Mañé, J. Ignacio. "Los Allendes de San Miguel el Grande." *Boletín del Archivo General de la Nación* 2, no. 4 (October–December 1961): 517–556.

―――. "Los Unzagas de San Miguel el Grande." *Boletín del Archivo General de la Nación* 2, no. 4 (October–December 1961): 557–568.

Ruxton, George. *Adventures in Mexico and the Rocky Mountains.* New York: Harper & Bros., 1848.

Salm-Salm, Felix. *My Diary in Mexico in 1867, Including the Last Days of the Emperor Maximilian; with Leaves from the Diary of the Princess Salm-Salm.* 2 vols. London: R. Bentley, 1868.

"Sánchez Navarro Papers (1658–1895)." *The Library Chronicle of the University of Texas* 1, no. 1 (Summer 1944): 31–32.

Sánchez Navarro y Peón, Carlos. *Memorias de un Viejo Palacio (La Casa del Banco Nacional de México), 1523–1950.* Mexico City, 1951.

―――. *Miramón: El caudillo conservador.* 2d ed. Mexico City: Editorial Patria, 1949.

―――, ed. *La Guerra de Tejas: Memorias de un Soldado.* Mexico City: Editorial Jus, 1938.

―――, ed. *Tres Cartas inéditas Del Emperador Maximiliano.* Mexico City: Vargas Rea, 1944.

Santisteban, J. B. de. *Indicador particular del administrador de hacienda: Breve manual basado sobre reglas de economía rural, inherentes al sistema agrícola en la república mexicana.* 2d ed. Puebla: Imprenta Artística, 1903.

Schurz, William L. "The Royal Philippine Company." *Hispanic American Historical Review* 3, no. 4 (November 1920): 491–508.

El Siglo Diez y Nueve (Mexico City), September 24, 1868, October 12, 1876.

Smith, Ralph A. "The Scalp Hunter in the Borderlands, 1835–1850." *Arizona and the West* 6, no. 1 (Spring 1964): 5–22.

Smith, Robert S. "Sales Taxes in New Spain, 1575–1770." *Hispanic American Historical Review* 28, no. 1 (February 1948): 2–37.

Spell, Lota M. *Research Materials for the Study of Latin America at the University of Texas.* Austin: University of Texas Press, 1954.

Stein, Stanley J. and Barbara H. *The Colonial Heritage of Latin America: Essays on Economic Dependence in Perspective.* New York: Oxford University Press, 1970.

Stevenson, Sara Yorke. *Maximilian in Mexico: A Woman's Reminiscences of the French Intervention, 1862–1867.* New York: Century Co., 1899.

Strickson, Arnold. "Hacienda and Plantation in Yucatan." *América Indígena* 25, no. 1 (January 1965): 35–63.

Tamarón y Romeral, Pedro. *Demostración del vastísimo obispado de la Nueva Vizcaya, 1765.* Edited by Vito Alessio Robles. Mexico City: Antigua Librería Robredo, 1937.

Tamayo, Jorge L., ed. *Benito Juárez: Documentos, discursos y correspondencia.* 11 vols. Mexico City: Secretaría del Patrimonio Nacional, 1964–1967.

Tannenbaum, Frank. *The Mexican Agrarian Revolution.* Washington, D.C.: Brookings Institute, 1930.

Taylor, William B. *Landlord and Peasant in Colonial Oaxaca.* Stanford: Stanford University Press, 1972.

Thomas, Alfred Barnaby, ed. *Teodoro de Croix and the Northern Frontier of New Spain, 1776–1783.* Norman: University of Oklahoma Press, 1941.

Tovar Pinzón, Hermes. "Las haciendas jesuitas de México, índice de documentos existentes en el Archivo Nacional de Chile." *Historia Mexicana* 20, no. 4 (April–June 1971): 563–617, and 21, no. 1 (July–September 1971): 135–180.

Towne, C. W., and E. N. Wentworth. *Shepherd's Empire.* Norman: University of Oklahoma Press, 1945.

United States. House of Representatives. *Correspondence between the Secretary of War and Generals Scott and Taylor, and between General Scott and Mr. Trist.* Executive Document No. 56, 30th Cong., 1st Sess. Washington, D.C.: Government Printing Office, 1848.

———. ———. *Treaty between the United States of America and the Mexican republic, concluded at the city of Mexico, December 30, 1853.* Executive Document No. 109, 33d Cong., 1st Sess. Washington, D.C.: Government Printing Office, 1854.

———. Senate. *Affairs of the Mexican Kickapoo Indians.* Executive Document No. 215, 60th Cong., 1st Sess. 3 vols. Washington, D.C.: Government Printing Office, 1908.

———. ———. *Claims on the Part of Citizens of the United States and Mexico under the Convention of July 4, 1868, between the United States and Mexico.* Executive Document No. 31, 44th Cong., 2nd Sess. Washington, D.C.: Government Printing Office, 1877.

———. ———. *Message from the President of the United States, Communicating, In Answer to a Resolution of the Senate of the 25th Ultimo, Papers Relative to Mexican Affairs.* Executive Document No. 11, 39th

Cong., 1st Sess. Washington, D.C.: Government Printing Office, 1865.

————. ————. *Report of the Special Committee of the United States Senate on the Irrigation and Reclamation of Arid Lands.* 4 vols. Washington, D.C.: Government Printing Office, 1890.

————. ————. *Treaty of peace, friendship, limits, and settlement between the United States of America and the Mexican republic, concluded at Guadalupe Hidalgo, on the 2d day of February, in the year 1848.* Executive Document No. 52, 30th Cong., 1st Sess. Washington, D.C.: Government Printing Office, 1848.

Vasconcelos, José. *Don Evaristo Madero (Biografía de un patricio).* Mexico City: Impresiones Modernas, 1958.

Vizcaya Canales, Isidro, ed. *La invasión de los indios bárbaros al nordeste de México en los años de 1840 y 1841.* Monterrey: Instituto Tecnológico y de Estudios Superiores de Monterrey, 1968.

Wallace, Ernest, and E. Adamson Hoebel. *The Comanches: Lords of the South Plains.* Norman: University of Oklahoma Press, 1952.

Weddle, Robert S. *San Juan Bautista: Gateway to Spanish Texas.* Austin and London: University of Texas Press, 1968.

West, Robert C. *The Mining Community in Northern New Spain: The Parral Mining District.* Berkeley and Los Angeles: University of California Press, 1949.

Wislinzenus, Adolphus. *Memoir of a Tour to Northern Mexico Connected with Col. Doniphan's Expedition in 1846 and 1847.* Senate Miscellaneous Document No. 26, 30th Cong., 1st Sess. Washington, D.C.: Government Printing Office, 1848.

Wolf, Eric R., and Edward C. Hansen. *The Human Condition in Latin America.* New York, London, and Toronto: Oxford University Press, 1972.

Zarco, Francisco. *Crónica del Congreso Extraordinario Constituyente, 1856–1857.* Edited by Catalina Sierra Casasús. Mexico City: El Colegio de México, 1957.

Zavala, Lorenzo de. *Ensayo Histórico de las Revoluciones de México: Desde 1808 hasta 1830.* Edited by Alfonso Toro. 3d ed. 2 vols. Mexico City: Oficina Impresora de Hacienda, 1918.

INDEX